IN THE WIND

IN THE WIND

ONE WOMAN'S AMAZING SPIRITUAL JOURNEY

MAUREEN SAJNA CLARKE

To order additional copies of this book, contact:
Xlibris Corporation
1-888-795-4274
www.Xlibris.com
Orders@Xlibris.com
42515

❀ DEDICATION ❀

To my precious children Ariss, Solomon, and Jesse, in hope that some day they will understand.

❀ DISCLAIMER ❀

"In The Wind" is an autobiographical account of my affiliation with a religious cult. The names and places outlined in this manual are true and are a testimonial of my experiences under the influence of 'mind control.'

The narrative in this book can at times be an intense read, but it is not my intention to sway peoples' beliefs, or to indoctrinate my readers to the ways of this, or any religious group. In order to appreciate this book, it should be read in its entirety. The final chapters reveal how I discovered that I was under the 'control' of the sect's leaders and their beliefs and how I found my way out of the cult, as well as the struggles I endured while trying to find my way in the 'real' world again.

If any intentions at all are to be made by my manual, it would be that in sharing my experience, I might be able to enlighten others who 'may be' or 'may become' subjects of mind control, either within the confines of a religious, a political group, or a personal affiliation. It is also my intention to show how powerful a hold brainwashing techniques can have on an individual. Perhaps I might be able to dissuade present or future victims from becoming ensnared in groups, or affiliations that use the control techniques I have outlined in this book.

❊ ACKNOWLEDGEMENTS ❊

I thank God for all He has provided to finish this project.

My husband Don has been my backbone throughout this endeavor. Thank you!

I am so grateful to my mom and dad for caring for my children and helping me out of mind control.

Much appreciation is extended to Allana Sullivan, Pat Barclay, Charles Wilkins and Susan Sajna for their editing advice and expertise.

Thanks to Margaret Pert and Ellen Mastrangelo for their perseverance and patience in word processing.

A special thanks to all my family and friends for their encouragement and belief that I could complete such a monumental task.

I shall be forever grateful to the Explorations Program of the Canada Arts Council for awarding me the funds needed to develop my manuscript into publishable form.

❀ PREFACE ❀

This is my story, what happened and how I thought and felt about it. I kept no diary during my experiences, yet my memories are so strong that I felt compelled to relive them on paper.

In opening up my life and sharing these experiences, I hope to bring a clearer picture of the strong net of power and control which exists to ensnare searching souls like myself. When I awoke to the fact that I was in a cult, which had manipulated my mind, I found technical books on the topic of brainwashing hard to understand. Books about others' personal experiences were much easier to relate to, but they often left me with more questions. I wanted to know more details about the beliefs, the mental conflicts, as well as what happened to the writer after leaving the group.

Therefore, in my book, I have attempted to provide explicit details of the ideas and events which led to my involvement with the Christ Family. I also describe the outward adventures, inner conflicts, thinking processes while under mind control, as well as the cult's doctrines and way of life. Finally, I include the traumatic experience of being kidnapped and deprogrammed and the years of readjustment that followed.

I don't claim to be an authority in the fields of psychology, or brainwashing. I am simply one individual who has experienced living under this type of repression. By sharing my story, I hope to enable others to draw their own conclusions.

❈ INTRODUCTION ❈

Disillusioned with society and obsessed with the possibility of nuclear disaster, I was driven to find truth and safety in an alternative way of life. Initially, my quest took me from my home in a small northern Canadian city, south through the United States, Mexico, Central and South America, to the incredible Andes Mountains of Peru.

This treacherous trek, motivated by the promise of a secret valley and spiritual enlightenment, brought me to the remote villages of the Ancient Inca, literally above and beyond modern civilization. I came face to face with endless adventures and hardships, heightened by pregnancy and the dependency of my baby daughter still in diapers.

Yet the search for the Valley of The Blue Moon was only the beginning of my story. Convinced that this time I had finally found 'the truth,' I walked barefoot, dressed in a white robe believing I was a disciple of Jesus Christ. I had to give up everything and everyone I loved. With no home, no money, no shoes, I lived on the road, 'in the wind,' like the early believers, having faith that God would take care of my needs. I experienced many adventures and challenges, like sleeping in drainage tunnels, graveyards and freeway ramps. The battle of the mind was a constant inner struggle and to meet the demands of these new beliefs, my perceptions of the world, and myself, had to undergo a dramatic change. This compelling mission had me believing that I was sacrificing my life for mankind!

This book is a sharing, not only of actual events, but also of my innermost thoughts and feelings while experiencing them. The mystery of brainwashing is difficult to understand. So come with me through these pages and perhaps they will shed some light your way.

❋ CHAPTER ONE ❋

Night fell upon the day; the leaves of gold and crimson turned to grey. The season was changing. I could hear the last storms of autumn approaching in the bitter winds that howled outside the house.

I have often felt a part of the dazzling power of lightning storms, the searing flashes of light burning cracks in the looming darkness, allowing one to see clearly for a brief moment. Sometimes my life seems like one continuous lightning storm.

"It's your turn again, Mom," Sol's voice sounded with an edge, bringing me back abruptly to our game of cards. "Why do you keep staring out the window?"

"I'm sorry, kids," I told them as I threw my hand down. "I just can't concentrate on cards tonight." I looked at the two of them, Sol, now seven, and his nine-year-old sister, Ariss, and remembered a time when they were very young and our lives had been so different. The children ran playfully down the narrow hallway of our home. "Quiet, or you'll wake Jesse," I called after them.

The beckoning wind seemed to draw me inwards. Memories whirled through my mind, bringing with them feelings of disbelief that I could ever have experienced the extraordinary spiritual journey that had occupied so much of my life. The past kept slipping into the conscious present. Why, after so many years, was I still unable to let the past go?

I moved from the table to the couch and feeling a cool draft, wrapped a white blanket around myself. The lightning storm raged on, the winds even wilder now, the flashes of light taking me by surprise each time they pierced the darkness. I thought about the many lightning storms I had witnessed when I lived on the road. One in particular passed through my memory. I'd had no shelter, but a piece of plastic, mounted overhead as a roof. I felt so much a part of the storm that night, not merely an observer.

Images of the man who called himself "Lightning Amen" came to mind, to whom I had not only given my life, but my entire heart, soul and mind.

Ariss and Sol interrupted my thoughts, snuggling beside me on the couch. I wrapped them in the blanket. We huddled together in silence, watching the storm.

Then Ariss, perceptive as always, leaned over to me and said, "Mom, why do you look so sad? What are you thinking about?"

"Well, Ariss, memories keep bombarding me. Like these flashes of lightning, they become so clear, so real, it's like I'm reliving them. So much has happened in my life over the last few years. I guess I'm still sorting it all out," I told her.

"Some day, I would like you to tell me the whole story, Mom; everything that happened to you and why," she said, her blue eyes filled with concern.

I threw my head back and let out a sigh. "Boy, I really wouldn't know where to begin, honey."

But, later that night, Ariss' question remained etched in my mind. What was the whole story? What had happened to me, and why?

Back in the mid-seventies, I was troubled by many of the things I saw. War, rape, murder, child abuse, sexual abuse, lust, greed and selfishness thrived in this world. The almighty dollar seemed to have more say in the running of world affairs than did those elected as leaders.

Most people didn't seem to be aware of, or care about what was happening, either. They were so caught up in the systems of the materialistic world, working at jobs they hated to support their plush lifestyles and habits. It seemed to me that the more people had, the more they wanted and advertising would surely convince them that they needed it. But, where was all of this leading? There has to be more to life than this, I thought.

Unrest in the Middle East, earthquakes, famines, wars, all prophesied, were now being fulfilled. It seemed as if anyone who tried to make a difference was murdered, like Gandhi and Martin Luther King Jr. All through history, so many saints and prophets had been killed.

Humans were literally peeling the skin off the earth, polluting it, abusing it, destroying the perfect balance of nature. I could visualize chemical waste dumps oozing their poisons into water sources that would eventually become people's drinking water. What right did 'they' think they had; to take and not give? What intelligence had fabricated bombs that could destroy the entire planet? This was not intelligence to me; this was insanity! It showed no understanding whatsoever of the true essence of life. I was concerned with the imminent reality of a nuclear war.

One day, as I sat pondering all these heavy questions, I felt a tug at my long skirt and looked down into the yearning eyes of my one-year-old daughter, Ariss. Embracing her, I thought of the news I had just received from my doctor, of the new life forming within me. I wasn't quite sure how I felt about this. Was it wise to be having babies at such an uncertain time? What future lay ahead for my children? What suffering would they have to endure? At that thought, I squeezed Ariss tighter. I loved her so much. What could I do to save my babies from the impending disaster? Yet, I too was supporting 'the system' by living here and was also guilty of destroying the earth by enjoying so many luxuries obtained at its expense. I wanted to find a way to live in peace with nature. Realizing this, my soul reached out in search of truth and meaning.

As a child, my parents had planted the roots of Catholicism deep within my conscience. Love and security flourished in our home. As the oldest of three children, I learned responsibility at an early age and was an obedient and trusted daughter. I worked hard in school to reach top marks and by the age of thirteen had earned my grade eight piano diploma from the Royal Conservatory of Music.

Thunder Bay was a friendly town to grow up in, situated right in the centre of Canada, surrounded by wilderness. An abundance of lakes, rivers, waterfalls and forests was ours to discover. Every summer my dad took us camping and each year my appreciation for nature grew.

As a teenager growing up in the seventies, I came to realize that the world around me was not as unblemished as I had once thought. I started to separate my values from those of 'the system's' and began my search for deeper truths. When I was sixteen I took my first step against 'the norm' by becoming a vegetarian. It was around this time that I met Will, an intriguing man who seemed to have an amazing amount of wisdom and spiritual insight. He introduced me to a whole new way of looking at the world and I found myself casting off my secure cocoon and rebelling against most things I had once believed in. The seed of discontent grew until I saw myself as part of a huge leech that was sucking the lifeblood from the earth.

In June of 1976, Will and I were married, although he wanted to just live together. The fact that I was pregnant influenced our decision. I was only 18 years old.

Will had set himself apart from the views of the world. He completely rejected the materialist 'illusion' that so many fall for, believing instead that the only reality was spirit, or who we truly were, 'inside.' His way was peaceful, but his manipulative use of language left many speechless at times. His mother and siblings had nicknamed him "The Preacher Man," which suited him well for he was very opinionated and outspoken about everything.

Will was my mentor. I was the student who drank from his fountain of wisdom with unquestioning thirst. He was teaching me so much about true giving and universal love. A naive nineteen-year-old, I was also easily influenced by books on spirituality.

Many that I read seemed to point to an 'end of the world' scenario. One of them, "Survival into the 21st Century," strongly influenced our diet; as we were now moving from being vegetarians to eating only fruit. Even when I read the Bible, I kept opening it at random to sections where Jesus warns His disciples about the signs to watch for that will mark the end of the world.

One book in particular that Will was reading had a great influence on both of us. He read parts of it to me and told me the rest. It was called "The Secret of the Andes" by Brother Philip (London: Neville Spearman, 1974). This complex piece of literature proclaimed a philosophy that was alien to most. It spoke of a hidden valley in the Peruvian Andes Mountains on the northern tip of Lake Titicaca. This valley's exact position and altitude gave it a warm semi-tropical climate where fruits and vegetables could grow to a phenomenal size. Here in the ancient land of the Inca, masters of other planets had manifested into physical form and communicated with residents there. These advanced beings were spiritual helpmates for those who wanted truth more than anything in this material world. There was a monastery there that was made of gigantic blocks of stone. It was a repository of Lemurian science culture and Arcan knowledge; a mystery school which held truths and hidden understanding of Adoma, Atlantis and other advanced civilizations. The valley of the monastery of the Brotherhood of the Seven Rays was known as the Valley of the Blue Moon. The author, Brother Philip, claimed to be the guardian sent to escort to the valley those who had made the treacherous journey to the 'sky village' at the summit of one of the highest mountains. Only those guided by God would safely find it, for the way was dangerous and difficult. There were references to "The Christ" coming to the valley to gather the inhabitants when they were ready.

This must be the place Jesus spoke of when He said *". . . flee to the mountains . . . ,"* *(Mathew 24:16)* we thought, for sheltered by immense mountains, this utopia was one of the only places on earth that would not be affected by nuclear disaster. Another valley in the Tibetan mountains was mentioned as the only other safe place. The people who gathered in Peru lived simply, without modern conveniences. They made their own clothes and tools, grew fruits, nuts, and vegetables, and lived communally, sharing what was needed. To us the valley was a preparing ground, a school of 'the spirit.' This way of life seemed to be more real and perhaps what I was looking for.

My brother Ed and I had always been close and he came to visit Will and I often. We all shared the same beliefs. We agreed that the world was about to undergo dramatic changes and we refused to ignore the signs. We had a burning desire to know the inner life of truth, to understand the reason for our existence. All of us were interested in Eastern philosophy. Yoga and Zen were a part of our lives, yet there was something missing; some answer was out there, or in there, just beyond our grasp. Will had been talking about going to live in South America for some time now and reading "The Secret of the Andes" had changed his vague feelings to firm convictions.

"I feel a strong calling to find the valley," Will told us one evening.

"There really isn't anything here for me. I no longer want to be part of this scene," Ed agreed.

"Our income tax money will be coming soon, so I've been thinking about buying an old school bus for the journey," said Will, his icy eyes shining with anticipation and excitement.

Their conversation faded as my thoughts grew louder. My heart was with them, but my head was questioning. Was I spiritually strong enough for such a journey? Was God really calling me? I was especially concerned for Ariss. The journey would be hard on her. Her choice was in our hands. Furthermore, I was two months pregnant. Where would I give birth? Could I live through the hardships ahead? Could I really survive without modern comforts and all the luxuries I'd grown accustomed to? It would be hard to leave all those I loved. Suddenly a loud knock interrupted my troubled thoughts.

"I'll answer it." Getting up from my cross-legged position, I went to answer the door. "Hi, Tony. Good to see you. Will and Ed are in the living room." I looked into his dark eyes. Tony had been my Brother Ed's best pal since early grade school. Tony was as outgoing and fun-loving as Ed was quiet and introspective, each of them absorbing a bit of the other's personality over those impressionable years of youth. Being the youngest and quite a bit younger than his brother and sisters, he was his mother's 'breath of life.' I'm sure there were also plenty of times when he made her hyperventilate.

For instance, I could remember a few years back, when streaking was 'in' and Tony and Ed streaked right through the centre of the A&W restaurant parking lot, which was packed with cars and on through a busy intersection and down a few long blocks to my parent's home. Meanwhile, I held their clothes, laughing as I watched their naked bodies run, Ed's lean, tall form and Tony's stout, shorter one accelerating in the excitement of this daring event. All three of us were sworn to secrecy. Plenty of people saw, but the way those boys ran like the wind, they arrived at home base without getting caught! Tony was like a brother to me, he was at our home nearly as often as his own. His black Afro hair and olive skin revealed that his ancestors came from the toe of Italy. Now, he followed me to the living room and I continued on to the kitchen to make some herbal tea. The aroma of fresh mint filled the air as the last rays of sun streamed in through the window.

Returning to my friends, still deep in discussion about Peru, I noticed that Tony, too, was absorbed. He sat motionless, listening to Will. "This endeavor is not a vacation from which we will return with pictures and gifts. This is a journey with a purpose; one we have no intention of returning from. This is a quest for truth, a chance for us to find ourselves and the essence of our existence."

I looked at Will as he spoke, so utterly expressive, his blue eyes glaring and his eyebrows struggling to keep up with his many facial expressions. Fair hair, full and wavy, covered his broad shoulders. He sat with his back humped over, cross-legged on the beige rug and waved his pointer finger around as if he were conducting an orchestra as he spoke . . .

✳ CHAPTER TWO ✳

Everything seemed to fall into place in preparation for our departure. We bought an old bus from a Bible group which was painted light blue with "SPONSORED BY JESUS CHRIST" in white lettering along both sides. Perhaps this was one of the signs that God was pointing us in the direction of the valley. The bus had already been set up for traveling, with carpeting throughout, comfortable airplane seats, a closet and a space for a mattress in the back.

We had put our beliefs into action by letting go of our material possessions; stereo, couch, beds, dressers, pots and pans, dishes, towels, wedding gifts, mementoes, even the sheets off our bed. People came to our apartment yard sale by the dozens. Money was not the main issue; a lot of our stuff was just given away to those in need, for we ourselves needed only enough money to get us to the valley. I became lighter, less preoccupied, with each string I let go, more in touch with 'the spirit.' We kept only the basic necessities and a few trading goods.

My parents must have been distressed. We didn't talk much about it. Perhaps they felt helpless, knowing we held little respect for their advice at this time. They felt that Willy had influenced me in a bad way and disagreed with his ideas. We asked them to come with us as we did all of our friends, but most didn't share in the urgency of our belief in the system's imminent downfall. Don, a good friend, considered coming with us, but thought South America was too military and decided to go to Hawaii in search of a simple life. Tony told us he wanted to join us, but waited until the last week, giving his decision much thought.

In the dreary month of March, 1978, on a cold bleak night, we said our farewells to my beloved mother and grandmother. Their melancholy, tearful faces haunted me as we left our birthplace for what we believed was forever. Will was so anxious to leave that he could not wait for my father to come home from work so that we could say goodbye to him. I wanted to wait for my dad and felt uneasy about leaving without seeing him for the last time. My dad and I had a deep-rooted understanding of each other that still remained, underneath all of this misunderstanding. As we drove away, the fog hung heavy in the air and I wondered if this was an omen and that we should have waited. We drove in silence plunging forward into the unknown, each of us alone in thought.

We met the first of many difficulties at the American border. Suspicious of the hippies in the bus, the guard thoroughly searched our belongings in an effort to find an illegal 'stash' somewhere. Unsuccessful he still refused us entry because we had quit our jobs and thus posed a threat to U.S. society. Will's voice expressed the disappointment of us all, "That's what we get for being honest in this world of lies."

"What do we do now?" I asked.

"Why don't we try the Fort Frances border and tell them we still have our jobs," Ed suggested. "If they won't accept the truth, then we'll have to lie."

The snow blew wildly, making it hard to see. As we turned onto the highway going west, the wind picked up, driving the large flakes into a swirling whiteout. Tension grew. Suddenly, Will hit the brakes and we swerved into the ditch, landing with a jerk and lurching forward in our seats. Ariss awoke screaming. I had known the journey wouldn't be easy, but I hadn't expected all this adversity on the first day!

Will then turned to us. "Satan is going to put blocks in front of us because he's losing his grip on us," he said firmly. "He's trying to keep us from 'the truth.' Try to look at this as a challenge of strength and faith."

After some effort and help from a passer-by, we resumed our travels, crossing the border just as the horizon gave a hint of light. We didn't spend much time in the United States, for we had no time to lose. To us, the States was a modern Babylon and surely 'the system' would fall apart there first. We felt such an urgency to get out of modern civilization. The holocaust seemed to be right behind us, biting at our heels. We took very few breaks, not even stopping the bus to switch drivers at times. If Will was driving and needed a break, he would call Ed, or Tony to hold the steering wheel as he got out of the seat and the next driver got in. This made me a bit nervous.

Watching winter turn to spring and then summer was fascinating. As we drove further south, the snow-covered hills gave way to budding trees, blue-green pastures and vibrant colors. A parallel to the scenery came to mind as I pondered how life seemed to quicken for me in the past few years, with so many changes in so short a time. I had gone from being a dutiful daughter and conscientious honor roll student with hopes of a nursing career, to a non-conformist teenager, thrown into a shaky marriage and early, unplanned motherhood.

Now here I was, riding in this bus, heading for a secret valley in a foreign land. I had just said goodbye, forever, to everyone I loved except Will, Ed, Ariss and Tony. It had been so hard to leave them all behind.

Ariss spent a lot of time sitting on my lap and together we looked out the window at the wondrous sights. This kept her amused for a time, but the constant traveling was hard on a child so young. Fortunately, the rocking motion and the humming of the engine tended to lull us both to sleep. Being in the first stage of pregnancy, coupled with my susceptibility to motion sickness, I was in rough shape. I tried positive thinking and visual imagery to ease the physical discomfort. It helped a bit, but the queasiness was always there.

Hitchhikers added interest to the long hours on the road. We picked up all sorts of people going to all sorts of places, for all sorts of reasons. I enjoyed talking to them and discovering what was important to them. We told everyone we gave a ride to about our quest and offered to bring them along. No one took us up on the offer.

One day, Ariss and I snuggled under a blanket in the back of the bus. The mattress we had put there fit perfectly, making a comfortable bed. The sound of the motor rumbled on, fading as I drifted off . . .

"Maureen, wake up." Ed's soft voice nudged me awake. Ariss was already outside. I could hear her muffled laughter.

"O.K. Ed, I'll be there in a bit." I felt disoriented and needed some time to get grounded. I stretched, yawned and wondered how far we had driven while I slept. As I left the bus the sun greeted me with its warm rays. Closing my eyes and tilting my face toward it, I took a deep breath. The air was light, with subtle hints of newly-sprouted grass and flowers.

"We've just crossed into Texas," Will reported.

Gazing at the rolling green pastures and grazing cows, I replied, "It's beautiful isn't it? The sun feels fantastic."

"We should make it to our cousins' today," said Ed, looking at me. "I hope Raymond will be there, we've never met his folks."

"Mexico is just around the corner." Tony's voice rang with excitement. "Buenos dias, Senora."

"Buenos dias, Senor," I answered him, practicing the bit of Spanish that Tony had been teaching us.

We arrived at our relative's home later that day. The house was nestled among fruit trees and situated on acreage of farmland outside the small town of Fayetteville, Texas. A middle-aged woman came out to greet us. A friendly smile arched over her weathered face. "Howdy, can I help you?" Her eyes quickly glanced over us and fixed on Ariss. "What an adorable child!"

"We are John's children," I said.

"Oh my goodness, you came all the way from Canada. You do look familiar; Raymond has pictures of you all. Too bad he's not here. He moved to Kentucky; finally settled down. Please come in, you must be tired and hungry."

We followed her into a huge, bright, country kitchen. Rows of preserves lined the walls. Bread was rising, giving off a scent of yeast that filled the room. My aunt, puzzled by our strange diet, soon worried about how little we ate. I tried to explain our reasons for wanting to eat only fruit and sprouts, but she just shook her head in disbelief.

"But, the baby needs milk, needs meat, needs potatoes and everything. She is growing. Fruit is not enough for her," she said to me, concern flaring up in her eyes. We were fruitarians because we believed that it was the healthiest way to eat. It didn't take any energy from the body to digest it, but rather gave energy. Being the original food that God gave to man, it was man's perfect food. It was also the most peaceful food to eat, involving no slaughtering of animals, no ripping of vegetables from the soil, no taking; instead it offered itself freely, falling from the tree when ripe. No cooking or preparing needed, it came in a perfect, biodegradable package, so we didn't add to the world's pollution problems.

Our uncle, a kind-spirited, hard-working man, was pleased to see us. He proudly showed us around the farm, pointing out his fig trees, which were nearly ripe. One of our cousins gave us a Canadian flag, which he suggested we tape to the window in the back of the bus. "Mexicans hate Americans. This will let them know you're not American," he advised us.

The next day, we said our goodbyes and headed for Mexico. As we came to the border in the late afternoon, the muggy heat of the day lingered in the air and mixed with the scent of salt water that we could almost taste. Our passports were stamped for one American dollar bill and with no questions asked, after which we soon found ourselves back on the highway heading south along the Atlantic coast. That night we slept on the beach, under the starry sky. The soft sand molded to our bodies, making the most comfortable bed. The sound of waves making love with the shoreline lulled us to sleep.

In the morning we stayed on the beach, relaxing in the sun's heat and the healing salt waters until our skin began to exude that unique odor of tanning bodies. Ariss loved being naked, running along the shoreline and playing in the sand. I sat on a rock, eyes fixed on the infinite mass of water. The moods of the ocean were so diverse. Last night it brought comfort; today, the power of the waves crashing over the beach was so intense it was almost frightening. I wondered if its power was part of God's plan for the end of the world. Would the primordial sea rise to reclaim the earth?

Further down the road, we traded our toaster and electric kettle for a stash of avocados, papayas, mangos and bananas. The fresh fruit tasted great, no preservatives and perfectly ripe and natural.

Twilight poured its magic on us just as we caught sight of the oil refineries lighting up the coastline of Tampico Bay. The fuel-filled air hung heavy, dulling our senses as we crossed the bay on a ferry. Reaching the other side, we pulled the bus over to the side of the road for the night.

For the next few days slashing rain, carried by wild winds, challenged our driving skills. Groups of Mexicans, gathered on the side of the narrow road and waved us down as we passed, thinking we were one of their country buses. We thought they were hitchhiking and as we stopped to pick up a few, the bus slid off the road into the ditch. Ariss let out a frightened shriek as we came to a sudden stop. We were jolted around a bit, but there were no casualties. The bus landed nose up in tangled brush. A group of wet, smiling natives came to our rescue with shovels and picks. Handing out the machetes, our guys joined in the rescue. Ariss and I watched them all work together in the torrential rain. Finally, a farmer pulled us out with his tractor.

Loud grunts and snorts aided the bus to freedom, as a chorus of claps and "yeahs" accompanied the finale. We thanked the Mexicans, but failed in our efforts to get our tools back. So, giving up as gracefully as we could, we pulled away from the dark, smiling faces and all those hands tightly clutching their new tools.

"It's not wise to trust anyone in this country." Tony's voice was agitated.

"Well, maybe they thought it was pay for helping us out," I said. "Besides, they probably think that we have lots of material riches because we are from Canada."

"It's all behind us now and in a day or two we'll be in Central America. We're over halfway there," Will added.

As we approached the City of Palenque, the rain let up. Close to the Mayan ruins was a campground run by some American hippies. Parking the bus for the night, we walked around to explore. On the way to the ruins we discovered a cascading waterfall, sheltered by lush jungle. We stared, awe-struck. Gigantic light green ferns bordered its banks and danced in the slight breeze from the rushing water. Glistening rubber plants grew under towering tropical trees that yielded only glimpses of the sky above. Sunlight filtered through in a perfect balance of shade and shine, giving hints of endless blue beyond. Bouncing streams flowed into a crystalline pool, inviting us to refresh our dusty, sweaty bodies.

Simultaneously, we took off our clothes. Tony gave a Tarzan howl, as he grabbed hold of a vine and swung back and forth over the falls. Ed and Will followed. It was fantastic watching their bodies fly freely through the air into the water and listening to their primal screams. Ariss and I swam in the warm pool, laughing with sheer delight. I felt like Eve in the Garden of Eden. It was so wonderful to be surrounded by the dreamlike setting and mesmerized by the sound of rushing water over rocks, the sun making rainbow reflections on dancing water.

Evening brought with it a star-filled sky; our roof of heaven. Snuggled in sleeping bags, we gazed at the continual meteorite showers, Ariss giving cries of excitement with each one. We talked a bit about life on other planets and then shared the light show in silence. Suddenly, a sound shattered the stillness of the night. It was a gun shot, quickly followed by the cry of an animal. Shrieks and howls continued through the long night unceasingly. As we left, early next morning, we asked about the cries. We were told that the "federales" (police) had shot a howler monkey and the cries we'd heard were the mournful protests of her mate. She was shot for fun. How can people be so cruel? Our little remaining faith in mankind lessened as we rode away in silence. Anger overcame me as I sat deep in thought about the state of the world. Why was there so much cruelty, I wondered. Why do we humans choose evil over good in so many instances? How far we have come from the Garden of Eden! How sad it was. I felt a deep ache in the pit of my stomach. I'm so glad to be leaving this cruel world, I thought, and tried to ease the pain by imagining the Valley of the Blue Moon.

"It's all behind us now. Let's keep our eyes to the future," said Will, as if reading my thoughts.

"Yes, the valley. Can it really be as beautiful as in my mind?" I asked.

"It won't be long before we see. According to this map, we will be in Guatemala today," Tony informed us.

Two hundred miles later, the bus slid off the road again. We waited in the ditch for a few hours before the Mexican Automobile Rescue Unit, popularly known as "The Green Fleet," came to help. The Mexican roads were incredibly narrow and rough, making it difficult to control the large school bus. Will, who did most of the driving, was getting quite annoyed at the situation. He and Tony stayed with the bus as Ed, Ariss and I walked to a nearby hut where a native woman and her children were watching us with inquisitive black eyes. I had brought a bag of toys and baby clothes with me and proceeded to hand out these gifts to the apprehensive, yet delighted, youngsters. Smiles spread across their dirty little faces as they sheepishly said, "Gracias." The women called to someone in the hut and another woman came out. The scene looked like something out of a "National Geographic" film. Their long black hair glistened in the sun. Their tanned broad faces displayed infinitely black eyes. Loose cotton skirts and blouses concealed their figures. They were barefoot. The children's clothing was dirty and ragged. As I looked at their humble hut with its dirt floor, I couldn't help thinking of the society we had left behind and what most people there call the 'necessities.' How very little we really need, I thought. I did not feel pity for these people, for their eyes smiled.

We had taken Ariss' little wooden rocking chair with us on the journey. My mom had made cushions for it out of yellow fabric with a pattern of dainty red flowers. Ed and Mom had redone the chair itself, restoring it to even better than its original state. It had been mine when I was a child. When we 'liquidated' our possessions I just couldn't give it up. It represented so much to me, an heirloom and a gift from my mother, a part of my childhood. Ariss loved it, too. She sat in it even while the bus was moving.

It was time, though, to shed a few of my last attachments. I had learned that true giving involves giving away something you really value. So I walked back over to the bus and picked up the tiny rocker and two of my favorite long dresses. The women's eyes brightened even more at the sight of these gifts. I put the rocker down and handed them each a dress. Then I walked away, feeling great. "There's something about giving that's ironic. The one doing the giving feels like she's received," I said to Ed.

❋ CHAPTER THREE ❋

Night fell, descending on us just as Ariss and I were lulled to sleep by the humming engine. Strange threatening voices invaded my slumber and I awoke with a shock to see three men in army uniforms, carrying machine guns, herding the hitch-hikers we'd picked up earlier off the bus like cattle about to be branded. I felt afraid for them and for us, too. A lieutenant strutted on to the bus, wearing a red baseball cap and holding a copy of "Swat Team," an American comic book, in his free hand. I had to find out what was going on. I boldly came forward, addressing him with: "What do you want?" I spoke to him in English, assuming he could speak it. He couldn't hide his ignorance for I saw through his mask, like the blank look of a dog when it turns its head from side to side, trying to understand you. Then in a whirl of arrogance, two other men boarded the bus and roughly searched through our belongings.

Will sensed my confusion. "We came to a road block. I think someone escaped from jail, or something. We are only a few miles from Guatemala," he told me.

A few minutes later, the men left as rudely as they had come and we were free to go. Will anxiously turned the key, but the pitiful whining of the engine was all we heard. "The battery!" He moaned. Tony went to talk to the Guatemalan border patrol and they ended up pushing us down the hill into their confused country.

In Guatemala City, infiltration of American ways was everywhere. Fine-suited businessmen and women, clutching tightly to their briefcases, rushed through streets lined with soaring office buildings. Their Hollywood clothes and hairstyles seemed so out of place, almost a disgrace, when beside and beneath the skyscrapers lay dilapidated huts, with clotheslines running over the street and dirty-faced children, roaming about barefoot. The bit of native culture that had still survived the Spanish and American onslaught was upheld in the city's colorful cotton-clothed poor.

At the laundromat we were unable to use the machines because they only worked with American quarters. The woman working there didn't have any so we headed for a bank, feeling quite put out. Armed guards, their faces hidden, protected the bank with fingers on their rifle triggers. Their black helmets reminded me of the Dark Force in the movie "Star Wars." "It's so ironic, such heavy protection for money in a country that has none," I said to Will.

At the marketplace we traded some of our clothes for Guatemalan ponchos and colorfully embroidered shirts. We also traded our sleeping bags for hammocks. This was a decision that we would come to regret. Ed and I didn't like the confusion of the market place and found ourselves allowing Will and Tony to do most of the bartering.

The driving conditions in Central America reminded me of bumper-car rides at the fair. Will was the main driver and was getting frustrated with the narrow roads. Honking horns, weaving cars, confused intersections and downright dangerous driving, with a cumbersome school bus in the middle of all that and what do you have? You have a bus sitting in front of a hotel in El Salvador with a "FOR SALE" sign on it.

We stayed in that hotel for about five days. It was a much-needed rest. I gave my wedding dress to our maid. It was an unconventional wedding dress, simple, but beautiful, with layers of lace set in white cotton. Every day she admired it and her face lit up with excitement and disbelief when I handed it to her and said it was for her.

After selling the bus for five hundred El Salvadorian dollars, we took a country bus through the rest of Central America.

Transit systems in that neck of the woods were strange. Chickens, pigs, natives and the odd foreigner shared the long hot hours. A hundred body odors filled the stifled air. Running water and soap were luxuries for these people. The constant perspiration made me feel clammy. By this time I had become practically an expert at fighting off the constant urge to vomit that prevailed throughout our travels. "Mind over matter," I'd tell myself. I was still travel-sick, but if I didn't mind, it didn't matter. I sought solace in dosing off as we jostled down the winding dirt roads that were called highways.

The border crossings into the remaining countries on our journey were quite the ordeal. Armed officials pranced on the bus as if they owned it and all of us in it. I watched the people cringe with fear as their facial expressions became watchful and subservient. We waited in long line-ups, frying in the sun, to be cross-examined, approved and stamped. Vendors set up food booths to entice the weary travelers. Litter, although scattered everywhere, was not a problem. Pigs roamed about, eating anything and everything. I watched amused as one pig actually leaped like a dog after a bone to catch a corn cob being thrown. Another ate Will's straw hat.

Many dark eyes peered at Ariss. Her ivory skin, blue eyes and blonde curls were so unusual here. "Que bella niña" (that beautiful girl), echoed as people nodded to me, their smiling faces addressing her with universal baby talk.

We slept in 'hotels' along the way. They consisted of a few rooms in native family homes. Will, Ariss and I shared a room with two old dusty cots and dirty cement walls and floors and crawling creatures everywhere. But, the warm welcomes we received from the families made the unclean conditions bearable.

From Panama, we took a flight to Ecuador because we did not have enough money to fly to Peru. There we learned that to enter Peru, there is a law that one must have a return ticket. Our funds were nearly depleted. There in the shadows we stood, unnoticed and misplaced, apart from the hustle of the airport in Quito, Ecuador.

"Well, where do we go from here?" I asked, echoing the prevailing concern.

Tony piped up, "I still have my income tax money back in Thunder Bay. There must be some way we can transfer it here. My brother would sign the check for me."

"Yes, but all that takes time," I said. "We only have enough travelers' checks to last a short while. Where do we stay in the meantime? We can't afford a hotel and we don't know a soul here." Exhausted and plagued with the "I'm Pregnant Blues," I was deep in self-pity. My head hung low; I closed my eyes in prayer.

Time came and went, yet we remained there, waiting and wondering. Then suddenly I looked up and saw a native woman staring at us. She came up to Ariss and looked at me with compassion etched in the lines on her brown face. "Hola! Como esta?"

Tony and our rescuer, whose name was Theresa, spoke to each other while the rest of us waited to be clued in. "This woman has invited us to stay at her house, she has two rooms that she rents out for $2.00 a day," said Tony excitedly.

Our faces lit up as we gathered our stuff and followed her to her car, for Theresa was a cab driver. I sent a silent thank you to God for sending her to us. The city air reeked of diesel fuel that burned my nose and churned my stomach as we drove to a suburb on the edge of town. Massive cast-iron fences with daggered peaks surrounded the houses. Howling, barking dogs gnashed their teeth through the spaces, threatening anyone passing by.

Finally the car stopped at the iron gate where Theresa's dog was chained. He eagerly sniffed each of us as we passed by into the house. Ariss burst into tears of fear as we went past, making the dog bark and Theresa lose her tight grip on him for a nightmare of a second. He leaped at us, which made me scream and she yelled at him, pulling hard on the chain until he coughed.

The kitchen surprised me with a fridge, stove and sinks with running water. In the centre of the living room, beside the woodstove, was a small black and white T.V. There was even a bathroom with a shower, although as Theresa had explained; the water pressure was not good. If we desired the luxury of soap and toilet paper, we would have to buy our own. Ed and Tony shared one bedroom and Will, Ariss and I, the other.

Each room contained two cots and a dresser. Putting our clothes into the dresser gave me a good feeling; we were home for a while. But, then I noticed that the money bag I carried around my waist was gone! I panicked. Most of our money in traveler's checks was in it. Now, we were almost broke.

That night I phoned my parents. My mother's voice strained to contain her relief as we touched over the miles. "Maureen? Where are you? How are the baby and Eddie?"

"We're all fine," I told her. "We're in Quito, Ecuador, rooming in a nice woman's home," I reassured her. "How's everyone there?"

"Oh, missing you."

"We are sort of stuck here, Mom. We are nearly out of money. Tony has an income tax return for $500.00 that should be in by now. He called his brother and arranged for him to cash it and give the money to Dad and you. Could you send us the money now, as a loan, until it comes in?"

"Well, I don't know, Maureen, you'll have to talk to your father." Her voice grew cold with disappointment. She had probably been hoping we'd changed our minds and were coming home. I felt like comforting her somehow, but I didn't know what to say. It surely was never my intention to hurt my parents. I loved them. Nevertheless, I had to follow what I believed was true. All too soon, everything was arranged for the money to be mailed to us at the Quito post office.

Day after day, we ventured out on the long bus ride to the centre of the city where the post office was. Bus stops were unheard of and so was bus stopping! People just walked along the route, waved their hands and the bus would slow down enough for them to jump on. Once on it, they were fortunate to find a seat. Packed tight like corn nibblets in a can, the passengers anticipated their stops miles before and squeezed their way to wait beside the door.

On one such ride, a man tried in vain to get on a full bus and fell out, screaming, as it ran over him and kept on going! No one said a word; as if they hadn't heard! Every day we came home without the letter. We were more street and bus-wise, though.

The marketplace where we bought our food was about seven blocks from the house. As we walked there every day, the fierce barks of dogs behind fences and the agitated crowing of roosters tied to hydro poles echoed through the streets. "Why are they tied up within inches of each other?" I asked one day.

"They are fighting cocks, Mo, tied up to get good and angry so they'll give some demented mind a thrill when they kill each other," Will told me.

Fresh fruits and vegetables lined the marketplace and farmers stood proudly behind their tables of produce. We bought huge avocados, papayas, bananas and many other kinds of fresh fruits. In the middle of all this living food lay a massive pig, bugs and flies feasting on its dead flesh, an apple stuffed in its mouth and grapes arrayed on its back. The crowd thickened around it as if honoring this grotesque offering. "How can anyone eat dead flesh?" Ed said looking at me with a face filled with disgust.

"I don't know, Ed, but I'm sure glad we don't." I looked at him, friend of my childhood! My brother and I, despite being only a year apart, had always been close. Instead of feeling the common sibling rivalry, Ed and I got along well throughout our youth and had remained close friends into adulthood.

Ed never wastes words, I thought. He thinks about everything that comes out of his mouth and never says a bad word about anyone. This I admire. Some would say he's shy, but we had often had great one-on-one conversations, especially about mysticism, or spirituality. Ed is a peacemaker and over all, a gentle and beautiful being. There is a calmness about him that always makes me feel good. I remember a story Ed told me about an incident that happened to him a few years back. He was at camp, playing with a gun belonging to one of his friends. They were aiming at birds and Ed shot a sparrow. The bird was still alive and in pain, hanging onto a string of life. Ed's heart sank. He walked over to the dying bird and picked it up. All he could think of was how he could save its life; the life that God had given it and that he had just taken away. The bird died. Since then, Ed has never picked up another weapon. He has never taken another life. The very next day, Mom was stuffing a chicken for supper and Ed saw it for the first time in his life. A bird, once alive and free, now lay stuffed on our table, flat on its back, legs up; a dead carcass. Ed couldn't eat it. All he could think of was the bird that had died in his hands. He never ate meat again. When I asked him why he had been refusing steak at dinner one night he told me, "Maureen, I just realized what it is. It's not food to me anymore; it's an animal that was once alive, with feelings and big brown eyes."

From that day on, every piece of meat I ate had big brown eyes and a few months later, my mom had two vegetarian teenagers to contend with. At that time, neither of us knew there was such a thing as vegetarianism. We were alone in our conviction. Ed and I, against the world! I looked at my brother admiringly. Boy, how I loved this man!

Quito, a city that seemed as large as San Francisco or Toronto, was burdened to extremes. The Catholic Church, laden in gold and rich hardwood and garnished with stained glass windows and crystal chandeliers, stood out against the pitiful shacks.

In Theresa's house, the small T.V. was almost constantly on. "Bionic Woman" and "Six Million Dollar Man," dubbed in Spanish, played three times a day. They were the only American shows we witnessed while there. What an image of North America these programs must have given the natives!

One day, Will, Ariss and I took a hike through the hills behind the house where we were staying. The sizzling equatorial sun bronzed our exposed skin as we climbed the winding trail. After about forty minutes, we came to a flat ledge overlooking the hills and valleys below. The morning sun burned through the haze in full brightness. "Let's sunbathe for a while," Will suggested, as he pulled off his shirt.

"You don't have to talk me into it," I said. "There aren't too many things I enjoy more, especially here with not a soul in sight."

The sun caressed our bodies with its healing rays. Even Ariss sat quietly. Then Will broke the silence "Let's walk a bit further," he suggested.

"Oh no, it feels so wonderful here," I moaned.

"Well, then, you stay and I'll take Ariss with me. We'll be back in a little while," he said.

"O.K., see you guys." I reached over, kissed Ariss on her rosy cheek and watched them stroll away. The solitude was welcoming. I relaxed in a peaceful meditation, feeling a part of nature. Then a noise in the bushes behind me startled me back to consciousness. Turning onto my stomach to inspect, I gasped. There, hovering over me stood two young native men, eyeing my slim, but well-endowed pregnant body with their lustful mouths contorted in sensual leers. I lay paralyzed. My mind was too stunned to think. The older one, whom I guessed was seventeen, reached for my smooth skin with a quivering hand. "Oh Lord, help me!" I prayed.

Then suddenly, I noticed the gold cross dangling from his broad neck and flashing the crucifix I wore at him, I quickly said, "Dio aqui" (God is here). Taken by surprise, he stepped back as if hit by God Himself. The look on his face gave evidence of his internal struggle between good and evil. I took that moment to throw my clothes on and stand up, all the while gibbering all the broken Spanish I knew about God and Jesus, sensing that Christian morals had been drilled into them since birth. I told them that my husband was near as they both approached, their eyes revealing clearly that their groins had won the battle with their Christian ethics.

"Que bella Senorita," one of them said, in a voice that made my skin crawl.

"Think fast!" The words splashed across my brain, as the adrenalin rushed through my veins. With brow creased, I stared over their shoulders and pointed. As they turned to see what I was pointing at, I quickly ran away, spitting up dust with every stride. I could hear their heavy breathing and footsteps right behind me, just as I turned a corner and smacked into Will and Ariss! The boys halted and then ran off like dogs with tails between their legs. Will looked at my scarlet face with questioning eyes.

When I was able to speak, I couldn't stop. "Don't ever leave me alone again! They almost raped me! People appear out of trees when you think you are alone, lurking to take advantage of you. I don't feel safe here . . . I want to go to Peru, I want to be in the valley."

We spent a month in Quito before the money finally came. Theresa was wondering if we were ever going to pay her and move on. I was able to get reimbursed for the lost traveler's checks, which blessed us with food and toilet paper.

❊ CHAPTER FOUR ❊

The muggy air hung heavy as we waited with the crowd for acceptance into Peru. The border stipulations were the toughest we had come across. A ticket out of the country had to be presented before entry. Refused and feeling blue, we stood on the street wondering what to do. I went to the restroom; an outhouse with foot holes to squat over, leaving Ariss with Will and many admirers. As I walked back, I noticed a splash of blonde clutched in a native woman's arms as she swiftly moved away. Ariss? Whipping my head in Will's direction, I felt my panic crystallize. She was not there.

Spinning around to where I had last seen her, I barely felt my body as I ran through the crowd, bouncing off anything in my way, yelling, "Mi niña (my child), in a frantic voice, searching wildly for my precious baby. I could feel my vision blur as the world reduced to the search for my child. Where was she being taken and why?

After what seemed an eternity, I heard the sound a mother recognizes so well; the cry of her child. Instinctively I ran in its direction. There she was, trapped in a stranger's strong grasp and struggling to escape from the shawl that now half-covered her head. Reaching them, I grabbed the abductor by the arm and clutched her greasy black mane with my free hand, holding her tight. Her black eyes glared coldly at first, but were soon melted by the sting in mine. I snatched Ariss from her and shouted, "Mi niña," just as the crowd thickened and Will, Ed, and Tony arrived at my side! My whole body convulsed in gasps of emotion as the gate of relief opened wide releasing my tears. The woman quickly disappeared.

Our second attempt to cross into Peru was successful, even without the stipulated return tickets. Our visas were stamped for a $5.00 American bill.

A warm wind rearranged the dry, sandy dunes beside the road as we walked along the desolate highway into Peru. My feet shook with excitement as they touched the soil of our future homeland. Before us, the Andes Mountains stood, in lofty isolation. They seemed as welcoming as they were threatening; the same way hope loomed above the shadows of all our struggles. Here we were, five searching souls with all of our earthly possessions on our backs, not really knowing where we were going except for a few hints written in a book. Yet each of us truly believed, with every stride we took, that we were closer to our destination: The Secret Valley of the Blue Moon.

A man in an old, beaten up pick-up truck gave us a ride to the capital city of Lima. Diesel fumes, mingled with the scent of greasy food cooking, filled the air. Thousands of food carts roamed the city, day and night. Peddlers sold jewelry, clothes and crafts. Litter was everywhere. In one part of town people threw their garbage out of the windows. Once again, dilapidated shacks struggled to stand in the shadow of towering riches. The contrast between poverty and prosperity was like black ink on white paper.

After a day or two in Lima, we boarded a plane for Cuzco, a city high in the Andes. The stewardess warned us, "It's important not to walk fast, or run in Cuzco, for we are many miles above sea level. The people who live here are accustomed to the lack of oxygen. You must be careful to sit and rest if faintness occurs."

As we walked from the tiny airport, the sights surrounding us arrested our attention and we stood in awe. Powerful mounds of jutting rock lay in every direction. We were in a valley of luscious green hills carved with ancient stone pathways. Cuzco, the capital of the Incan Empire of old, contained fascinating ruins of stone and inlaid gold. I felt a sense of their mystery and power. History was truly alive here.

Tony spoke to some people and found out about a tourist train that ran every day and went higher into the mountains. "We can take the train ride to the highest point and get off there," he suggested. The train ride was great. I felt as though I was riding through the 'wild west,' before civilization stretched its arms across North America. The ancient steam engine reminded of the ones you see in western movies. The hills folded into snow-peaked ridges, where llama and alpaca roamed free. I felt deeply content.

The village where we got off the train stood nestled below grand mountains. Cool, crisp air filled our lungs as we walked through the streets in search of a resting place. Tony made an arrangement with one of the villagers, who took us to his home and put us up in his extra room which was separate from the house, a one-room affair with a shed off to the side that served as the 'hotel' of the village. Three sets of bunk beds were squeezed into the tiny room. The toilet was an outhouse, down the hill.

The following morning we bathed in the bubbling waters of the local hot spring. "Sure beats Banff," Will grinned.

I smiled, tickled with the sensation of it all. After about five minutes in the water, Ariss turned limp as a rag doll and lay in my arms enjoying her bath. Later that day, he bought some alpaca blankets, hats, gloves and ponchos in preparation for our climb into the mountains.

Tony, absorbed in a conversation with a local man, met us back in our room later. He bounced in, beaming with excitement. "I met a man who knows about the sky village." He pulled a piece of paper from his pocket. "Here's a map of the climb and the names of the villages we will have to pass through. God sent us a messenger!"

"Right on," Will said, as he took the hand-drawn map and examined it. As the men huddled together, discussing plans, I stole out into the night for a moment to myself.

Looking up into the dark blue vault of the night sky, I was awestruck! I had never seen the stars so brilliant, or so close. The concept of infinity touched me, in knowledge, born of 'the spirit.'

The next day, we took a ride on the only transit system out of town; a cattle truck. We squeezed in amongst the natives into the truck's open back. Dirt spat up from potholes as the massive wheels plunged onwards and upwards through the mountains. The pulse of the engine echoed through the vast unpopulated surroundings. "Quite different from the Greyhound, isn't it?" I whispered to Will. He nodded and returned his attention to playful games with Ariss.

Black, questioning eyes glared at us as we changed her diapers. I'm sure that Ariss and I were just as strange to them as they to us. They had probably never seen a woman in blue jeans, nor a fair-haired child. These women held their babies' bare bums out over the side of the truck every so often so the kids could do their business, for diapers were unheard of up here. Some mothers wrapped their children in colorful hand-woven blankets and carried them on their backs. The women were all variations on a theme, with broad, bronzed faces and oiled cast-iron hair that gleamed in the midday sun. Hand-woven skirts in primary colors, full and long, concealed their figures. Most were barefoot, with feet tanned and toughened from a life-time spent plodding ancient Inca stone pathways. In contrast to the more primitive attire; a black hat, like a shorter version of a top hat, called a fedora, crowned each female head. The men wore woolen caps with ear flaps, decorated with brown and black llama or alpaca designs. I wore the same, calling it my 'Rocky hat' because it reminded me of Rocky's hat on the T.V. cartoon show, "Rocky and Bullwinkle." Most of these people had bulging cheeks, full of coca leaves. Coca is abundant in these parts and chewed regularly. It is said to numb hunger pains and make breathing easier at high altitudes. Pieces of chalk are put under the lip to absorb the excess moisture that the coco leaves produce.

We sat close together on the truck floor, the wooden sides rising far above our heads. My view was restricted to sky and soaring mountain peaks. The nauseating diesel exhaust burned the inner lining of my nostrils. Worse, the constant bumping motion added to my nausea and the unborn child pressed against my full bladder. Unable to control it any longer, I desperately yelled, "Banjo" (bathroom)! The truck stopped. Struggling over packed bodies, I reached the rear of the truck bed, jumped off and looked around. There was not a tree or bush anywhere. Where was I to go? Edging my way closer to the truck, I bared my bum nervously. Looking over my shoulder to make sure no one was watching, I gasped. Several dark male faces, eyes smiling, leered at me from over the truck's wooden railing. Too nervous to pee, I squatted there in humility for what seemed like forever. I knew then why the women wore long full skirts.

The mountain atmosphere was luminous. Except for the truck, all was quiet and still. No one spoke a word, as if we were hypnotized by it. As night descended, the sky above us seemed ablaze with stars floating in the blackness. The only sound I heard in the whole world was hot tires on cold gravel. Using my packsack as a pillow, I snuggled amongst the warm bodies, holding my sleeping babe against my chest.

After three days of riding, we were let off in a small village, in the dark night. Cold, tired, dirty and hungry, we roamed about the sleeping town. We came to a church and asked the caretaker if we could sleep inside, but the door slammed in our faces. The chilling damp air made Ariss scream. I wanted so much to comfort her, but I was just as much a victim of circumstances as she. Lying on our blankets on the churchyard ground, I held her on my chest and rocked her to sleep. "Boy, we were stupid to sell our sleeping bags," I blurted out. "How unprepared we are."

Morning brought life to the town. We found a tiny restaurant, but because of our strict vegetarian diet we didn't find much too eat. Already we were too high up for fruit. Even though I didn't like fried foods, I did order some fried potatoes for Ariss. We made arrangements for two guides to lead us to the next mountain village. Two mules carried our packs. As we trudged along the mountain pass, the scenery changed from jungle-like forest, to bushes with berries, then to sparse brush and finally tundra. The air grew thinner, making climbing difficult. Our guides' bodies were strong and their lungs accustomed to the reduced oxygen. They walked swiftly, constantly turning to us gringos and yelling, "Rapido" (faster)!

The stone and dirt pathway became lost in rough terrain and rocky ledges. Climbing was exhausting and hunger clawed at our hollow stomachs. Meanwhile, the sky darkened with clouds as the last hint of sun sank behind a western peak and cold silence descended from the surrounding rock. Stumbling in the darkness, we followed our guides, hoping our village destination was nearby. But, when the guides started arguing, we knew for certain what our minds had feared for the last few hours.

We were lost! The cold wind seemed to blow right through me and the sky poured. With the night too dark to see even inches in front of us, we stopped right there. On top of a hill, unsheltered from the elements, we covered our bodies with blankets and our spirits with resignation.

Morning brought more challenges. We came to a land bridge that connected two mountains like a bridge about fifteen feet long, three feet wide, with drops of several thousand feet to either side with nothing to hang onto. Like an isthmus, it jutted out boldly. I've always admired tight-rope walkers, but my fear of heights squelched any desire to emulate them. Now I watched the men, one by one, walk over the narrow ridge with seemingly effortless ease. Casually, Will took Ariss across, neither of them flinching. The gap between us seemed to stretch for miles as I stood there on the other side, the only one left to cross.

"Come on, Mo, just don't look down." My brother's voice broke my trance-like state, but I couldn't talk. I was numb. A barrage of wise clichés sprang up in my mind like pop-up targets on a shooting range: "There is nothing to fear, but fear itself"; "Fear is an illusion"; *". . . If only you had the faith of a mustard seed you could move mountains . . . ,"* *(Mathew 17:20)* yet fear shot holes in all of them. Flashes of recurring dreams I'd had as a child, all involving being afraid of crossing a bridge, came to me. How could I do this? I prayed for guidance as my feet allowed me to take that first step. The vastness and the peaks below on either side were impossible not to see, unless one had tunnel vision. Then a scattering of pebbles and small rocks broke lose and slipped over the edge. Too scared to look, I focused straight ahead and listened and listened, straining to hear the echoing chatter as they bounced off the rocks below. But, only silence answered. This sent shivers across my skin and my feet stuck to that spot as if they were glued. Ed, sensing my panic, started back across towards me. Reaching out his hand, he encouraged me in his soft voice and guided me the rest of the way. I held onto his hand long after we made the crossing.

After hours of climbing steep cliffs and struggling through matted bushes we found the trail. It was so much easier now, that the descent passed quite quickly. Then suddenly, around a corner of a cliff, stood a tiny village nestled in a crown of imposing peaks. Patches of green flowed down to it. Llama grazed freely. Grey stone walls bordered along either side of the pathway, which turned to rock as we approached the settlement. There were several thatched huts surrounding a stone church and a well. Corn, fava beans and potato plants grew in the yards. Cows, pigs and chickens roamed at will. Our guides brought us to a vacant hut beside the church, as inquisitive villagers peered out at us from their shelters.

Once inside, we began to light a fire. This took effort; one of us had to blow on the embers constantly or they would go out. We discarded our wet clothing and placed it near the fire to dry. One of the villagers kindly brought us some coca leaf tea, corn and a type of corn bread that was wrapped in the husk, called tamale. We were so hungry at this point that it tasted like nectar from heaven. To show him we were grateful, Will gave him a pair of blue jeans which fit the man perfectly. He beamed. Spanish was not spoken much up here. "Quechua" sounded to me like a cross between Chinese and Spanish. We weren't able to communicate in words, but somewhat understood.

The Catholic priest who circulated in this region arrived later that day. He was from France and also spoke Spanish. Tony had a lengthy discussion with him and when he had finished he shared this with us: "This priest is really concerned about us. He told me he met other white people who had come searching for the valley." One of them, a woman wearing a white robe, was killed falling off a cliff. Others were reported dead, too. Some disappeared. Some went back home. The climb from here is apparently treacherous, impossible for a pregnant woman." Tony looked at me, his eyes filled with doubt and concern. "I don't know you guys, he seemed genuinely worried."

"I think he's just one more obstacle that Satan is putting in our way to stop us from reaching the valley," Will said. "Why come this far and give up?"

No one else said anything. I wondered if the priest was right, but to turn around now would mean failure. Where could we go? What would we do with our lives? Did we not believe that God was leading us? He had to be, He had helped us in so many ways like, guiding us across the ridge and sending the messenger with the map.

The next day Will, Ariss and I went for a walk and found a secluded waterfall. Bathing in the ice water was painful, but refreshing. The warm sun dried our dripping bodies; then we put our soiled clothes back on. We washed Ariss' diapers as best we could without soap in the stream bed.

When we returned, Ed ran out to greet us in a panic. "The guides took off with the mules, some of our blankets and some other things!" He gasped. "I tried running after them, but they rode out as fast as those mules would take them. To top it all off, Tony is nowhere in sight, I've looked everywhere for him."

I gave my brother a loving hug and we went inside to investigate and fumble through our few belongings. My wallet and hiking boots are gone," Will announced. "Well, there's nothing we can do about it now. Mo, do you have some money and the map?"

"Yes," I said. Not much money, but we shouldn't need to go much further 'til we reach the valley, I hope."

"But, what happened to Tony? Where do you think he is?" Ed asked. "Maybe he's talking to one of the villagers," Will suggested.

Two nights passed and Tony did not return. Our spirits were low; our unity was broken; our brother was lost. I could not figure out what had happened to him. If he had planned to go on to the next village, he would surely have told us. Could the guides have kidnapped him? This mystery would puzzle us for days to come.

That morning, while Ed and Will went to find another guide, Ariss and I quietly sat in a hut watching two women weave a colorful blanket. One of them liked the Jesus beads I wore. My mother had given them to me before we left. The woman fondled them admiringly. I took the precious wooden beads off my neck and slipped them over her head as her dark eyes questioned my motives. "For you," I said, hoping to be understood. Her eyes filled with tears and she pulled at her wedding ring, attempting to give it to me. I held her hand, shaking my head. "No, not a trade, I just want to give them to you," I said. She somehow understood and hugged me while muttering something in her own tongue.

Later that day we ventured on to the next village in hope of finding Tony there waiting for us. We hired a guide and rented four horses, so each of us had a horse to ride, with a fourth one carrying our packs. Will and I took turns carrying Ariss, although he ended up with her more than I. Riding bareback and holding onto the horse's mane and a rope for balance was quite a challenge.

Our guide walked faster than we rode. His body was strong and his chest, broad, to hold his enlarged lungs. He carried a whip, which he used on the horses when they slowed down. Every time he whipped them, we all yelled at him in disapproval. Many times we dismounted and walked beside our horses to lighten their burden. At some points in the day, comedy ruled. The three of us rode in single file, very close together, and with every step the horses farted, the loudest I've ever heard, in all different keys, after which they would sigh in relief. Sometimes their farts would be a prelude for the bigger stuff, which would come gushing out while they walked so nonchalantly, blissfully oblivious to it all.

Throughout our journey, extremes prevailed. One moment I would be laughing and the next, in panic for my life. At one point, losing his footing, my horse slipped and his back leg slid over the edge of a cliff, placing both of us in a horizontal position. I clutched onto his mane with one hand and wrapped my other arm tightly around his neck in a desperate attempt to avoid being swallowed up by the canyons below. Closing my eyes, I said a quick prayer asking God's forgiveness for all my sins. In a second, we could have been carried away.

All I could do was hold on for life and hope I wouldn't choke the animal while doing so. Leaning forward, I struggled along with the horse as he miraculously regained his footing and found the trail. It was as if the very hand of God pushed us back on track. I remained clinging to my friend for a while. He seemed to enjoy the comfort, for I'm sure he'd feared for his own life, as well. Something bound us in those few moments, as woman and beast suffered together equally at the mercy of fate.

Because I was the last one in our caravan, no one had seen what happened. Then Ed turned around to find me lagging behind and waited for me to catch up. "I nearly died, Ed," I told him quietly. "My horse's left leg slipped over that ridge over there, we could have gone over. God helped us. It was as if angel pushed us back up. Good thing Ariss wasn't with me; boy, it was all I could do to hang on as it was." His eyes widened. Are you all right?" I nodded, "yes, a little freaked out, but I'm O.K." We carried on our way.

As we climbed higher, we were gradually concealed in mist; truly in the clouds. Icy rain began to fall and we shivered in the unforgiving cold. The lack of oxygen made us light-headed and Ariss' cries echoed through the canyons, piercing the pervasive silence. Her basic needs were not being met. She was hungry, wet and dirty. I felt so guilty. Will kept telling me to think about how we were saving her from the greater hardships of when the bombs would come; but, a mother's instinct to provide comfort for her young is strong. I had to think of the valley and how good it would be for her there. I tried to make the journey bearable for her. She ate before we did. We pounded her soiled diapers against rocks to clean them because the streams were too cold to keep our hands in. I tried to play with her when we rested, but I knew this was no place for a year-old baby.

At the top of the mountain, there were three white crosses. They marked the halfway point between villages and meant another descent began from here. Our horses ran down the pathway over jagged rocks making our ride uncomfortable, so we got off and walked beside them. In the gathering dusk we eventually deciphered the outlines of a few huts.

As we approached the village, a man and a woman came out to greet us. The man was dressed in a military outfit, the woman in modern clothes. They were happy to see us, or perhaps, the civilization we represented to them. "Hola, buenas noches," we greeted each other. We communicated quite well with them for the limited amount of Spanish we knew. We had all depended far too much on Tony for this. The woman, Maria, spotted Ariss on Will's back and fussed over her the way women do. Philip and Maria invited us into their hut where we shared some lemongrass tea and bread. The hut looked the same as the rest from the outside, but contained a table and chair set, a Coleman stove and a radio. Philip, a border guard, was stationed for a year in this village on the Bolivian-Peruvian border. He and Maria were from Lima and found the change of lifestyle hard to adjust to; Maria especially.

They took us to the jailhouse to sleep. It was a huge stone hut with eight army bunk beds along one wall and no windows. It felt so good to snuggle up under the blankets that night, with the silence of the mountains penetrating even the stone walls. During the night I was awakened by a strange noise. It sounded as if someone was groaning in pain. Was there another person in here with us?

In the morning, enough sunlight came through the door to reveal the mystery. A man lay on the cold dirt floor, groaning in pain, unable to move. Just then Philip came in and answered a few of our questions. He suspected that the injured man had a broken rib after falling from quite a height on his way to the village the previous day. Philip had already called for a doctor on the radio. No one knew what to do in the meantime. I asked Philip to bring me a cotton sheet and we wrapped it around the man. Will and I tried to massage his leathery feet, but were unable to penetrate his thick calluses.

Then I rubbed tiger balm on his forehead and temples and he muttered something in Quechuan. Philip told me that he had said, "Thank you, doctor." I protested, but Will said to let him believe I was a doctor so that he would start healing naturally through positive thinking. I looked at his eyes, staring at me with such faith and felt so helpless. I wished I could truly heal this child of God. Ed suggested that if we could get him off the damp floor into the sunlight it would do him good. So, on a handmade stretcher we lifted him into the sun's healing rays. A smile creased his weathered face.

The sunshine, warm and inviting, lured us to explore the village. We sat by a grand eucalyptus tree and gazed at the tiny, ancient settlement. It reminded me of pictures I had seen of Europe, with ancient cobblestone fences, well-trodden pathways and thatched huts. The wind seemed to whisper ancient stories no living soul could know.

Ariss ran around happily, discovering sticks and rocks. Maria came by and played with her, fascinated with her beauty. She made sure Ariss' bottle was full and gave me some soap and a place to wash her diapers. That evening Maria brought us boiled potatoes, a root vegetable similar to potatoes, and some eucalyptus tea. She told us not to drink the stream water. Maybe that is why I had the runs? I gave her my sewing case, a pressed flower necklace and some clothes. She was delighted with a jar of colored buttons. There was a friendship between us that had an old familiar feeling to it.

Philip arranged for a guide to take us to the next village, although both he and Maria tried to discourage us from continuing our quest. He told us that the author of "The Secret of the Andes" had written the book right there in the jail hut that we were staying in. He claimed it was pure fiction. He and Maria tried hard to persuade us not to go and I sensed their genuine concern.

Yet, as the sun rose in the mist-filled sky next morning, we began a new climb along the stone pathway. Maria's eyes filled with tears as she and Philip waved goodbye, reminding me of my mother and grandmother that night back in Thunder Bay. How far away that seemed to me now. I wondered how they were and ached at the thought of never seeing them again. I couldn't help but wonder if these kind people were right and the book in which we placed our trust was pure fiction. Were we in great danger, as they had said? Would our suffering and endurance be in vain? But, there could be no turning back; the world was going to end and what choice did we really have? I had to put these questions and doubts out of my mind, or I would not be able to carry on. Common sense would just have to be ignored for the time being.

Focusing on our dreams of the hidden valley and enjoying the moment, I walked through the most spectacular scenery I'd ever seen. Mist hung from the peaks like phantoms. A pearl-grey river, flowing into a narrow gorge of rushing, falling water, lay far beneath us. Silence echoed from the surrounding mountain cirques, making us strain to hear something other than our feet against rock. Cold winds rolled off the slopes, bringing snow with them as we moved on in anticipation of the next group of white crosses. The bitter damp weather chilled us to the point where our shivering became uncontrollable. My nose was constantly dripping and my lungs felt heavy with what seemed to be early bronchitis.

At one point we had to climb a wall of boulders greased with a treacherous film of slippery moss. On my hands and knees now, I kept slipping, unable to make any ground. Frustration overwhelmed me as I watched Ed and Will get ahead of me once more.

I felt terrible. My body ached, my stomach was so hollow that its growls echoed through the silence; I was downright exhausted and weak. I didn't want to climb anymore. I wanted to just sit back, relax and eat something. The threatening mountains closed in on me. I felt trapped inside my physical body; a body so tired and sick and weak. I had too many limitations. I sat on the edge of a huge cliff and looked down at mountain peaks and clouds. I felt a dark cloud hovering over me as I anticipated my plunge over the edge. Then I thought of how God would feel about me willingly destroying my life, a gift He gave me. I thought about Ariss, Will and Ed . . . . I knew I couldn't do it. It would be just my luck to survive the jump; bones crushed against the hard rock and slowly die in great pain. The thought made me shiver. I hated pain.

Then I heard Ed's voice calling me. "Maureen, the white crosses are just up ahead over this ridge. We've almost reached the highest point. Come on." Holding my hand, he helped me climb the rugged cliff, pulling me up at places where I kept slipping. The three white crosses represented hope, for the descent began from there.

I watched Will and Ed jump over the slate rocks along the stone pathway. They seemed to fly over them with grace and surefootedness. Having Ariss on his back didn't hinder Will at all. My own movements were slow and jerky as I hung onto the ledges for fear of falling. I tried many times to let go and dance over the rocks like the men, but something inside kept me from it. So once again, I lagged far behind. At one point I could see Will, as small as a mouse, walking around a ledge far beyond me and I found myself running to catch up and being able to jump over the rocks with much more ease. Will was very much a believer in each of us carrying his or her own weight. He wasn't going to wait for me, or help me just because I was pregnant, or frightened. He wanted to make me stronger, more independent. At times I could see his point, but I sure could have used his help now.

Day rapidly turned to night and we were still traveling; cold, wet, hungry and exhausted. Through a veil of mist and a narrow gorge between sloping hills we could barely make out the outline of two huts. As we approached, a breath of wind carried the scent of burning wood. Our guide took us to one of the huts and then disappeared into the darkness.

"Can this be the village?" I asked.

"I don't know. The villages have been getting smaller as we climb," Will answered. "He must have meant for us to sleep in this hut." Will knocked on the huts wooden door. No one answered. He opened it slowly and went in. The door squeaked as it closed behind him. Ed and I looked at each other with yearning eyes. We both hoped we would be able to rest in this shelter.

Will's voice carried through the hut, "Come on in, there's no one here. You guys have to see this, what a 'set up.'" I followed Ed slowly, careful not to wake Ariss, who was sleeping on my chest in her pack. The warm glow of the fire welcomed us. Hot tea, milk and corn nuts were placed by the fire. A bunk bed covered with two woolen blankets lay across the room. The dirt floor, partially covered with a woven mat, was like cobble-stones in a castle to us.

"Well, don't just stand there, come in and receive the gifts that are here for us," Will said.

Although I wanted to believe him, something in me felt hesitant about the whole situation. Perhaps whoever owned the hut would come back and find us there, intruding. We drank the warm tea and sipped the milk, giving most of it to Ariss. Our fruitarian diet seemed less important now. Survival was the issue, not purity. The corn nuts tasted great yet taking someone's food made me uneasy. I felt like Goldilocks eating porridge in the bear's hut.

The early morning sun broke through the haze as we left our resting place. We met a young man and asked him if this was the village of Saci. He shook his head "no" and pointed to the east, where we caught a glimpse of a village in a valley. It looked to be about three miles away.

"I guess our guide dumped us early," Ed said. As we walked down to the village, the sun was swallowed by dark clouds and our hike became very wet. I had been sick with a cold and the runs. Having to go pee every few steps put me behind the others once again. As the luxury of toilet paper did not exist up here, moss or little shrubs had to do. I thought more and more about the things I used to take for granted. How many North Americans were thankful for a bathroom, toilet paper, water to clean with, food to eat and a warm place to sleep? We have so much, yet we are so discontented and ungrateful.

A man and his children came out to greet us as we entered the village. They welcomed us into their home and offered us some tea and boiled potatoes. I was too sick to eat, but Ariss made up for me. She grabbed handfuls of the plum-sized 'papas' (Spanish potatoes), shoving them into her little mouth as fast as she could swallow them, eyes wide open, face covered in them, practically snorting because she didn't take time to breathe.

I felt terrible about putting my baby through all these hardships, yet at the same time I wondered how long 'the system' would remain the same back home. Surely it would be much worse for her there, in the midst of destruction and nuclear havoc. We would not likely survive, especially in such a cold climate. If the holocaust hit in winter, everyone in northern Canada would freeze. So, in comparison, this was just a bit of temporary suffering on our journey to permanent safety.

We expressed our gratitude as best we could and moved on to the heart of the village. There, we spread Ariss' diapers out to dry over the stone ledge around the church and we discussed our goals.

"We'll stay here overnight and try to find another guide and two horses to take us to the next village," said Will.

"It doesn't look like Tony's here, either," I said. "What has happened to him? Did the bandits take him with them when they stole our stuff?" No one answered, but the sorrow we all felt in losing him was completely understood and felt.

Ed went for a short walk and when he returned he told us of a hut that was boarded up, close to the church. So with sticks and metal spoons we worked on getting the boards free and after much struggling, we were able to enter this dusty old shelter. It was much smaller than the one we had rested in the night before. There was a fire area and a bare narrow wooden bench, or bed.

A few sticks had been left so we lit a small fire, enough to take the edge off the cold and to dry our socks. We stripped off our soaked clothes and put on dry ones. We had to keep blowing on the fire to keep it going. Spreading a blanket on the cold dirt floor, we huddled together for warmth, using the other blanket and our ponchos to cover us. I just couldn't get warm. We were truly chilled to the bone.

We awoke to an audience of villagers who gathered by our door, peering in at us with dark round eyes. I thought about these strangers whose lives were so different from anything in our civilization. Their lifestyle was simple and mainly peaceful, but they were ignorant of ways to improve themselves. They seemed to have lost the spiritual magic of their ancestors. They watched us attentively and laughed when I changed Ariss' diapers. I felt uncomfortable and wished they would leave us alone.

I told the guys: "I dreamed about food last night. I was eating Peanut butter sandwiches, pizza and fresh fruit. I've never been this hungry before. My body is craving a good meal. I must be about six months pregnant by now and I still fit the jeans I left in. I'm worried about this baby. Will; I haven't felt him move yet."

"You worry too much," he said. "More positive thinking is what you need, even more than food."

I could see his point, but mine was valid, too, so Ed and I went on a food hunt. A farmer gave us fresh cow's milk to fill Ariss' bottles and although I dislike the taste, I drank some of it for my baby's sake. Then he brought us to a barn where he made cheese that looked like tofu, but was harder in texture. We bought some from him. On the way back, we shared a piece. It was very salty, but my body welcomed the solid food. As we ate, we sat by a lively stream that gurgled and sang. We bent down and drank from it, getting our faces splashed by the cold water. "I love you, Ed. You've been my companion all my life," I told him.

Ed looked at me and I understood that he felt the same. "Do you imagine what the valley's going to be like?" He asked.

"That's what keeps me going. I see a place almost like the Garden of Eden. There will be clean air, peace, home-grown food and simple huts for sleeping in, but most of our living will be done outside, except for the studying in the temple. I can see Ariss and her baby brother or sister, playing with nature's toys and learning to be 'seeing' beings. I could go on forever about my dreams of the valley."

To our surprise, the French priest whom we had met several days ago came to sit with us. He was a village missionary who traveled through these parts. Once again, he warned us of the dangerous journey we were taking and tried to get us to turn around. He walked us back to our hut where we found Will and Ariss about to go searching for a few mules and a guide.

Just then, music came from one of the huts and a man came out and invited us in. The place was filled with drunken, dancing men, who played with an old phonograph player like children with a new toy. They were drinking "chicha," a type of alcohol made from corn roots. I felt uncomfortable there, but we managed to leave with a guide connection for the next day.

The following morning, two mule horses stood outside our hut, a black one and a white one. One was to carry our packs and the other was for Ariss and me to ride. Drawn to the white one, I mounted it, but the guide opposed my choice and helped me get on the black one. I was happy to be leaving this village, where the people were always laughing and staring at us. In a way, this horse I was to ride seemed as wild and mysterious as these people. Will held onto the rope guiding us and the crowd thickened, watching the circus. Will bent down to fasten his sandal while stepping on the rope with his other foot and all of a sudden the horse took off, bucking like a wild bronco. Ariss and I were thrown to the ground while all the locals laughed. Was this a joke? Eddie was furious. His usually shy and quiet nature erupted into swearing and yelling.

Will took Ariss out of her packsack, checked for broken bones and tried to calm her. I had hit the ground right on my tailbone. We left the village of Saci, shaking the dust from our feet as fast as we could. The fall made me hemorrhage and I thought for a while that I would lose the baby, but the bleeding stopped after a few days. I felt that the child I carried was a boy and thought about naming him Sol, which means 'sun' in Spanish.

Visions of the hidden valley filled my mind as we climbed. I imagined everything, from the weather to the people. The people would be filled with the love of Christ and have peaceful energy. Some would be healers and if anyone was sick, they healed him, or her with herbs and the love of God, just as Jesus did. I had a strong desire to be a healer myself and hoped I'd be given the gift. My vision of the valley fulfilled my idea of paradise on earth. We would still work, but it would be work we enjoyed that would lead us to greater spiritual growth and harmony.

Once again, drizzle turned to icy snow and the snow-covered peaks looked like huge teeth gnawing at the sky. This was the last climb we would have to make, for the sky village lay ahead. The book said the hidden valley was ten days down from this last peak. We had nearly completed the treacherous passage through the Andes, overcoming the tribulations of the journey.

Near the top of a glacier-tipped mountain, two huts hugged the jagged ground. Was this the sky village, at last? Unsheltered by mountains, the tiny community was exposed to the cold winds as the glacial chill of evening poured from the peaks. No one was there to greet us so we laid out our blankets behind a stone hut, somewhat sheltered from the icy chill of the wind. Exhausted and past the point of hunger, we huddled together, heads under the blankets for warmth. I dreamed about Thunder Bay that night. In my dream I flew into my parent's home while they were eating and watched them eat. Then I tried to talk to them and partake of the food, but I was invisible to them. I flew out through the glass window, without a cut, in an effortless plunge and soared high up into the air. The desire for food was far behind me.

Next morning the sun tried to make its way through the mist to this mountaintop town. This could be the day. Yet the future hung in the air like the heavy mist. A man came by and we talked to him in Spanish and were relieved he understood. When we asked him if he knew Brother Philip, he pointed to the second hut a few yards away. My legs shook with excitement as we approached it. My entire body was numb with anticipation. This was it. We had overcome all the dangers that had tested the strength of our faith. I knew that all these were behind us now. Brother Philip, or another person from the valley, would be in the hut waiting for us and would escort us to our destination. Could this be real? Were we finally here?

The three of us stood outside the thatched hut for a lingering moment; then Will knocked on the door. The sound echoed, then fell into silence. We waited a moment and I called out, "Brother Philip?" Will excitedly opened the wooden door. Sunlight poured into the dark hut. Empty. How could this be? Where was our guide? We needed one of the valley people to lead us through the secret passageway to the hidden valley. The book said the valley was a ten-day walk down from the sky village.

"Maybe the man meant for us to stay here while he went to get Philip," I said.

"But, maybe he didn't understand us and thought we asked him for a place to rest," said Will. "I'm going to find him and try to communicate better."

Minutes, then hours, passed, before Will returned with the man. He brought us a pot of chuna soup made from dried potatoes. We thanked him for his kindness and asked him again about the valley. He looked at us with troubled dark eyes and shook his head from side to side. From what we could understand, he was telling us he knew of the valley we spoke of, but that others had come looking for it and it didn't exist. Will asked him what the jungle was like, down from this point. Once again, he shook his head gravely and quite clearly made the point that a tribe of cannibal Indians lived beneath us in the jungle. He said if we wanted to live, we should turn around. Then he left us with troubled hearts and minds.

"I think we should go from here ourselves. God has led us this far, He'll guide us safely to the valley," Will said.

I wondered what Ariss' choice would be if she could talk. "But, there's no trail and no guide. Will, that's suicide," I said. "What if all these people are not tools of Satan to keep us from finding it? What if they're just trying to help us? How can you be so sure the valley does exist? From a book that may be fiction? I never even read the stupid book, I just believed you."

"Calm down, Maureen," he ordered. "You're not the only one who's disappointed. But, I haven't come this far to give up on it now." Ed just looked at us, but never said a word.

"What do you think, Ed?" I asked.

"I don't know. Maybe we should wait here for a day or so."

"Yeah, we should," Will concluded.

Perhaps God would lead us to the valley. But, perhaps God had nothing to do with the valley. This I had never considered until now. Disillusioned, I sat in that cold, dark hut, the damp air so wet; it gave off a strong moldy scent. The sound of hogs, snorting just outside echoed through the silence. I am so tired, I thought–beyond hunger, body aching, chest laden with mucus, intestines still cramping with diarrhea. How much abuse can a body take? Was the baby within me growing? Was this fair to Ariss? Where was Brother Philip, or the guide? The valley was a ten-day walk down through jungle and would be impossible to find without this guide, or so the book said. Could it possibly be all just fiction as Marie and Phil had told us? As for the priest, could he be right and was our journey in vain? If, just if, there was no valley, where would we go? What would we do? I was too afraid to say more to Will about my doubts. I had no energy for arguing.

We laid our blanket out on the cold dirt floor of the thatched hut and our heavy, tired bodies on it. Ariss' screaming subsided into muted sobs and then, finally, restful breathing as I rocked her little body back and forth on top of me, trying to soothe her. The two blankets we covered ourselves with barely took the edge off the icy chill. The four of us slept close together for body heat, covering our heads with the blankets for added warmth from our breathing. We never really got dry or warm for almost the whole mountain trip. I would lie there shivering, night after night, until sleep rescued me, freeing me from awareness of my physical state. Usually, I was so exhausted it didn't take long.

Tonight, the dark, cold room filled with rhythmic breathing as I lay there, my mind unable to rest. I thought about the valley and what it represented to me; peace, love, harmony, developing my inner self and becoming Christ-like. It meant living side-by-side with nature instead of abusing it. It meant safety from an insane civilization about to blow itself up. I wanted my children to be brought up in the light of truth and peace. I recalled our journey so far. We had walked along the stone pathways of the Inca, touching a part of history that remained etched in rock, unchanged by technology. How peaceful this land was. So why did I not feel peace? Why was I in such disharmony? Why did I want to go to sleep and not wake up?

At last, I sobbed my misery into a state of prayer. Then, like a ray of light breaching the horizon, these words and understanding came to me. "... *The kingdom of heaven is within ...." (Luke 17:21).*

I had been searching on the physical plane for a state of inner being. I had heard the statement, "... *Heaven is within ...*"thousands of times in my childhood, but I had never understood it until right now. This was why I was not at peace, even though I was away from everything I blamed for my unrest. I had carried my state of mind and heart with me, from Thunder Bay; a searching, unsettled, unsatisfied mind and heart. So the scenery had changed, but inside I was the same. I had gone through the physical journey of climbing mountains without realizing that we all must go through such a journey on the 'inside.' I was beginning to see that happiness was not a place you arrive at, it's a way of traveling. I still felt that I had to be prepared for the end of civilization, but now I thought it might be possible to be prepared inside that civilization.

I could also see another point of view. If the world ends, it doesn't matter where you are physically, as long as you're spiritually with God. The physical is temporal anyway. I thought about Thunder Bay, my parents, family and friends. It would be hard to return there after telling everyone we would never come back. Could we be wrong about the end being so near?

Realizing this didn't make the situation any easier; we were literally caught between a rock and a hard place. Going ahead to try and find the valley meant wandering for weeks, maybe months, without a trail, or guide, through unknown jungles. Also, we had no way of knowing where the valley was, or if we would ever reach it. That is, if we didn't get eaten by cannibals!

Our second choice wasn't much better. With no food or money, we would have to go back through all those mountain trails, ridges, cliffs, unfriendly villages and the wet, cold weather we had just labored through. I had barely made it this far. I couldn't fathom doing it again. I didn't want either choice. It was like choosing between cancer, or leprosy.

❀ CHAPTER FIVE ❀

The next morning we sat on the mountain top, gazing through the mist at a view that went on forever. Even Ariss sat quietly on my lap, mesmerized by jutting earth and encroaching sky. Never had I seen them so close together. Never before had I touched the clouds.

There was reluctance in all of us to turn around. Even Will must have had doubts, or he might have gone on without us. Perhaps it was the temptation of being so close to the valley. Was it really there beneath these soaring peaks? Perhaps, after all, our guide would come.

We sat there, each of us alone with our thoughts. What was going to happen to us from here? Would I be able to make it, up and down through all the mountains we had just climbed? Would I survive? I had barely had the strength to make it to the sky village. Journeying back through all these mountain paths would be even worse than the trip here, because the prospect of the valley was no longer urging us on. Was I being weak, not wanting to venture down into the jungle to look for it? That vision I'd had, that 'the truth' is in my heart; was it just an escape my mind had concocted because of the extreme physical denials I was experiencing? What about the end of the world. Did I now care more about getting a square meal? I thought about how your perspective changes when you are starving.

Will broke my thoughts, when he spoke. "I think we should aim for Cuzco. We can live there until we find out exactly where the valley is. Perhaps a guide can take us all the way. There was some land for sale real cheap," he added. Will wasn't about to give up on this so easily. I could see the determination in his piercing, ice blue eyes.

"That would mean going all the way out of these mountains, then turning around and coming all the way back up," Ed stated, with a subtle moan. Will grinned revealing the wide spaces between his front teeth. "Yes, but by that time, we would know these mountains a whole lot better. We'd be faster too," he said.

"Truthfully, guys, I can't imagine even surviving the journey out of here, let alone back again. I know it's not too noticeable, but I am pregnant and very sick," I said. "And, did you ever consider Ariss and all the suffering we have put her through? I'm tired of all this torture. I'd rather get nuked back in my warm bed at home. I want to go home." I felt like Dorothy in the "Wizard of Oz." How I wished all I had to do was click my heels and wake up from this nightmare, back in my warm bed. "Well, you know something, Will, I sure would love an apple and a peanut butter sandwich right about now," Ed said. "Thunder Bay seems real good to me."

"We'll just have to see what opens up for us, just don't close any doors. The valley may exist, after all. Let's just go day by day, O.K.?" Will answered.

So, with the valley in our hearts we began the long hike back down, through the great Andes Mountains. Night fell upon us with a blackness that allowed no sight. Again I fell behind Will, Ed and Ariss. Stumbling in the darkness, I felt my heart stop with shear terror. ""I can't see! I'm all alone in this foreign place." I thought wildly. I fell into an icy stream and landed on my knees and elbows, bruising them on the sharp rocks. I started weeping, feeling like a lost and hurt child in need of comforting. Only silence answered. I prayed to God for help.

As I attempted to stand, someone appeared from behind me, helping me up. He took my hand and led me back onto the path. "Ed, is that you?" I asked. He never answered. Who was this, an angel? His hand was large and calloused and very much composed of flesh and bone. He mumbled something and I recognized the tongue. It was Quechuan. Where did he come from? There is only one trail. God answered my prayer! Together, we caught up to Will and Ed in no time; this man knew his way. He guided me until we reached his hut, all the while holding my hand.

My rescuer shared his hut and food with us and we slept there with his wife and seven children; all of us huddled together in his humble, one-room home. The candlelight was soft among the shadows. It allowed me to see this good-hearted stranger who had rescued me from the darkness. He stood tall and strong; as if chiseled, high cheek-bones and broad nose stood out on his weathered face. Ageless, dark, inquisitive eyes looked into my soul. He was not sophisticated, nor claimed to be Christian, yet his inner beauty shone. He gave freely of what little he had. We didn't speak the same tongue, yet our spirits shared an understanding greater than words.

There was much laughter that night; the children were laughing in the loft, creating an atmosphere of joy which was healing for us. It was a very special night. I felt secure and safe for the first time in a long time.

The hut stood alone on a ridge, about four miles from the cruel "Saci." I didn't recall seeing it on the way. How I dreaded passing through there again. The family stood outside their hut waving to us as we left. He himself came with us to show us the trail, walking with us until he was sure we knew the way. I turned around to see his silhouette against the mountain peaks and sky. I hoped he knew how much I appreciated his kindness.

Every step I took was labored. By this time my body was on its way from pain to numbness. I doubled up in coughs and sneezed repeatedly. My bowels were still leaking. Fever from my bad chest cold told me it was probably pneumonia now. I was so dirty and itchy. We had not had a bath, or a change of clothes in weeks, or more.

I felt sore and weak all over, yet here I was climbing one of the highest mountain ranges in the world.

Willy's body remained strong. He was much quicker than Ed and I. Even with Ariss in a pack on his back, he sped along the dirt and stone pathway effortlessly and disappeared.

Ed had 'the runs' along with me by this time. I think we both had diphtheria, from drinking the stream water. I could tell he wasn't feeling too hot, either. We both were staggering along the trail like a pair of drunks, half delirious. At one point we were too dizzy to stand up, so we sat on the side of a ledge. I looked around. I was touching a part of the earth that modern man with all his knowledge and technology had not yet prostituted. There was no pollution, no noise of planes, cars, trains, machines, voices . . . just silence; echoing silence. Mountains, valleys, waterfalls and streams, mist, rain, snow . . . yet, I was not at peace. The words *". . . Heaven is within . . ."* came to my mind once again.

"Beautiful, isn't it," Ed said to me. "But, you know what Maureen? I can feel even a greater sense of awe and peace at Dad's camp at Sturgeon Bay."

"I know what you mean, Ed. It's a state of mind and heart, isn't it? Do you think we'll ever make it home?"

"I don't know, Mo." His last words stuck in the air as we struggled to pick up our weary bodies and continue our walk, hanging onto each other for stability. "Remember all the things we took for granted back home, Ed?"

"Yeah, most people have no idea how good they have it, eh?" He answered. "They have a warm dry bed to sleep in, a bath whenever they want, a flush toilet and toilet paper, drinking water, clean clothes and food! I dream about food. I've never been so hungry!"

"I dream about food too, Ed. Think of all the food we refused to eat; bread, rice, beans, nuts. I'd eat a peanut butter sandwich without question right now if someone offered me one."

"Yeah, and people complain about money and wanting new cars and dishwashers!" We both laughed. All of that was so incredibly unnecessary and seemed silly to us, especially now.

Willy and Ariss were waiting for us just before the village of Saci. We walked right through there without stopping.

It was getting dark by the time we reached the two huts up on the hill, a few miles beyond the village. The first hut we came to was abandoned. Will opened the door and we all went in out of the drizzle. All of us were soaked and Ariss was screaming from discomfort.

"I'll try and make a fire so we can warm up, then I'll go look for some horses," Will told us. Ed, Ariss and I huddled together on the small wooden bunk. We kept Ariss between Ed and me for warmth. She was still crying, her tears stinging my heart with such pain and remorse. I wished I could wave a magic wand and make everything comfortable for her. I felt like an idiot for subjecting her to this stupid journey. I started sobbing at first, but then let go and howled and cried like a baby. The three of us lay in that hut, hungry, cold and sick, rocking back and forth and crying like babes in the wilderness!

The door blew open as an old hunched-back native man came into the hut. Anger glared in his eyes. One of his eyes was lazy and stared off to one side in an eerie way. I felt as though I was watching a horror movie when he started hitting us with the stick he used for a cane. Was this his home? Why was he so violent with us? He poked me in the stomach with his stick, making me double over with pain. "You stupid idiot, she's pregnant, you old fool," Ed yelled at him. "Let's get out of here, Mo!" The man hit Ed across the knees as he stood up. I screamed frantically. Ariss was still crying. Will showed up just as we got outside and the man pulled out a large knife, threatening us with it. Then Will produced some money and threw it at him and he backed off. I could still hear him yelling at us as we walked out towards the pathway into the next mountain pass.

The rain poured on us now; it ran off my face and mixed with salty tears. I couldn't think anymore. All my energy was focused on lifting my foot to make the next step. Ed held on to my hand as Will led the way, through the darkness.

Maria came out to greet us at the border village. Her face was full of pity for us weary travelers. It was so good to see her. She took us to the jail hut and I collapsed on the lower bunk.

Having returned with chuna soup, buns and lemon grass tea, she nursed me. I couldn't remember when I'd last eaten anything. She mothered Ariss for the next few days that we rested there, allowing me to drift in and out of sleep. I wondered what month we were in and pondered the fact that my twentieth birthday must have passed without notice. So young yet so old, I thought.

Food passed through me nearly as fast as it went in. My bottom was raw by this time. Lying down for two days just seemed to make the mucus in my chest thicken. I was not getting well.

Philip told us of another route we could take back that would be faster. It was off the trail, but there would be other people leading the way. We would try to meet a truck. It passed through the area once a week and tomorrow was the day.

Our caravan consisted of five women, nine men and the four of us. I rode on a horse with Ariss and we put our packs on the other one. We traveled on a path for awhile, through a mountain pass and over rolling hills. We would never have been able to find our way without these people. We followed them to the spot where the truck would pass by. The thought of not having to walk anymore was so exciting. We waited and waited. Then the man who seemed to be leading us stood up and started walking a different way. We had missed the ride. My heart sank.

The new route took us past a glacier lake and came closer and closer to a glacier on a mountain peak. The icy wind blew through us and a man, seeing how I was shivering, gave me his poncho. The cold in my chest made me cough every few minutes and my body ached all over. I'd probably have been in the hospital if I was at home, but here I was out in the frozen rain, next to a glacier! I was so delirious that I found it funny. Night came in a matter of minutes and it became pitch black. I clung onto the horse's mane, frightened and not knowing where I was going, until a man came and guided my horse. The women started to wail and cry out, making an eerie echo. Were they frightened too? Were they cold and hungry?

At last we came to a mountain cliff. We slept under the glacier that unforgettable night, huddled closely for warmth, strangers with a common goal; to survive the bitterly cold night. Ed told me later that the women were crying because we were walking on the edge of a narrow cliff in the darkness. I didn't see the cliff at all.

The frost-bitten morning brought little relief to our aching bodies. The horses' hooves kept breaking through the thin ice onto the frozen ground. We came to a steep hill where we dismounted and climbed up on foot, at almost a ninety degree angle. My ankles and feet were double their normal size, so swollen, making it difficult to walk. Each step was a tremendous effort. It was well worth it, though, for a short way over the top lay a good sized village, with a road!

The first thing we did in the village of Putina was order toast in a tiny diner. Just as we walked out, we saw the "Camion" (passenger truck) with people piling on. So we hopped on and let the truck do the climbing for us, all three of us grinning at the luxury. We traveled night and day. I don't remember most of it because I slept a lot. We passed through Pucara and arrived in Juliaca, where everyone got off.

Juan, the leader of our caravan, invited us to his home. His wife prepared us a meal of corn and bread, which we accepted gratefully. Juan wanted to help us out, so he bought our wedding rings from us. We were completely broke and owned nothing of value except our gold rings. He also brought us to a cheap motel where we stayed for two nights. There was an outdoor shower. The water was cold, but it felt great to get somewhat clean. I hadn't bathed in a month and my hair was so greasy it stood up on end. I had never been so utterly filthy!

In Juliaca, we went to the police and told them of our robbery in the mountains and that we had no money. They gave us three train tickets to the city of Puno. Our plan was to catch a bus from Puno to Lima and there contact the Canadian embassy, in the hope that they would provide us with a way home.

In Puno, we boarded the bus and were assigned seats on the left side. We drove through the night and all the next day, with short stops for food and the bathroom. We bought fruit whenever possible. It tasted fantastic.

The air here was very hot and heavy. It was hard to get used to the drastic change in altitude, for we were at sea level now. I thought about life's contradictions. Here in the lush forests was plenty of fresh food and the beautiful ocean, but there was also hot, humid air and bugs. In the mountains, there was clean, fresh air and no modern civilization, yet it was cold there and no food grew.

On the second night, the back seat of the bus was empty so I went back there, leaving my seat in the front with the rest. I was able to stretch out and lay down there. Many people got on the bus the next morning and I had to sit up to make room. I glanced up to the front left where my party was sitting in hopes of returning to my seat, but someone had already taken it. I was seated on the right side, next to the window. Glancing out, all I could see was fog, so I drifted back to sleep. The next thing I remember is strange, scattered and unclear. I heard people screaming and crying. I heard Will come over to me and say, "Is she alive?" I felt pain and then I was spinning through space. I saw pure white sand.

When I regained consciousness, I saw doctors and nurses, all in white, talking in a language I didn't understand. I was lying in a bed with a woman holding my hand. I thought she was my Aunt Dodie. Touching the right side of my face, I felt a bandage covering my eye and upper cheek. The area was wreathed in pain. So was my neck. I asked this woman where I was and what had happened and, in English, she told me all about the accident.

"My name is Sister Anna," she said. You have been in an accident, a very bad one. Two men have been killed. One of them sat in front of you. You are a very lucky girl; angels are watching you."

"Where is my family, my baby?" I asked.

"They are all fine. No one was hurt but you. They are staying at the convent with me and the other sisters. Your daughter is beautiful," she answered, in perfect English.

"Where am I and how did it happen?" I asked her.

"You are in Arequipa. The accident took place between here and Lima, but closer to here. A large truck didn't see the bus in the heavy fog. Both vehicles swerved to avoid a head-on collision and the truck hit the back of the right side of the bus right where you were sitting. The doctors say you will be fine. You had glass in your eye and face and they fixed it all up; a bit of plastic surgery, I believe. Now no more questions, just rest," she demanded.

I liked Sister Anna. She was the mother I needed at this time. I obeyed and drifted off to sleep. When I awoke I could see a little better, although seeing from one eye was a skill that took time to acquire. I was in a large room with eight beds in it. All of them were occupied, but one.

"Buenos dias, bella Chiquita (Good day, beautiful girl)," a rather large, jolly women said to me.

"Buenos dias," another voice echoed. This one was very strange and I turned in the direction of the voice to see where it was coming from. The voice came again and I realized it belonged to a parrot. He was sitting on the shoulder of one of the patients. A parrot in a hospital, speaking Spanish! Will, Ariss and Ed walked in just then. Ariss climbed on me, giving me a big hug. "I brought you an avocado sandwich on dark rye, Mo." Will smiled as he handed me the sandwich.

"What a treat. Thanks." Diving into the sandwich, I asked them to tell me everything.

"We found you all curled up under the seat in front of you. The way your legs were bent, we thought they were broken. You sure have been blessed. Two guys were killed. Both of them sat near you," Will explained.

Just then a man in a white suit came in with another man who spoke to me in English. "This is the doctor who is looking after you. You are a very lucky girl. A lot of glass was taken out of your face and eye, but everything else looks intact."

"How is the baby? I am about seven months pregnant."

The translator relayed this to the doctor, who immediately took on a look of surprise and concern. He spoke to the man in such rapid Spanish that I caught only the last word. "The doctor did not know that you were pregnant. He wants to examine you right away."

"Wait a minute. Before you go, I want to know if I will be able to see from this eye," I asked, pointing to the bandage on my right eye and cheek.

"The doctor says he can't say. It's too early to tell, but most likely you will."

The thought of losing my eyesight frightened me. I also wondered what my face looked like, under the bandage.

The examining of the fetus was done in another room. Afterwards, I was told the baby was no more than the size of a three or four month-old fetus. The doctor said it was impossible that I could be seven months pregnant, but then, he had no idea of what I had just been through. I felt afraid for my baby, but I knew that worrying wasn't going to do any good. I decided to try to make things right, from here on in and began by 'pigging out.' The kitchen staff realized that I was a vegetarian after about a week and stopped giving me meat and began piling on the veggies. The other ladies who shared the room gave me the portions they didn't want and Will and Ed brought in sandwiches and fruit every day. It seemed as if all I was doing was eating. Talk about extremes. One week I'm starving and climbing all day long to a point past exhaustion and the next week I'm lying in bed and stuffing my face with all kinds of food. I loved it! It was like an exotic holiday for me. I thought about hospitals back home and how everyone complains about the food and the food is ten times better in Canada, than here. Yet the only thing I really minded was not having hot running water. I was still so dirty and a sponge bath wasn't enough. They weighed me after three days of eating and I was forty three kilos (94 lbs.). Not much for being five feet, seven inches tall and seven months pregnant!

Visiting hours were anytime and children were allowed, so little Ariss came with the guys. I missed her so much. Will was anxious to get to Lima and arrange something with the Canadian Embassy, so he arranged to have me moved to a hospital there.

We drove from Arequipa to Lima in a taxi. The ride was bumpy and unpleasant and I didn't feel good at all. Lima smelled of diesel mingled with the dirty scent of a big city. Neon lights flashed propaganda while beneath them, barely standing, were shacks with ropes of laundry hanging on them. My heart went out to those people. I knew the pain of hunger, but seeing this seemed to make my own pain grow lighter. Rows of fig trees grew on either side of a beautifully kept street. This must be the high class section of town, I thought. The cab stopped in front of a huge, white building that didn't look like a hospital at all. It looked more like a manor house on a rich estate. Tropical gardens surrounded the building.

The bus company covered the bill in Arequipa and the one in Lima. They also provided a hotel for Will, Ed and Ariss, but it was so far away from the hospital that it took them over an hour of riding on buses to get there.

This hospital was different from the last one; it reminded me of a hotel. My room had two beds and a private bathroom. There was a shower down the hall. The bed on the other side of the room was empty. I lay down to rest and a young man in a bell boy's suit brought me dinner on what looked like a silver tray. I wondered if I were in the right place. Somehow there must have been a mix-up, because the hotel provided for the guys was in the slums of the city. After hours, Ed, Will and Ariss came in beaming and handed me three sandwiches on dark rye.

"Guess what, Mo?" Ed asked me with a smirk. "The bus company has given us an open credit at a restaurant. We can go in at any time and eat anything we want without paying a cent. Little did they know we were starving for almost a month!" We all laughed. It felt so good to laugh.

Here I also ate and ate and went to the bathroom a lot. After a few days the patch came off and I was able to see. Blurry, but I could see. My face was so puffy and looked weird without eyelashes or eyebrows, but it would heal. Near the end of my stay there, Will left Ariss with me for a whole day. The nurses just loved her; they put a tiny hospital gown on her. She looked like an angel. One of the nurses took me outside to see the beautiful flower garden surrounding the yard. At first she insisted I go in a wheel chair, but later we walked together.

After ten days of healing, I was dismissed from the hospital and we went to the Canadian Embassy. Will said they had been giving him the run around. I really didn't know what was going on. In the embassy we met a couple from Canada.

"What city are you from?" The woman asked. "It's a place in Northwestern Ontario called Thunder Bay. It's in the middle of nowhere," I answered.

Her eyes got really big and she was so excited that she practically yelled. "So are we! Can you believe this; we're from the same town!" The conversation moved on to streets and high schools and people. Wendy gave us her phone number and told us that she and Gordon rented a room from a really nice Peruvian family. They both wanted to get together with us again.

After the visit to the Embassy, we had an appointment with the bus company and had to go. "We can sue them for permanent damage to your face, Mo," Will informed me. "So, we have a settlement of money to deal with."

Inside the office, a young Spaniard in a business suit sat at his desk peering at us with dark, untrustworthy eyes. Standing next to him stood a woman who spoke English. They brought out a paper with fine print, all in Spanish. She translated what was on it and we were told that until we had a doctor back in Canada to see me, the settlement would be open. We asked for enough money to get back home by air and she said there would be no problem if I signed the paper in front of her. They gave us five thousand soles, which sounds a lot, but amounts to about thirty-five dollars in Canadian funds. That was all we ever got from them. The paper I signed was a release form. They duped us.

The next day Wendy and Gordon came and picked us up. A drive through the rich section of Lima was interesting. The home they stayed at was beautiful and wealthy by local standards, but comparable to middle class by ours. The people who owned the house fell in love with Ariss and invited us to stay there until we left for Thunder Bay. They had hot running water and a huge bathroom upstairs. A hot bath felt so luxurious! A servant girl did all the cooking and cleaning. She lived in the attic, which was reached by outside stairs and separate from the house. The girl was Indigenous, the owner's Spanish and I watched how differently she was treated. She didn't eat with the rest of us, nor did she use the same dishes or utensils as the rest of the family. What amazed me was that she didn't mind at all. It seemed to be proper and accepted behavior. The people were kind who opened their home to us and I was very grateful.

❋ CHAPTER SIX ❋

We phoned our families and they volunteered to send money for the airfare home. When it arrived after a few days, we bought our tickets.

As we boarded the huge jet, I turned around and looked at Peru and thought of the valley that I was taking home with me. In a sense, my journey had just begun. The long hours air-bound gave me lots of time to contemplate. I recalled all that had happened over the last four months. It seemed more like four years. I wondered why so many hardships seemed to come my way, while Will and Ed didn't have to deal with as many. I knew that being brought up in a middle-class family in the 'new world' had sheltered me from the reality of true suffering. Willy, ever since I had known him, had been trying to 'toughen' me by letting me stand on my own two feet in every sense of the phrase. That was why he had walked ahead and didn't help me over the difficult places. He believed in each of us carrying our own weight and was coming from a place of no pity in his own heart and mind. Perhaps, I thought the journey was different for Will and Ed because so much of what we perceive has to do with our 'inside' world of fears and beliefs. Perhaps more suffering had come my way because I was the weakest of the three, or perhaps it was because I needed these trials to grow. Or, maybe common sense got the better of my faith at times and the resulting doubt made my heart and focus falter. In contrast, Will was like an arrow flying straight for the centre of the target, always walking with his 'will' pointed in the direction of the valley. Ed seemed to be somewhere in between Will and I.

I also thought about what we were going to do when we got home. We had given away all of our possessions, given up all of our hopes for the future of our society. What would we do now? I was sure Mom and Dad would welcome us into their home for a while, but we had left telling everyone we would never return. A lot of pride was about to be swallowed. I felt a longing to love people and to try to see the positive side of things. I prayed for guidance and direction and for the health of the baby inside me.

When the jet stopped for a few hours in Miami, we walked around in the sunshine and strong winds. I watched palm trees bending, almost in half, from the powerful winds and thinking that they looked as if they were going to break. I compared them to myself and what we had just been through. From Miami we flew right to Thunder Bay. As we passed over the familiar area, almost in a dream-like state, I suddenly realized we had made it! A vision of us up in the sky village surfaced and I remembered wondering if we would ever make it home. When we finally stepped off the plane a sense of accomplishment, tainted with a feeling of failure and humility, filled my heart.

Seeing some figures up ahead, I recognized Will's family as he walked over to them. I caught sight of my mother's nervous smile and eyes veiled with tears as we drew near. She took Ariss from my arms and my Dad kissed and hugged me, muttering, "My prodigal daughter has come home. Praise God!"

"You look so skinny; all I can see are your big brown eyes!" My mother exclaimed.

"Let's go home and put some meat on your bones, son," Dad said to Ed. Will went home with his family and Ed, Ariss and I went with ours. As we drove through the familiar streets, I thought about how everything had remained the same, yet I had been through so many changes. It was now the end of June, so the grass was deep green. Flowers were in bloom everywhere and the air was moist and heavy. As we pulled into the driveway of my parents brick bungalow, an old sense of security wrapped around me.

"I have supper all prepared for you," Mom informed us excitedly. "We're having salad, broccoli, beans and potatoes."

Ed and I smiled at each other. A home cooked meal. What a blessing.

We described some of our journey through the mountains. My mom, dad, sister and grandmother were a captive audience. I was so happy to see them all, especially my grandmother who held such a special place in my heart. After supper my mom and I gave Ariss a long bath. She was happy to be home, too. Mom was worried that she might have rickets from malnutrition. "We'll take her to the doctor tomorrow."

"Mom, don't worry," I said.

"You'll all be going to the doctor. I've already made appointments for you," she replied.

"Thank you Mom, thank you for caring and loving," I said affectionately. There seemed to be a bonding taking place. I had not felt close to my mom since my teenaged rebellion. Will hadn't gotten along with my parents and I had always felt caught in the middle. But, Will eventually had won out and I, as a result, was not nearly as close to my parents as I could have been. "Thanks for letting us stay here, Mom," I added.

"Oh come on, Maureen, this will always be your home, too." As she spoke, Ariss was blowing bubbles in the water. Her laughter lightened my spirit. "I don't want Willy here, though," Mom continued. "Tony told me how terrible he was to you."

"Tony! Tony is here? Why did he leave without telling us?" I asked.

"Well, you'll have to talk to him, but as I understand it he left for two reasons. One, he didn't like the way Willy was treating you, and two, there was a priest who told him the valley wasn't there."

I ran to find Ed to tell him about Tony and then returned to Mom and our conversation about Will. She was dressing Ariss in a pretty pink dress and combing her hair. "Mom," I began, "I know you have a hard time accepting Will, but he's my husband and her father," I said pointing to Ariss. "If he's not welcome here, then we aren't, either."

"Well, by the way Tony talked about it; I'm surprised you want to stay with him. I'll discuss it with Dad."

"Mother, in less than two months I will be having another baby. I do love him and I want to give this marriage my all. Perhaps this trip has settled him down a bit," I said hopefully.

She looked at me, her face full of doubt. "Let's forget about it for now, go enjoy your bath," was all she said. Boy, did I enjoy it. I was taking very little for granted anymore.

My parents agreed to let Will stay with us and I appreciated their generosity. I felt so humble that I told Mom I would be her servant, to work for our room and board because we had no money. She was quite puzzled by this. I helped her out as much as I could with the household chores. My dad was elated to have us home. Never given the opportunity for strong family ties in his youth, he had become very family-oriented as a father. His children meant the world to him. We had good talks about our journey and he would tease me and say, "So where else do you want to travel, Maureen?"

"I don't want to leave here. I've had it with car sickness and adventures. I've done enough traveling to last a lifetime," I replied and really believed I meant it.

Tony came to visit and we shared our stories of what had happened after we separated in Peru. He'd experienced quite the adventure, getting back home. Someone tried to kill him in Lima. Traveling alone in those countries with little money wasn't very wise. He told us that Don, our friend who went to Hawaii, and another guy, had been in town since a few weeks ago, dressed in long white robes. Don had told him that Jesus was back on earth and that they were following Him. I watched Will's face light up at the news and my heart cringed with the fear of losing him. There was no way I was going to believe anything off-the-wall anymore. Tony never did tell us why he left and we just accepted that he must have had his reasons.

Our doctor's appointment revealed parasites living in us all. It turned out that I was extremely anemic and Will had hepatitis. I went for daily iron shots. My parent's grocery bill must have been atrocious! We ate so much food.

Will and Ed cut their hair short and shaved their beards to achieve a more acceptable social image and ventured out to find jobs. Ed found one at the local paper mill and Will at a men's clothing store. It was strange to see him dressed in a suit and going to work. It was quite the culture shock.

As for me, I was still unable to ignore the corruption and suffering in the world. The futile lifestyles that so many seemed trapped in, still gnawed at my heart. I tried so hard to be satisfied with the typical, North American dream, but something was still missing. Although all the physical comforts were provided again, my heart ached with questions. What kind of life was I to live? Was I to dive right into the material world and forget about my ideals? Was I meant to be just an ordinary Canadian mother, absorbed in the struggles of child rearing? Although I now realized that heaven was in my heart, I was unsure where my spiritual search would go from here. A part of me wanted to quiet that searching nature and just 'be.' To push back that part of myself that felt I was selling out for the comforts of food and shelter. Why was I not content?

One day as I stood at my mother's sink doing dishes, I gazed out of the window at a seagull gliding in the cool late summer breeze. How free it danced through the air. I'd always wished I could fly. My yearning spirit surfaced again and I went deep in reflection about Jesus and the messages he tried to bring to us. Why after so many years is mankind so far away from them? And where am I supposed to find 'the truth?' The churches seemed just as confused as me, I thought, as I wiped a pot. I knew that 'truth' was lying inside my heart waiting to be realized, but I wanted to 'know' now! Like most of my generation I was looking for instant enlightenment. I said a silent prayer asking God to show me the way.

A knock at the door brought me out of my thoughts. I opened it and stepped back in surprise at the spectacle in front of me. I nearly swallowed my heart. Barefooted, in a long flowing white robe, stood a man who looked like an angel! Beams of light seemed to pour from his bright blue eyes, captivating me. Had God answered my prayer that quickly? Then I recognized him. He was our friend Don and I remembered that Tony told us he was now a follower of Jesus. I couldn't believe the change in Don. His face was so relaxed and peaceful, his eyes so powerfully magnetic. His entire aura was mystifying.

"Hey, Don, it's good to see you." I plunged forward to give him a hug. "Love without touch, sister," his words stopped me. I was surprised by this strange comment. What did he mean? I led him to the family room where Ed was.

"Howdy, brother," Don greeted him.

Ed's eyes gave away his surprise. "So how was Hawaii?" He asked.

"Hawaii was great! I met an angel there who gave me the keys to heaven," Don replied, in a smooth-flowing voice full of confidence.

I couldn't get over his eyes. I remembered him having beautiful eyes, but something about them was different this time. They were filled with a light that seemed to draw me into it. I thought about how much he looked like the paintings of Jesus, I'd seen. I had to know what he was all about.

"What are the keys to heaven?" I asked.

"No killing, no sex, no materialism; the life of Christ," he told us seriously. "They are a way of life, the guidelines to follow if you wish to dwell in heaven. Heaven is in your heart, a state of consciousness. It has always been within us. When Jesus came to earth two thousand years ago, he tried to teach us that. The first step towards heaven is not to kill. It involves being non-violent with man, or the animals. Therefore, a pure vegetarian diet is important. You guys can relate to that. That includes not stealing from the animals, so no milk, eggs, or honey. God's people don't eat carcasses, or wear dead skins. Their consciousness is beyond death. We are barefoot because the ground we walk on is holy. The concept of no killing goes much deeper than that, but as you live this life more secrets are revealed to you."

What he said made sense to me. I had just been learning that heaven was in my heart. Being a vegetarian for years, I agreed with his ideas about not killing the animals. Wearing leather, or furs, hadn't really occurred to me though, because I thought animals were killed for food and their skins were just used so as not to waste them. Since our return from South America we had been eating cheese and milk. They seemed pretty harmless to me. Yet what he said struck me.

Don continued, "Fruits, nuts, grains and vegetables were the foods God originally gave man to eat. Can you see Adam slaughtering animals in the Garden of Eden? There never was, or ever will be, killing of anything in paradise. *Genesis 1:29* says *". . . Behold I have given you every herb bearing seed, which is upon the face of all the earth, and every tree in which is the fruit of a tree yielding seed; to you it shall be for meat . . . ."* There is an abundance of live food. There is no need to kill, or steal. The second key is no sex and is pretty straight forward. God loves us all, equally. In truth, we are all brothers and sisters, because God is our Father and the earth is our Mother. Jesus didn't take a wife and multiply his seed. He is our example. It's time to rise above the desires of our flesh and learn to truly love. The world is coming to an end, so it's not the time to be bringing more flesh bodies into it. It's time to multiply in 'the spirit'!" Don's words flowed from him without hesitation, or doubt. All at once I felt ashamed of my protruding belly.

"No materialism means no attachment, or ownership," he continued as Ed and I remained captivated. "We don't work for man, or money; you can't serve two masters."

Jesus sent his disciples out and said, *". . . take no shoes, no two coats, no purse worthy of a thief and follow me . . . ." (Mathew 10:10)* His disciples traveled from town to town preaching the word of God. Where they were received, people shared food with them and where they weren't; they shook the dust from their feet and moved on. That is what we are doing; we are living the life of Christ because he is back here on earth gathering his flock. His new name is Lightning Amen, for he has come like lightning from the east to the west. Last time Jesus came, the seat of corruption was Rome in the East. This time, it's in the West. Babylon, the great whore, is the United States of America, the seducer of all nations." Don spoke with such conviction.

"But, the Bible said that he would come in the clouds and every eye would behold him," I said.

"You're right, sister," Don continued coolly. "He has come in the clouds in man's eyes, for every eye shall see him, but few will know he's the Lord. He's the most beautiful, loving being I've ever met, but most 'earthlings' see some nut dressed up in a sheet."

"You mean you've been with him?" Ed asked.

"Yepper, I sat next to him and listened to him preach," Don nodded. "The Second Coming of Christ has happened on earth, right now, and we are either with him, or against him. Read the Book of Revelation, man. Jesus said He'd come back and collect his bride. His bride is whoever loves God more than this world, more than their own life. So this white robe is my wedding gown." Don pointed to his robe.

"But, how do you know this guy really is Jesus? How do you know this is the real thing? You could be led astray," I said.

"How do you know what a peach tastes like unless you take a bite? You can't really explain the taste of a peach, can you? When someone takes a step toward God in blind faith and stands on the foundation of truth which is the 'life of Christ,' God opens their eyes to what is righteous. You know He's Jesus because the Holy Spirit reveals it to you as you live this way." Don spoke so calmly, yet strongly. The words flowed from his mouth so naturally. He didn't fumble, searching for words. They were always there and they were always right. He truly believed what he was saying. I wondered why he was here. Was what he told us true? Did God really send him to us, or was Don in need of straightening out? How would I know if this guy Lightning Amen was Jesus? And if he really was, how could I not follow him? But, what about the false Christs that Jesus warned us about? Just then Ariss came running into the room. Don smiled at her and said to me, "Ease your mind. Be like a little child." Did he read my mind?

After a while Don stood up and asked if we could go outside for some fresh air. We all went out to the back yard. It was a cool, sunny day with the leaves on the trees giving a hint of color. I looked at Don in bewilderment as he pulled out a can of tobacco from his white sack and rolled a smoke. Suddenly his angelic purity diminished before my eyes.

"What are you doing?" I exclaimed. "You are defiling the temple of God!"

"No, I'm just partaking of an herb of the earth. God never said anything about smoking. It's the world that says it's bad for you. I don't believe in the ways of the world, sister."

"But, Don, it's a stupid thing to do. I can't picture Jesus smoking," I said.

"Well, he does sister. And he smokes herb, too. Just to blow your mind," he added, "*. . . You're not defiled by what goes into your body, but by what comes out . . . ." (Mathew 15:18)* He threw another Bible quote at me.

"I can't see Jesus Christ smoking. There is no way. He'd be beyond an addictive habit," I told him almost angrily. Willy came walking up the driveway and they started talking, but I'd had enough. That smoking bit put a damper on everything Don had told us earlier. I went back to the house, back to the real world and my image of a Jesus who doesn't smoke. I helped Mom with supper and she invited Don to join us. Shortly after the meal we said our farewells and watched Don walk out of our lives.

He was heading south for the winter to preach the word of God where his bare feet wouldn't freeze. I wondered what Will and Ed thought about his ideas. Then Will told me Don had asked him to go with him, but he'd answered that he didn't want to leave me. I was happy to hear him say that. It gave me a sense of security that I had never felt with him before.

As the days passed, I became engrossed in preparations for childbirth. The baby took extra time to grow and was at least a month overdue. In two months I had gained twenty pounds! My life was becoming very predictable and I was happy that way.

On September 18th, 1978 on my mother's forty-second birthday, I gave birth to a beautiful baby boy. He weighed seven pounds, five ounces and was in perfect health; our miracle baby. I knew he would be all right, even though I was confronted with other peoples' doubts. The baby took every bit of nourishment I had in my body. He had deep blue eyes and peach fuzz, white-blonde hair. That little "Mr. Magoo" was beautiful to me. We named him Solomon, meaning "peace." We often called him Sol, which is Spanish for "sun." I remembered thinking about giving him that name while I was traveling through the Andes.

Since the visit with Don, something subtle had been happening to me. Many times when I'd take the children for a walk, I'd look down at my feet and feel guilty for wearing leather shoes. One time, I actually felt my feet burn in them. The same guilt came up when I was eating cheese, or yogurt. A part of me felt it was wrong. I gave my leather shoes and boots to my friend Laurie and she bought me a pair of white vinyl snow boots. I felt much better without animal skins on my feet.

In October, we moved into a beautiful home. Brian, a friend of my parents, offered to let us stay there. We were only required to pay the utility bills. The rent was free. What a wonderful gift Brian gave us. He was traveling, doing missionary work for a year. This home had four bedrooms, a fireplace, dining room and a cellar full of fresh preserves that Brian welcomed us to. He called the house "Pooh Corner" because he had pictures of the cartoon "Winnie the Pooh Bear" in almost every room. I was so happy there.

Ariss and Sol were my main concerns and they were growing, happy, healthy children. I loved being a mother. Sure it was stressful at times, but the joy I felt melted the negative aspects. I felt so blessed. I had two beautiful children, a warm shelter that was more than I ever expected, food to eat whenever I was hungry, hot water to bathe in, a toilet and toilet paper, a warm bed to sleep in. I appreciated all of this so much. Ariss, Sol and I would have baths together nearly every night. Then we would sit in front of the warm fire and wait for Will to come home. I was starting to feel a contentment that I never felt before. God was showing me how to serve Him, in my own way, through my children.

Sol was a good baby. He seemed much more contented than Ariss had been at a month old. For hours he would lie on Will's lap and stare into the dancing fire. He had such a calm spirit.

Ariss was so much happier here. The first month we were home, she was too weak to walk much. Now she ran everywhere and was into everything that toddlers do. She made me laugh when she pulled up her shirt to breastfeed her dolly while mommy fed the baby. She was a good help for me, too. She still awoke screaming in the night quite a bit, though. At six a.m. every morning she would wake me saying, "Soup, soup." She wanted soup for breakfast for months.

Will came home from work one cold November evening and told me he had bumped into Don. "He's staying the winter in town now because his sister Judy was hit by a car on the highway and badly hurt. Judy, Les and a guy named Jerry put on white robes and went with Don when he was here this summer. Don's going to wait for her broken arm and leg to heal and then they'll all leave together," Will told me, his excited tone showing me he was interested in this strange group that Don was a part of.

"Do you think these people are really following Jesus?" I asked him.

"I don't know, Maureen. It is a good possibility, though," was all he said.

The next day, Don came to our home. He was so full of love and positive energy, being in his presence was like taking a breath of fresh air.

"God has a mission for me, here in Thunder Bay," Don told us. "That's why he 'set-up' the accident. He wants us here for awhile. I have a strong feeling there is lots of 'open heart surgery' he wants done here," he smiled at me as he spoke. I wondered what he meant.

Don's visits soon became more frequent. I knew when he was knocking at the door because he knocked and walked so softly. The other visitors made a lot more noise and Will's feet were heavy compared to Don's. I felt excited each time he came over. I loved being around him. His energy was healing. Maybe I could learn something from him without having to believe exactly what he does, I thought. What made this man so different from anyone I had ever met? Peace, love and harmony seemed to emanate from his being. Nothing depressed, or upset him. He was so patient, so centered and so kind. He possessed all the virtues that I wanted.

Other friends of ours, Les and Jerry who had traveled with Don, Don's sister Judy, my brother Ed, Tony and Cheryl visited often. We shared many meals together, talked about God and sat in front of the fire in silence. Everyone was intrigued with Don's way of life. Many evenings we sat listening to Don preach and tell stories of the Christ Family and his adventures traveling. He left all of us with a feeling of awe; I could see it in everyone's eyes. As for me, he looked and acted just as I imagined Jesus would, except for the smoking, of course.

One snowy evening, the nine of us sat around the fire listening as Don talked to us about the deceptions of the world. "Humans think they're a superior form on the planet; weird. I don't see seagulls punching clocks, worrying about taxes, or spending their existence chasing illusions. And, we call them scavengers? Nonsense! They're the cleanup crew and they're still flying while people plod along like idiots, afraid to lift their feet too high lest they lose 'control' over the 'uncontrollable.' This society is bred in fear and conditioned to continue to teach their children the same things that they were taught, how to fit in with all the other 'earthlings.'" Don's blue eyes sparkled with life. At times I could swear I saw beams of light flash from them. "By the way, God's got a pecking order," he went on. "The first will be last and the last will be first. That means the servant has front row seats, while the kings of the world are in 'Standing Room Only.' That's justice; perfect. So if serving others is the higher position, do it. You don't know about love by reading about it, singing about it, talking about it. Live it, brothers! Let love guide your lives and transform your selfish natures into a new Godly nature."

Such passion for love and faith in God, I had never witnessed in anyone. I was amazed at how pearls of wisdom seemed to just fall out of Don's mouth each time he opened it. I could clearly see that these words were not a calculated sermon that he had memorized. It seemed as though he didn't even know what he was about to say next.

"The Holy Spirit gives us the words we need to speak in the moment, so you never have to worry about what you're gonna say." He smiled at me as he spoke. Even though I had grown accustomed to Don answering my thought questions, before I had a chance to verbalize them, it still blew me away each time it happened. It felt like magic, or something.

"No one can be farther along the path than they're supposed to be," he continued. "As long as we give up our fears, doubts and misconceptions, we free up space for trust, certainty and truth. When we give up violence, lust and greed, we get peace, love and all we will ever need. When we give up our will, we get it back dry cleaned. God isn't forcing anyone, but He'll purge you with fire if your layers of worldly scrunge gets too thick. The farther you get away from the light of love, the darker and scarier it gets. When we turn around and seek out the light, no matter how far away it may seem, there will always be enough glow to show the way." His message hit my heart.

The extra company brought added cooking, baking and washing dishes. Don was very helpful and we often ended up in the kitchen together. We talked about the world and 'the truth' as he knew it to be. I watched him closely and listened carefully to his stories. I asked many questions, thinking up ones I thought no one could answer and he answered them all to my satisfaction. This amazed me. His words seemed to flow from somewhere deep within him, effortlessly, as if from some holy fountain of wisdom in his soul.

Within a short while, Ed and Tony were totally convinced that the Christ Family was 'the truth.' They wanted to join these followers of Jesus and they sewed up hand made white robes from cotton. Les, Jerry and Judy had already traveled in robes, so the only ones without them were Will, Cheryl and I.

Cheryl was the friend who seemed to be the least influenced by Don. She came over about once a week to visit, yet I could see that yearning look in her eyes. She and I had been close during high school and we had kept in touch, even though our life paths went in different directions. As for myself, I didn't feel that I would join the group. I just wanted to be more like Don. The children were my main concern and traveling around the world was no life for babies. I had learned that one the hard way.

A woman that I knew, Allana, came to stay with us for a while. She had a daughter close to Ariss' age named Melissa. Intrigued with Don and his ways, she was attracted to the Christ Family philosophy like a child to water puddles. She was a born-again Christian who was experiencing doubts because of the rivalry between the various churches. One day she brought Bruce, a friend of hers, over to meet Don. Bruce and Don had quite the debate, in which a lot of good points were brought out along with the Bibles. I watched Don breeze through it all, shining and unshaken. He knew what he knew and it was 'the truth.' Although Bruce's stubborn nature made him hold onto some of his own beliefs, he wanted to follow Don. Allana did, too, but when she went to talk to some of her Christian friends and leaders of her church, they talked her out of it.

One of the many things I found intriguing about Don was the way he would ease into meditation and prayer. Several times during the day I saw him sitting, eyes closed, peace emanating from him like a golden aura. He seemed to be so in touch with the 'inside world;' with God. And, every now and then he'd go to that source. He'd close his eyes to the illusion that we call reality and go into what seemed like another realm.

I had never experienced being that in touch. Curious, I questioned Don on one such occasion. He and I were sitting by the fire, with Ariss in my lap, Sol in his, and all of us watching the dancing flames. We had been discussing something; then, practically in the middle of our conversation, Don closed his eyes. The firelight on his face gave it an angelic glow and a feeling of utter peace and love vibrated from him. I waited until he opened his eyes again, all the while wondering what he was experiencing.

"Brother, what do you feel, where do you go when you meditate like that?" I asked him.

He looked at me for a minute, his blue eyes full of soft light. "Communion," he said. "Being at one with the Father. When your eyes are open, there are countless distractions. It's important to touch home base, to lose all false fears and just 'be.'"

I wanted to experience communion with God, too. I wanted to lose all the petty trivialities that bombarded my mind daily. My mind seemed to be filled to the brim with so many unimportant details and here was Don, tapping into a source of life and truth that I yearned for.

Another aspect of his personality that attracted me was his incredible patience. One day, he helped me paint a dresser and chair for Sol's room. Blue and white were the colors we chose. I watched as Don sat there, meticulously making perfect stripes of blue and then white on the tiny, spiraled legs of the chair. He sat for hours without moving; a totally relaxed expression on his face the whole time.

His kindness and thoughtfulness amazed me. This man was so utterly unselfish, always giving and always bounding with positive energy. His insight and awareness surprised me. Somehow he seemed to have an inner sense of how he could be of help.

For example, I would be heavily laden with physical chores and child-care routines and he would just come into the room and so naturally take over a chore that I was about to do. He was so incredibly aware. A few times I would be exhausted in the afternoon from two babies in diapers still keeping me awake at night and Don would come in, take over my work, play with the kids and tell me to go for a nap!

I had never met anyone so giving in my life. This man was incredibly beautiful, an angelic being. I had not seen him in a bad mood, angry, or struggling within. He was always tuned in, patient and peaceful. Whatever had transformed this human being into a God-like creature?

❈ CHAPTER SEVEN ❈

Gradually, I began to see changes in the group that gathered at our home. There was an ever-growing sense of brotherhood emanating from us that I had never experienced before. We served each other, truly cared about each other. I felt that I was becoming almost selfless. There were so many lessons to learn; lessons in humility, in giving, in having faith and not doubting. I felt as though I was taking a crash course on love. There were actually days when I felt crystal clear. I was bounding with positive energy; never had I felt so good. My daily chores transformed into joys. As I emptied my cup, it was being filled. I saw everything in a different light. I was in love with everyone and saw each person as being Jesus Himself. *". . . Loving your neighbor as yourself . . ." (Mathew 22:39)* was becoming less of a struggle for me. It seemed to come naturally now. The transformation was incredible!

I wanted to ride the crest of this wave forever. There were moments when we sat by the fire in silence, an inexplicably high and completely comfortable silence. I felt like an apostle of long ago. Yet, there was still a part of me that remained cautious. I wanted to observe, to not get totally drawn into it so that I wouldn't lose my perspective. Besides, I wasn't planning on leaving to 'hit the wind' as most of the others were. I now felt I could accept the fact that Willy might want to leave to travel. It was his choice. I no longer felt as clinging as I once did. I felt strong within myself.

Over the winter, I witnessed changes in Will and Ed. Their gestures and movements flowed with a new calm. Even their eyes had changed. They seemed to be filled with light. They both began to talk like Don and even to look like him somehow. No words came out of their mouths that weren't good, or true; no swearing, gossiping, or small talk. In fact, nothing was talked about unless it was godly.

A part of me was looking for a crack in the armor. There had to be something that wasn't right. This was too good to be true. Were all of these changes, a result of the possible reality that Jesus Christ was truly back on earth? Was this idea absurd? These were the 'end times,' so why not? But, did I have some sort of scenario engrained in my brain of what the Second Coming would be like? Would this image hold me back from accepting the real thing? That's what happened the last time Jesus came, wasn't it? Everybody was waiting for a Messiah and when He arrived, most people never believed Him. Would all my doubts make me miss the boat? Maybe I was truly being called to be Jesus' disciple. If not, in what way had God fashioned me to fit into all of this?

I had just been through so much pain and hardship searching for the elusive valley in Peru. Had that whole journey been a preparation for what was happening now? I had realized then that heaven was within me; now I was experiencing that realization bloom. I felt a deeper sense of understanding this with my heart now and not just with my head. I wanted to do God's will.

The fact that everyone else in our flock took to smoking roll-your-own cigarettes still bothered me. If there was a crack in the armor, this was it. I secretly clung to the image of a Jesus who didn't smoke. One evening I took Don aside into the den to talk with him alone. "Jesus doesn't really smoke, does he?" I asked, like an innocent child. "That is just your own personal belief, isn't it, brother?" I was smiling, hoping for a confirmation of what I so badly needed to know.

Instead, with eyes blazing, he commanded, "Get behind me, 'Satan'!" His impact was so powerful, I nearly fell over. Never had I seen Don so angry. In fact, I had never seen him angry at all.

He glared at me, walked out of the room and left me alone, as confusion stretched its dark presence around me. A cold shiver convulsed my body. It was the same feeling I used to get when I got in trouble with my parents as a child. I've always hated that feeling. Why did he call me "Satan?" Was he deliberately directing a blow to my doubting mind? And why did I doubt more than the others? Judy said she smoked because it was one way of 'dying to her old self.' Well, I liked that part of my 'old self' that didn't smoke. How can I know for sure that Don is preaching the 'truth?' Should I close my doors to it? But, what if Jesus is truly leading this movement? I will be doomed if I am being called by God and I ignore His invitation. I can't deny the immense love that we all share. I can't deny how much more joy there is in my life. How can this be false? I'm experiencing it! Then I thought about my parents, who were on a vacation and wished that I could talk to them.

I walked upstairs to my bedroom and threw myself down on the soft mattress. The springs squeaked and moaned. The room was dark except for the blur of the street lights that filtered through the frosted windows. The subtle smell of sandalwood incense lingered in the air. "God, please help me!" I called out. "I want to do your will, but I'm confused as to what it is. Please tell me if the Christ Family is where you want me to be. Is it 'the truth?' Direct me!"

I lay there waiting for a voice, or a sense of knowing, but I heard nothing but the crunching of hard snow under heavy tires and muffled voices from downstairs. I felt nothing, but confusion and anxiety. It had been so long since I had felt like this. Waves of emotion triggered a storm of tears as I lay in the dark room, alone.

Then I remembered what Don had told us at dinner that day: "We are not just worshipping Jesus who roamed the earth two thousand years ago and trying to live like the disciples did. Jesus is roaming the earth in the flesh right now and we are His disciples!" I envisioned the group around the dining room table that night and counted twelve of us, including Ariss and Sol. Were we merely acting out a role based on historical events, or were we receiving a genuine 'call'?"

I flicked on the light beside the bed and picked up the Bible sitting on the table next to it. In desperation, I opened the book and let my shaking fingers flip through the pages. I closed my eyes, hoping the Spirit of God would direct them to a message, a direction and an answer. Opening my eyes to see where my finger pointed, I read: *". . . And as you go, preach, saying the kingdom of heaven is at hand. Heal the sick, cleanse the lepers, raise the dead, cast out devils, freely you have received, freely give. Provide neither gold, nor silver, nor brass in your purses, nor script for your journey, neither two coats, neither shoes, nor yet staffs; for the workman is worthy of his meat. And into whatsoever city or town you shall enter, enquire who in it is worthy; and there abide 'til you go from there . . . ."* (Matthew 10:7-12)

I felt as though a lightning bolt had hit me. I was electrified! This was exactly how the Christ Family lived. They traveled from town to town barefoot, in white robes, with no money or, 'script.' People who were worthy were called 'connections' and the Christ Brother would be welcomed into their homes and provided with the physical necessities. *'. . . The workman is worthy of his meat . . . ,'* seemed to perfectly describe the reason the Christ Family lived without working, just exactly as the Scripture said. The Christ Family even preached that the Kingdom of Heaven is at hand. Their 'work' was to heal the sick hearts and the 'spiritually' dead.

I sensed God was telling me that all this was 'the truth.' I resolved in my heart to believe my brother Don from now on, even if it made no sense to me. Besides, what did I know, anyway? I was just a new babe to this way of life. I didn't even know how to crawl yet. Don was right. The 'three keys' were the tools that we needed to be able to see spiritually. I walked down the old oak staircase and into the living room where Don sat speaking to Will and Ed. I sat down on the floor beside them to listen.

"The ways of the world are often the opposite of our true nature," Don was saying. "All anyone really wants and needs are to feel and give love, yet the world teaches us to put the gathering of earthly possessions ahead of caring for each other. Instead, we are taught competition through school systems that judge all our abilities on the basis of earthly knowledge, not on the knowledge of God. Whoever ends up on top of the biggest heap of stuff is the most valuable in the eyes of the world. Yet they'll never find fulfillment at the top of a homemade 'Tower of Babel.'" The soft glow of the fire created lights and shadows across Don's face. Even in the dimness his eyes glowed with inner light. His long, wavy, sandy-colored hair flowed over his broad shoulders and the firelight highlighted the blondness in it. His high cheekbones flowed down to a strong narrow chin covered by the neatest-looking beard that I'd ever seen; a very masculine face, yet so soft, so holy . . .

Don continued: "It's not as complex as some might think. Actually, if a child can't understand something, I'm really prone to wonder about its validity. You see, we're all 'family' so why aren't we treating each other like 'family?' God is our Father, the Earth is our Mother and we are all brothers and sisters. People who don't align their wills with God cheat themselves out of their birthright. Blinded by their own self-importance, or false ego, they miss out on experiencing the finest moments of a joyful life, because their cup is full of confused lies, jumbled and fragmented thoughts and a whole mess of unanswered questions! They won't find joy in their temples and synagogues either, where 'Pharisees' pull the wool over their flock's eyes, teaching the doctrines of men. God's people have no podium, no temple and no prefabricated sermons. No, they preach on street corners to the lowly. Their words and deeds are given freely, straight from the one worthwhile source, the Holiest of Holies. The new song being sung by God's angels is that the innocent are free from judgment and that God's law was not, is not and never will be restrictive. It sets us free. It allows us to be all we truly are!"

I looked at Ed and Will. They were practically hypnotized, as if breastfeeding on every word that came out of Don's mouth.

"'Earthlings' shouldn't waste their time looking for worldly wisdom. It's rags in the eyes of God. Empty your cup with a bowed head. Ask Him what you need. Trust that God never misses a single prayer. 'Kick back' and let the Master be in charge of all the details that you now foolishly think you have control over. How can anyone be anything but optimistic about the outcome of this movie? Are you blind? Don't you know who's directing it? What if it all fell apart tomorrow? Praise God! His will be done on earth, as it is in heaven! And no, I'm not talking about a physical place we all fly up to when we die. I'm talking inner space, a state of harmony with all creation. Heaven's in the heart, brothers, so get out of your head!"

I felt as though he was speaking directly to me. I knew the Holy Spirit, speaking through him, aimed his words at me because they seemed to hit me right in the heart. I felt so humbled. "Lots of 'earthlings' think they believe in God, but you know a tree by its fruit," Don continued, the words flowing from him like a stream. "God's not interested in what you think you believe. He wants it all. Your heart, mind and soul, one hundred percent of you! Be and live in God's will. You see, what goes around, comes around; you get what you give and it's not like we have to figure this all out ourselves. God's never gonna expect anything from anyone without giving them all they need to accomplish it. All we have to do is align our will with His, empty all of our trash and be an open receiver to 'the spirit.' Allow God to lead you, let go of doubts and fears. All the rest will be given in the moment."

I knew Don was right. I learned so much that winter. A whole metamorphosis took place inside me. Bad habits, unclear thoughts and attitudes; all were looked at closely and converted to righteousness. Many battles took place in my mind. I felt my 'old self' fight back every time I commanded it to go away. At first, 'old' words and phrases would come out of my mouth automatically. Then I would realize what I had said was wrong and consciously try to correct myself. As time went on, I began to cut off the 'old' thought pattern before it came out of my mouth, changing it in midstream. My personality, myself as I knew me, was changing and I liked the changes I saw. I was much more joyful, giving and unselfish.

I was learning how to shut off my doubting mind which Don told us was our greatest enemy. I was learning the depth and reality of the understanding, 'Be here now,' which meant enjoying the moment to the fullest without anticipating the next. To this way of thinking, 'now' is the only true reality. To truly live in accordance with this, there were so many concepts and habits that had to go.

I learned what was considered acceptable and unacceptable language. Little phrases like, "I'm sorry," "Thank you," or "Excuse me" were not to be used because if you're tuned into 'the spirit,' you didn't have to say you were sorry. All thanks go straight to the Father and "excuse me" is merely small talk. All such polite inventions are the world's programming. I had to consciously stop the habit of using them and replace them with new phrases. "Thank you" was replaced by "Praise God." "Children" was replaced by "hobbits." Sleep was replaced by "rest" because a 'Christ mind' never sleeps. "Woman" or "man" were also replaced by "brother" or "sister." So, Ed and I began calling our parents by their first names and viewing them as siblings. Ariss didn't call me "Mom," but "Mo," and was taught that I was her big sister. These changes in our language and habits created a void between the world and us and gave us a feeling of being special; being set apart.

Following the three keys of no killing, no sex and no materialism seemed to come naturally to me. I was already a strict vegetarian, having given up the fruitarian idea after our trip to Peru. I didn't feel the desire for sex at all and I shared whatever material things I had with others. With all of us reinforcing each other's commitment, the whole thing seemed more real.

There were other fundamental rules that we followed, as well. For example, the physical body was not to be adorned, or given too much attention. This involved not wearing makeup, or fussing with night creams, or facials, not wearing jewelry, not shaving legs or armpits and not being involved in clothing fashions. The brothers didn't cut their hair, or shave their beards. We gave the physical body just the amount of attention it needed to be healthy, nothing more. We looked at our true selves as entities that were separate from our bodies. We were merely riding in our bodies. That's why Don called his body "the horse," or "the creature." We also had names referring to different parts of the body, "the paw" for hand, "the beepers" for eyes, "the mane" for hair. Whenever possible, the words "I" or "me" were left out, creating more of a gap between the body and the true self, or who we believed we really were. We were in a physical body, but we knew the true self was not the physical body; it was 'the spirit' inside. This way of looking at things took away much of the personal ego involvement in any situation. I felt so removed, as if I was watching a movie, except that I was acting in it as well. I had total trust in the 'Director' to tell me where to go and how to act. This viewpoint also increased my sense of security within. In reality, the only control we have over many situations is how we choose to react to it. Therefore, if events got really crazy on the outside, I would still have home base to run to, the sanctuary within. I had faith and trust that God had everything covered and that He knew what was going on even if I had no idea. This faith and trust grew stronger the more I let go of my doubts and analytical thinking.

By springtime, we were all practically living together at "Christ Corner." We had converted the name from "Pooh Corner." We were preparing to 'hit the wind,' meaning to live in faith, on the road. Don told me that there were other young children in the Christ Family camp in Oregon. He had heard some brothers and sisters talking about setting up a sort of day-care operation, 'a hobbit farm' where they would take turns caring for the children and going on the road. I felt that I would be a good candidate to care for a child care centre.

We sewed our white robes, tote sacks and bedroll straps by hand. Ariss and Sol sat with us, not knowing what it all meant. I felt happy to be able to lead my children to Jesus. I imagined other children in the 'Family' and a happy, joyous environment for them. Don told us stories of the Christ Camp in Oregon and I imagined a heavenly brotherhood, such as we had, only on a large scale.

Tony and Les got 'itchy feet' and left before us. They headed west, 'in the wind.' Tony left us his truck and we fixed up the back like a camper. We were waiting for Judy to get her cast off. She had been on crutches since her accident. We knew, in reality, it had been set-up by God. Don would never have spent the winter here otherwise. We believed there were no such things as 'accidents.'

During this time, Judy and I became close. We loved each other; loved helping each other along the road to enlightenment. I knew she loved my children as her own. She was an example of such strength and righteousness. She felt God had allowed the accident so that she could preach to the people in the hospital and to teach her not to be so attached to her physical body. I wanted to wait and travel with her so that I could help her to walk. I admired her childlike innocence, for although she was in her mid-twenties, she had such a sense of wonder. Her face glowed! She was truly a Christ Sister.

My parents felt very uneasy about Ed and I being involved with this group. I wished they would come along with us and see the light too, but they sensed something very wrong. When they came back from their trip and found us deeper than ever into it, they panicked. Brian the missionary, who owned our house, came back to Thunder Bay for a visit. One day he and my parents came over with the intention of calling the demons out of us to straighten us out. They laid their hands on me and prayed for all the lies to be revealed to me and for Jesus to stop me from joining the group. Nothing happened and Brian, in desperation, offered to sell me his home for one dollar if we did not leave. But, by then I was too far into it to be persuaded. I felt Brian's offer was like Satan's tempting of Christ in the desert with material riches. I must admit it was tempting. The house was beautiful. I told them that unless they had a better truth, I was going. Their arguments were nothing compared to what I was experiencing. They must have left with such a feeling of helplessness.

Later that evening my grandmother called, trying to talk me out of it as well. I loved her dearly, but I had to stand up for what I felt to be 'the truth.' Don told me that it was important to leave your birthplace because your close friends and family would keep you attached to your 'old' mind and self.

Music had always been a part of my life, from early singsongs with the family to choir practice and piano lessons. I remembered that Don played the guitar quite well and wondered why I had not seen him play at all this winter. Ed and Les were not playing music, either. Then my mind flashed to earlier, in late autumn, when Don brought over an oil painting he had painted for his parents and he and Will made a frame for it. When I went up to it to admire his fine work, Don looked ashamed instead of proud and said to me, "It's a sin to worship 'graven images,' sister. This is the last painting I will ever do and I really should not have done it, but I promised it to my earth parents."

I didn't really understand how a beautiful work of art could be a sin, or why he felt so ashamed of it. Until now, I had never thought about how we were going to have to give up all of our talents. So I asked Don about playing music and why he didn't play anymore. He looked at me with those shining eyes of his and in no uncertain terms said, "There is too much ego involved in playing music. The glorification of your own self, the illusion of accomplishment, sinful pride, all take your focus off God and put the spotlight on you. That is vanity. There is a much higher music that can be heard if you have the ears to hear. It surpasses anything of this world. The angels' voices are the perfection of music. When you give something up for the Lord, you receive something better."

"Have you heard this music that you speak of, Don?" I asked. He smiled at me and nodded affirmatively, then closed his eyes as if he had gone inside that world and was listening right then.

The thought of never playing the keyboard again bothered me, but if this was necessary in order to please God, I would do it. As for listening to music, the only tapes we could relate to and played were those of Bruce Cockburn. His lyrics were full of truth and love for Jesus. I'm not sure if Don felt totally comfortable with Will and I listening to them, but he never mentioned it.

Sometime in midwinter, Bruce Cockburn came to town and gave a concert at the University. Don babysat Ariss and Sol while Will, Ed and I went to hear him sing. He walked on stage with his acoustic guitar so humbly, dressed in blue jeans and a plaid shirt. He seemed almost shy. His choice of material met the approval of the roaring small crowd. I sang quietly along with him, knowing every word. During the break, I met my friend Allana who was walking over to speak to Bruce's manager. She wanted to ask him if Bruce would come and sing in a Christian coffee house where she worked. As I walked with her, I sensed 'the spirit' telling me to arrange to talk to Bruce, who was a seeker of truth. Allana talked to his manager and he muttered something along the lines of "We'll see what we can do." We both knew what that meant. She went on to ask if she could talk to Bruce himself, but it was no use. Ignoring my inner voice, I walked away with her, not saying a word.

The next set was just as dynamic as the first. All through it, that little voice kept nagging me to tell Bruce "The Truth." Now how was I to do that? Run up to him before he left the stage and blast him with it? I kept trying to think of a way to get to see him, then concluded God would have to make it happen and cleared my mind. Then suddenly, just as if something was guiding me, I found myself walking up to his manager. "I have a message to share with Bruce. It's from God. I'm just the messenger," I said to him honestly, as I looked him straight in the eye. He looked surprised, yet he seemed to believe me because he told me to meet him by Bruce's room after the concert. I smiled and walked away, feeling so good. I was working for the Lord and He was directing me, setting everything up. All I had to do was to be in His will and empty my mind of confused thoughts to hear the messages.

The crowd around Bruce's dressing room was thick with reporters, camera-men and local musicians. It looked hopeless for me to get a chance to see him. After all, I was nobody in the eyes of the world. I had no business there. Then the manager came out of the dressing room and had everyone line up. He spotted me near the back and called me forward. I walked past all those people, right into the dressing room and sat down beside Bruce Cockburn! It was so fantastic both to 'watch the movie' and be in it, at the same time. I smiled inwardly and thanked God for 'setting it up.' My knees were shaking from excitement as I sat inches away from my favorite music artist. I looked at Bruce and told him as honestly as I believed, "I am just a messenger from the Lord. Jesus Christ is back on earth." My voice was clear and steady and my gaze never left his eyes. "The Second Coming has already happened. You see, He said He would come in the clouds and He has, for the clouds are in man's eyes and only those with eyes that see inward will recognize Him." He looked at me in disbelief. "Where is He?" He asked.

"He's 'in the wind,' brother, wearing a long white robe, barefoot, traveling around gathering 'The Chosen.' He has given us three keys to live by, along with all the teachings He taught two thousand years ago. "No killing, no sex and no materialism; deny the world of the flesh and open the doors to 'the spirit.'"

I can't recall what he said to me, but I remember walking away, feeling so high. I was an open vessel for the Holy Spirit to work through and it felt so good.

For the last weeks before we left, we wore our white robes. Putting mine on for the first time was like putting on a wedding gown and that is what it was, for I was married to Jesus now. I was His bride and servant. I remember walking in the cool spring rain with little Ariss splashing through the puddles. I felt like a child, my mind clear of worries and all the garbage with which we adults fill our heads. Everything was so new. I gazed at the flowers and saw miracles all around me that I was blinded to before. I was passionately in love with life!

Cheryl was the only one of us who still seemed to be caught between two worlds. She still went to work, wore makeup and fashionable clothing and kept her boyfriend. She came over often to listen to Don preach, but never gave up her old life, or sewed up a robe. I wanted her to come with us so badly, but Don told me not to pressure her.

If she was meant to come, she would. I wished there was some way I could convince her to see that our vision was real. She was already partly drawn to us and could see 'the truth' in our ways, yet she was not ready to make that incredible commitment to give up everything for God.

Once again, we gave away our possessions. It amazed me to see the volume of 'things' that had accumulated in such a short time. My plants were the most precious to me and an interesting event happened regarding them. My friend Ann wanted them and when I drove over to her house to give them to her, she wasn't home. We were leaving the next day and I had to find a home for them immediately. I sat in front of her home and waited for awhile and then felt a 'pull' to her neighbor's house. So I went next door and spoke to the woman, asking her if she was in need of some houseplants. She looked at me so surprised, as if I were reading her thoughts and said, "As a matter of fact, my roommate moved out a few days ago and took all the plants. I was just thinking how bare it is in here without them." I smiled and went to the truck and pulling the plants out by their hangers, two by two, walked into her humble home with them. "I can't believe this," she said. "I have a hook for every one of them. How much do you want for them?"

"They are a gift from God, sister," I answered, knowing the 'set-up' was providential. When she found her tongue, she yelled to me as I reached the truck, "Thank you."

"Praise God, not me," I answered. A new door had opened for me with that experience. I could feel the same love for that stranger as for my friend. I was learning to love as God loves us, equally, with no favorites.

Our white robes turned a lot of heads and attracted attention. Some kids from nearby St. Pat's School used to come over and ask us questions. One of the boys, Bernard, seemed especially interested and the night before we left, he begged us to take him with us. He told us he was sixteen and his tall stature supported this age claim. Don assured him it would be all right for him to come and we arranged to pick him up at his home the morning we would leave.

Then the difficult task of saying farewell to my parents was at hand. Dad tried to talk me into leaving Ariss and Sol with them, but leaving my precious children was unthinkable.

In the early part of May, on a rainy day, a little over a year from our departure for Peru; Don, Judy, Will, Ed, Bruce, Bernard, Ariss, Sol and I said our goodbyes to "Christ Corner" and to Cheryl, who was standing in front of the house. A few minutes earlier, inside, I had begged her to come with us. I couldn't imagine her being left alone. I sensed she wanted to come, but something was holding her back. My last attempt to persuade her had failed and now she stood watching us pile into the truck, tears mixing with the raindrops on her face.

Don saw my disappointment as we drove away. "She just isn't ready yet, Mo. She must have more lessons in the world to burn out on yet."

As we approached the highway out of town, I felt the strings of attachment being broken and new wings being formed. I was on the road of truth, that long and narrow road that few follow. I was actually following Jesus Christ! I had made my marriage vows to Him and was now "Maureen Christ." I felt so blessed to be chosen as an apostle of Jesus. I knew it would be a hard life on the road, especially with two small children, but I also knew that God would give me the strength that would be needed to carry out His mission. Ready to do the Father's will, I was now 'in the wind.'

❊ CHAPTER EIGHT ❊

In the small town of Fort Frances, Ontario, Bernard was taken away by two policemen. They told us that he was a minor and that his parents wanted him back home. Don reassured us, "Everything is perfect in God's time; once in the robe, always in the robe. Bernard's right where he's supposed to be. Don't question the 'Will of God'."

We cooked our meals on a Coleman stove. Pan bread, rice, boiled beans and potatoes were regulars. Peanut butter and jam sandwiches were our favorite. The stars were our roof at night. Each of us had bedrolls. Even Ariss had a little one. Sol slept with me. My robe was especially designed for breastfeeding. There were two slits and flaps that crossed over them with snaps. It was nicely concealed, yet easy to open.

Don did a lot of the driving and I sat beside him much of the time. He mentioned that some of the brothers and sisters had been given 'spiritual mates' to travel with.

I secretly hoped Don would be my 'spiritual mate' and we'd always travel together.

Along the way, we picked up hitchhikers. They must have been surprised to see us all in white robes when they opened up the back door. We had built a box on the back of the truck for any 'dead animal skins.' So if anyone wanted a ride he had to take off his leather and put it in the box until he left.

Somewhere near Revelstoke, B.C., we stopped for him. He was just another hitchhiker laden with leather. One of us opened the back door and welcomed the stranger in. For a few moments he stood there motionless, eyes wide, mouth hanging to his chin, as he gazed upon the brilliance of white-robed beings; then he grinned and let out a chuckle, saying, "So, what's this all about? Who are you guys?"

Will was the first to speak. "First of all, we don't believe in killing, brother, so will you take off all your leather and put it in this box." He pointed to the box attached to the truck. The stranger hesitated, gave him a strained, curious glance, but he did as Will requested. Off came the black leather jacket, then a belt, a watch, and lastly, big brown leather boots. His jacket gave off the smell of brand new leather and for a moment filled the truck with its disgusting scent. "My name is James," he said, holding out his hand.

"The handshake is in the heart, brother; we aren't carrying weapons," Ed said to him smiling. We didn't believe in the custom of shaking hands, because of its origin of making sure that any stranger wasn't carrying a weapon.

"Do you guys mind if I smoke?" He asked, almost expecting us to say no.

"Not at all brother; I'll roll you one," Will said, as he took out his pouch of tobacco.

The look of surprise on James's face was priceless. Here he was, sitting with a truckload of white-robed, barefoot beings that looked like angels and they smoked, but they made him take off his leather goods. He sat quietly for a quarter of a mile or so, then couldn't stand it anymore and spilled out question after question.

Because I was sitting in the front, I could only hear bits and pieces of the preaching he received in reply as we rode through those indescribable Rockies. In fact, the vibration level seemed to rise with our climb until we all knew that James was receiving 'the truth.' This was confirmed when we stopped at a restaurant dumpster a few hours later and James took all his leather out of the box and one by one, threw the items into the garbage. When he came to the jacket, he said, "You know, I just bought this yesterday, it seems wrong to throw it out. Perhaps I could give it to someone."

"No brother, we wouldn't want to give away something dead, to anyone. We should offer them life instead," Don told him.

James wasn't totally convinced, but he threw it in, anyway. He did want to be a Christ Brother and this was the first step. I was looking forward to watching how God would 'transform' him. Our first task was to get a robe on him and we had the material from Bernard's robe-to-be, good heavy denim, tightly woven for maximum strength. Judy and I started sewing it that evening in our camping ground, as we sat around the campfire after a dinner of potatoes and beans.

That evening, we watched in silence as the 'Divine Artist' painted a pastel sunset in hues of pinkish blue. The tranquility was shattered by a loud shriek. I ran over to the truck to pick up Sol, who had fallen out right on his baby-soft head. For some reason I had taken my eyes off the sunset and glanced over to the truck just in the split second that he had rolled out. I scooped him up in my shaking arms and cried with him.

Will came and took him out of my arms, muttering, "Oh he's a big boy. You're O.K., aren't you, Sol?"

Sure, he's a big boy, I thought to myself; he's all of seven months old.

Don glared at me with fiery eyes that seemed to burn a hole to my depths. Had he heard my thoughts? In a stern voice, he said, "A Christ Sister doesn't let emotion overtake her. You have to die to that mother-bear instinct, sister. You are an example to the whole world of a true woman, a reflection of Mother Mary. You have to remain calm and peaceful at all times. Where is your faith in God? He's taking care of Sol and all of His children. No attachment sister!"

I took my scolding like a trooper, knowing that Don knew best. I couldn't help feeling like a little child, though, as if I had just received a spanking and, like a good little girl, hadn't talked back. Instead, I silently prayed for the strength to be unattached to my children and to be rid of old emotions and habits.

That evening there was further discord among us. Bruce took out his Bible, which he had secretly concealed from us and pointed out certain passages in an attempt to prove some of our concepts wrong.

Don had told us we weren't supposed to carry the Bible, because we were the 'Living Word of God.' The Bible was 'yesterday's newspaper,' written centuries ago and so many people had distorted its truth by interpreting it with blindfolds on. It was written for those who have the eyes to see, he said, but so much had been lost over the years. Anyway, Brother Don and Brother Bruce had quite the showdown that starry night. There seemed to be sparks flying from their fingertips as they waved them around in the debate. I listened carefully, for there was a part of my mind hungering for proof that I was truly following Jesus. Don answered all of the questions with ease and a sense of clarity, while Bruce seemed so confused and uptight. The next morning, he was gone. No one said anything, but I felt the cloud of anxiety lift.

We were heading south to Oregon where Don had last seen the Christ Family camp and had met "Lightning Amen." It felt funny to call him anything but "Jesus" and I didn't understand why he took a new name, but I was sure there would be an answer; there always was.

Near the Canada-U.S border, we caught sight of a white-robed person walking on the side of the highway. What a sight it was, his white robe luminous in the sunlight was flowing over his form like an angel. We stopped to pick Bruce up. He climbed into the truck and we continued down the road.

On the edge of the town of Yakima, Washington, we rented a lot in a campground for a few days. There was a store, a playground and restrooms and showers. It had been so long since I had bathed in anything but cold mountain streams. It was great to be stationary for a while. Traveling was so tiring. I was still car sick most of the time. It was especially hard on the 'hobbits.' Ariss, now two and a half, wanted to be on the move discovering things. To sit still all day long was almost like being in jail. Sol, who had just learned to crawl, was also in captivity in the back of that truck. Here, in the playground, they played in the sandbox and on the swings. They were so happy.

That night, in our mansion under the stars, Don told us stories of different adventures and miracles. I felt warm and secure with my baby at my breast, my little girl beside me and surrounded by people I loved. All of them had the same desire as I had, to serve God with our whole heart, soul and mind.

Will was now like a brother to me and my love for him had been transformed into brotherly love, as well. We had not had a personal, heart-to-heart talk in a long time. There was no room for that because we had to die to our egos, or false selves. Our lives were supposed to be a reflection of righteousness. To allow any personal 'trips' or doubts would be blowing it. We were the saints. We were reflections of Jesus Himself, so there was this perfection image to live up to. Anything less had to be shut out. Even when I wasn't feeling good, or high, I had to praise God every moment of every day. That was our commitment. That was our duty. I often wondered what was going on in the others' minds. Instead of the peace and holiness I tried to project on the outside, my mind was sometimes a literal battleground. I felt lower, less worthy than the rest because of this.

One reason for the battle between 'the spirit' and the flesh that seemed to rage on, may have been the fact that Judy and I were the ones who looked after two small children, with all their physical needs. While the brothers sat in bliss. I was breastfeeding, changing diapers and sleepers, washing diapers and clothes by hand, feeding babies, cooking and sewing. My mind was absorbed with physical duties. I had so much yet to learn about spirituality and the life of Christ. I knew deep inside, that there was a way to perform physical deeds with spiritual intent and I was determined to be totally open in order to learn it.

Staying put for a while gave me more opportunity to break in my feet. Walking barefoot was a completely new experience for me. I had always worn shoes or sandals, even in the summer. My 'pads' were as tender as a baby's bottom and walking those first months was like learning to walk all over again. I was aware of every step, concentrating hard for an action I had been accustomed to perform automatically for nearly all my life. If my mind became distracted by anything beyond the 'here and now,' a sharp rock, or piece of glass would remind me to keep on track. I discovered a reason, beyond reason, for the command that we walk barefoot. It forced me to keep my mind clear and aware of everything around me and walk softly on the earth. Don assured us that the soles of our feet were symbols of our spiritual souls. The longer we walked on the enlightened path, the tougher they both became. We weren't supposed to feel our feet, or 'give in' to the flesh and I tried not to 'space' on my feet.

One night, we sat around the campfire and listened to Don tell us one of his road stories. The light from the fire seemed to hypnotize us; all eyes were drawn to the dancing flames as Don spoke. "There is a place in the Oregon hills where there is a white dome, nestled in the woods on the side of a clay hill. There is a garden and a sauna dug into a small knoll with a primitive outdoor shower beside it. I saw Christ Brothers and Sisters everywhere, walking barefoot, back and forth between their 'mangers' (sleeping areas) under the trees. It felt like heaven. Lightning Amen was there, along with Moses, Abraham, Sarah, Mary, Martha, Archangels Michael and Gabriel and a whole host of angels on both planes; physical and spiritual."

Ed put a stick on the fire and poked at the remaining wood and ashes as Don continued his story. "I was in the dome. Solomon's temple it was called, because Brother Solomon had given this property to the Christ Family when he 'transformed.' Late one afternoon, Brother James and I were doing dishes and looking out the open window above the sink, listening to some other brothers talking about God's business and feeling really blessed to be there. Then a brother approached me and quietly stood beside me. He was a new brother. His name was Stephen, but he was later to be named Joshua. I could tell he hadn't been with the 'Family' long by his short hair, skimpy beard and crisp white robe without a battle scar to be found. Still, his eyes had a shine that hinted at his joy of being in the Lord's Army. Almost timidly he asked me if I would take him out on the road. He said he needed the lessons of the wind and the experiences of living the life of Christ. My initial feeling was that I don't want to leave this beloved place for anything, or anybody. I truly felt I was in God's arms there. James, the brother drying dishes next to me, noticed the indecisive look on my face, but never said a word. I told Stephen that I would give it some 'space.' If there was any trace of disappointment in his heart, it never showed on his face. He just smiled and walked away. I felt guilty for not saying yes right away. I felt selfish for not wanting to leave a place so full of love and light."

Ed put another piece of wood on the campfire and it shot a trail of sparks into the cloudless sky. Bugler tobacco was rolled and passed around. Don went on with his story. "A short space passed before I spoke to James beside me. I asked him what he would have said. He just smiled and started telling me a road story." Don's voice changed slightly as if James himself was there to tell his own story. "I was in an apartment where some 'earthlings' had 'transformed;' about four of them who all put on the robe at the same time. There was also a large group of seasoned brothers hanging out having already 'liquidated' the new brothers' possessions and sewn up robes for them. Everyone was real comfortable, with lots of money for righteous food, Bugler and showers. It didn't seem like anybody wanted to take these new brothers and sisters on the road and they sure needed it. That's when Lightning showed up. He walked in, rolled a Bugler and talked to the new brothers and sisters. They told him how much they wanted to be 'in the wind,' learning the lessons of the life of Christ, but no one wanted to leave the space and take them. Lightning never even finished his Bugler; he jumped up and almost yelled, 'I'd be honored to take you brother. Let's 'hit the wind'!"

"I let the water out of the sink," continued Don, in his own voice this time. "As I dried my hands I thought about the message of the story I had just been told. What choice did I have, but to follow the Lord's example? Right on, brother, I hear you! I told James and next morning we set our sails for adventures on the high seas. Stephen and I rode in such high space. I had poured out my cup and God had filled it before I'd even noticed it empty." I loved listening to Don's stories. They always taught me lessons of the heart.

The next morning, Don took us all by surprise, telling us that he and Bruce were 'hitting the wind.' Bruce had been acting strangely, ever since that heated debate on the road back in Canada. Don felt he had to get him away from the rest of us and let him experience 'some wind' to blow his 'finite mind.' I guessed he had been letting us know, in a way, by the story he had chosen to tell us the night before. My heart sank. Don, being the 'older brother' in the group, was our leader and we all looked up to him. I didn't want him to go. Yet, a part of me remained removed from my feelings and cut them short with my 'inner sword.' Attachment to one brother was not right. I must follow God's will, not my own, I told myself. They gathered their bedrolls, tote sacks and army-blankets and started walking.

As he left, Don turned to us and said, "'In the wind,' brothers." Then the brother who had brought me the gift of truth walked away, his white robe flowing with his gentle walk, as my own sword and shield did battle with a barrage of emotions. Would we ever meet again? I glanced over at Judy, caught a glimpse of tears welling up in her dark blue eyes and was overcome by a sense of righteous pride at my ability to hold back mine.

A sense of loss hung in the air like mist over water. I experienced déjà vu as I remembered how we had felt when Tony disappeared in the Andes Mountains. But, here we were, the saints, who had to be righteous reflections to each other and to our fellow man. There was no time to waste on 'earthly' emotions, or attachments.

The next day we 'hit the wind' ourselves, heading south to Wolf Creek, Oregon where Don had last seen Lightning Amen and a number of the brothers and sisters. We were looking for the dome on some acreage of land that Brother Solomon had given to the Christ Family. It was the place Don told us would be the 'hobbit farm,' where children were. It was also a rest stop for the brothers; somewhere to wash off the dust from the road and to 'catch some space.' I hoped Lightning would be there. I wanted to meet him with a passion.

At times, doubt still nagged at me, though. Was Jesus really back on earth? I felt like "Doubting Thomas" in a way, because I just had to see him. Feelings of guilt would swarm around me and I would fight it, but it was always there, in the shadows. All I really had to go by were the stories Don had told us about him.

According to these stories, Lightning had a virgin birth in San Diego, California, some forty-odd years ago. When he was three years old, he planted an apple seed in his backyard and the next day, a full-grown, fruit-bearing tree was in its place. In 1969, he went out into the desert to fast for forty days and nights. This was when he fully realized that he was Jesus, reborn, and God gave him the three keys to heaven. From there, he went out on the road preaching, dressed in cut-off jeans, a white T-shirt and an army blanket. The robes came later. One of the miracles he performed after he started his mission occurred when he walked into a hospital room where a woman lay crippled from a disease. He told her to get up and walk and follow him. To the amazement of the doctors, she did just that and is still by his side now. Her name is Cher and she is believed to be the reincarnation of Mother Mary. I was told that Lightning Amen chose his new name from certain passages in the Book of Revelation, which named Amen, the faithful and true witness of God, the Father of all creation and claimed that He would come like lightning from the east, meaning Jerusalem, to the west, California.

Another story we heard was that one day Lightning was given over a thousand dollars by a wealthy man, but that night he sat at a campfire with a group of brothers and burned each bill in the fire, to teach them detachment from the physical and material world. Another time, a pilot of a jet plane saw a man flying outside the plane beside him. Don told us that was Lightning in his light body.

Although fascinated by these stories, I seemed to be the only one who had trouble believing them. For one thing, I didn't understand why Jesus would have to be born again and go through a second carnal life. The Bible tells us of his appearing to us when He came for the second time. Also, why would He have to change His name to Lightning? To even harbor these doubts was a sin, for 'believing your brother' was a rule right up there with the keys. Also, we were not supposed to think independently with our old mind. We were taught to accept without questioning the wisdom of an older brother. To question was to allow Satan to plant the seed of doubt in your heart. The seed of doubt in me wanted to grow, but I kept cutting it down with my 'sword of truth.'

Finally, we arrived in Wolf Creek and asked a man at the service station if he knew how to get to the white dome. He told us the directions and muttered other things about the group. I can't remember what he said, but I know how it affected me. I was shot into a space of such great doubt and fear that my whole body shook and the last words of my mother rang in my ears: "Don't do this Maureen, can't you see this is false?"

It was too much to keep inside and I confided in Ed. He reassured me, saying that my doubts were only my 'finite mind' rampaging in its last efforts to stay in control, because the 'finite mind' does not like the unknown and 'freaks out' when faced by it. "Just 'watch the movie,' Mo. 'Kick back' that old mind and see what's really going on," he told me. We had been taught to view reality as if we were watching a movie that we were also taking part in. In this way, we remained detached enough to be in the world, yet not of it. My brother's advice, reminding me of this, was soothing. As we drove down the rough dirt road to the dome, a sense of excited anticipation filled the air. I conjured up images of what it would be like. The brothers and sisters would be so full of peace and love. Lightning would welcome us and tell us he had been expecting us. There would be other little children for Ariss and Sol to play with. I imagined it would be like a part of heaven. Then reality rudely struck as the truck got stuck in thick mud just a mile away from the dome. The brothers started digging out the back wheel, but it looked as if they would be a while. I turned to Judy and said, "Do you mind if I walk up ahead, I'm so 'juiced' (excited) to see everyone."

"Sure, I'll watch the 'hobbits,' you go on," she replied.

"Praise God for your love," I answered.

The sun was high in an endless blue sky. My feet sunk into thick mud as I walked down that country road to meet the Lord. Now, more than ever, I had to meet him; the desire burned inside me. No thoughts kept me from walking the fastest I had ever walked barefoot. I honestly don't think I even felt my feet. My heart practically pounded out of my chest when I turned onto the long driveway and caught sight of the dome nestled among trees in the distance. A smile etched my face which was now dripping from perspiration.

The pungent smell of wood smoke, mixed with the fresh scent of wild flowers and trees, contradicted the apparent desolation of the place. Everything was hauntingly quiet. Not a soul in sight. The wind made the trees bend and creak with an eerie sound. I could hear my heart beat. Now I was within feet of the dome and still no one was about. Could the smell of wood burning be coming from a neighbor's house? No one was here. The place was deserted. Everyone must have 'hit the wind,' I thought to myself. But then, just as I approached the dome, I was taken by surprise by the presence of a sister. Her black hair and eyes were in sharp contrast to the color of her robe which was stained with the red clay of the area. "Praise God! A sister!" She said, as she smiled at me warmly and added that her name was Sister Alice.

"Where is everyone else, Lightning and the others?" I asked her, feeling insecure about how new my robe was.

"Everyone 'hit the wind' except for Solomon and me. Would you like to meet him? It's so good to see you, sister," she added, as I followed her into the dome.

There he sat, on a large royal blue pillow, with four other pillows around him making up his throne. An air of majestic arrogance and apparent wisdom emanated from him. His beard hung below his chest and blond hair covered his shoulders. He wore a blue satin patch over his right eye. I sat down in front of him and Sister Alice rolled him a Bugler cigarette, lit it and handed it to him. He took it from her with no show of appreciation for the gift, as if it were expected of her. Then she got up to work in the kitchen while he and I talked. He asked me who I was with and I asked him where all the other brothers and sisters were.

"In your heart, sister," he answered authoritatively. He spoke to me as if I was an inferior creature. He treated Alice like a slave. Don had never treated Judy, or me with that kind of attitude. I wondered if the sister's subservient role was the norm for all Christ Sisters. Then he suddenly said, "A sister's role is to humbly serve her brother." I looked at him, surprised by this comment. Had he read my mind? He went on. "Every brother is a reflection of Jesus, so a sister serves him as she would serve the Lord Himself. She is to obey and 'keep her head covered' (refrain from speaking unless spoken to). The brother creates the space and the sister fills it with joy. Eve deceived Adam and caused him to fall out of perfection, so now, she must follow him back into the garden."

Just then Will, Ed, James, and Judy with Ariss and Sol came into the dome. They were impressed by its construction and began talking with Solomon about it. I realized that in my excitement I hadn't really noticed the building at all.

The window and door frames, triangular in shape, were open so that fresh air was constantly blowing in. The inside of the building was divided into three levels. The sharing of meals took place on the top level. The second level was the cooking area, which consisted of a woodstove, a sink and a wooden counter, and the bottom level was used as a resting area. The floor was interesting; it was made from logs cut in three inch pieces. The circles of wood were set in cement.

While they were talking, Sister Alice took me aside and explained a few things to me. Several months prior, Solomon had taken off his robe because of doubts and his attachment to his young son. All the other brothers and sisters had left him alone to work it all out. Then, a month ago, two brothers and Sister Alice had passed through and found Solomon with his son. They talked him into putting his robe back on and following the Lord. The two brothers left, but Alice stayed behind to serve him. She was a beautiful sister, so humble and ready to give of herself. I pondered the story she told me. I had never heard of anyone taking off their robe before. She told me it was called 'flip flopping.'

That evening, Judy, the children and I rested inside with Alice and Solomon while the brothers slept outside. As usual, both Ariss and Sol awoke in the night crying. In the groggy state I was in, I just about jumped out of my skin when I heard a deep voice bellow out in the darkness, "... *woe unto them that are with child and that give suck in the last days! ..." (Mathew 24:19)* 'The king' had been awakened. To top it off, this scripture had haunted me through our whole Peru journey. Hearing it now made me feel doomed, unworthy to be a disciple of the Lord. So after the 'hobbits' had settled down, I lay awake, battling my mind in the darkness. This place was nowhere near what I had expected; what Don had described to us. How I wished he were here. This Brother Solomon did not vibrate love to me. Something just wasn't right. This wasn't the same as the oneness and love we had shared at "Christ Corner."

The next morning, Solomon informed me that 'the hobbits' were not permitted in the dome, unless they could be seen and not heard. He brought me out to a shack that was in the yard and said we could rest in there. "You're not strict enough with them sister," he said accusingly. "When they cry for no reason, put them in this shed, lock the door and walk away. Let them cry it out. They have too much control over you. You must stop feeding their negativity!" His orders seemed so off the wall, inhuman, without compassion. But, was he being directed by God?

That night in the shed, Judy and I opened up to each other shedding our facades. "I don't feel the love of God here. The vibration isn't right. Instead of a clear space, I feel confusion," she said to me.

"Judy, I'm so glad you told me that. I feel the same way. If Don was here he would know what to do. Do you think all the other brothers and sisters are like this?"

"I don't know, Mo, but I don't think so. Don may be here soon. He told me he would meet us here if it was the Father's will. You know what? Solomon may be taking the frustration he feels over his own attachment to his son out on you and the 'hobbits.'" I gave her an affirmative nod.

"Praise God for you, Judy," I said. Judy still couldn't walk with her bad leg. Crutches helped, but walking barefoot was so hard on her since all of her weight had to be put on the one foot. I felt very protective of her and helped her as much as I could. Just the simple act of squatting to take a pee was nearly impossible for her, unless I held her up. We had a beautiful sharing. I felt blessed to travel with her. Solomon, Ed, Will and James went to town for food and on their return, brought someone with them. They pulled up in an old school bus. The newcomers were an older man named Joseph, a middle-aged woman, Mary, and a young man, Mark. Joseph had crazy blue eyes and long white hair. He wore loose clothes made out of burlap, leather sandals and a colorful braided pouch. He spoke with authority and sureness, coming across as a man with much wisdom and knowledge. He told us he was Moses and Mark was Aaron and that he was going to lead the people out of the wilderness and darkness. They had picked up Mary on the road and she became one of his followers. Joseph was like their guru and had them hanging on every word that came out of his mouth. I balked when Solomon allowed them to enter the dome wearing leather. These people were strange. I didn't think Joseph would be willing to give up his reign as Moses and lower himself to be a mere Christ Brother, but you never know. They all sat in the 'communion area' debating truths while Sister Alice buzzed around serving everyone.

The next morning, Ariss and Sol were not living up to Solomon's expectations of children and he ordered me to lock them in the shed and walk away. I felt tormented. I was supposed to obey him, but I knew in my heart he was wrong. What was happening? I wanted to talk to Will, but I couldn't find him. Ed and James were absorbed in Solomon's preaching. I asked Judy to watch the 'hobbits' so that I could take a long walk and talk to God. She said that would be fine. I just had to get away from the whole scene.

The rocks and stones poked the tender soles of my feet, but in a strange way, I enjoyed the physical discomfort. It diverted my attention away from the mental anguish I was experiencing. I sincerely wanted to totally believe that Lightning Amen was Jesus, come back to earth. I had experienced wonderful changes in myself over the winter. What was happening now, I believed, were only 'the storms' that Don had warned us about. There would be hard times that brothers would have to endure in order to break through the doors of realization and reach new levels of awareness.

Going through a 'storm' was like being thrown into the fire to become a refined vessel of God and all my hardships and confusion were necessary tests of faith that would make me stronger. Besides, if Jesus Christ was back on earth and you truly believed it, how could you turn your back on Him and not follow Him?

Meanwhile, in getting away for a few moments to myself, I had no idea where I was walking, but I was moving fast. I called out to God, asking for direction, asking Him to send Don, or another brother who would bring clarity to my mind. I prayed for the eyes to see spiritually and the faith and wisdom to know where to go and what to do. I passed by a farm and a man came out to greet me. "Hi there!" He called to me.

"Howdy, brother," I replied.

"Do you know what you're into?" He asked.

"Why, yes, brother, I'm living the life of Christ; 'no killing, no sex and no materialism.'"

He laughed, throwing his head back, his long beard almost hitting my face. "Well, I can't see that Christ would condone deserting little children." He turned and called to a young child who was playing on a swing. The little blonde-haired girl couldn't have been more than four years old. Her eyes shied away from me as she approached. "This here is Sandy; we took her in last year. One of your sisters just left her to fend for herself." I'm sure my mouth must have dropped open in disbelief. I told him that I had two children and that I would never leave them. They were a gift from God and He wanted me to bring them up in the light of 'the truth.'

On the way back to the dome, I struggled with what the man had told me. Was this a general practice that the sisters followed, to leave their little ones behind? It was not right. Why would God want us to do it? Don never told me I would have to leave my children. There is no way I could do that. Hadn't he had mentioned a 'hobbit farm?' All the way back, I prayed for clarity. When I reached the dome, I tried to talk to Will and Ed, but they were both rapping with Solomon and Joseph. I went to see Judy and the children and told her what the farmer had told me. She shook her head in disbelief. I held Sol in my arms, feeding him from my breast and felt such utter love for him. How could this love be wrong?

Then Judy left the shack for a while and when she returned, excitement filled her. "A sister and two brothers just blew into camp," she announced. "They are talking to Solomon right now. They seem to be putting him in his place. Mo, they feel like right-on brothers and sisters."

My prayer had been answered. "Praise God," I said.

After a few minutes, the new sister came to the shed. "My name is Sister Laura," she told us. "'The spirit' directed us here to clear things up. Someone must have been calling out. Solomon is not riding in a clear space right now. This is no place for new brothers and sisters. We are going to split this scene soon. We also heard something in the ethers that had to do with a mission to Canada." She looked at me and said sternly, "Sister, we have to talk, follow me."

Her eyes were so powerful they drew me into them. She spoke with almost military force. As I followed her out of the shed, Ariss ran after me, crying and tugging on my robe. When I bent down to pick her up Laura ordered me not to, saying authoritatively, "No, don't give in to her, sister." Meanwhile Ariss was screaming at me, demanding that I pick her up and throwing her little arms up towards me. "'Kick back,' Satan!" Laura yelled and pointed her finger at Ariss. Her impact was so strong that Ariss actually fell over!

My first instinct was to run to my baby and pick her up and tell Laura to leave her alone. Seeing my struggle, Laura placed her hand on my chest holding me back from rescuing Ariss and ordered Will, who had just shown up, to take the screaming 'hobbit' inside. I felt so torn. I then remembered Don scolding me for being too attached to my kids.

"'The spirit' has told me to talk to you about something. Let's go into the woods where we can be alone," she said. Obediently, I followed her into the forest. "Giving into feeling and emotion is a trap," she told me over her shoulder. She walked fast with sureness in every step, like someone wearing shoes. We came to a beautiful spot where the sun beamed into the forest in a golden ray of light. I could hear birds singing in the distance. Then Laura looked me straight in the eyes holding me with her stare. I found myself admiring her strength and sureness. It seemed as if she had it all together. I knew I had been the one whom they heard calling out 'in the ethers' and that God had sent her to me.

"The Christ Family is the Lord's army, sister. We are His soldiers. It's a battleground out there and we must be strong. Satan and his army feel threatened by us and will try to defeat us," she explained, still fixing me with her gaze. "We need all of our energy to be focused on 'the truth' and on serving the Lord. You can't serve two masters. You must choose! You can't serve your 'hobbits' and Jesus too. The Bible even tells you. Jesus said it Himself: *". . . those who do not leave mother, father, sister, brother and children for My Name's sake are not worthy of me . . . ." (Luke 14:26).*

I felt my vision blurring and lost the fight to hold back tears. She was telling me I had to choose between my children and Jesus!

"It's not fair for the 'hobbits' to be brought up in 'the truth.' They have to go back into the world and experience sin before they can choose to want to live without sin. I had two children, also, and know what you are going through. You'll be able to see why you must give them up as you live this life and experience more."

Before I had time to think, we were all packed up and in the truck, ready to 'hit the wind.' My mind was a whirlpool of grief and confusion. Numbed by what had happened. I felt as though I was dreaming. I felt totally helpless and frightened. I had no say in the situation at all. I didn't want to leave my babies. I loved them so much; too much, I guessed. I had never thought that God would ask this of me. Was I really strong enough to give Him all that He required in order for me to follow Him? Why had this decision been made for me? Perhaps I do love them more than God. I am new in this life and these brothers and sisters know what is best for me. I have to believe my brothers. When I called out for direction, God sent them to me. But, how can I live without seeing Ariss' little face smiling up at me? How can I live without touching Sol's soft hair? How can I possibly live without them? How?

The truck came to a sudden stop. "All attachments must be broken," Laura's bark jolted me out of my mental struggle. Ed, Will, James and I were let out on the road a little way down the highway. Laura had said that Will and I had to be separated also. So, she ordered us to travel apart in groups of two. Ed was to go with me and Will, with James. Judy had decided to stay and take the trip back to Canada with Laura, who said that they would bring the children to my parents. So, Will and I signed a piece of paper giving my parents custody of the children and Laura the right to take them. She asked for our I.D. and any money that we had and we gave her everything, except for my passport. We also gave her the truck. I don't think she knew Ed was my flesh brother and I wasn't about to tell her, either. As we said our goodbyes in the truck, I looked at Judy, Sol and Ariss and wanted to hug and kiss them all. Sol looked happy as usual in Judy's arms, but Ariss sensed I was leaving and cried out when I left the truck.

"No, Mo!" Laura slammed the door as Ariss lurched for me.

"'In the wind,' brothers," she told us, sternly.

I hesitated. Ariss cried out, "Willy, Mo!!!"

"Just go," Laura commanded. "Serve the Lord."

Will and James walked on ahead. I wondered what Will was feeling about leaving the children. Ed and I waited until they had a good lead on us and then walked onto the hot pavement of the highway. Immediately I wanted to run back and say, "I've changed my mind." But, the Bible story of Lot's wife, who was turned to stone for looking back, came to mind and I dared not turn around. Full faith in God, I told myself. Silently, I recalled two verses from the Bible: "*. . . If any man comes to me, and leaves not his father, mother, wife, children, brethren and sisters, yea his own life also he cannot be my disciple . . .*" and "*Whosoever does not bear his cross and come after me, cannot be my disciple . . . .*" (Luke 14:26-27). I wanted to be a disciple; I wanted to do God's will. I thought about the Bible story of Abraham and Isaac; how Abraham had waited so long for a son and how much that son meant to him. And God had told him to sacrifice his beloved son on the altar. Now I could relate to how hard this must have been.

Meanwhile, the sun was setting, casting its warm glow upon us. Ed and I walked on in silence into the twilight. I felt very light; very strange. I didn't know where I was, or where I was going. I was totally letting God lead me. I had given up everything for Him. "*. . . Take no shoes, no two coats, and no purse worthy of a thief and follow me . . . ,*" I thought.

❄ CHAPTER NINE ❄

S ome woods a little way off the road served as our resting place for the night. I lay there in my bedroll, gazing at the infinite stars that stayed awake with me. The most intense pain pierced my entire soul! I felt empty, lonely and inexplicably lost. No solace came to my full, leaking bosom. No warm little body snuggled up to mine. I felt a hollow, aching numbness. The sound of the wind rustling through the trees drowned my weeping. Thoughts raced through my mind uncontrollably. Perhaps God is just testing me, as He did with Abraham many years ago. Now that He knows I love Him more than anything in this world . . . maybe He'll give my babies back to me . . . . I guess I'm still attached to them. Physically they are gone, but the attachment is much deeper . . . so deep. I already missed them so much. How could I live another moment without them?

Then guilt settled in, like a dark shadow. All attachments to this world must be broken, I reminded myself. I cried out in prayer for strength and for God to fill this emptiness with His Love. He knew I gave my babies up for Him. He knew how hard this was for me.

Next day, I walked behind my brother on Highway Five, heading south. We had no idea where it would lead us. The sun rose higher in the morning sky, staining it with pinkish gold. No home, no job, no bills, no bed, no plans, no kids, no husband; I had nothing but the earth and sky and the Father's guiding hand. Hours passed as then the noon-day sun blazed overhead, burning our heads and feet. We both instinctively started walking on the white margin line, off the burning black pavement. Cars flew past. No one stopped. As time slipped away, my stamina weakened and the physical and mental anguish became unbearable. My mind, a battleground, kept fighting off the need to grieve over the loss of the children. My tired, hungry, thirsty body, with blisters on my feet and full, aching breasts, all added up to sheer misery. A 'space change' would certainly help.

So I called out to God for a ride and within minutes, a red pickup came to a squealing stop and Ed and I climbed in. Ed preached to the driver who was kind enough to give us a ride to a small town and a few bucks for a meal. He really wasn't very interested in our cause, but he was generous, nevertheless. If anything, the preaching was for me, for it made me 'high' and reconnected me to who I really was and what my purpose was. God was answering my prayers.

"Well, Mo, the old stomach is calling out for some peanut butter sandwiches. There's a grocery store right there." Ed pointed across the street and we both started walking towards it, anticipating food.

"I really feel like a juicy peach," I told him. "Sounds great," he replied. Inside the store, we realized we had only enough money for a loaf of bread and a jar of peanut butter. Stuck on the peach idea, I went to the produce man and asked him if he would give freely of two peaches in the name of Christ. He refused and I had to give up my peaches.

Ed and I went around to the back of the small store and found a piece of green grass where we spread out a poncho and sat preparing our sandwiches. "I can't stop thinking about the 'hobbits,' Ed," I said. "I miss them so much. It's tearing me apart." I knew I wasn't supposed to use the words "I" or "me," but this was my brother, he would understand.

Ed looked at me, his hazel eyes revealing a tinge of empathy. "They are right where they are supposed to be, Mo. Everything is in God's hands. You have to believe this. Carmel and John feel they have lost two children, you and me." It seemed strange to hear Ed call our parents by their fist names. Ed continued, "Ariss and Sol will replace that loss for them, they will replace us. This will make them happy; more complete."

I looked at him, digesting his words. I had never thought of it that way before. My intentions were not to hurt anyone and if, instead of being a burden, the children would make my parent's pain ease, it would help me feel a little better. Ed continued, "The world as we know it is on the verge of disaster. When it all comes down, everyone will see that we are the saints and understand what seems unreasonable to them now. John and Carmel will then feel blessed that we are their children. 'The truth' is so far away from the ways of the world. Ariss and Sol are your brother and sister. God is our Father. He loves them. He'll guide them. Place your faith in Him. Keep focused on God, Mo. You have given everything to Him and He will bless you."

"He already has, Ed, I'm traveling with you!" I said. We both smiled at each other lovingly. Ed's words were like a bandage on a child's cut. The wound still hurt, but the presence of the bandage somehow made it feel better.

Voices just behind us caught our attention. We both turned around to see three teenaged boys climbing into the dumpster behind the store. One of them noticed us, his face showing his surprise as he gazed at the two white-robed strangers. Inquisitive, the boys walked over to us and I offered them a sandwich. They accepted and sat beside Ed and me.

"So, what are you guys all about?" One of them asked, as he took a bite of his sandwich.

"We are followers of Jesus Christ, brother. We have forsaken everything in this world to travel and preach His word," I answered.

"What word?" Another asked.

I looked over at Ed and he answered, "Peace on earth and living life to its fullest. You see, it all starts with the individual. If everyone was at peace with themselves, they would be at peace with their brothers and with all life." Ed then looked at me, giving me the floor.

"That's why we don't partake in killing of any of God's creatures. We are strict vegetarians. We don't even kill flies or bugs," I said.

The conversation lasted for some time and the young men seemed to be absorbing every word. When they got up to leave, one of them pulled out a can of peaches from his bag and handed it to me. I looked at Ed in surprise. "Can you believe this Ed? God gave me my peaches! I'd already forgotten about them."

"Give it up and you get it back, even better than you imagined. That's how the Lord works, Mo," He said, with a grin that could have melted any frozen day. I couldn't help but wonder if God would some day give the children back to me.

On the road again, refueled spiritually and physically, we continued our journey. Once again, hours passed and cars swept by us as if we were invisible. The sun sat red and low, resting on the horizon like a tired air balloon. Once again, physical weariness led to mental stress over the little ones. I wondered where they were, if they were being treated well, what Sol was eating, how Ariss must be missing me. Knowing Judy was with them was soothing, but I still had to fight all the concerns. Then a van pulled up beside us and the door flew open. "Wanna ride?"

"Praise God," I said in almost a whisper and Ed and I climbed in. As the vehicle pulled away, it hit me. There were two Christ Brothers and a sister in the van! I was so spaced out, I hadn't even noticed that they were all dressed like me.

"I'm Sister Margaret," the woman with long, golden-red hair, sparkling sea-green eyes and a freckled face told us. "Driving is Archangel Raphael and the brother beside him is Brother Richard."

The driver turned his head and nodded to us as she mentioned his name. He wore sunglasses that concealed his eyes, but his grin showed a happy character. His hair, speckled with grey, hung down just over his shoulders in a gentle wave.

Then Brother Richard turned around and flashed his magnificent baby blues at me and I was immediately taken by this brother. He looked just like my mental picture of Jesus. He emanated love and peace. His face glowed, as did his eyes. His blonde hair reached his shoulders and his auburn-blonde beard was full and hung down past his chest. I felt the presence of the Lord. So this was why all those cars hadn't picked us up. What a miracle, a ride with an Archangel! Sister Margaret sat in the back of the van with Ed and I. It was fixed up nicely with lush blue carpeting covering the raised floor over storage space underneath. Royal blue curtains decorated the windows. Everything was 'zenned to the max' (totally neat and tidy).

I tried to explain to the sister how sore my feet and breasts were. She cut me short, saying, "Don't get into your physical body, sister. Praise God for everything. It's all good."

She spoke abruptly in a military fashion that reminded me of Sister Laura. I asked her a few questions, trying to get to know her, but again I was cut short. "I don't like to talk about the past," she said. "Just be here now and dwell in the present and experience the love of God right now." I felt like a little kid being scolded. She seemed like a cold fish to me. I hadn't expected to be made to feel this way by one of our own kind. I'd thought we had a corner on love and truth. Her attitude confused me, but being a new sister I knew I had a lot to learn, so, I meekly obeyed.

After some miles, we stopped to pick up two hitch-hikers. They turned out to be James and Will! Now we had seven brothers and sisters all together. This was great. Not wanting to be reprimanded for small talk, I bit my tongue and nodded to them, fighting off all the questions that I wanted to ask Will.

We were in California now, in the land of the giants. It was an enchanting place. I felt as though I was in a fairytale. The redwood trees were humungous, stretching towards infinity. The width of some of them was unbelievable. A house could easily fit into one. It was dark now and the shadows in this wonderful wood set the stage for an amazing rest under the giant trees. After a meal of boiled potatoes, we lay in our bedrolls and gazed up at massive trees that seemed to touch the heavens. The sky looked so far away I could barely see a star, here, or there. This gave me a better perspective of the distance between earth and sky. It was truly, inexplicably, amazing. I felt so small, so insignificant. This was a spiritual lesson for me about self-importance and I smiled to myself, thanking God for opening my eyes.

We traveled together for a few days in the van which Raphael called the "P.T. Boat." This stood for patrol and tactical, because we were in the Lord's Army. We stopped in parks for meals and we asked a lot of churches and police stations for gas money. We were new recruits learning the means of survival while traveling in a group with wheels. We didn't view any of this as begging, we were working for the Lord and asking for our needs in His name. "... *Ask in my name and you shall receive ...*"; *(John 14:13)* "... *A workman is worthy of his meat ....*" *(Mathew 10:10)* We also believed that in return, we were giving people the opportunity to receive our message.

While traveling with these seasoned brothers and the sister, I listened to and watched them carefully. There were a few things that confused me. For instance, all the brothers and sisters smoked 'roll-your-own' Bugler tobacco. The can was aqua with navy blue graphics of an army soldier standing at attention and playing the bugle. Along the bottom of the can was a ring of tents. I was told that the Bugler can was a symbol of the Lord's Army and the end of the world. The soldier playing the bugle represented Archangel Gabriel on the last day. What confused me was that we were not supposed to support 'graven images' at all, yet the graphics on the can were 'graven images.' Back in Thunder Bay, I had gotten rid of everything that had 'graven images;' any clothing with a pattern, the kids' stuffed toys, paintings, picture books, etc. I was told that these man-made things defiled God's creation, by trying to reproduce His wonders.

Another issue that bothered me was that Raphael told me it was all right to hug a brother or sister once in a while, if you were coming from 'clear space.' He said that some of the brothers were giving each other massages, too. But, Don had taught us to love without touch. We weren't supposed to touch each other in any way. When I questioned Raphael about it, he told me that the Christ Family had gone 'through a long phase of judgment' when they were all very strict, fiery and military. At the time, there were only a few members and they were at war with Satan's army, so no slack could be cut. For this reason, they very seldom brushed their teeth, or combed their hair, bathed, or washed their robes. All this was done to deny the physical body as much as possible and put all their energy into spirit.

"A few months ago, Lightning put a new message out to the brothers. Be nice, rejoice and enjoy," Raphael explained. "This new phase has opened up many doors that were locked before. We are now able to keep our bodies and robes clean without being accused of vanity. And language has become more relaxed; saying 'my' and 'me' is O.K. now." Raphael's eyes sparkled as he spoke. He seemed to be always bubbling with positive energy.

"I've just retrained my brain to stop saying those words and now you're telling me that it's O.K.?" I asked him.

"Yepper!" He replied. "Give it up and you get it back."

I thought about what he had said. It was a bit awkward to say 'this one' instead of 'me,' and 'the horse,' or, 'the creature' instead of 'my body.' Meanwhile, Margaret was training me to be a righteous Christ Sister by telling me what was accepted and what was not. She was molding my thoughts and actions. If I tried to confide in her and tell her how I ached for the 'hobbits,' she would cut me short. "There are no snivelers in the Lord's Army," she would say. "It's the survival of the fittest." I felt she was being too hard on me and her ways contradicted what Raphael had told me about being nice and rejoicing. I concluded that I must have needed to be put through the fire to become more pliable, so that the Lord could mould me into the being that He wanted. I still had much to learn.

Will and James got off somewhere in Central California. Richard and Raphael felt that James needed some 'wind,' which meant he wasn't yet giving up his free will totally and needed to experience the miracles and hardships of the road. Will and I had been practically ignoring each other in an effort to break our attachment and to love each other the same as any other brother or sister. As I watched James and Will walk away, with my emotions outwardly well under control, my sense of 'righteous pride' fell for a moment. Will I ever see him again? I wondered. Well, it's the Father's will, I told myself.

As we continued on in the van, Brother Richard remained a perfect example of a Christ Brother. His gentle nature and peaceful gestures filled my heart with yearning to be like him. He seemed so happy, so full of joy to give his life to God. I wondered what he had been like before and how long he had been living this way, but I dared not ask after the scolding Margaret had given me.

One day, as we rode along the highway, he came over to sit by me. I was battling with my grief over Ariss and Sol, trying hard to conceal the pain. He looked long and hard into my hurt brown eyes as if reading my thoughts and feelings. "Sister," he said softly. "I know how you feel. I had to give up two 'hobbits,' also."

I looked at him, surprised at how he knew my thoughts. A bond started to form right there. He told me he had been in the Christ Family for three years and had experienced many miracles. Before, he had been a railroad worker, an engineer. He owned a huge home in the country outside of Ben, Oregon. He loved his wife and children dearly and wished they had joined the 'Family,' also. But, they didn't, so he had to leave them behind. I admired him. He touched my heart with his compassion.

At night Raphael and Margaret slept inside the van while Richard, Ed and I rested under the stars. Richard told us bedtime stories every night and I found myself anticipating them. They were stories about the Christ Family, of course. Lots of them were his adventures and miracles. I found them fascinating and looked forward to similar experiences. Through these stories, Richard taught Ed and I a lot about the group and confirmed our stand that this was truly 'the truth.' I couldn't help but wonder why the other two rested apart from us. There definitely was a hierarchy and this bothered me a bit because we were supposed to believe in equality.

One day, a conversation came up about marriage. Margaret told us that she and Raphael had been married in the physical sense, before they joined the group. I asked why they were allowed to travel together, telling them how Will and I had been pushed into separation.

They looked at each other and smiled. "We went through that phase too, sister. We didn't travel together for a year or two, but we gave it up and got it back," Raphael explained to me. "Also," he continued, "Lightning and Cher, the lady by his side, were married before they 'transformed.'"

His words hit me with such force that I was thrown into a state of confusion and doubt. That doesn't seem right. Jesus didn't marry the first time, why would He this time?

"I don't get it, why did Jesus get married this time?" I asked him. They remained unflustered, enjoying my little moment of doubt as if it were a test of their faith.

"He had to experience sin to be able to truly relate to us," said Raphael and went on to support his reasoning, but I was still not totally satisfied. I was torn between my own reason and believing my brother unconditionally. Doubt was of Satan. We were not supposed to question, for our 'finite minds' were Satan and questioning only fed the fire. I didn't understand, but finally I had to shut my mind off, put it on the back burner.

Later that day, the van pulled into the parking lot of a department store and whipped around to the dumpster in the back. Raphael and Richard hopped out with grins on their faces. Ed, Margaret and I watched as they climbed into the 'hopper' and disappeared. Every once in a while we saw a head pop up for a second and an object being thrown to the ground. Then two young boys came walking by just as

Richard and Raph climbed out of the dumpster wearing space helmets with pink antennae. We laughed at the sight of these white-robed, barefooted space-monsters! Richard, being about six foot four, looked like a giant to the young lads, who upon seeing him, screamed and ran as fast as they could go. By this time, the trio in the van was hysterical with laughter as the spacemen joined us, bringing pens, hats and other toys. Raphael was always pulling stunts like this, lightening up the space. I loved him for that. He was a wonderful brother and as time went on, I could see that Margaret was a beautiful sister, too.

I know I would have enjoyed traveling with them more if I hadn't been going through so much physical and mental anguish. My breasts had been filling up regularly and the pressure had been almost unbearable after breast fever had set in. By now, it was about two weeks since the children and I had been separated and finally, the swelling and pain were subsiding.

Ed, Richard and I, 'hit the wind.' I had left my breastfeeding robe with Raphael and Margaret. Raph had given me his 'play robe,' an older, extra robe he used when working on the van. Although it was soiled and thin, I really felt honored to wear the 'archangel's' robe.

All that day, I found my thoughts wandering to my cousin Kim. Perhaps this was because we were so close to where he lived in Modesto; perhaps because he was thinking of me. The more I thought about it, the more convinced I was that we should go to him and bring him the gift of 'the truth.' Perhaps he would join us. I asked Ed what he thought and he agreed, saying that he had been thinking of Kim, too. I mentioned it to Richard, who was sort of our leader, and he said we could project to head in that direction, but it was in the Father's hands where we went. I was satisfied with that.

The California afternoon sun scorched the pavement, our bare feet blistering as we walked on. Ed and I struggled to keep up to Richard's long, swift strides. I lagged farther and farther behind. I would take a few steps in agony, then throw my bedroll down and rest my burning 'tootsies' on it for a few seconds, then run a few more steps and hop on my bedroll to cool my feet again. Richard and Ed marched like soldiers, showing no signs of suffering from the heat. I felt ashamed. I was failing the Lord by putting energy into my physical body, dwelling on the pain and thus intensifying it all the more. "Get out of your feet, sister!" Richard commanded.

Oh, how I wished I could. "Please God, help me rise above this pain," I prayed. It felt so good to reach them finally and I sat on my bedroll cross-legged, my aching feet, finally off the stove-hot pavement.

"You're just breaking in 'your horse'," Richard said with a glitter in his blue eyes.

"You're going through the tender foot space. Your feet are like your soul. The tougher the soles of your feet get, the tougher your soul gets."

I remembered Don telling us that. Brother Don; it seemed like an eternity since I'd last seen him. Would I ever travel with him again?

"Wanna Bugler, sister?" Richard asked, holding a roll-your-own smoke in front of me.

"I don't smoke, brother," I answered.

"You will," he said, almost laughing.

Every brother or sister I had met so far, smoked. It seemed to be almost a ritual. They all smoked at the same time. It was a sharing, like a meal. I wondered what the significance was. Then Richard got up to start 'trucking' again and my heart sank. I had just sat down. I wanted to speak up and say, "Can't we sit a while longer?" But, I knew better than to go against my elder brother's wishes. Limping, trying not to walk on the worst blisters, I followed my brothers down the road.

In Modesto, a smile softened my lips as I stood in front of Kim's window. I'd always loved surprising people. Now, peeping into my cousin's bedroom window, I felt like a child. I wanted to make sure Kim was home. I felt his father, my uncle, would not be pleased with me. As I pressed my nose against the pane of glass, I saw him. He stood in front of the mirror, admiring his half-naked, firm, muscular body. Kim's good looks and tall, powerful form, coupled with his witty charm had always had the women flocking around him. He did look like a Greek god. I stood there watching him admire himself and I saw the false ego at play as I had never seen it before. It hit me with a double edge because I felt the sting from it, too, as I saw it operating in him. I, also, was conceited about my good looks. I had just never been aware of it before. Becoming aware of self-conceit is the first step towards eliminating it.

Kim caught my image in the mirror and whipped his body around with surprising agility to stare at the figure adorned in white sackcloth that seemed to resemble his cousin. His brown eyes opened wide and his jaw hung low in disbelief and shock. I smiled at him and waved, confirming that it was really me. He moved closer to the window and told me to go to the door. I motioned to Ed and Richard, who were waiting on the front lawn and they followed me.

Kim's composure was still rattled as he welcomed us in, saying, "I was thinking about you guys, but usually I get a letter, or I'll phone you. A personal visit, I didn't expect."

He seemed to be chattering to hide his nervousness about our strange attire. He welcomed us to use the shower and the laundry facilities and we really appreciated this luxury.

While our robes were in the washer we all sat out in the back yard, wearing our army blankets. I was sweating and itchy from the wool against my skin. Birds chattered, plum trees and flowers adorned the yard. Kim seemed to be restless while Ed preached to him, as if anticipating something. Then a woman, dressed in a sleazy, red, acrylic dress with a slit up one side and wearing an over-abundance of makeup, slithered into the yard and over to Kim. She looked totally uninterested in the crazy people her date was with, giving ample evidence of her impatience as she tapped her high heels.

As she and Kim left for their date, Richard said to her, "Some day you will see that taking your brother's eyes off God isn't where it's at, sister."

She looked at him, wondering what he meant, but her heart understood. I could see it in her eyes. I'm sure her face would have turned red if it hadn't been masked in so much paint.

So, Kim isn't going to come with us, I thought. He's got a long way to go before he'll be ready to give up the ways of the world. He has a lot to burn out on, yet.

As we waited for our robes to dry, my Uncle Denny came home. He was outraged to find us there and immediately started yelling at me. "Where are your children?!" He bellowed, in his Italian-American drawl.

"In God's hands," I answered calmly.

"You mean you don't know where they are? You terrible mother, you're a child deserter! You disgust me! Get out of my house! You're not welcome here! Get out!"

We grabbed our wet robes from his dryer, slipped them on and left. My body was trembling. His energy was so intense. I was shocked at the intensity of his reaction toward us. This was my uncle. And when Kim had phoned his sister, my cousin Janet, for me earlier, she wouldn't even talk to me on the phone. Ed and I were being rejected by our own family. Richard assured us that this was a common thing with the Christ Family.

"The only family you have now is the Christ Family. No one else in the world really knows what true love is, sister. Jesus said He would come with a sword. Families would turn against each other," he reminded me.

Yes, I thought, this truly was a lesson for me. The Christ Family is my true family.

We walked through Modesto to a park just as the sun was setting. There we sat, watching an ever changing sky splashing gold and pinkish lavenders into eternity. We sat in totally comfortable silence. I loved this about this life. When friends were together 'in the world,' everyone felt uncomfortable if no one talked. Now, there were so many things that were understood and words were not needed. Richard rolled a joint and we shared it. I still didn't like to smoke herb either, but Richard always persuaded me to have a little puff. "Join in the 'communion'," he'd say.

I would puff it to satisfy him, but just hold it in my mouth without inhaling. I guess the fact that I held on to my own belief about smoking bothered him, because I wasn't totally conforming to the group's way. After he had rolled the joint, he handed me the little pouch of herb and said," It's the sister's job to hold the herb and the Bugler and to roll. You're gonna have to learn how to roll. I'll teach you."

I felt uneasy about carrying the herb because it was against the law. A few minutes later, my fear manifested when a policeman came up to us. I wondered if I'd brought him to us with my fear and felt ashamed for feeling it. My heart was pounding as he spoke to us.

"You can't sleep here," he said. I stared at my tote sack where the herb was, trying not to seem uneasy in his presence. I was happy that I didn't have to speak, knowing my voice would crack if I did.

"Do you know where we can sleep then, brother?" Richard asked him.

"Well, if you move to the end of the park, I'll pretend I didn't see you," he said, as he pointed to a dark, wooded area.

"Peace be with you, brother," Richard answered. The man walked away.

When we were settled in our new resting spot, Richard turned to me and said, "Sister, when you have full faith in God, it eliminates fear and worry, because you know that whatever happens is God's will and you are right where you are supposed to be. It's only when men think that they have total control over their lives that stress comes in. Nothing that happens to you happens without God's will. Even if you were thrown in jail, there would be someone there who needed to be 'wired in' about 'the truth.' You see, 'the truth' does set us free."

I smiled at him, wondering how he knew my thoughts. We lay there, with the sky ablaze with stars for our roof and the temperature perfect. My feet were on fire, but it had felt so good to get off them and to lie down. I thought about Kim and how worldly he had seemed. He was caught right up in the rat-race. I knew he had a spiritual side, but he wasn't feeding it much energy at this time, it seemed.

The next day, Will and James came walking into the park. It was so good to see them again. We spent the day and night together and rested in a fruit orchard. Kim found us that day, also, and tried to talk Ed and I into staying in Modesto and leaving the group. He left discouraged. After he had gone, Richard sent Will and Ed on a mission for some food while James, Richard and I sat in a circle talking.

All of a sudden, Richard stood up and said to me, "It's time to 'hit the wind.' Follow me."

I got up hesitantly and followed him. Without a word to James, we left. I wanted to ask him why he didn't want to tell Will and Ed that we were leaving. I wanted to ask him where we were going. But, I knew better. So, I just 'kept my head covered' and 'watched the movie.'

As we arrived at the freeway, a car stopped for us. It was a white convertible with its top down. I'd always loved convertibles. Richard smiled at me, his long, blonde hair blowing wildly in the wind. "Lightning quick," he said, as we drove. "The Lord breaks attachment just to blow your mind. You were attached to Ed even more than to Will. Now all your people attachments are broken."

I looked at this man, who seemed to know me so well. I felt very strange, but very free.

❋ CHAPTER TEN ❋

The cool wind off the ocean brought a refreshing change from the heavy heat of the valley, as we rode across the Golden Gate Bridge in the white convertible. The huge bridge was bustling with traffic. Our driver let us out in the centre of San Francisco.

Richard and I walked the streets until dark, when we found a small park and rolled out our bedrolls among a few bushes. The noise of the city was astounding.

Sirens, squealing cars, yelling, screams, honking horns and hordes of other noises echoed through the streets. I lay there beside Richard, feeling very strange. Who was this man next to me? What was I doing here in this strange city? Everything was entirely new and I was so disoriented. There was nothing left for my 'old' mind to associate with except memories and habits and those two things were continually being reshaped and cut down. If a thought came to mind of wanting to be with the children, I would cut it short and say to myself, no attachment. Who they really are, is spirit. In truth, they are with you. Don't fall into the illusion. They are not their flesh bodies and neither is this flesh body, me. If I felt pain, I would do the same thing. Any negative thought from the 'finite mind' became the enemy. The result was a battleground inside my head.

As time went by, I learned to cut down thoughts before they totally formed. At first, Richard would tell me if I had said something that wasn't 'right on.' He told me of a magic 'converter-button' that we all have inside us. This was an imaginary button that shifted your awareness, enabling you to see things in a different light. It turned negative to positive. We practiced walking down the street, 'converting' everything we saw, or heard. I had never met anyone with whom I shared so many inner thoughts. The inner communication between us was truly extraordinary. Of course we were both tuned into 'channel seven' (the Holy Spirit). If I was having doubts, or 'taking a dive,' Richard would feel it and tell me to push my button. I also would chant "no killing, no sex and no materialism" in my head if I was really having to battle Satan.

Riding on an underground subway for the first time was quite the adventure. Waiting for the train, I heard a sound like a large rushing waterfall as the train rumbled towards us. Hordes of people came bustling through the door, rushing to wherever. We were lucky to get a seat. Many were standing. It reminded me of the buses in Ecuador.

The next night, we found a churchyard to sleep in. The air was fresh and cool, a perfect temperature, and my body was warm under my sleeping bag. The churchyard Richard chose for our resting spot was wonderful. A hedge rose high on all sides, sheltering it from the street. The grass had just been cut and the scent of fresh grass still lingered in the air. Our spot, perfectly flat, was so comfortable. Honestly, at that moment I felt I was in heaven.

We lay there in silence, enjoying our roof of infinite stars. I wondered what was beyond this universe and what the stars looked like from behind, facing our way. I wondered about God and the subject of free will. "Brother," I said to Richard, "I don't understand the matter of free will. If God has given us free will, then how could we be living totally in His will? Is anything we do of our own accord? Do we take any responsibility for our actions here?"

"Well, sister," he replied, "when you chose to live this life and go for 'the truth,' you surrendered your will to God. When a person consciously does that, God sees the gift and returns it, purified. Therefore, everything that you do becomes His will. Your will and God's are now aligned. What could be freer than to do God's will? We are truly free."

In a park on the edge of town, a young man came up to us. His body was tall and slender and his dark skin shimmered in the sun. "Hi! Where are you guys from?" He asked, with a tinge of nervousness evident in his quivering lips.

"The Kingdom of God, brother," Richard replied.

"What do you mean?" He asked.

"Come and sit by this tree with us, brother, and we'll tell you."

I took out the can of Bugler tobacco and rolled smokes as Richard preached. "We have been raised out of the flesh into eternity. We are no longer attached to the earth and are here in physical bodies to preach 'the truth' and gather the chosen ones. We are the disciples of Jesus Christ. We heal the sick and raise the dead, in the spiritual sense."

The man sat attentively, absorbing Richard's words like a sponge in water. I loved to hear Richard preach. It was a high. I still had lots to look forward to because I knew I wasn't 'there' yet, but I could see that Richard was.

Richard gazed into the newcomer's luminous black eyes as he continued. "We have forsaken all earthly possessions; all flesh attachments, even the attachment to our own flesh bodies, to follow the Lord one hundred per cent. We have died to this world and are being transformed into perfect reflections of Christ. We have already died and gone to heaven. You are in hell and hell is getting hotter. Satan is the God of this world. The angels are holding back the four winds and at any time they can

104

let go and it will all come down. The end of the world is closer than you think. Are you prepared?"

I lit two Bugler cigarettes and passed them to the brothers. Brother Guy was not debating Richard's words the way most of our other 'connections' did. He seemed to be entranced by us. He was receiving the word of God. "I've got the feeling the end of the world is coming, too," he said.

Richard continued. "We've already detached ourselves from the illusion, the physical world, but those who believe it is real, sure are in for a surprise when it ends. Praise God for opening our eyes to 'the truth'!"

"What is 'the truth'?" Guy asked.

Richard smiled with knowing eyes. "'The truth' will be revealed to those who live the life of Christ and understand His words of wisdom. 'The truth' is a way of perceiving what is real in life from what is illusion. The flesh will pass away, but the part of us which is real shall forever be. Therefore, we follow three rules that guide the flesh into purity, allowing our true selves, our spirits, to see truth, to truly love. No killing, no sex and no materialism are the three keys to heaven. These were the original laws that God gave to Moses. The blindness of the people of that day would not allow them to receive them, so Moses broke the tablets and made the Ten Commandments instead. These original laws included the Ten Commandments and more. In no killing, we extend it to the animal kingdom. That is why we don't eat, or wear animals. You see, all living things are connected by a golden cord of life. When you kill, you are, in essence, killing part of yourself. Our diet consists of fruit, grains and vegetables, the foods that God originally gave to man." Richard then quoted from the Bible, saying, *". . . Behold, I have given you every herb bearing seed, which is upon the face of all the earth, and every tree, in which is the fruit of the tree yielding seed, to you it shall be for meat . . . ." (Genesis 1:29).*

"Man was a vegetarian until after the flood, when God allowed Noah to kill because of necessity. It is time for us to start walking back into the Garden of Eden. Perfection is here if you choose to go for it. You reap what you sow. If you give life and freedom, you will receive life and freedom. If you kill and cage-up, you'll feel dead and caged. Look at most people today. They work at a job they can't stand, eating dead flesh and feeling awful, eating eggs and feeling just as caged as the chickens. They don't even know what life is, yet! The world is opposite to 'the truth.' They call death 'life' and life 'death.' You must die to the world and to your carnal self before you can taste life. There are so many wonderful things to eat; there is no reason why man has to kill."

"We are pure vegetarians, brother," Richard went on earnestly, "no milk, eggs, cheese, or honey. Animals are cruelly treated and misused so that we may be gratified with dairy products. The baby calf is torn away from his mother the moment he is born, without being allowed to feel her warmth and drink her milk. If it is a male calf, nine times out of ten he's made into hot dogs, or hamburger. If it's a well-bred female, she's put into a stall all by herself, fed soy milk and eventually becomes a milking machine, just like her mother. Cows and chickens even have natural procreation taken from them. They are artificially inseminated. We don't believe in supporting a system of abuse to the animals. God gave man dominion over the animals. This is not righteous dominion!"

Guy looked deep and hard into Richard's blue eyes as he preached. I handed both of them another Bugler and smiled inwardly at the feeling of the moment. I was in heaven. Ecstasy embraced me as the words of 'the spirit,' speaking through Richard, caressed my soul. I knew that this was just as much for me as it was for Guy. My consciousness was being lifted also. It was so wonderful to see this searching soul taking it all into his heart. So many preaching confrontations turned into big debates on right or wrong, but Guy just looked at Richard, speechless.

"No sex is the second key," Richard went on. "There are many reasons for this. One is that Jesus is our example and He is not involved in sex. He loves everyone equally and that is how we are to love. True love is far beyond what the world views as love. Sex is a flesh trip, that's had its time and space. Look at all the problems in the world that root from sex. Unwanted babies, abortion, child abuse, divorce, adultery, pornography, starvation, over-population . . . it is no longer time to procreate. We are living in the 'end times.' The curse of sex has been lifted for those who have eyes to see and ears to hear. Sex was the original sin. Satan deceived Eve and told her that she could be like God if she had sex with Adam. Sex was the downfall of man. From then on, we became aware of our physical bodies and were thrown out of the Garden. Man had to work by the sweat of his brow and woman had to bear children in pain and sorrow. Now is the time to return to the beginning, to purity, simplicity and oneness with God."

Suddenly, a bird overhead burst into song, as if agreeing with Richard. He had Guy and me hanging on every word.

"The third key to heaven is no materialism." Richard smiled at Guy with a twinkle in his eyes as he preached. "It is time to share and give freely. We forsake all of our material possessions and follow Jesus. It goes much deeper than not owning material things. You may just have a robe and nothing else and still be materialistic. No attachment is what it really means, to be able to have and use things without attachment to them, without the concept of 'this is mine.' No attachment to the flesh, also. We don't work for man, or money. We don't support the system of greed. The world takes God's free gifts and puts a price tag on them. Then they make you work like a slave for what's yours in the first place. The system is the 'beast' that is written of in the Book of Revelation," he added, with utter conviction.

"We work for God, not man. We are disciples of the Lord and He told us to ask in His name and it will be given. We are the children of the first resurrection; we are the saints. We have come to take over the world with love, God's love. Jesus Christ is walking the earth in a physical body. But, He is not that physical body and He knows it. This is the Second Coming. He is wearing a long white robe, walks barefoot and is living the three keys. He has come in the clouds in men's eyes. He has come from the east to the west like lightning. He is spirit. He is king. He is Lord and he is calling you to follow Him." At these words, Guy stood up. He was ready to follow Jesus.

As we walked to his place, I noticed that Guy's feet were a bit deformed and he had a hard time walking. He walked over on his arches quite badly, which made his knees buckle. In his dark and run-down room, Richard gave him his extra 'play robe.' Even though it was short, Guy looked wonderful in it. All we took with us was some money he had and the white sheet off his bed.

All three of us walked single file on the burning highway, heading east. I could feel the blisters forming on my feet as I tried to keep up to Richard's fast pace. Guy was singing from his heart some black, spiritual, gospel songs, limping on his crooked feet, lagging far behind. I wondered why Richard was 'trucking' so fast. I kept turning around, wishing I could help Guy. What a sight he was. A tall, thin man, the white robe hung luminous against his dark skin, limping on the scorching hot pavement, trying to keep up. No complaints crossed his lips. My own pain faded as I watched his struggle.

"Follow your brother!" Richard snapped at me. "Your position is right behind me. If he's a trooper, he'll make it. If not, he's not strong enough to be in the Lord's Army." I obeyed him, but inwardly I questioned his lack of compassion.

The next few days found us walking long hours. I barely felt the oozing blisters on my feet. They were nothing compared to the hard time the new brother was having. But, I followed Richard, focusing all my energy on the 'inside' to help Guy walk.

We settled down in a park to 'rest' (sleep) one night. I prepared us a sandwich of peanut butter, canned green peas which I mashed up and mustard. Despite how this combination sounds, it really did taste great. It became one of our favorite sandwich spreads. As we ate, we watched an exquisite sunset.

Soon the sky was ablaze with stars. I loved resting outside under the stars. I felt so much more a part of nature, so real. Just as we were about to 'blast off' water began falling on us. Puzzled, I looked up at the clear sky as Richard ran a short distance and called me to bring my wooden bowl. The water from a nearby sprinkler, redirected with the bowl, flooded over our feet. The moon rose in the sky, shedding light across us in beams, creating a dreamy mood as we washed each other's feet. We stared at each other without a word, enraptured by feelings of goodness in the presence of God.

In the morning, Guy told us that he couldn't follow us anymore. Tears welled up in his eyes as he said farewell. I felt like hugging him and telling him that it was all right, that God could see the goodness in his heart. I felt so much compassion for him.

"'In the wind,' brother," Richard said, as he turned to leave.

I had to hold back my emotions not to cry. As we walked on down the road, Richard assured me that everything was in the will of the Father. "Once in the robe, always in the robe," Richard assured me. "He just has some karma, or desire for something worldly, to burn out on yet. He'll be back."

I did notice how much easier it was to travel just with Richard. I felt lighter. We flowed so wonderfully together in God's river.

"Can you feel the 'space change,' sister?" Richard asked, as if reading my thoughts. "When you take a new brother down the road, it's like 'taking a dive.' The spiritual level is lowered. Along with a new brother come a lot of negative vibrations, because he has just come out of the world, or the carnal state. Satan and his army try to tempt him back and a spiritual battle takes place. Each time a saint is pulled out of the world, it gets uglier and more evil."

"It feels really good to be with you, brother." I looked admiringly up at Richard. He was very tall and thin. Balding on top, the lines on his face gave evidence of his age. I guessed he was in his late thirties. His chiseled features were extremely attractive and his deep blue eyes, seemed to be filled with light, giving him the look of a holy man. I felt honored to be with him.

❊ CHAPTER ELEVEN ❊

As the days flowed into weeks, we became closer and at times our telepathic communication was so strong, it seemed we almost merged into one. When we walked, I concentrated on being in step with him. When he preached, I heard the words in my mind at the exact same time as they left his lips. He knew when I was tuned right into him, too.

"I felt you 'juicing' me on the 'inside,' sister. Praise God," he'd say.

One night in Las Vegas, Nevada, in the home of one of our 'connections,' before we fell asleep I heard a conversation in my head. It seemed as if I was talking to Richard, but it was strictly my own inner voice, speaking for both of us. Out loud, I asked Richard if he had been talking to me in my head. He answered by smiling on the outside and saying, on the 'inside,' "Yepper." I felt so elated. I had always believed telepathy was real, but had never experienced it to this degree. Richard told me that he had experienced it with others, but not as powerfully as with me.

As we walked through the town we came to a movie theatre. "Wanna see a movie?" He asked.

"Sure, brother sounds right on," I answered.

We followed the line-up into the theatre and Richard asked the girl at the ticket box if she would give freely of a movie in the name of Christ. "Go on in, see anything you like," she answered. It was such a high feeling to just walk in and not have to pay. The theatre was huge. About ten different movies were playing at the same time. I followed Richard into one and we sat near the back. The movie started out to be real mellow, but as time went on, I began feeling something wasn't quite right and by the middle it was turning into a horror flick. That's when we walked out. I felt really off center as we came out into the night.

There was a church down the street a ways, with all lights on and singing coming from an open window. Richard and I went in and sat near the back. The church was full. The preacher held his audience captive with his charismatic, calculated words and antics and I found his performance amusing. He had people crying, yelling and coming forward to be 'saved' and bathed in the blood of Jesus. His dark skin and eyes made his silver-white hair nearly fluorescent. His heavy southern drawl magnified everything he said.

After the performance, a woman came up to us. "You are part of the Christ Family, right?" She said. "No killing, no sex and no materialism; you follow Lightning Amen. I know; I was once where you are. I used to be a sister. You have to believe me when I tell you this. It is a cult. It is not 'the truth'. Please reconsider, leave the movement!" She pleaded.

Richard didn't feel any pull to talk to her and he split the scene. I followed him to a river bed in the town, where we rolled out our bedrolls and I wondered what the woman had been talking about. I had never heard the word 'cult,' and couldn't imagine what it meant. I felt so disoriented. What a night; the movie, the preacher and now, this woman. Doubts were creeping into my belief structure. It was more than I could fight off. I couldn't handle it. I actually felt sick to my stomach from it all. If only I could have met Lightning, I thought. Then I'd know what to believe right now.

"Brother," I said reaching for Richard to pull me out of the quicksand I was sinking in. "I am full of doubts, I don't feel right. What if Lightning Amen really isn't Jesus? What if this isn't 'the truth'?"

"Satan sure is having a heyday with you tonight, sister," he answered kindly. "Be strong; don't allow him to get to you! Shut off your thinking mind and just feel, just be. It is real. You are a living witness to the very reality of 'the truth'."

During the next few weeks we traveled through California and Nevada to Utah, walking along the roads in silence. We had many 'communions' (conversations about God) and 'connections' (people who had received the word and would see to our physical needs). People picked us up on the freeway as we walked. Some would take us to their homes, give us a meal, a shower, let us wash our robes and give us a place to sleep for the night. We met all kinds of people, living in all kinds of places. Our physical needs were always met. This, in itself, was a miracle to me, proof that God was taking care of us as we did His will.

In Salt Lake City, we hung out in one of the largest and most beautiful parks I had ever seen. This park stretched across seven city blocks one way and about three the other. Various trees provided lots of shade and homes for birds and squirrels and a huge zoo on the side of the park kept many different kinds of animals captive.

"Do you have any I.D. with you, sister?" Richard asked as we strolled through the park.

"Sister Laura took my birth certificate and driver's license when she left us in Oregon to take the 'hobbits' back to Canada," I answered. "But, I still have my passport."

"Can I see it, sister?" Richard asked.

"Sure." I pulled out my passport and handed it to him. We looked through the pages of colorful stamps; Mexico, Guatemala, El Salvador, Costa Rica, Nicaragua,

Panama, Ecuador, Peru . . . my mind journeyed back through all those places, conjuring up faces and traces of events gone by.

"It's time to get rid of this," Richard stated. "This Maureen no longer exists," he added, pointing to the picture. "If God wants you to travel abroad, He'll make it happen. We don't follow mans' rules."

We came to one of the garbage cans. Richard stopped walking. He then handed me the passport and with a glimmer in his eyes said, "Rip it up and burn it. You are now Maureen Christ."

I obeyed. Richard lit a match and grinning, set my picture on fire, the photo melting and curling, coiling in the heat. The litter can was bare except for the burning passport, which was quickly consumed by the flames. I felt a surge of energy rush through me as the last remaining physical evidence of my old identity was transformed into ashes.

All of a sudden, the sounds of fireworks blasted overhead and the sky lit up with a blaze of color that was to last for hours. "You see, God is pleased with you, sister," Richard exclaimed, his face beaming. We both stood there gazing at the sky, two white-robed angels yearning for flight.

All the captive animals pulled at my heartstrings as we walked through the zoo. We stopped at the monkey's cage for quite some time, enjoying their human-like antics. One particular monkey held me in a near-hypnotic stare. He then proceeded to tell me about his life, moving his arms as he spoke, his facial features so expressive. With eyebrows arched and mouth puckered, he ran abruptly into his cave and then back over to me carrying a banana peel in his hand. He then stuck it out of the cage, offering it to me and I received his gift. As I did so, he smiled at me and let out a squeal with his lip curling up to reveal his yellow teeth. As bizarre as this may sound, this monkey did communicate with me. It truly seemed that I had actually understood him.

After a while, a girl who was working in the park picking up trash came over to talk to us. She insisted that we come home with her and told us we could stay as long as we liked.

Lil lived in a small one-bedroom home with her boyfriend, Gary. They were quite the characters. Lil had only been educated up to grade two because she had lived on river boats with her dad and had always been traveling. Gary, a motorcycle gang member, wore black Harley shirts, and chains, and spurs on his pointed leather boots. They both liked to smoke pot, which suited Richard just fine. Was this their common ground?

They gave us full dominion over their pad. Lil was happy that I liked to cook. I baked bread, cakes and cookies and made spaghetti dinners and other vegetarian meals. Richard especially loved pinto beans, cooked with a whole clove of garlic. Lil and Gary enjoyed my cooking and liked the way I cleaned their house, while at the same time, hot meals and clean bodies were a real treat for us. A few times when we talked, it seemed as if Lil wanted to follow us.

During this time, I fought many inner battles. I thought about the 'hobbits' quite often. My heart ached to be with them. Living on the road, with its constant change, had kept me from thinking about them every moment of every day. Yet there were many times when the solace of "being in the will of the Father" wasn't enough to keep the immense pain of separation away. One such night, Richard and I were 'resting' on Lil and Gary's front lawn. I couldn't stop my mind from feeling the anguish and I started sobbing quietly. I knew I was giving in to the flesh, but I couldn't control it this time. All of a sudden, Richard jumped out of his bedroll, grabbed my hand and started running as fast as he could down the street. I felt a rush of excitement overwhelm me. I found it amazing that I kept up with his lengthy strides. The night was black and quiet with everyone in dreamland, as two white-robed figures ran through the deserted streets. I knew Richard must have felt my pain and taken me running to shake me out of that sad space. It worked.

We had many 'connections' in Salt Lake City and much 'C-weed' (pot) was given to us. Richard said we were given so much of it because I hadn't let go of my convictions against it yet. Usually we smoked it at night. It relaxed me and helped me sleep. Around this time, I also started to smoke Bugler tobacco. Richard told me that by not wanting to smoke, I was holding onto my 'old self,' the part of me that was very health conscious and obsessed with what was good for the body. We weren't vegetarians for health reasons. We didn't concentrate on the flesh. We lived in 'the spirit' realm.

Walking along the wide open stretches of Wyoming's vast landscape was a test of faith. My body was in pain and run-down and the few cars that passed by ignored us. We walked on, through the blistering heat with no shade trees in sight. Richard felt my pain. I didn't say a word, but he knew. He walked down the shoulder of the road and I followed him into a drainage tunnel.

The tin culvert, dry and cool, was to be our home for the next few days. Our only food was a jar of peanut butter which we mixed with water to make peanut pudding. We shared it with the mice that also occupied the tunnel. The first thing we did was clear out a few pieces of garbage and unroll our bedrolls. The culvert was barely wide enough for both of our bedrolls to fit across. It was such a relief to lay my bones down. Richard let me rest and he rolled us each a Bugler. The evening found us singing songs to God and listening to our voices echo off the tin walls. My heart was full of praises while combating the 'creature features' (body illnesses) I was trying hard to ignore.

The next day we rested. Unfortunately this only magnified the intense spasms that were now ripping through my abdomen. What was I lacking spiritually? I wondered. I was sure that disease meant 'dis-ease' with God. Finally I realized I had to get up and do something to get my mind off the pain. Richard didn't feel like coming for a walk so I ventured down the culvert alone, hunched over as I walked to avoid hitting my head on the roof. The culvert ran under the highway before it gave way to sunlight and the air beyond. The sun nearly blinded me when I reached the end and was able to take a deep breath of fresh air. Eyes now adjusted, I gazed in awe.

I was standing in the most peculiar stretch of land. It was like the bed of a river that had mysteriously evaporated overnight. This canyon-like abyss where I stood had cracked clay walls that stretched far above my head on either side. I felt as though I had just stepped into a mythical 'Land of Giants.' Walking through this prehistoric crack, I found it miraculous that little splashes of colorful wildflowers had erupted through this unforgiving and otherwise barren land. They stood so out of place, as if defying their harsh surroundings. Good fruits can be found in the most unlikely places and in infertile soil, I thought. Another lesson God was teaching me.

I lay down in the dirt, just a being on the face of the earth. Silence enveloped me. Not realizing the intensity of the sun, coupled with the infection I was fighting, I became dizzy, weak and unable to move. I opened my parched mouth to call for Richard, but found I could not utter a sound. I felt my consciousness drifting like the ebb and flow of the ocean. I remember thinking that I had to get out of the sun and heat, but my body had become heavy, limp and motionless. All my attempts to yell for Richard failed. So I cried out for him 'on the inside,' concentrating my focus on getting my message to him.

"Sister, are you O.K.? I heard you calling me." The sound of his voice made my cracked lips arch into a painful smile. He scooped me into his arms and carried me back to our shelter. He nursed me with the last bit of water in our canteen. "We have to get to a town and have a doctor look you over," he said. Was that concern I heard in his voice? I wondered.

"Richard," I said, when I was able to speak, "you told me you came because you heard me calling. Did you physically hear me call you?"

He paused for a good space before answering me, thinking about the question. "I heard you in my head, sister," he said at last. "It was more like a strong pull, a feeling that enveloped me. You were calling me on the 'inside.'"

I nodded affirmatively. "I was trying to use my voice, but I was too weak to yell, or even speak. When I focused all my energy on you and called out for you in my heart, you came," I said. "I believe God set this all up to teach me a lesson about how much faith I still have locked into the physical illusion. Praise God for His infinite wisdom. I believe this abdominal pain is somehow entwined in that lesson, too."

As we left the shelter, I prayed for a house 'connection;' somewhere where we could wash our bodies and robes and have a good meal. Just as the last rays of sun shone across the desert plain, we caught sight of a mobile home court on the horizon. As soon as we arrived in this tiny village, a man called us over and invited us into his home. Inside the trailer we met his wife and two children. I was attracted to these children, who were close in age to my little ones and I praised God for letting me hold a baby once more.

That night I shared with Richard a revelation that God had given me. "I love the 'hobbits' here in this home with the same intense love that I feel for Ariss and Sol. I'm starting to experience equal love, brother; God's love."

"Praise God, sister." He smiled at me. "Equal love is the highest form of love. God has raised us above the flesh, beyond the world and its ways. We are getting higher with each day that we live in God's will, even though we sometimes take two steps forward and one step back."

That night I thanked God for all His gifts and asked Him to mould me into a reflection of true love.

The next day, we got a ride with two well-known rodeo riders. These guys were really rough characters. We lay on a mattress in the back of their pick-up. They told us they were going to Idaho, but when they stopped and let us off, we were back in Salt Lake City! "There must be someone calling out for 'the truth' here, sister," said Richard calmly.

Although we dreaded walking the same old streets again, we knew God was controlling our destiny and He wanted us back here. I was still in pain, so we decided to go to the hospital and give the old body a tune-up. At the hospital office, I asked if they would give freely of their services in the name of Christ and they agreed and gave me a form to fill out. They must have questioned my answers, Name: Maureen Christ. Address: In the wind. Age: Eternal. State: Bliss! A doctor gave me a prescription for hormone pills and we took it to a pharmacy and asked the druggist if he would give freely in the name of Christ and he did.

We were walking down a quiet street and Richard said to me, "I just received a 'beeper' that someone is calling out." He stopped for a moment and suddenly changed direction as if being led somewhere. He came to a halt in front of a rundown house. A man sitting on the stairs smiled as we approached him.

"Welcome, care for some tea?" He said, his eyes twinkling. My 'finite mind' still couldn't believe what was happening, but my spirit was soaring and my convictions and beliefs were being reinforced. There were two women and two children inside. The house was bare and had boxes piled in every room. They stared at us in awe as we walked in. Then we all sat around in a circle on the floor, listening to Richard preach the word of God.

Everyone agreed about 'no killing.' "The first step to take against cruelty and violence towards animals is to become a pure vegetarian," Richard told us. "Don't eat, or use anything that comes from animals. Read all labels carefully. There are a lot of bad spirits that enter you if you eat flesh, or the products of captivity. So don't wear leather, or use feather pillows."

All three adults started going through their possessions, throwing away shoes, purses and soaps and feeling really good about it. Richard went on preaching the other keys, but only one person, a woman named Samantha, was ready to receive them. She went and gathered a sleeping bag and a toothbrush and comb and told her friends that she was leaving with us. There was great confusion as the other two freaked out and tried to talk her out of going.

At last Richard spoke up, saying, "'In the wind,' sisters," and we followed him out of the house as the others screamed, "Don't go!"

We got part way down the street when her friends pulled up in a car. The man, whose name was Terry, got out, took angry steps toward Samantha and said, "Don't go with them, Sam. We need you."

"I want to serve God, Terry. I belong with these people," she told him soberly.

As she turned to walk away, he frantically grabbed hold of her hand. She broke loose from his tight grip and walked towards us. The car drove reluctantly away. We walked in silence. Then Richard stopped in front of a house and told us to wait for him as he knocked on the door and went in. He came out with a white sheet.

"Here's your robe, sister. We'll go to a park and sew it up for you," he said to her.

The next day, when we had finished, she put it on. She looked like an angel. Her fuzzy auburn hair blew in the wind and her sea green eyes sparkled with the excited enthusiasm of a child.

"I feel so good in this robe," she told us.

Richard looked at me and said, "Praise God, for another has given her life for him."

The next few days were a training period for our new sister. I took her into a grocery store and showed her how to check the labels for 'unrighteous ingredients.' I showed her how to ask freely for a loaf of bread in the name of Christ and explained to her why we did it. I taught her how to roll Bugler tobacco and warned her about 'keeping her head covered' and listening to her brother without any feedback. We corrected her when she used words, or phrases that were not cool and replaced them with ones that were exclusive to the Christ Family. We explained to her that the 'finite mind' is Satan. We told her about the battle between the flesh and 'the spirit' that she would experience. There were many other things that had to be refined in order for one to become a seasoned Christ Brother or Sister. It was a sort of art; every move we made, every word we spoke, was a reflection of the Christ Family perfection that we tried to achieve.

Samantha, we discovered, had a hard time letting go of her false ego. She didn't like to be told what to do and how to do it. But, we gave her as much energy 'on the inside' as we could and saw that day by day she made progress in adapting to our way of life.

Richard again heard a 'beeper' and followed it in a certain direction. This time we almost walked by the 'connection,' but stopped when a woman called out to us. This woman, Heather, was intrigued by us. She wanted to know everything about us and asked if we would stay with her for a few days. Heather was middle-aged, lived alone, worked in an office and loved to sail. We talked to her for hours in the evening when she got home from work. During the day we cooked and baked. I even made Samantha a birthday cake because she was now 'born again' in 'the spirit.' Heather told us that she wished she had the faith to be able to come with us, but she didn't. She admired us greatly and was full of remorse when Richard said it was time for us to move on.

"Please come back whenever you pass through town, stay as long as you like," she told us. "I feel so good when I'm around you guys."

On the road again, we headed north towards Montana because Richard felt a 'pull' in that direction. He walked ahead, while Sister Sam and I walked side by side behind him. It was nice to be with a sister. The road taught us many lessons and 'connections' filled every day.

Sam was having problems with huge hives that spread over her entire body. They were intensely itchy and she was really having a hard time ignoring them. I was still having problems with my periods and also with abdominal aching. My first period after my pregnancy with Sol had lasted for over a month and I felt weaker as time went on. Both Sam and I went to a free clinic in one of the towns we passed through. The doctor gave Sam some pills for her hives and he prescribed a birth control pill for me. I found that really ironic, a Christ Sister on "The Pill!" The doctor had given me three month's worth and said that my problem should clear up by then.

Monthly periods were always a hassle for me. The boxer shorts we all wore under our robes meant that tampons were the only option we sisters had for sanitary 'ammunition' during our periods. One morning I awoke to find myself sleeping in a pool of blood, my white robe stained with red blotches. We were sleeping on a cement slab in front of the side doors of a school. Luckily, the janitor had left the doors open. I found a washroom, took off my robe and boxers and commenced to scrub them with hand soap. What a job that was. Sweat and blood dripping, I tried to hurry in case the janitor came in and caught me. I put my pink, damp robe back on and Richard, Sam and I ventured to a 7-11 store.

"Can you give freely of a box of tampons in the name of Christ?" I desperately asked the man in charge.

He looked at me over the top of his newspaper, appalled by my attire and request, and said, "No, if you can't pay for them, beat it." I continued to try to talk him into it, wondering all the while where the next closest store was, but he repeatedly refused my request. "Brother, I need them!" I told him sternly as I stood there, leaving the desperate evidence of my blood on his floor. He got out of his seat, angrily grabbed a small box of tampons and threw it at me. "Get the hell out of my store, you weirdo!" He yelled.

Richard and Sam were waiting outside when I finally emerged with my precious tampons and from there we ventured to find a public washroom. It was after this experience that I learned to be prepared and carry a few supplies with me. Also, in grocery stores' employee washrooms, there were always a few extras that no one would miss. I don't know how I justified the stealing part of it, but I did and I never again found myself begging for tampons. Later I was to learn that after belonging to the Christ Family for a while, many sisters found that their periods had stopped.

Somewhere between Utah and Montana, Samantha left us. It was a dark, rainy night and the three of us had taken cover under the eaves of an abandoned old store. "I want to go on a pilgrimage alone," she told us. "I feel I need a solo."

"We love you, sister!" I yelled to her as she trucked off, bare feet splashing in the puddles, the dark night consuming her. My heart felt heavy at her parting. "I hope she doesn't go back into the world," I said to Richard.

"There's no such thing as 'hoping' sister, it's all in the Father's will. She was having a hard time believing her brother. She may have more lessons to learn before she can live this way."

Sam would voice her opinion when being told something, instead of humbly receiving it. But, for sisters, submissiveness was a must. It was looked upon as righteous and holy. I had felt the battle she went through in trying to give up her individuality and 'clean her closets' to become an open vessel for the Holy Spirit. I too was still battling my 'old self.' I felt a part of me departing with her as Richard and I stood in silence, watching her walk off into the stormy night.

It was well into summer now. One day I asked someone what month it was and he told me, "July." Another birthday had passed unnoticed. I must be twenty-one now, I thought to myself. Then I corrected my thought. "No, I'm eternal. I'm 'the spirit' force inside of this flesh."

Later, while walking through a small town, we came to a park and laid out our army blankets. Using our bedrolls as pillows, we lay down under the trees for a rest. It felt so great to get off my feet and be horizontal for a while. The sky was powder blue, with a few feathery clouds passing by now and then. The sound of the breeze whipping through the leaves was so comforting. We lay there side by side, praising God for opening our eyes to the little wonders that so many were blinded to. I remembered my life before I had been 'reborn,' and how busy I was with laundry, cooking, cleaning; the perpetual picking up of toys . . . one chore led to another and time to just 'be' was non-existent. I had been a slave to my material possessions, having to care for them . . . I felt so blessed to be here now.

"Sister," said Richard, breaking my train of thought. "A Christ Sister wears the same garb as a brother; a white robe, boxer shorts, army blanket, bedroll and tote sac."

I wondered why he was telling me this. "Yes?" I answered.

"Well, then, it's time for you to throw away your bra," he stated.

I felt a little embarrassed, wondering how he knew I still had it. My breasts were still producing milk, but the pressure had decreased as time went on. I was no longer engorged and in pain, but I had never felt comfortable without a bra. I didn't want to give it up. I didn't see the necessity. But, it was a matter of obeying my brother. 'Believe your brother' was a rule that was just as important as the three keys.

I walked into the park restroom, took off my bra and threw it into the trash can. Without support my breasts sagged into their natural position. It felt strange. Was it my ego that was once again being shot at; pride? I walked back to Richard and resumed my position beside him.

"Praise God," he said as he smiled at me.

That evening we rested in a graveyard just on the outskirts of town. Graveyards were one of the safest places to rest. There were usually no underground sprinkler systems as there often were in the parks and the chances of our sleep being interrupted by drunks, or policemen were slim.

That evening, while lying among the tombstones, I had to fight a barrage of 'old tapes' (old programs or memories) that tried to infiltrate my mind. Fears and visions of horror were attempting to shake my space. The moon rose above us, full and luminous, adding an eerie sense to the place. I wondered if I would choose to sleep here if I was alone. I knew that fear was not of God and that this whole 'movie' had been 'set up' to help me overcome fear. Eventually, I was able to feel at ease resting among the thousands of dead bodies.

Montana reminded me of Canada. The trees and foliage were much the same. I wondered if I would ever be in Canada again. I didn't feel comfortable with the thought of passing through Thunder Bay; I didn't know if I was strong enough to see Ariss and Sol and then leave again. I feared falling back into the world. Richard told me that it would be like falling from heaven into hell. My spiritual consciousness would be wiped away and I would be lost in the darkness once again. Only worse this time because I had once seen the light and had turned my back on it. I would be doomed forever.

That night I dreamed that I was back in Thunder Bay, with the kids. It felt so wonderful to feel the warmth of little Sol's body, as I cuddled him and nursed him. Ariss' innocent face broke out in a smile as she saw me approaching her. She ran to me, arms open, smothering me with sloppy kisses. I had missed them so much. Now I was with them, their mother once again. The only thing that tainted my bliss was the fact that I had turned my back on Jesus, in order to gratify the need to be with my children.

I awoke, disoriented. I was surprised to see Richard and to find myself in my bedroll. The dream had been so real. We were by the doorway of a school, sleeping on the stairs under an overhang. It had been pouring that night and the cold concrete was an inviting alternative to the cold and wet. Richard's face was shining, he smiled at me and handed me a Bugler. I sat up and began telling him my dream. I was in hell, because I turned away from 'the truth,' but it felt so good to be with the 'hobbits' again, I concluded. "I'm sure glad I woke up to find myself here with you."

"We are all working a lot of things out, sister. God uses our dreams for His lessons, too," he assured me.

❈ CHAPTER TWELVE ❈

We got a ride to Spokane, Washington with a lovable old soul in a pickup truck. When we arrived, he treated us to dinner. He didn't want to see us go. People usually reacted to us in basically two ways. They were either repelled, or attracted. Those that were attracted to us were sad to see us move on. We explained the rejection and attraction in this way, since we were dwelling in God's love; we carried with us positive energy. The good were attracted to the light and the evil, repelled. When we spent time with someone, we took on their negative vibrations and converted them to positive. Thus we would bring people's consciousness levels up into our space and they would feel really high. Many times, Richard and I would feel drained afterwards and have to be by ourselves for awhile.

As we walked through a railway yard in Spokane, Richard turned to me with a twinkle in his eyes and said, "Do you wanna check out riding the freights?"

"'Right on,' brother sounds like fun."

A minute later we were sitting on a small platform in the open space between two box cars. I felt my stomach churn with excitement as the train started picking up speed. I'm sure my knuckles were white from my tight grip on the steel. The wind blew stronger and stronger, disarraying my long auburn hair. It was so strong, my eyes watered and I had to turn my head to the side. We passed by forests and rivers all undisturbed by man, except for the railway line.

I thought about the beauty of the countryside. Why does man, who is supposed to be the most advanced being on earth, destroy most of its natural beauty? Why couldn't humans live in harmony with all other living things? It was nearly too late for the earth to remain in this form. At any given moment, I was expecting the holocaust to bear down on us. Yet fear had no claim on my heart. I knew that I was 'right' with God; I was living 'the truth' I had given up everything of this world, so I was no longer attached to the illusion of the physical. I knew that everything was energy and energy cannot be destroyed, just transformed.

I was anxious to see the 'transformation' of the new earth. I remembered a few weeks back when Richard and I were in someone's home, listening to the news.

There was concern about a meteorite that was going to fall to earth somewhere near California. Richard and I were excited about the news. Later that evening, in our bedrolls, we talked about the possibility of this being the beginning of the end. The Bible did say that fire would fall from the sky.

Richard told me that he had been an engineer on the railroad. He was working when he first met the Brotherhood. Two brothers were riding the freights and they baptized Richard with 'the truth.' He took the brothers home with him, hoping his wife would want to leave with them, too. A couple of days later, he was following them down the road in a white robe.

We saw many hobo jungles nestled in brambles near the tracks. When we got off the train, some hobos jumped off, too. They were surprised to see us and laughed at our robes. "You won't stay white for very long riding these suckers," one of them told us.

Richard and I walked through the little town, catching every eye we passed. Someone gave us enough money for a loaf of bread and a jar of peanut butter. We shared our humble meal in a park with those same hobos.

Mealtime was very sacred to us. It was a quiet time. The food itself was just a 'prop' to help us in our meditation. Most of the time, we ate outside in parks, so it was like having picnics every day. We believed that we were also eating the vibrations of the food. It was given to us, which was a positive feeling; and it was vegetarian, so it was alive.

Living on the road, I was amazed at the few, bare necessities, one needs to survive. The average house and all of the possessions one collects over the years seemed so far away from me now. We believed that each attachment held you to the world and lowered your vibration. That is why Jesus said it was hard for a rich man to enter heaven. We traveled light and simple. We did not acknowledge the concept of time. We ate when we were hungry; we slept when we were tired. Most of the time, when the sun went down, we rolled out our bedrolls, too. I'm sure there must have been times when we went to sleep as early as 7:00 p.m.

Richard felt right at home, riding the freights. We were now riding in an open boxcar bouncing around with the other cargo. Then, abruptly, the train stopped and a tall husky man came walking down the tracks alongside it. He was halfway past our car when he spotted us. His facial expressions went from fear to surprise and then to open friendliness.

"Richard? Is that you, old buddy? I heard that you joined some Jesus freaks, left the wife and kids behind . . . Well; I see you never got the railroad out of your system, huh? He said, with a nervous grin.

"Good to see you again, Roger. I'm doing great. "I've never been happier in my life," Richard told his friend.

Roger glanced at me and winked at Richard. "She's a beauty if I ever saw one."

"Well, she's my sister, Roger and that's the way I treat her." Roger looked puzzled, but all he said was, "Listen, the train is going to stop again in a while, so why don't you two come on up and ride first class? I'm in the second engine." Just then the train started up again and he nodded quickly at us and disappeared.

Richard turned to me, "I'm so grateful to God that he pulled me out of the world."

"Right on, brother. I feel the same way. I don't understand why I've been chosen, but I praise God constantly for allowing me to see the light," I answered.

We rode in silence for a time, rocking with the rhythm of the bumpy old boxcar, absorbing the wilderness that sight allowed. The train slid to another squealing halt. Richard's eyes were sparkling with the mischief of a child. He grabbed his tote sack and bedroll and hopped off. "Come on, we don't have much time," he said, holding out his hand to help me.

"Ouch! These rocks are sharp," I blurted out. I wasn't supposed to say this, but it just came out. Richard pretended he didn't hear and started high-tailing it over the sharp, jagged rocks as if he had shoes on his feet. I gazed ahead to our destination and realized that we were about three quarters of the way back towards the caboose and the second engine was way up there. I started following him, but my steps were slow and clumsy as I tried to protect my feet. Richard turned to see me lagging far behind and yelled, "Get out of your feet, sister."

How could I get out of my feet? I thought about the movie "Kung Fu" and how the hero, Cain, had walked over hot coals. I thought about Jesus and the pain He had endured. I wanted to follow Him more than anything, more than protecting my feet. This was just my physical body, anyway; the illusion. I held my head straight and focused on Richard's robe, sparkling in the sunlight. I didn't look down at the sharp rock ballast, or my feet. Directing my will straight ahead, I could almost feel an invisible cord pulling me. I walked swiftly. My feet no longer existed.

Ahead of me, I could see Richard climbing up the ladder to the engine. The train started and I still had three more boxcars to pass. Was I going to have to hop a moving train? We weren't supposed to feel fear, but I was. I could feel my body running flat out over the sharp, jagged ballast. It was as if I was watching a movie that I was also in. The brake released and the train lurched forward just as my foot stepped onto the rung of the ladder.

In Bend, Oregon, we got off the train and walked through the streets of the quaint town. Richard had grown unusually quiet, so I asked him if he was O.K. He seemed to be in deep thought. We were standing right in front of a movie theatre. He looked at me rather oddly, I thought, as he said, "Let's go in and see a movie." The ticket girl looked surprised at our clothes, just as everyone else did, but Richard just looked her straight in the eye and said, "We are traveling Christians, sister. We have forsaken all our earthly possessions to preach to the world, the word of God. But, even we like to have fun every now and then, so would you give freely of a movie in the name of Christ?" She just stared at him in awe and nodded for us to go through! Then the ticket boy saw us, he looked at her for directions and she said to go get us a bag of popcorn and let us see whatever we wished! Walt Disney's "The Jungle Book" was our choice and it had us singing their song "The Bare Necessities" for days.

It was such a high feeling to have people give to us. They felt great, we felt great, together we were defying the notion that 'money rules.' We went into pizza places and other restaurants and asked for a salad, or pizza without cheese. Nine times out of ten, it was given. It allowed us a chance to clue people into vegetarianism and gave them an opportunity to give. Jesus told us to ask for anything righteous in His name and we did. Bakeries gave us bread, donut shops and coffee shops fed us, people gave us money to buy food and hotels gave us rooms. This confirmed my belief that it was all real; Jesus really was back on earth and we were His followers. God was taking care of us through his earthly children and at the same time teaching them lessons on giving freely. He had it all covered. His divine plan was so grand. I felt like a child again, totally trusting my Father to take care of me and direct me along the right path. It was very freeing. We called it 'being in the Father's will.'

That evening as we snuggled in our bedrolls on some freshly cut grass in a churchyard, Richard said, "This was my hometown. This is where my wife and children still live."

"Do you want to go see them, brother?" I asked.

"No, not this time. I've been back here before to try and tell them why I'm doing what I'm doing and to ask them to come along, too, but Debbie always freaks out and doesn't understand. She still has lots of worldly lessons to burn out on first."

I put myself in his place. "I couldn't pass through Thunder Bay without seeing Ariss and Sol and my family," I confessed.

"I know," he said. "That's why we aren't in Thunder Bay." He smiled at me, but I sensed turmoil under that warm smile. I rolled us both a Bugler, lit them and handed him one. No words were spoken, but I knew we were both thinking about our children.

The closeness and unspoken understanding between Richard and I was constantly growing. It was such a joy to serve and share my life with him. Richard was usually the first one up in the morning. He would sit watching the sunrise patiently, waiting for me to 'blink in.' When I awoke he would hand me a lit Bugler. The last thing I felt like was a smoke first thing in the morning, but I took it anyway, trying to burn out on the 'old self.' Then, we would brush each other's hair. I usually braided his in a French braid. The sunlight made his hair look like sparkling gold. Sometimes we rubbed each other's neck and back. This was now permitted, as long as the 'sex space' was nowhere in sight.

The very idea of sex seemed almost ridiculous to me at this point. I felt so far away from the carnal flesh trip of sex. It didn't haunt my mind at all; no desire whatsoever. My love for Richard went way beyond that type of expression. He was like Jesus to me. I trusted and obeyed him totally.

Even so, having to relentlessly observe my every thought was often a shattering experience. It pulverized my false ego, humbling me in a way I had never experienced before. I felt ashamed of the many unrighteous thoughts that passed through my mind. I thought about the children far too much. If anyone needed repentance, I did.

I felt guilty for having taken so long to finally decide to join the 'Family.' I had been one of the most stubborn ones at "Christ Corner" that winter. If it hadn't been for Don's patience, I surely would not have seen the light. Now, more than ever I was becoming aware of cutting down my reasoning mind by using my 'sword of truth,' my 'helmet of salvation' and my 'shield of faith.' These were my spiritual armor and they were all very real to me then. In fact, many thoughts were cut down before they ever fully formed. Each one was a victory over Satan.

One day, in the late afternoon, we went again to a railway yard and climbed into one of the box cars. We had a few provisions with us, a full water jug, taco chips, bread, peanut butter, a can of peas and a squirt bottle of mustard. We sat in the box car and dined. It was a grand meal. I thought about the lady in the store who gave me the chips. She was frightened when I first walked in and called me a wolf in sheep's clothing. After preaching to her a bit she warmed up to me. "Be aware of false Christs. Many shall come in his name and claim to be him," she yelled to me as I walked out the door. Yes, I thought, but I know I'm following the real Christ.

"Kings and Queens," Richard said. "We have such fine food to eat."

After what seemed like hours, the train hitched up to our car and we pulled away into the night. We unrolled our bedrolls and crawled into them, heads facing the car opening and gazing at the infinite stars in the dark sky. The clicking hammer of steel on steel lulled us to sleep. "Now this is first class," was the last thing I remembered Richard saying.

We were awakened abruptly by our box car banging into something. Richard got up and went out for a minute. "They've dumped us," he said when he returned. "We're in the middle of nowhere."

We rolled up our bedrolls, threw them over our shoulders and jumped out. A railway guard told us there was a town about twelve miles away and pointed us in that direction. In the dark, with tired cold bodies, we walked in silence. It poured rain, but we just kept walking.

Very few cars passed and no one stopped. My wool army blanket poncho became heavier. The tips of the corners were now dipping into the puddles that were past my ankles. The rain was cold. My body shivered uncontrollably. Flashes of my journey in the Andes Mountains began to flicker across my 'memory-screen.' This feels hauntingly familiar, I thought. I wished I could be in a warm bed with a nice hot cup of herbal tea beside me.

Whenever I would experience hardships, or 'stretches' like this, my mind would conjure up an 'I wish' situation. Then guilt would come. I felt guilty for being selfish and thinking about comforting 'the flesh.' I was feeling shame for giving in to my own weakness. Jesus died on the cross for me and endured more pain than I can possibly imagine. I scolded myself and prayed to Him to give me strength.

All night we trudged through puddles in the stinging cold rain. I no longer felt sorry for myself. I felt blessed, for God had chosen me to be one of his messengers.

I remembered a verse in the Bible: *"... A certain man said unto him, Lord I will follow you wherever you go! And Jesus said unto him ... 'Foxes have holes, birds of the air have nests, but the son of man has nowhere to lay his head ....'" (Matthew 8:19-20).*

We arrived in a small town just as the sky gave a hint of light and the rain subsided. Finding an open cafe was warming to our feet and hearts, for the women who worked there gave freely of two cups of coffee.

After warming up a bit we ventured to a nearby grocery store and did our routine of looking in the 'hopper,' or 'salad bowl' (garbage dumpster) for thrown out goodies. I was craving an avocado sandwich and lo and behold, we found a gold mine of avocados. I filled my tote sack with the 'primo' (good) ones. We were given a loaf of bread at a nearby bakery.

People got such a good feeling from giving that most of them said thank you to me. Since "thank you" was a phrase we didn't use, I would answer with, "Praise God for your love."

At first, I felt uncomfortable going into a store and asking the person working there if they would give freely of a loaf of bread, or a cup of coffee in the name of Christ. It seemed like begging to me and my pride didn't want me to do it. When I first traveled with Richard, he must have sensed how I felt because he was constantly telling me to go here and there to ask for things. Now, however, I could see that I was actually helping these people by giving them a chance to give because in giving they would be blessed.

We were in Northern California now, where we were invited into a few homes in a small town by people who were receptive to the word of God. With summer on the wane though, the south was looking better with each passing day. So after a few more days, we hit the wind again aiming our sails southward.

Many times, as we walked along the road, people would yell at us from cars, "You brainwashed idiots!" Richard would just smile and yell back, "Yeah man, our brains have been washed clean, Praise God."

I followed Richard down the highway. We were in between two towns now and had been walking quite fast for hours. He never said a word to me this whole time.

Then Richard surprised me by heading off the highway just at some evidence of civilization. He turned to his right, down a dirt road filled with sand spurs that stuck to our feet. The road gave way to a plum orchard. I followed my brother in silence, wondering why he was going to this place. Were we going to pick some plums? We walked through the centre of the orchard and then Richard stopped. He turned around, looked me in the eye and ordered, "Take your robe off sister."

I stood there stunned. Why is he asking me to do this? I thought. Is he testing my obedience?

Sensing my confusion and hesitation, he added, "Do as I say, take it off!"

I was shaking, now. Obediently, I untied my sash and pulled my robe over my head.

"Your boxers, too," he commanded.

I stood there, completely naked. He looked at my body for a moment and then pulled off his own robe and boxers.

"Spread your army blanket out and lie on it," he ordered.

What is happening I wondered in panic? Is he testing to see how far I'll go? 'Believe your brother' is a rule, but no one ever said what to do when your brother tells you to go against one of the keys! 'No sex' is part of the very foundation of our beliefs. I had never ever even thought of going against it. But, now, not knowing what else to do, I meekly lay down on the blanket as he had commanded me.

He lay on top of me, entering me, defiling us both. I wept uncontrollably. This is worse than rape, I thought. I am committing incest. This man is my brother. He is my idol. He is screwing me and I am letting him! Was I supposed to have obeyed, or was I supposed to yell "no sex!" at him and run away? I had given my trust and obedience totally to this man. Now I couldn't understand what was happening. I was so confused. I didn't enjoy it one bit! I had no feelings of arousal at all. Instead, all I felt was torment and shame. After this animalistic act, Richard got up and put his robe back on in silence. His face gave evidence of guilt and his own inner turmoil, yet he didn't share his thoughts with me. I felt terribly alone and confused.

I put my robe back on and followed him out of the orchard. No words were spoken. I wished there was somewhere I could wash. I felt like I imagined Eve did in the Garden of Eden, after her first experience of sex with Adam. This was the original sin. I had just fallen from heaven and I now felt the heat of hell.

Reaching the city, we connected with some people and Richard began preaching to them. I couldn't believe that he could actually preach 'no sex.' I couldn't begin to 'juice him' on the 'inside.' I was drowning in guilt and confusion.

That night, before we 'blinked out,' he said, "I was lusting for you in my mind. Jesus said that thinking about it is just as bad as the act. I felt if I physically did it, I would burn out on it and stop thinking about it. Still, you should have not allowed me to. Don't you know the difference between when your brother is speaking to you and when Satan overpowers him?"

From then on, I was never quite sure what I was supposed to believe and what I was to obey. The possibility of Satan overpowering Richard seemed absurd to me. I thought he was with God, one hundred percent. What did he mean by that? Were there times when I should be on my guard? Yet, what did I have to judge by? If I didn't 'believe my brother,' I would be going against the foundation of our beliefs. Which was I to obey, my much more experienced brother, or my own judgment?

There were always reasons for things that could surprise the reasoning mind, things that seemed to be 'set up' especially to blow your mind. Was this one of them? Were we supposed to learn a lesson in forgiveness, on being able to let go and truly forgive ourselves, burying the past? Or, was God telling us just how human we still are? Was what had happened a way of helping us to relate to our fellow 'earthlings' better? Was I unconsciously the temptress, the one to blame for taking my brother's eyes off God?

As days went by, I could not live with the confusion any longer and tried very hard to force the doubts from my mind. It was 'yesterday's newspaper,' anyway. Living in the moment was the only reality and each new day brought plenty of adventures.

After a few days in the city, we connected with a preacher who offered us a meal and a place to rest in the basement of his church. We really appreciated the shelter, for the winds and rain were wild. There was a piano in the basement and I asked Richard if it would be all right if I played it, already knowing that we really weren't supposed to. Much to my surprise, he said, "Sure," and I sat there and played for hours. Richard enjoyed it and smiling, he said, "Give it up and you get it back." We weren't supposed to play music, or do artwork because of the false ego that is often involved and the sense of accomplishment that goes along with it as well. Too many people forget to give all praise and glory to God and puff themselves up instead. When I played, it was a prayer in itself, so I felt justified. It may also have been a healing experience for both of us, to be able to release some of the guilt through the music.

In the morning, Richard and I were told that a Bible class was being held so we had to leave. We sat on a cement slab under the porch overhang and watched the lightning storm. The energy was electrifying. As we sat there, I kept getting the thought of Bakersfield. I had been there once a few years ago, with Kim, my cousin, but I didn't remember anything special about the city except that as its name suggests it was really hot. I ignored this thought at first, but for some reason it wouldn't let up. Finally, I caught on that 'the spirit' must be giving me the message to go to Bakersfield.

"Brother, I have been getting a 'beeper' to go to Bakersfield. Are we very far from there?" I asked, almost timidly, not quite sure if it was a sister's place to direct where we went.

Richard looked at me without answering for a while and then said, "You sure are beautiful. Here I was, asking the Father where He wants us to go from here and waiting for an answer, but none came to me. Instead, He uses you and teaches me a lesson through it. Bakersfield is about a day's drive from here. As soon as the storm clears, we'll make our way toward the highway heading south, unless the Father has other plans for us."

He did, too. Only a few minutes after Richard spoke this, a police car stopped in front of the church and two officers ran towards us in raincoats. One of them said, "We have been getting complaints about you two from the neighbors. What are you doing here?"

"We are disciples of Jesus Christ, brother, and we are here for you," Richard answered. "It's time to lay down your weapons and live in peace. It's time to stop killing and eating animals."

The policeman interrupted him and said, "It's time to come for a ride with me." Then they escorted us to the car.

I wondered where they were going to take us. Were we being arrested? I looked at Richard and he winked at me. His composure wasn't ruffled in the least. "Just 'watch the movie.' We are in the Father's will," he said.

"We'll let you off just beyond the city's limits; any particular direction you're heading?" The officer driving asked us.

"We are going south, brother," Richard replied. Richard didn't preach to them while we rode and they didn't ask any questions. The rain had lightened up quite a bit when they let us off on the highway.

"No hitch-hiking, or walking on the freeway, now," one of them said with a grin and they left.

"Well, Papa really wants us to go to Bakersfield, doesn't he?" Richard said, just as a transport truck stopped to pick us up. He gave me a boost up the steep step to the cab, where the trucker welcomed us with a smile.

"So, where are you people heading and where are you from?" He asked, in a southern drawl. "We are heading for Bakersfield right now, brother, but usually just blowing 'in the wind'," I said.

"Bakersfield? Well, this is your lucky day. I'm passing right through there and it's my next stop to refuel. Make yourself at home, rest in the bed there if you want. We've got a long ride ahead."

He was a jolly character, I thought. "Right on, brother, praise God for your love," I replied.

I crawled up into the sleeping berth and lay on my stomach with my elbows holding my head up. Richard sat in the passenger's seat. It was great. Not only was I comfortable, but the view while riding so high off the road was amazing. Richard and Ben, the trucker, talked, but I could barely hear their voices over the rumble of the engine and I enjoyed this for a change. I was feeling blown away by the events that had just transpired. We had been sitting at the church watching a thunderstorm. First, I tell Richard that I feel a pull to Bakersfield, then second, the Lord sends the police officers as our free taxi service to the freeway. And, we wait barely five minutes before this trucker picks us up and is taking us straight through to Bakersfield! What a miracle. I felt so excited, like a child going to the fair for the first time. Everything was a marvel to me. I thought about how true this is in life, but how blind most of us are to it. People fill their lives with routines and they can only see the misery they have created for themselves. It's as if they have tunnel vision. All the child-like wonder has gone from their sight. I was rediscovering the kid in me and I loved it.

A dark, still Bakersfield welcomed us. Ben let us off next to a park where we rolled out under the stars. I was still 'buzzed' and restless. Richard and I shared a joint which helped to relax me and we 'blasted off into space.' That night, I had a dream about Lightning Amen. I remembered it and told Richard about it in the morning. He said he'd had a similar dream, too. Had we shared the same dream? I asked him what Lightning was like.

"He is just like you or me to look at with physical eyes, sister, but, he is the Lord," Richard assured me. We both caught a glimpse of a white-robed being walking at the other end of the park. I could feel my heart quicken as we walked over to see him. The brother saw us coming towards him and came to greet us. His long, black and wavy hair were evidence of years spent in the group. His eyes shone with love and light. Was he Lightning Amen?

"Brother Thomas, good to see you again," Richard addressed him. He smiled at us and said, "We are camping a few miles from here in a campground by the river. There are three buses and a few other vehicles. Lightning and Cher and the sisters are there, too. I've come in for some supplies with Sister Joe. We'll pick you up here when we are done and bring you to the camp."

"Right on, brother," Richard said.

I was numb. This was blowing my mind. God has brought me to Lightning Amen, I thought. He really is Jesus and I'm going to meet him! I was also going to meet the prophets and the saints that I had heard of and read about. We believed that the Christ Family members were the reincarnation of the holy men of the past. Don had told me that he had met Moses, Abraham, Isaac, Martha and many other biblical characters.

I was finally going to see them all with my physical eyes. God has a sense of humor, I thought. Who does he send to pick us up, but St. Thomas, who had to see Jesus and touch his wounds to believe that He had risen from the dead? In the past, I had felt an affinity with Thomas because of my own doubt and need to see Lightning with my physical eyes. Lately, I had been learning so many lessons that now I no longer felt the need to see Lightning in his physical form. Once again, the theory, 'give it up and you get it back' has been proven true. This was Jesus whom I was about to meet! He knew my every thought. Was I worthy of even being in His presence? God must have thought so, or He wouldn't have set this meeting up for us. But, he knew Richard and I disobeyed the 'second key' in the orchard. How could I face him? He knew everything.

Thomas and Richard rode in the cab of the truck while Sister Joe and I rode in the open back. I was so nervous and excited that I wanted to scream. I took it all 'on the inside' and prayed for the wisdom and grace that were needed to be a true Christ Sister and to be in the presence of the Lord. Each moment was truly a new life. He had forgiven us because Jesus doesn't dwell in the realm of guilt and the past. He was truly living in the moment, for the moment. It was up to me to forgive myself and Richard. I did right by obeying my brother yet wrong by going against one of the keys. If I disobeyed my brother and refused I still would have done wrong . . . I prayed for God to wash my hands clean of the whole situation and pushed the issue out of my mind. Besides I was about to meet Jesus!

❧ CHAPTER THIRTEEN ❧

Sunlight, reflected on white robes, gave the whole camp an unearthly brilliance. Everywhere I looked I saw angels. Here were all the prophets, saints and apostles of old. I would be meeting Abraham, Noah, Martha, Mary, Matthew, Luke, John . . . I could see that not all the brothers and sisters were here. But, quite a few were, enough to blow my mind into oblivion.

I got out of the truck and just stared. Everyone was so beautiful! Their eyes shone with light. They walked slowly and gracefully, as if in tune to a spiritual song. The air was filled with a peaceful, serene calm. Everyone was flowing. It was like watching a beautiful ballet. There was very little talking and when there was, it was in a quiet voice. I had never seen anything like it. It was almost as if it was orchestrated; everyone had assigned duties, yet there was also a definite sense of freedom. In my experience, whenever there had been a large gathering 'in the world' there had always been so much noise and confusion. This was incredible. Everyone was of one mind, of one accord. Just being there immediately heightened my consciousness and gave me a light-headed, high feeling. I had finally made it to the true Valley of the Blue Moon. This was how I had dreamed the feeling in the valley would be.

Richard spoke to a brother as I roamed about, absorbing it all. The campsite was surrounded by mountains covered in brown earth. I imagined that in the spring they might have been green, but as this was now autumn, they had been exposed to the scorching California sun all summer. We were east of Bakersfield by about twelve miles. The sounds of the city were far away. The Kern River ran through the campsite to one side of it and down a slope. Cottonwood trees lined the riverbank and were basically the only trees around. Up from the river were three school buses, two trucks and a white car. I was surprised to see so many vehicles. One school bus, called "The Royal Coach," was where Lightning, Cher and a few of the older sisters rested. The second was the "Kitchen Bus" which carried the food supplies. It had two stoves and ovens built in and lots of cupboard space. The third was called the "Trooper Bus." It was fixed up with lots of storage space under the raised floor.

On the 'trooper bus,' I met Sister Theresa. She had been a friend of Don's and was with him in Hawaii when he met the brother and sister who had brought him 'the truth.' Theresa had 'transformed' with him there. She told me that she had been traveling in Canada with Will, Ed, James, Don and Judy. It was good to hear about them all. I secretly felt a special love for my brothers and sisters from Canada. We had all been so close when we were getting into the Christ Family. Theresa also told me that Cheryl, my old friend from Thunder Bay had been in the camp and had just left a few days ago. After trying to 'let go of the world' three times, she had finally left with Theresa. I was elated to hear that Cheryl was now 'in the wind.' I must admit I felt disappointed that I had just missed her, but I knew that if the Father willed it, we would meet again.

Outside the 'kitchen bus,' two brothers and a sister were making fresh grape juice from grapes. I watched them turn the handle of a homemade press they had fashioned from an old barrel. The pulp squeezed through a screen-like sifter, producing pure grape juice. In the 'Family,' alcohol was forbidden. We called it 'the devil's brew,' or 'rotten grain.'

"New wine, pure and unadulterated," one of the brothers said to me as I watched the process. "Howdy, sister! I'm Gabriel, but you can call me Gabe," he said, wiggling his eyebrows comically. I liked Gabe right away. He reminded me of Raphael, who'd had a similar sense of humor. I found out that Gabe was also an archangel, although he didn't act as though he was above me. His tall, wiry form moved with grace. His dark eyes flashed with light. Bushy eyebrows arched above them like halos. Long, thick curly black hair cascaded down to his back. His smile was wide and uninhibited, very warm and loving.

"I'm Sister Miriam," the sister standing beside him told me, smiling.

"I'm Edmond," the other brother said.

"Sister Maureen here, at your service," I saluted them and helped make the juice.

"You two look alike," Gabriel said to Miriam and me. "Were you two relatives in the world?"

We both shook our heads "no." I could see what he meant. It was like looking into a mirror, peering into Miriam's dark eyes. We both reached about the same height, we both had long dark hair and high cheek bones. Our olive skins were tanned very dark. I knew that the resemblance went deeper than flesh, though. I felt a definite affinity with Sister Miriam.

We talked for quite some time. She had also become a fruitarian before she joined the 'Family' and she had also ventured up into the Peruvian Andes after reading "The Secret of the Andes!" It was extraordinary how we had traveled the same roads. She never found the valley either and shortly after was drawn into the Christ Family.

"The brother I was traveling with disappeared up in those mountains," she told me. "We were in one of the native huts because the mist was too thick to travel that day. He wanted to go on, to find the trail to the next village. I didn't, so I sat in that hut for days waiting for him to return. He never did, he probably fell off a cliff. I felt that he had 'dusted' (died). A space later, I saw a 'hobbit' of a friend of mine. "I knew that the 'hobbit' was him reincarnated," she said. Miriam's dark eyes gave a hint of such inner beauty.

Looking around me at all the beautiful, white-robed people, I noticed how we all walked, talked and even moved the same. Squatting had never been a favorite position of mine; I found my legs got too sore. As time went on, however, I found comfort in 'the squat' as did all the other brothers and sisters. It was a popular position in which to make a fire, to wash dishes in streams, or to just 'rap'.

The dinner bell rang and everyone gathered in a large circle on the ground for 'communion' (a meal shared). The food was passed in silence; wooden bowls full of rice and beans. No one started to eat until the last received his bowl. I gazed around the circle at all the brothers, my eyes searching for Lightning. He could be any one of them. They all looked the way I pictured Jesus. Spoonfuls of food were being passed from one to another. This feels like heaven, I thought.

Then a small, dark-haired woman seemed to come from nowhere and squatted beside Richard. "The Lord wishes to see you when you are done your meal," she softly said to him.

I looked into her face and saw such a beautiful being. Her brown eyes shone with intense love. She got up gracefully and started walking back to the bus, then turned and said, "You too, sister," smiling warmly at me. Jesus wanted to see me, too! I couldn't finish my food. Richard looked at me and we both got up and walked to the bus. I was about to meet Jesus Christ Lightning Amen.

His eyes hit me like a lightning bolt! It seemed as if he was looking at me from the inside out and I felt full of reverence, awe and bewilderment. Then he cracked a smile and with eyes now twinkling said, "Let's get drunk." and passed Richard a jug of grape juice. This blew my mind. Here I was, all serious and nervous about meeting my Lord and he blows it all away with his sense of humor. I felt so blessed to be in his presence. Since childhood, I had wished I could meet Jesus. Now here I was, sitting beside him and Mother Mary.

Studying his face, I observed his high cheek bones set in deeply tanned, weathered skin. His hair hung below his shoulders in straight, fine, blonde wisps. His long beard was speckled with grey. He was tall and thin and resembled Brother Richard quite a bit. They could easily pass for earth brothers. The most dynamic thing about him was his eyes, which were light blue and so powerfully magnetic. I felt totally naked in front of him. He knew me better than I knew myself. This was 'the spirit' that lived inside of me, whom I loved and followed. This was my Lord.

He got out a photo album and said, "Do you want to look at the 'Family' album?" It contained newspaper clippings, articles and pictures of different Christ Family members. I don't know exactly what I was expecting, but I wasn't expecting to look through an album with Jesus. He acted so human, so common. I guess I thought he would be preaching words of wisdom, or something, but my image of Jesus high on a pedestal was being blown to pieces and that's probably what He intended, since he knew my mind and heart. I hardly remember what we talked about because I was in such an ecstatic state.

Richard and I floated off the bus in search of a level piece of land to roll out on. We found a wonderful spot close to the river. The sound of water flowing and the crickets were like music to me. That night was profound. The moon was full and cast down a golden light. The illumination of the stars poured down from the infinite sky. I felt so 'juiced.' I just met Jesus, I marveled to myself. I am one of his followers. This is real, right?

One thing did bother me a bit, though. "Why didn't Lightning eat in the circle with the rest of us?" I asked Richard, as we watched the sky and smoked a Bugler. "Cher told me that his body has had a virus for a while so it's feeling a bit under the weather," he replied.

"But, why would the greatest healer of all time get sick?"

"He is in a physical body just like you and me, sister; he has not come to heal the flesh this time; he has come to heal 'the spirit.' That's what counts," Richard told me.

I still didn't totally understand, but that was good enough for now. I didn't want my mind to get full of doubts, I was enjoying being so high. I thought about the Tiger Balm in my tote sack and decided that I would give it to Lightning in the morning to rub on his chest and temples. I wanted to help him be well again. That sleepless night, I watched the stars disappear into a pink sky as dawn brought the promise of another day.

In the morning, I buzzed around camp helping out where I could. Two of the people I met were Sarah and Abraham. Abraham looked like Abraham, if you know what I mean. An older man, he had a long, grey beard and grey hair. Sarah was blonde and blue-eyed. Everyone seemed so beautiful!

The Archangel Michael, who was the second in command, reminded me of Will, in appearance and in the way he moved and talked. Sister Rachael was his 'spiritual mate' and traveling companion. Martha, Elizabeth and Naomi rested on the 'royal coach' with Lightning and Cher. They were very close to him. I was beginning to understand the pecking order of the group, but didn't really see why it had to be. The longer you were in the group, the more respect you got for being an older brother, or sister. It seemed that because I was Richard's 'spiritual mate,' I was ranked, with almost as much maturity as he. Even though I was a mere babe in the 'Family,' he had apparently picked me as his mate because I was able to 'cop the space.'

That day, I heard two older brothers talking about the end of the world being very close at hand. One of them even mentioned a date. Overhearing this made me feel excited and so blessed that I was appointed to be one of God's chosen ones. 'The end' would surely be tragedy for everyone except us. We already knew that the physical was an illusion, so to us the change was welcome. I did not fear the destruction of the world. I was looking forward to it.

I met a sister who everyone called Little Martha, to distinguish her from another sister, who was called Big Martha. Little Martha slept in a tent with her baby girl,

Robin. Robin was seven months old; the same age Sol was when last I saw him. Seeing the child and Martha breastfeeding her caused a barrage of emotions to surface in me. I noticed that the other brothers and sisters seemed to leave her alone. They were subtly disapproving of her keeping the child. I saw the struggle Martha was going through. I knew it so well. For the rest of the time we were in the camp, I helped her with her baby, watching Robin while Martha washed diapers, or went for walks. One day, I heard one of the sisters talking about Martha down by the river. "The attachment between mother and child is the deepest and hardest root to pull out. She's attached to the 'hobbit.' She has to give her up," she said. My heart ached for Martha and her baby.

After about three days in camp, Richard told me he wanted to 'hit the wind.' I rolled up my bedroll and followed him, a little disappointed to be leaving so soon. We walked into the 'royal coach' to tell the Lord we were leaving.

Seeing him again reconfirmed my beliefs that he was Jesus. His face was so like Jesus' face in the picture of a shrine that had been on display in a wax museum where Richard and I went, earlier that summer. Once again I felt totally exposed. I felt unworthy, but I wanted to be worthy. I wanted to be perfect.

Richard addressed him, saying, "Just wanted to let you know we are 'hitting the wind.'"

I wondered why he had to tell him. Didn't he already know? I thought He knew everything including all our thoughts. Then the guilt set in for having questioned. Why did my 'finite mind' doubt the Lord again?

Lightning Amen looked at us, eyes sparkling and said, "Sounds like a good plan, mind if I come along?" This guy was incredible. He was always so humorous, he was going to 'hit the wind' with us. Jesus wanted to travel with us. I felt so blessed, so blown away.

Word spread through camp like a brush fire and within twenty minutes the whole caravan was trucking down the road. Lightning gave Richard and I a truck to drive, an old 52 Chevy, royal blue and black. It was like being in a parade. All the buses were painted the same army camouflage brown, with a hand-painted Star of David and a lightning bolt on them. This was the 'Family' logo. The Star of David represented us, as the spiritual Jews, God's chosen people. The lightning bolt represented Lightning and also the way people would succumb to 'the truth' as if they had been hit by a spiritual lightning bolt.

Leading the parade were Amen and Cher, driving a white Cadillac. Big Martha and the other older sisters were second, in the 'royal coach.' The 'kitchen bus,' driven by Archangel Gabriel, was third, followed by the 'trooper bus' with Joy and Clyde in charge. Abraham and Sarah were in a van, Archangel Michael and Rachael in a truck and Richard and I in the caboose. The old truck we rode in couldn't go over 45 mph, but we didn't mind, we weren't in any hurry. All the 'Family' drove slowly. We called it Sunday driving because every day was the Lord's. Richard and I were so high. We sang songs. Our spirits were light.

Richard told me that we were heading to a spot on the Colorado River on the Arizona side, about 20 miles from Blythe, California. It was a place where the Christ

Family had set up winter camp for a few years; just somewhere that brothers and sisters could wash the road dust off their feet and refuel with spiritual food.

Our first rest stop along the way was by a river. I can't remember where, but I do remember that Amen had all of us captivated by his parables that evening around the camp fire. He was a great speaker. His words flowed out with ease, totally inspired.

"Everything that's happened in the past, all the way back to the Garden, is being played out again right now. Toward the end of a symphony the conductor gradually brings the music to a high point, called the crescendo. So that's the way it is. It's like in the days of Noah. It's like Sodom and Gomorrah. All of the events down through time are building right now, as God brings the world's song to an end."

I listened to my Lord speak, my mind void of thought yet nourished by his every word. His preaching enfolded us like an unseen cloak. "You see," he continued, "God gets you to heaven, He shows you the way to inner space. No matter how much you rack your brain, you're gonna find out that anything else is not where it's at. God is in your heart, brothers; not in your head. It takes the Spirit of God to alter and change you to the space where you can see, understand and know what 'the spirit' is saying. Without it, you cannot see. You're cut off, like night and day. It's a totally different life." Like a peaceful river, Amen's words swept away the mental debris of his listeners.

The next day, we drove along the desert highway outside Los Angeles. At a rest stop the troop gathered, while the 'kitchen bus,' the 'royal coach' and Abraham's van went to one of the towns to score some avocados. We were supposed to meet them at this campsite, but hours passed and there was no sign of them. Finally, Amen said to the small group of about 12 of us who were left, "Where are my children? Did they get lost?"

I found it strange for 'The Lord' to say that. Doesn't he know exactly where they are? I thought. But, his preaching soon wiped away my doubt. We all sat mesmerized, as Amen told us a story about one of the first brothers to follow him, his raspy voice piercing the silence.

"So this brother asked me, 'What are we going to do tomorrow for coffee and food?' I'd say to him, Today was sufficient for today, tomorrow will take care of itself. In the morning, the first thing the brother said to me was 'O.K, now, where's the coffee'?"

Amen threw his head back and laughed. We all laughed with him. He continued his story. "This brother must have been thinking about it all night long, you know, so I said to him, you haven't even got the fire started yet. So I'd go and grab some sticks and when we had the fire going he said to me, 'O.K., now where's the coffee?' and I said, put the water in the pan, man. So he went and got some water from the river and set the pan on the fire. Then I heard a motor boat go by; the camp opened right up to the waterfront. It was a beautiful little spot, there was a lake right off the river. So I walked down to the bank and this boat turned and came right up. The man stood right up, reached over to the bow of the boat, picked up a can of coffee and said, 'Here, I thought I'd bring this, you might need a cup or two,' and he winked at me. I took the coffee, he backed away, I held the coffee up to the brother by the fire and his knees got weak and he fell over. He said, 'The water's boiling,' and I said, the coffee's here."

"Things like this would happen all day long. He was blown away. So he said to me one day, 'I want to live like this!' and I said, O.K., but you can't occupy yourself. If you're going to move into the embryo stage you can't be occupied, an embryo just sits and grows. So I took away everything around him that he'd be distracted by. Boom, boom that's gotta go. Get rid of this. So when he peeled off all those doubts of the mind; attachments, the past, I was expounding, feeding him with the word of God and we would just live. You see, 'the spirit' works in such a wonderful way that everything is always right on time. It's perfect. He was ready to receive the word and experience the life of Christ."

Everyone sat listening attentively to Amen. His animated antics kept us all enthralled.

"So, one morning I said to him, O.K., and he'd say, 'O.K. what?' and I'd say, O.K. you're leaving. He'd be nervous, jumping around the camp and I'd say, jump in the water, roll up your bag, man, you're leaving. So he rolled up his bag, reached for a little thing of oatmeal and I'd say, put it back! Now we never had a food box no more than a foot square. We lived day to day. So he'd be standing there all nervous and I'd say, O.K. I'm going with you for a space."

"When we left there, all we had were a pair of shorts, a robe, an outer robe, a bedroll and that's it; stripped. So we'd 'hit the wind.' Now the main object was the faith that I would give him. He'd say, 'Man, we can't go to Florida like this, how are we gonna eat, how are we gonna this, how are we going to that?' So I'd say, just watch. We'd walk out on the road and I'd say, we're going in this direction and he'd put his thumb out. I'd say, kickback and sit on your bedroll, brother. And the cars would go by and he'd say, 'What about this car?' I'd say, our ride will stop and pick us up, he can't go by and he'd say, 'Aw, come on,' and I'd say, remember how the coffee and oatmeal came in, man? Just watch! See, he didn't have enough faith yet. So just then a car would pull over and we'd get in. The man who stopped had a good heart; he was the one we were supposed to talk to. I'd preach to him and after a few hours, he stopped and bought us lunch. The brother turned to me and said, 'I can't travel around like this, having other people feed me.' I'd say, let me tell you something, man, when God has you taking time out in your life to learn what He wants you to tell people and you go ahead and preach the word of God, you're not being a bum. You deserve everything you're getting and don't you bat an eye at it! The guy driving turned around and said, 'Yeah, I work eight hours a day at my job and I'm more than willing to do this if this brother can take the time out to bring me a message from God!' Same thing as in the scriptures, people would give the disciples things and they would trade them for food and such. A workman is worthy of his meat."

This story was one of many that Amen told to entertain us. It was special to be with him in such a small group. It reminded me of Jesus and the twelve disciples and here I was one of them!

On our way to Arizona, we picked up two Christ Brothers who were trucking down the road. One of them was James the brother who had traveled back to Canada with Laura, Judy, Ariss and Sol. He had been holding Sol the last time I saw him. My heart quickened at the sight of him now. I was anxious to hear where the 'hobbits' were; if they had made it to Canada and all the details. Another battle was raging inside me. Was it righteous to ask him? We weren't supposed to talk about the past. We weren't supposed to worry about our children. I was still attached. I knew that, but I was following the rules as best as I knew how. I was giving it my all! So I waited patiently for a sign that it would be O.K. to ask him about my children. I had been waiting for months and I could wait some more if that was the will of the Father.

Finally, when we gathered at a rest stop for a meal, Brother James came over to me and said, "The 'hobbits' are with your earth parents in Canada. Everything is O.K. God has it all covered."

I looked into this kind brother's deep brown eyes. "Right on, brother, Praise God," I said holding back hundreds of questions. I was learning. I was becoming Christ-like. I was denying the fleshly mind and desires. Emotion was not of God, it was a trap. I was learning how not to feed it, to take it all 'inside' and give it all to God. It was good to hear that Ariss and Sol were safe in loving hands, but I did miss them so . . .

Towards evening, we came some miles down a dirt road beside the Colorado River. This was the largest river I had ever seen. Dust rose like a huge cloud behind us as we made our way down the desert road. The buses and trucks stopped a few yards off the road, in a bowl-like depression that resembled a gravel pit.

"Well, here we are!" Richard informed me.

This is the desert camp? I thought. I had imagined something more permanent; a building, or something, but it was as wild as wild could be. It amazed me that the 'Family' had gathered here for years and left no trace behind.

Everyone busied themselves with setting up camp. A few tents went up in a circle. Richard and I loved sleeping under the stars, so we worked on leveling out a bed in the caked sand. I felt like one of the first human beings on the earth, making my bed of dirt so primal, so simple and so beautiful. The hot sun moved lower in the sky and everyone gathered around Amen who was sitting on a flat rock facing west. No one spoke a word as we watched, the desert sky flaming with orange and reddish gold, blazing as though on fire. Gradually, the color faded to bright rose pink, then darkened to maroon and pale pink until all that was left was a faint blush against the grey of the night.

Everyone was in a state of praise. The vibration was stupendous. That night was so warm that we rested on top of our bedrolls. The only sounds that broke the silence were the howls of nearby coyotes, echoing over the desert mesa.

Resting out under the stars gave me such a high feeling. Looking up at the heavens with thousands of worlds beyond our own, gave me a sense of humility. I was such a small atom in the workings of a whole, universal plan. This perspective is a constant reminder of the ego, I thought, for the ego would like to be the centre of the universe.

It often felt strange to have to explain to people outside the 'Family' that I was a saint and an angel. I didn't really feel that I deserved those titles. I could see the perfection in other brothers and sisters, but when it came to me, it seemed that I missed the mark somehow. Every day, I kept being hit with 'lightning bolts,' revealing realizations and deeper truths than I had ever seen before.

Revelations came in many forms, through media you would never guess. God was molding me, changing me and transforming me every moment of every day. "Praise God," was a term we repeated constantly. The lapses between my awareness of His presence came closer and closer together, until it seemed that I was almost always conscious of being in the presence of God. This left me with a deep feeling of reverence and awe. "Praise God," was the verbal expression of that exquisitely high feeling.

There was nothing left within me that wanted anything, but to do the will of the Father and follow Jesus. I daily brought Him my heart and will, offering my all to Him.

I had given up physical possessions, family attachments, every aspect of my 'old self' of which I was aware. I constantly emptied my cup before the Lord. I wanted to be one with Him, whatever the cost. I had to deny my own ways of thinking, feeling, talking and my desires, hopes, dreams and will. Emotion and rational thinking were traps laid by Satan. They were a part of his domain.

On our second day in camp, the brothers erected a teepee and we gathered in it for lunch. Rice and fruit salad were on the menu that day and I was grateful for the fruit, especially. After I finished, I wished that I could have more, but knew it wasn't cool to ask. Amen was sitting across from me. He looked me right in the eye and smiling, handed me his fruit. He'd read my mind! It was as if he had been right inside me, knowing what I was thinking. Of course he had, he was Jesus.

The desert was beautiful. I had never experienced such a strange land. Every day, the sun shone. Many different kinds of wild flowers bloomed here and there, pushing themselves up through the dry, caked earth and in between the rocks. This was a miracle to me, how flowers could survive the scorching sun with so little rain. Many were of the everlasting, or strawflower family and remained naturally preserved even after picking. I picked a bouquet for our headboard and one for Amen and Cher. Always intrigued with flowers, I had just started pressing and making pictures from them before we 'hit the wind' from "Christ Corner." So I saw these desert flowers as a gift and I praised God for them. Many times throughout our travels I would be surprised by flowers along the way and it was so nice not to be in a hurry to get anywhere and to literally "Stop and smell the roses."

In fact, I did more than smell them, I became them! Staring into a flower, or a tree, or a bug, I would feel the life within it at union with the life within me and actually felt as if the flower was 'in' me. This is hard to put into words, but it happened quite a bit and I loved it. I felt at peace and one with the life around me, as though the separation between human and animal, or plant was lifted for a few precious moments and a whole new dimension, a rift in my familiar way of looking at things, had opened up for me.

Usually we fill our minds with thoughts such as, "How am I going to get to work tomorrow, my car just broke down?" "What shall I wear to the party?" "I have so much to do today; shopping, basketball, a meeting and I have to try and squeeze in some time for my family and eat somewhere in between all of that." These worries and cares of the physical world occupy our thinking and leave our minds too full to see the other things around us. In silence, I found the presence of God. Silence is the opposite of the ceaseless internal dialogue that plagues our minds and keeps them distracted and unaware of the existence of a whole other world. In the Christ Family, I never had to worry about where I would go, or what I would eat. Everything was provided by the Father, with the result that I felt more and more like a child. In that state of mind, all of us 'freed up space' in our memory capacities and were able to use them to see and feel things that the average person missed.

On the third day, the 'kitchen bus' and the rest of the caravan showed up. Naturally drawn to the kitchen, I ended up helping with the serving of food and the cleanup. After a few days, I became the official bread baker and baked ten loaves of bread a day. I really enjoyed it. I had so much energy and I wanted to channel it through giving. My days in camp were busy and full; baking, cooking and washing dishes and robes in the river. I sensed that Richard didn't like me being so busy, though, and I felt torn between serving the others and serving him. This didn't feel right. I felt an attachment towards me on his part that seemed almost worldly.

One night, I dreamt about my brother Ed and told Richard that I had a strong feeling we would be seeing him again soon. The next evening while finishing the dinner dishes, I felt a strong 'pull' to look out the window. There, silhouetted against the dark purple sky, were two brothers walking into camp. I could barely make out their facial features as they approached, but I knew that one of them was Ed. A wave of excitement ran through me. It was so good to see him. I felt an urge to run up to him, hug and kiss him and tell him that I'd missed him, but I knew this would be worldly behavior. I had to love him the same as anyone else, with the equal love of God.

"Good to see you, brother," I said calmly as I greeted them.

"Aren't you glad to see me?" The brother with him joked.

"This is Brother Theodore, Sister Maureen," said Ed, introducing us.

Just then I realized that they were both wet. "What happened to you guys?"

"We took a short cut across the river," Theodore smiled, as he told me. "Quite enough excitement for one day, wouldn't you say so, brother?"

"Yepper," Ed answered him.

"We just finished the evening meal, I'll go and get you something to eat," I told them.

"Praise God," they both said.

I wanted to rest beside Ed that night, but I felt bound to my place beside Richard. I wasn't sure if I liked this 'spiritual mate' stuff. It seemed to equal being married, or going steady 'in the world,' and I really didn't want to feel bound to anyone. Then, on the other hand, I enjoyed traveling with Richard. We had learned and experienced a lot together. I was used to traveling with him and felt a sense of security in the familiar with him, as everything else in my life was so full of change. He was a beautiful brother and I was honored to be chosen to be his 'spiritual mate.'

The next day, the desert sun was scorching the dry earth once again as Ed and I took a long walk through the wilderness. Suddenly a road runner whipped by us at incredible speed and Ed and I both laughed at the images he reminded us of in the cartoons we had watched as children together. Yet, after this Ed was very quiet, even more than usual and I felt a strain between us for the first time ever. It seemed as if the closeness we had once had was gone. The problem was that we weren't able to express our love openly for fear of doing something that was not acceptable.

"Are you happy, Ed?" I asked him. He looked at me for a while, taking his time to answer, as he always did. He thinks long before he speaks and I have always admired that, although it would make me impatient at times. "How could I not be happy, Maureen, I've been chosen to be one of the Lord's followers," he said finally.

"Where have you traveled since last I saw you?" I asked him.

"Well, Will and I went up to Thunder Bay for a few days and I saw Ariss and Sol for a few minutes. They are doing O.K. Carmel wouldn't let Will and I stay there though. She was full of fear."

My heart pounded at the mention of their names. Sol must have had his first birthday, already, and Ariss would be three years old soon. I remembered how when she was a baby, I would imagine what she would be like when she was three and how I would be able to have conversations with her; how we would be friends. She was probably talking fairly well. I wondered about all the phases in growth and learning that I was missing. Sol would be walking by now. I never did see him take his first step. I wasn't there when he first opened his eyes in search of his mother. The hot tears welled up in my eyes. I knew this was unacceptable, so I shut out my emotions, cutting them down with my 'sword of truth,' keeping them out with my 'shield of faith.' I wanted to ask Ed how our parents and sister and grandmother were doing, but I knew if I was going to keep my emotions and attachments under control, I could not feed them.

Ed abruptly changed the subject. "Lightning gave me a new name, he said I was Samson," he told me.

"Far out, but you better watch out for Delilah," I said jokingly. Ed and Samson of old were the same spirit, I could see it. "So shall I call you Brother Samson instead of Ed?" I asked him.

"It doesn't make any difference to me, Mo, call me whatever you wish."

"I love you, Ed." I just had to tell him. I wanted to break down whatever wall had formed between us. Why was it not righteous to be close to someone? Ed just looked at me and nodded.

That night I dreamed about Thunder Bay. In my dream I had to go back and see Sol and Ariss and when I did, I couldn't leave them. I was happy to be with the children again, but once again, I was tormented by guilt because I had turned away from Jesus and had fallen back into the world. I knew 'the truth' and yet I turned my back on it because I wasn't strong enough to give what it takes to follow the path of righteousness. The result was that I felt miserable and trapped by my attachment. Then Brother Don came to me. He wasn't angry, or upset. He was emanating pure love and understanding. His presence was so powerful in the dream that the thought of it stayed with me all through the next day.

That afternoon a few of us went to town to pick up supplies. As we passed by a park, I caught a glimpse of white. I told the brother who was driving to circle the park and sure enough, a brother was sitting under a tree. We got out and walked towards him. It was Brother Les. He didn't recognize me at first, but when he did, a big grin arched across his face.

"Brother Don and Sister Judy are walking down the road to the camp. I was left here to scout out the area for any Christ Family members and see if we could set up a ride to camp. Judy's leg still keeps us trucking at a slow pace."

Les has never spoken so many words at one time in his life, I thought.

"We'll pick them up, brother," Sister Theresa said. She also was excited to see Don. They had been in Hawaii together when they 'transformed.'

I thought about the dream I'd had last night, awed that my subconscious mind had known Don was near, just as it had with Ed. I was looking forward to seeing him and Judy again. We picked them up near the beginning of the dirt road that led to the camp. Judy was walking with quite a limp, but she was walking. She looked so different, hardly like the same person. She had lost lots of weight. Her face was so narrow and tanned and her eyes looked bigger and bluer. Don was also thinner and bronzed. I wanted to jump up and hug them both and say, "Hey everyone, this is the brother that brought me 'the truth.'" But, once again I had to act appropriately and I just smiled and told them it was nice to see them. Don seemed distant.

Back in camp, I wanted to rest with them in the teepee, but once again felt bound to Richard. I wanted to get close to Don and talk to him like we used to, but it seemed as if all of us had built little walls around ourselves so we wouldn't get snared into emotion. Richard seemed uneasy around Don, a very subtle uneasiness, but I picked up on it right away. Don seemed to stay away because Richard was my 'spiritual mate.' It was so strange. I remembered the times we had shared up in Canada and how much freer I felt then. What had changed? Why were we so distant now? I remembered wanting to be Don's 'spiritual mate.' Now there was such coolness between us. I didn't like it, but it would have been unrighteous and worldly to talk about my feelings. These feelings were a trap, my old mind trying to take over again.

Only a few days after they arrived in camp, Ed, Don, Les and a few other brothers 'hit the wind.' Part of me wanted to jump in the open back of that old pickup with them. But, I stood beside Richard and waved goodbye, wondering if I would ever see them again. "That is a worldly thought," my 'Christ mind' interjected. "You are in the Lord's Army sister, remember that!"

Judy and I hung out together somewhat, but between us, too, there was that strained feeling of holding back. Were we trying too hard to show no attachment to each other? She did tell me a bit about the trip to Canada with Laura and the 'hobbits.' She avoided answering my questions about them, sensing I still had an open sore in that area. She was being a righteous sister by not giving my emotions anything to feed on.

Mealtimes proved to be vast learning grounds for giving, sharing and self-sacrifice. All of one's best qualities and shortcomings lay in full view of the encircled angels of supreme holiness. With such power present, the fulfilling of physical hunger was merely a 'prop.' 'Communion' was the main objective. Partaking of spiritual food was what was really happening.

I usually felt uptight and uncomfortable, during mealtime. There seemed to be an underlying current of pressure not to eat much. Questions paraded across my mind. Should I give my first bite away, so as not to appear selfish? Should I pass my bowl to the others before I'm finished? If I don't, will they think I'm not spiritually tuned in? I didn't eat much while in camp and usually ending up passing my half-full bowl of food, all the while ignoring my growling stomach.

At one such mealtime, Archangel Michael, the highest commander in the Lord's Army, preached to us about the importance of spiritual food.

"Brothers," he stood towering over us as he began; "Some of you are not carrying out your duties to the Lord. Why are we here, to hang out in the comfort and security of camp? Too many are attached to this space. You are in the Lord's Army, man! Your duty is to be 'in the wind,' preaching to the world. Too many brothers have softened with the 'kick back' attitude of camp life and three meals a day. Anyone who asks for second helpings of food needs some wind. Where is your faith? Food is just the 'prop.' 'Communion' is where it's really at." By now he was bellowing. His blue eyes glared at the dinner circle, his pointer finger out in accusation. "Keep your heart on what your mission is, man! No attachment! Not to food, not to your bedroll, not to your brother, not even to one blade of grass, man! It's all illusion. Don't you know who you are? The only reality is God and the life He has chosen you for. No killing, no sex and no materialism, man; space on that. It goes deep . . ."

As I cowered off to do the dishes that evening, the vision of Michael's piercing eyes and battle-scarred face, coupled with his message, haunted me. I felt as though he had directed his tirade at me. I was filled with feelings of guilt for staying in camp.

The sisters had formed a choir and each night we climbed up the mesa in the back of the camp and sat in a circle to sing songs of praise. Big Martha was inspired to write most of them and she taught them to us. One of my favorites was called, "Look Above." "Look above and you'll see his crown in the heavens. Lightning's come and he's brought his reward with him. Are you prepared to fly and enter in the kingdom? Are you prepared to fly and enter in the kingdom? In the song, the rhythm of creation, in the flow, forget yourself, seeing God in all things. Are you prepared to fly . . . ?" Our voices echoed through the desert. It was a privilege to be able to sing and I enjoyed this new space that was opened up for us.

One night, I dreamed about my old friend, Cheryl. In my dream we were talking openly about the past, partaking of one of the forbidden fruits. Once again, my premonition manifested and Cheryl trucked into the camp with Brother James, the first brother we picked up in the truck back in B. C., Canada. It was great to see them both. It was so good to see Cheryl finally in a white robe. She came right up to me and hugged me. I shrank back at her openness unconsciously looking around to see if anyone had seen us. She was freer in her speech and actions than most Christ Sisters. She seemed to be more in touch with her feelings, more open to say what was on her mind. A proper Christ Family member would disapprove of this, but I found it refreshing in a way, although I felt it was my duty as her sister to straighten her out. She spoke openly about 'falling out of the robe' with James in L.A. and wearing 'funny clothes.'

She was still a new sister and hadn't yet learned all the tricks of the trade. I remembered that not too long ago, I had been just like her. But, Sister Margaret let me know in no uncertain terms what was cool and what wasn't. So now I looked at Cheryl and noticed for the first time, how much I had changed. I felt good about these changes because I wanted to be a righteous example of Christ, no matter what the cost. It was a high price, too.

The very next day, Richard wanted to 'hit the wind.' I felt he was being unfair. He knew how close I was to Cheryl and yet he wanted to leave. I never questioned his decision verbally, though. I was very disappointed. Perhaps God wanted to separate Cheryl and I for His own reasons, I decided. So our reunion was cut short and Richard and I walked out of camp. After a few miles, we rested by the river. Here I experienced fire ants for the first time. We hadn't realized that the hill we were sitting on was infested with large, red ants that take little chunks of flesh with them when they bite and when they bite, they don't want to let go. Flicking them off doesn't work so you actually have to pull them off. Being peacemakers, we would be sinning to even think of killing these little creatures, so we not only had to pull them off while they were stinging us, we also had to do it carefully so as to not harm them. What a test of patience and reverence that was. Anyone in their right mind would have freaked out and I did, on the 'inside,' but on the outside, I remained as cool as the situation would permit. Richard and I were covered with ant bites as we continued down that dusty road, hoping for a ride. Fortunately, in a short space an elderly couple in a camper picked us up. They gave us refreshments and fruit as we drove to Tuscon, Arizona.

We found many 'connections' in Tuscon. One was a group named, "The Rainbow People," who invited us to one of their pads to share a joint. Afterwards, one of the guys there, wanted to talk to us some more, so he invited us to his place for the evening. The preaching went on all night. There were times when we could feel him receiving 'the truth' and other times when his mind would click in at full force and deny it. It was interesting to observe this human consciousness play by play, as it flipped back and forth in the battle between 'the spirit' and the flesh. In the end, he gave in to his flesh and didn't come with us, but I'm sure his life was never the same again.

❋ CHAPTER FOURTEEN ❋

It sure was good to be on the road again. The excitement of the constant change was refreshing, partly because it required more faith than staying in camp. When we rested under a tree in a park it felt fantastic just to 'be.' Towards evening, we roamed about to find a safe place to rest. Richard always picked the resting place and this night we roamed for hours in search of a suitable spot. As we walked past a few houses in a residential area, Richard suddenly picked out the most peculiar place. He walked over to a little patch of green in between two houses. "Don't ask why, but this is where we are supposed to rest," he said.

So we rolled out our bedrolls and spent the night. In the morning, we awoke to find two police officers, poking us. They were shocked to see how we were dressed when we stood up. "The neighbors are complaining that two bums are on their property. You better come into the station with us," one of them said.

So we rolled up our bedrolls and it was then that I noticed a woman next door on her sundeck, staring at us. She called the officers over and when they came back, they told us we were free to go. After they had left, she called us over to her. "I'm sorry, I thought you were bums. I can see that you are people of God. You must be here for me. I was praying to God last night to send me some company. I'm so lonely, you know, my husband died a few months ago. Will you stay for breakfast? I have the porridge on. Charles always liked his oats in the morning," she said.

"We sure will, sister. Praise God for your love and your sight, to see that we are here for you," Richard told her. She beamed at this confirmation of her words and went into the house. She was an elderly woman, in her sixties, I guessed, and with a heart so open and beautiful. She shared much of her life with us while we just listened. I was glad that Richard didn't feel the pull to preach to her much. What was discussed, was our diet. She found it strange, but understood our stand for peace. We spent the day with her while she gave us food, washed our robes and let us have a shower. Then she begged us to spend the night and we did. The next day, she gave

145

Richard a special gift. Her husband used to smoke a pipe, so she gave Richard one of his pipes and some tobacco for it. Tears floated in her eyes as she thanked us and said goodbye.

That day we got a ride to New Mexico which I found to be full of wonders and beauty. Mountains and desert mingled with all types of native traditions in this place where there was so much creative energy and many interesting people. Ironically, we found that it was the poor people who gave to us most of the time. We were treated like royalty in a humble Mexican restaurant where we were invited to eat as many beans as our bodies would permit.

Yet the wind itself seemed to blow us back to the desert camp. There must be more lessons to learn here, I thought to myself.

Sisters and brothers blew in and out of camp all that winter. Cheryl and James were gone. I wasn't supposed to, but I felt a bit disappointed; then guilt set in for feeling so worldly. That was always the way it happened if I felt an emotion that wasn't cool, it would soon be followed by feelings of guilt and unworthiness. I continually felt that I was lower spiritually than the others. They all seemed to have it together. As time went on, though, I learned different. I remember one particular incident that shocked me. I was down by the river, washing robes and a few of the sisters came down to bathe. Two of them I had never met before, so I guessed they had just arrived in camp. Well, they were such chatterboxes; I had never seen sisters carry on that way before. From their discussion I learned they were not 'new' sisters as I had suspected, but on the contrary, had been in the Christ Family for years.

I couldn't believe what I was hearing; a group of Christ Sisters gossiping about other Christ Family members. That was so utterly worldly; so wrong. I thought we had risen past all that stuff. I thought we truly loved each other. I sat there in silence, wondering if all this was happening to show me a lesson about judging my neighbor.

Was I the one in the wrong here, because I had been so quick to judge them? Now I was totally confused! I scrubbed the desert dirt out of those robes 'til my fingers ached. Sister Miriam came with a bucketful of soiled robes and left them soaking in a bit of soap. She didn't bother sticking around to wash them. I wondered why? Was she rushed with other things to do, or was she also disapproving of the sisters' behavior? I wanted to walk with her back to the camp and ask her, but if it was going to turn out that I was wrong, then I would feel even smaller than I already did. Besides we didn't do that kind of thing. We usually only showed each other the holy side; the righteous actions. It bothered me that I felt this hesitation to approach my sister and tell her what was on my mind.

Eventually the other sisters left gibbering down the road. I wondered what they thought of me and if they felt I was snobby for not joining in their gossip. I sat there alone, confused and a little disillusioned. After all we were supposed to be the saints. We had been sent to lead the world out of the hell state of mind into love consciousness. Was I a righteous reflection of Christ? Meanwhile, the river bubbled and swirled past and I almost heard it whisper something to me, but not in words. I knew that whenever I felt hurt or confused, the best remedy was to give. To get out of self. So I walked over to the bucket of soiled robes that Miriam had left and I started scrubbing. It felt so good to do this. This was true giving, I thought, no one would know that I had washed the robes, so I wasn't doing it to look holy in man's eyes, or to be thanked. I was doing it out of love with no strings attached. God talked to me while I washed those robes. I was learning a lot about giving and life. While hanging the last bit of laundry on the line, I realized that time had slipped away and I had left bread rising in the kitchen bus. A feeling a bit like worry began to gnaw at me as I walked faster than usual, back to camp.

As I approached, I could see Brother Edmond's face peeking out from the doorway of the bus and looking in my direction. As I drew near, I could see his expression was anything but friendly. "Where were you, sister? You have responsibilities here. The bread is already in the oven. Good thing I was around to see to it, or we wouldn't be eating it tonight!" He yelled at me harshly. I was taken completely by surprise. He actually yelled? I knew I couldn't tell him why I was late because my gift of giving would have been adulterated if I had tried to justify myself, so I just humbly apologized. "I will be more aware next time brother," I said, and went on to help Rachel prepare the meal. As I made the salad I wondered why my brother had been so angry. If we were all tuned into the same spirit as I was told we were, why wouldn't he know that I was busy doing God's work; giving and learning many lessons? Why did he have to be so harsh with me? Where was the love?

Over the next couple of days, I became aware of a sister who would come to the kitchen bus after the meal, while we were cleaning up and ask us for a sandwich then. I noticed that she was never present during the 'communion' and that a pattern had formed of her coming to see us afterwards. Brother Edmond would be annoyed with her and unwilling to give her any food, but she always seemed able to talk him into it on condition that it would not happen again. Something was wrong with this sister. Her eyes had lost their sparkle and were filled with pain. Everyone else seemed to ignore her as she roamed about the camp and the desert beyond, like a lost soul. This was my sister. My heart went out to her. She didn't participate in camp duties, or anything and I wanted to know why. I wanted to help her if I could. So one day, I followed her as she walked onto the mesa behind the camp. "Sister," I told her, "I feel you are in pain. I am here to be a sister and a friend, talk to me."

I knew I wasn't totally following orders here, but my heart overruled at this point. She turned around and looked at me, her blue eyes filling with tears. She reminded me of a cherub, with her golden hair falling over her plump, white-robed body. "You mean there is a caring soul here?" She asked in a shaky voice. "I have roamed through this camp for weeks, totally alone in my pain and no one could care less. I thought we were supposed to be the saints. I thought we were supposed to love each other. Everyone is so caught up in image around here, they can't even feel anymore. I don't know why I stay, but maybe I do because the world is even worse."

I thought about what she said and knew there was some truth to it. I didn't want to get confused at this time, though, so I just filed it under miscellaneous and didn't let if affect me. "I care, sister, I feel your pain," I said to her.

She surprised me by hugging me and yelling, "Praise God!" We walked in silence for a while and then sat together on a slab of flat rock. The sun was low in the sky and the air was already starting to cool off. "Little Martha was the only one I could talk to before," she told me. "But, now she's gone to find a home for Robin, just like I had to find a home for my little one. I don't think it's right, the brothers seduce their sisters and then they get off scot free with a little slap on the hand, but the sisters carry the child, go through the pain of delivery, grow attached and then are expected to give it up like a piece of cargo. Of course, we aren't supposed to feel anything because we have transcended all the earthly emotions and all that, and if we haven't, we better learn to! So we give our holy babies born to the saints, back to Satan and his army because the child is not old enough to choose? Don't you think it had already chosen and that's why that particular soul was placed in a saint's womb? I want my baby back, sister! I want to bring her up in the light of 'the truth,' not the darkness of the world, although lately I've had my doubts."

I had never had such an open conversation with a sister before. She was being real with me, letting me see her torment on the 'inside.' I wished I could take her pain away. "Sister," I began, "I know how you feel. I had two babies when I joined the group. The brother who got me into this never mentioned that we couldn't keep our 'hobbits.' In fact, he talked about a 'hobbit farm.' I took them both on the road with me for about a month and then was told that I had to give them up. You see, you can't serve both your 'hobbits' and the Lord. They demand too much energy. We become too attached to them and take our eyes away from God. Besides, life on the road is not fair to them, it's very unstable. This is the Lord's work we are doing. You wouldn't take your kids to work if you were in the world would, you?"

"I don't know. All I know is that I've been told I'm a saint and I'm in heaven and what I feel is totally opposite," she moaned.

"You're just going through a storm, sister. Ride the waves, stay on course, God has it all covered. You have to have faith," I urged.

"I just don't know if I can make it through this one, sister. I feel as though the breath of life has been sucked out of me. The more I try to shut my mind and feelings off, the stronger they fight me. I am starting to wonder if this really is 'the truth.'"

I looked at this child of God; sister of my heart. Dark bags hung under her light blue eyes, evidence of sleepless nights. Her soft round face showed lines of confusion. What can I say to help her? I thought. What can I do? How clearly I could relate to her pain. "Sister," I told her, "you need some wind. The ever changing adventures and miracles on the road really helped me out when I stood where you are."

"Perhaps you're right. I don't know," she said doubtfully.

"Come on, let's go back to our roll-out spots and get some rest," I said. Obediently, she followed me back to the camp and then disappeared.

Throughout my time with the Christ Family, this sister always remained in my heart. When she 'hit the wind' the next morning a hint of light seemed to be back in her eyes.

That winter the brothers built a sauna, digging it into the side of a raised piece of land. Their workmanship was incredible. Inside, it looked positively royal. The resting bench was covered in royal blue velvet, which I thought illogical for a sauna, but logic wasn't highly thought of there.

Lightning and Cher seemed to keep to themselves quite a bit. One day, Cher asked me to French braid her hair. I felt honored, but I wondered if Lightning had told her to make contact with me because I had been thinking that they kept to themselves. She also asked me to wash their robes. This duty was an honor and a privilege. While washing Lightning's robes, I noticed that I was taking extra care to get them clean. Once again, the Lord was teaching me lessons through the laundry. I understood that He was telling me from now on to wash every robe with the special care and the attitude that it was a privilege. For, in truth, the Lord wants us to treat each other with the same respect and love that we show for Him.

Nights in the desert were becoming really cold now. Richard and I moved into the tent with Sister Laura, the one who took the children to Canada, and Archangel Gabriel, Sister Nancy and Brother Isaac. Each day that passed brought colder nights. Our thin bedrolls offered little protection from the frigid night air.

For our bathroom, we dug deep holes in the ground, placed two boards over each side where we placed our feet, had a plastic jug filled with water for cleansing and presto, 'la bano.' This method of eliminating wastes reminded me of South America. There were three 'banos' in camp on the outskirts of the circle, each with a tarp stretched partly around for privacy. Because the icy mornings offered us frozen water in our cleansing bottles, most of us 'held on' until the sun was hot enough to melt our liquid toilet paper.

Once again, I had a premonition that came to me in a dream. I dreamt about Will and he remained on my mind all through the day. "I had another dream, I have a feeling we will be seeing Will soon," I told Richard.

"I believe you are a prophetess sister," he said, smiling at me with a hint of pride in his eyes. Shortly after the evening meal, Will walked into camp with a sister. Although I felt excited at seeing him, I greeted him with the coolness and reserve of a proper Christ Sister. "I knew you were on your way brother, good to see you," I said to him.

"Howdy sister," he replied, nodding to me with the same coolness.

"Come to the kitchen bus and I'll fix you something to eat," I said, motioning to them both to follow me. I felt so uncomfortable with him. At one time, Will had been my husband. Now he seemed like a stranger. I think he was surprised when I went to the tent to rest beside Richard. Did he want me to rest beside him? Why didn't I feel free to?

Richard seemed a little uncomfortable with Will in camp, following me around. This was an awkward time for me. When we sat in our circle for our evening meal, both Richard and Will wanted me to sit by them. This was so strange. I felt torn between the two of them. One night, Will helped me clean the dishes and afterwards, instead of going to the tent, I went for a walk with him. We sat by the river watching the moonlight dance across the water and he asked me to 'hit the wind' with him.

"I'd like to travel with you, brother, to experience you as my brother instead of as my husband, but I also want to be with Richard," I said uncomfortably. "The truth is, we are 'spiritual mates' and he wants me by his side."

"You're free to travel with whoever you wish, sister, you shouldn't feel bound to anyone. Let's 'hit the wind' right now," he answered.

I thought about it for a long time as we sat there in silence. "I don't really feel bound. I enjoy being with Richard," I said finally. "He has a definite connection with the Holy Spirit. We can communicate without words. We have fun together." It was difficult to explain. Will had been my spiritual teacher, but God had now sent me a new brother to learn from. And when Richard told me we were 'spiritual mates,' I felt bound to him.

When I reached the tent after this conversation, the candle had been blown out and everyone was already rolled out. I felt like a teenager coming home after curfew. I literally snuck into the tent. Richard was awake, I think everyone was, but no one said a word. Tension hung thick in the air. I didn't sleep all that night. When I went to get the breakfast tray in the morning, the spot where Will rested was empty. I wondered if I would ever see him again and wondered if I had made the right decision.

After a few days, Martha gave us a ride into nearby Blythe, California and handed us the first copies ever to be printed of the Christ Family's "Declaration of Independence." It paralleled the American Declaration in the sense that the original phrasing had been converted to our way of thinking. Richard began reading it out loud.

"CHRIST MANIFESTO, Presenting the Alpha and Omega, THE DECLARATION OF INDEPENDENCE By the Freedmen of New Jerusalem In the Congress of the Host of Angels assembled. In the beginning was the Word, and the Word was with God, and Word was God. Let us move into the New Age with a PURE HEART and a CLEAR MIND. We hold this Truth to be self evident; that all living creatures are created equal, that they are endowed by their Creator with certain unalienable Rights. That among these are Life, Liberty and Happiness. When in the course of events it is revealed through a long train of abuses that evil has usurped the Rights guaranteed by Our Creator unto every living creature, it is the Right and the Duty of every being to oppose and abolish this evil.

A Perfect Union has been formed. We hereby separate ourselves from the nations of the world and unite in the Life of Our Lord Jesus Christ Lightning Amen, as One Nation under God, Indivisible with Liberty and Justice for ALL, AMEN. By LIVING HIS LIFE, which is the TRUTH and MANIFEST WILL OF GOD, we give Life, Liberty and Happiness to ALL Living Creatures. And for the support of this Declaration, with a firm reliance on the Protection of Divine Providence, We mutually pledge to each other our lives, our fortunes . . . and Sacred Honor. WE HEREBY UNITE TO MANIFEST HIS WILL ON EARTH AS IT IS IN HEAVEN, AMEN.

BEHOLD I HAVE COME and my reward is with me to give to every man according to his works. I AM the Alpha and the Omega, the beginning and the end, the first and the last. BLESSED are they that do His command that they may have Right to the Tree of Life and may enter in through the gates into the City, for without are dogs and sorcerers and whoremongers and murderers and idolaters and whosoever loveth and maketh a lie. I JESUS, have sent my Angels to testify to you these things in the churches. I AM the root and offspring of David and the Bright and Morning Star. The Spirit and the Bride say, COME. And whosoever will, let him take the Water of Life freely. THE BOOK OF LIFE is engraved in the HEART of OUR LORD. As all our names are in His Heart, so all our signatures are in One. IN ONE IS ALL-IN AMEN IS ALL MEN. KING OF KINGS, LORD OF LORDS." Richard's voice trailed off, but my heart was troubled.

❊ CHAPTER FIFTEEN ❊

I felt a little uneasy about this Declaration of Independence. We had been told that we were the 'living word of God' and that this was why there was no need to carry the Bible around with us. I couldn't see why we had to give out these pamphlets now, but I didn't say anything. Richard felt honored that Martha had given us the very first batch to circulate and I didn't want to spoil it for him.

After a few hours of 'billboard service' on the highway, we roamed about the city of Blythe, knocking on hotel and motel doors and asking the owners to give freely of a room, or some floor space in the name of Christ. But, no hearts, or doors were open to us that cold night and our resting spot was in the back of a super market; our bed, two pieces of cardboard, on the cold gravel. The desert night brought frozen air and I huddled my face under my bedroll with just my nose peeking out exhaling through my mouth for extra warm air. It was really cold. Just before dawn the body temperature drops and so does the air temperature inside our bedroll. I found this time of the morning almost unbearable, as we waited in anticipation for the sun to spreads its warmth on us. I compared us to the cold and dark world, waiting for the Lord to come and warm its heart.

Everything I thought of, or saw at this time was converted into some meaning of our truth. If I heard a song on the radio while driving in a car, I would understand the words to mean something relevant to the Christ Family. When I saw billboard signs, or neon signs outside restaurants, or stores, all had significant meanings or messages for me. If there was an earthquake in a town that a Christ Brother or Sister had just 'blown up' (reprimanded for not receiving the message), then we automatically assumed that the earthquake was because of us and that the 'bogus' stubborn people in the town would see they should have listened to God's people. To our way of thinking, we were the centre of the universe, we really believed we were the saints, that we were God's chosen people and that this was the end of the world. We also believed that we would be the only ones who wouldn't have to die a physical death; the Lord would take us up with Him in 'the spirit.' We believed that our bodies were going to turn into light; the more we denied the physical and experienced the spiritual. We would fall out of the physical the same way man fell into it, unconsciously. Because we had already died to ourselves and forsaken the world and all we once were, we would not have to experience dying a physical death. The 'higher' we became, the faster we vibrated and we would come to the point where we would vibrate at such a velocity that we would turn into light. I understood that when this time came, the whole 'Family' would gather in one place, altogether, and 'blink out.' I was looking forward to this 'rapture' with the excited wonder of a child. I wanted so badly to be free of the physical and to be at one, totally, with God. We didn't know when 'blink out' would be, but we were told it would be very soon and it was always there in the back of my mind.

That morning, Richard and I went to a garage to wash up and do our morning business. I always had battles in washrooms. I wanted to look into the mirror every time, but I knew that if I did, I would feel guilty because we were not supposed to feed our vanity at all. So I tried to stay away from mirrors. We weren't supposed to waste any more energy on the body than was absolutely necessary.

There were countless people who found it in their hearts to invite us into their homes for a meal and a shower. Actually, we often used food as a tool to introduce the first key, no killing. There were also scores of 'connections' who gave us money to buy food and many giving hearts behind counters in restaurants who served us a free meal. Pizza Hut had a good salad bar. A few Chinese and Mexican restaurants also gave us meals. It was such a high feeling to walk into a restaurant and be seated and served for free, in the name of Christ. These people would surely have been blessed for their kindness. And the fact that God was taking care of us through others, kept confirming my beliefs in the movement. If it wasn't vegetarian, it wouldn't cross my lips, or be used in any way. There were times when I'd be in the shower feeling so good to get clean after such a long stretch and the shampoo would have animal products in it. I must admit that once or twice the temptation was there, but I never gave in to it. I would rather leave my hair greasy, than defile the animals in any way.

One particular incident around this time puzzled me. Richard and I developed lice. We were invited into someone's home for a few days and the man gave us some money to buy shampoo and get rid of the lice. Richard said it was cool to use it, that he knew another brother who had done so. To me, this seemed a contradiction. What was the difference between killing lice and killing mosquitoes, or black flies? 'Believe your brother,' I told myself and put all doubt away. Besides, it was such a relief to get rid of the pests.

Richard and I loved to sing. I taught him the songs that Martha had taught the sisters in camp. Richard's voice was incredibly deep and we harmonized well together. He sang octaves lower than I did. We also sang many other songs, converting them to Christ Family meanings. I loved to sing. It felt so high. "The Bare Necessities," the song from the Jungle Book movie, was one of Richard's favorites and we both especially liked "Amazing Grace," "When the Saints Come Marching In," "Swing Low Sweet Chariot" and other Gospel tunes.

I felt like an innocent, trusting child again, singing with my brother, walking down the road, letting my Heavenly Father lead me. I had found the fountain of youth. Such times, when we rode in a high, clear space, it confirmed to me that this movement was 'the truth.' All the hard times I'd had, were just evidence of getting rid of my 'old self' in preparation for birthing into the new. God was working on me, little by little, giving me only as much as I could handle, showing me the way.

One day Richard told me that he had a 'pull' to head towards Apple Valley, California. His 'earth mom' had lived in a town near there the last time he saw her over three years ago. We were able to take a bus there when the driver gave freely of the ride. I was feeling a cold coming on and was thankful to be able to just sit comfortably and drift in and out of sleep for a while. At a phone booth in the cold, dark night, Richard made a call to his 'earth aunt' and much to our dismay, found out that his mother no longer lived in the area. By this time my feet were stiff and numb, my stomach ached with emptiness and my plugged nose let out a sneeze. "My earth dad's sister lives near here, brother. I can call her and ask if we can spend the night," I told him.

"Right on. Praise God. I knew there was some 'connection' here," he replied.

We believed that the needs of our physical bodies were only a 'prop' in our connections with people. That was why we still remained in our physical forms, for otherwise, we wouldn't be able to relate to people. And that was why we didn't really feel we were in need; rather, they were in need of the spiritual food that we brought.

Aunt Terry is a wonderfully giving person. Although it was something like one-thirty in the morning, she was at the phone booth to meet us within minutes. I felt uncomfortable not being able to give her the customary kiss and hug greeting. "Praise God for your kindness, sister," I said with a smile.

"You've come at the perfect time, Maureen. It's Thanksgiving today and most of your cousins are down for the weekend," she said. Aunt Terry and Uncle Richard had thirteen children, ranging in ages from thirty-something, to eight. The older ones were living in different cities and were home for the holiday, some with their mates and children.

The house was quiet with slumber when we arrived. Not being aware of time, we had no idea we'd called my aunt so late. In spite of the hour, she prepared food for us. I thought it was pretty ironic that 'the saints' had gone without food on Thanksgiving, while the rest of America was stuffing itself on dead birds.

The next day Richard gave me the space to preach to my aunt and cousins, because they were my family. I told her that I was a saint and that some day she would realize I was telling her the 'the truth.' She was very patient with me and accepted my words, although she didn't agree with me. Now, I can look back and see that she is far more saintly than I was, or ever will be. That woman breathed giving.

She told me that Richard and I could stay for a few days, as long as I gave my parents a call just to let them know that I was alive. I had a hard time with that and looked to Richard for approval. He didn't say anything, leaving it up to me. I wasn't used to making decisions. I just obeyed and followed. Well, the phone rang just then and I escaped my decision because it was my mom! It felt strange to hear her voice. To me, it seemed like centuries since I had been in Thunder Bay. Her voice was sharp and hateful. She was so full of rage and hurt. "How could you be so stupid?" She screamed at me. "How could you abandon your children? Don't you ever learn? Don't you know that you are following a false Christ; that you are in a cult?" This word still meant nothing to me. I had no idea of its implications.

Next my dad took the phone and in a patient, kind voice, asked me how I was and asked my permission to baptize the children in the Catholic Church. He added that my mother loved me and had been very worried about me, as was he.

"I'm following Jesus now, brother," I told him. "There is much more to see than with our physical eyes. The end of the world as we know it is at hand and I wish both of you would come and join the 'Family.' Soon you will see that I'm telling you 'the truth.' Then you will understand my actions. There is no intent to hurt."

My mom came back on the phone and I could tell she was crying. "You have no idea how hurt this little girl is, Maureen. There isn't a day that goes by when she doesn't ask me about you," she told me.

I was shaken by this, but I kept fighting off my emotion. Then she put Ariss on the phone! "Hi, mommy Maureen. I love you. We pray for you every day. When are you coming home? I miss you."

Her innocent voice, so sincere and fluent, caused my throat to close. I had never heard her speak in sentences. Forbidden tears won the battle with my will to contain them and fell freely from my eyes. In a cracked voice I replied, "I love you too, Ariss. Some day you will understand." She was so young, not quite three years old yet. What pain have I caused this little one? Guilt-ridden, I went into another room to ask God to forgive my weakness. After all this time, after all this praying and battling, I still had the human mother instinct. When would I truly give up this deep-rooted attachment? I felt unholy and unworthy. "Oh holy Father, heal me and make me whole; your will, not mine," I prayed. Thoughts of the children would remain with me for days after this episode. I fought the yearning to be with them like a warrior fights for his life.

Later that night Aunt Terry and I were doing the dishes. "Sister," I told her, "you will be greatly blessed for helping the saints." My aunt looked disturbed at my comment. "No, Maureen, I don't buy that. I can't see how I would get extra credit for helping a saint rather than helping a nobody." Her comment shocked me. I knew God loved us all equally. "Well, maybe you're right. I'll have to pray to God about that," I told her.

It was great to see all of my cousins, though. One of them in particular was interested in our theology and talked to us for hours asking many questions. I think this made my uncle very uneasy and finally he asked us if we would leave, giving us enough money for a bus ticket to Crescent City. Richard had found out that his mom now lived there. Meanwhile, Richard and I had been calling out to spend the rest of the winter in Hawaii if it was in the Father's will. My aunt confessed that she dreamed about going to Hawaii some day herself. "Join us and God will get you there," I told her. "He has given us everything we have asked for. Life is so different now. I feel like a blind man who is seeing for the first time."

"Well, Maureen, I can't agree with what you are doing, but I pray that God will reveal to us His will. Please don't make your parents worry, phone them every so often," she pleaded as we said our farewells.

On the bus to Crescent City my mind raced with the events of the past few days. Images of Ariss and Sol, Mom, Dad, Sue and Nana, my grandmother, haunted me as we traveled through the dark of night. I thought about the hurt they all thought I was causing them. But, that hurt was really caused by their ignorance of who I was. If only they knew, they would be proud; not hurt, I thought. I imagined the future, the day when the veils would lift from the eyes of mankind and everyone would see that we in the 'Family' truly are whom we claim to be. Then all those who had ridiculed us would understand we had been telling 'the truth.' I ached for that day of recognition, but I also realized that part of my aching was for the self, to prove I was right. This attitude was wrong. I knew that Jesus showed us this so clearly when He allowed Himself to be judged and ridiculed and hung on the cross. He didn't try to prove to his oppressors that He was the Messiah, even though He had the power to. I prayed for that kind of humility and patience.

While riding the bus, I had flashbacks of the bus accident in Peru. Fear tried to make its way into my space, but I shot it down before it had a chance. "Old tapes and fears," I ordered myself, "be gone," and they disappeared.

After two days of traveling, we arrived at Crescent City. The night was dark and bitter cold. Bronchitis, well on its way to becoming pneumonia, had been creeping up on me for weeks now and I could feel the heaviness of my body as it shivered from the inside out. We stood by a phone booth, as Richard tried to contact his mom to pick us up. My feet were numb, my body doubled over whenever I coughed, which was far too often. I didn't feel like an angel at all, I felt so human and vulnerable. I just wanted to lay my old body down somewhere and leave it behind. 'Creature features' is what we called it when our body was becoming sick. It seemed that I was continually going through some sort of 'creature feature,' or another. From breast fever to a cold, a toothache, female problems, backaches, foot aches, abdominal pains and now this. Boy, I was looking forward to the day when I wouldn't have to carry along this extra baggage they call a body. I would do just fine without all these body malfunctions, not to mention the perpetual car sickness that I faced in our life of traveling. I wondered if I was too attached to the physical and all this illness was God's way of teaching me to let go and dwell in 'the spirit.' Or, was He just showing me how to have the grace of being in silent pain? I used to have a bad habit of complaining. Was I riding out my karma?

We waited in silence by the phone until a jolly grey-haired woman came to pick us up. I thought she was Richard's mom until she spoke. "Flo is visiting your sister for a few days, Sonny. She told me to give you the key to the house and for you to make yourselves at home," she said, as we drove up a long driveway that led to a blue and white mobile home. It felt so good to know we were going to be in one place for awhile.

The home wasn't much warmer than the cold night and Richard immediately started to build a fire in the woodstove situated in the middle of the living room. His mom's trailer was neat and homey. Little knickknacks here and there and the colors of the furniture gave me a warm feeling about Richard's mom. For example, the bedspread on her bed was white. I liked that, the color white was very symbolic to us, meaning purity.

The warm glow of the fire as it thawed my frozen feet and hands, felt fantastic. The only sounds were the occasional draining of the fridge and the crackles and pops of the mesmerizing fire. The smell of pine filled the air. Richard and I just sat there. No words were necessary. No words would have described how good we felt. Even though my body was sick, I felt good. I felt awe at the way God was taking care of us, how He had set everything up; this home, this fire and even the fact that we would be there alone for a few days. What a blessing. What a magnificent Father we have. Praise God!

The next day we explored. The trailer was situated on a few acres, a couple of miles from town. There was a huge garden and a greenhouse which was still producing fresh tomatoes. The garden was pretty well finished except for potatoes, carrots, Swiss chard and the cornstalks were still standing. The air was clean and fresh. This was a glorious place and I loved being there. We took a long walk down the dirt road and came to a wooden float bridge. It crossed over a small brook. I've always loved moving water and we sat by the stream for a while.

Flo came home the next evening. She embraced her son with no inhibitions at all. His robe didn't scare her. Her rosy red cheeks and laughing blue eyes shone and her hair was pure white. Although she was seventy-three, she was so bubbly, agile and loving. I loved her from the first. "I'm so happy to see you," she shrieked excitedly. "Oh Sonny, I was so worried about you. Where have you been all this time? I'm so thrilled to see you."

Sonny? She called Richard, Sonny? I could tell he didn't really like the 'handle,' but he wasn't about to burst her bubble right then.

"Why are you wearing that white dress, dear," she asked him? "Introduce me to your lovely friend; oh my, isn't she cute?" This lady was incredible. She had so much energy; she wanted to be everywhere at one time.

Richard was very patient with her. "I am wearing a white robe, not a dress. I wear it because that is what Jesus is wearing and I'm following Him and living His life. This is Sister Maureen. We have been traveling together for quite a while now. I am here because God has sent us here," he told her.

"Well, God sure has picked the right time. Joe just died a few weeks ago, you know and I felt awfully lonely. I miss him so much. I miss you, too, Sonny and a day hasn't gone by that I haven't prayed for you. Have you been to see Debbie and the kids? They are so big now. Sonny, why did you just leave them like that? She was a good wife wasn't she?"

Richard's explanations faded as I put myself in his place and wondered if I would crumble at such a bombardment from the past and the old familiar self. I now understood why we had to leave our family and friends. They held all the links to the 'old self,' the 'old mind.' I remembered reading in the Bible that Jesus said a prophet is never recognized in his home town, because he is associated with the person he was before; *". . . Isn't that Jesus the Nazarene, the carpenter's son . . . ?" (Matthew 13:55)*. Thus, we label the ones we think we know and don't allow for who they might be today.

Flo and I got along really well. She reminded me of my grandmother whom I loved dearly and still secretly missed. Flo took me to her doctor who gave me medication for a bladder and yeast infection and also penicillin for advanced bronchitis. He told me I had a cyst on my ovary and Flo wanted me to have an operation. She fussed over me and made me rest for a few days, but after that you couldn't hold me down, my energy was boundless. I washed all her walls, cleaned out cupboards, polished windows, did all the spring cleaning. I also did most of the cooking, baking bread, muffins and cakes. I showed her how to bake without eggs, to cook without flesh. She ate vegetarian while we were there and she loved it. Richard chopped wood and helped with the dishes, but he relaxed there a lot more than I did.

I also picked some dried flowers and wheat and made a flower arrangement for her living room. It felt so good to sneak in that small creative energy.

Christmas was awkward. Flo's sister gave Richard and I each a pair of slippers. Flo gave me some perfume. But, we didn't use the words "thank you" in our vocabulary; we didn't believe in the world's tradition of Christmas and, of course, we didn't sing carols. I felt a sense of sadness, a feeling of missing something. I didn't reveal it.

Flo let Richard and I buzz around in her little blue car and we went for rides often. They usually led us to the ocean, where we walked along the beaches, or on colder days just watched the powerful sea eat up the rocky shore by the red lighthouse. One day, as we sat there by the lighthouse, we talked about the forbidden. He told me about his past, his life before and I told him about mine. We opened up totally. We talked about how neat it would be to live in a lighthouse if we still lived in the world. We talked about being together as a couple if we lived in the world. Being in love was unrighteous, because we were supposed to be in love with everyone, but between Richard and I there was an almost worldly love that sat uncomfortably with me. We were not free to have each other in that way; we were constantly fighting it.

Although we were not attracted merely to flesh, but to what we saw and felt inside the flesh body, I knew these feelings were more than what was acceptable. I knew that he shouldn't be looking at me that way. I knew I shouldn't feel so much towards him. I wasn't supposed to be any more special to him, than anyone else. Yet I could feel his hands quiver as he massaged my neck and back.

More and more I could see why the rule was, love without touch. Richard and I had gotten into the habit of massaging each other nearly every day. He would crack my back and neck and it felt so good. I brushed his hair and he brushed mine. Many of the other brothers and sisters did this, also. We saw it in camp. But, something wasn't quite right in our relationship and I felt it. For example, Richard wanted to sleep on the pullout couch instead of on the floor. I wanted to rest on the floor, but he insisted that my place was to rest beside him. Sometimes, he would hug me when we rested and I felt afraid of this and for the second time since we had been traveling I felt confusion about Richard's judgments. I was his sister and it was my place to obey, but I could feel myself pulling away a bit at his overwhelming love. Yet I knew I was attracted to him, felt more towards him than to other brothers. When I was doing dishes he would come up behind me and hug me, just like Will used to. This didn't feel right somehow, so I told him not to. This angered him and formed a subtle discord between us.

Another time, a similar thing happened and we argued just like husband and wife. Afterwards, I went for a walk by myself. I walked for hours, pondering what I should do about Richard and I. At last I decided to leave, to 'hit the wind' solo and let God heal me of this attachment. Soon afterwards, I got a ride with a guy in a pick-up truck. I didn't feel moved to preach to him. As we drove, my need was to stay absorbed in thought. But, suddenly he stopped the truck and reached over to me, his eyes full of lust and his hands trembling. "No sex, brother!" I yelled at him. As I pulled at the door handle, he pushed the button down. I glared right into his eyes and baptized him with the three keys, which I felt had power somehow: "No Killing, No Sex, No Materialism." "Jesus Christ is back on earth!"

Then, as he lurched over me, I flicked up the button, opened the door and jumped out. "Come back, sweetie. You're so beautiful," he called after me. I just kept running into the bush on the side of the road. Deeper into the forest I ran, my breathing heavy, my feet bruising up with every step. When at last I heard the truck squeal away, I collapsed on a moss covered tree stump. God was definitely telling me not to leave Richard. So I made my way back to the trailer, back to my beloved brother.

What was supposed to be a short rest stop stretched into the month of January, as Flo didn't want us to leave. I guess we felt justified in staying so long because she was receiving 'the truth' and eating vegetarian the whole time we were there.

One day, Richard and I cleaned up the garden for her. She had a huge cornfield full of dried stalks. Here in the cornfield, pulling up the old stalks turned into a symbolic spiritual cleansing for me. The roots of the corn plants were deep and it was a struggle to yank then out of the hard-packed earth. To me, every cornstalk became a part of my 'old self' that I was uprooting and casting away. Some were deeper and harder to pull out than others and it seemed as if the ones I had a hard time to uproot corresponded with how deeply rooted the sin, or attachment was in me. So here I was in this cornfield, the wind blowing wildly and making the air much cooler now, yet sweat poured from my body as I frantically pulled out the iniquity within me. "Jealousy!" I yelled, yanking on a corn plant, then, "Envy!" As I uprooted another one, "Self love!" As I tugged at a dried stalk, then heaved it over my shoulder. Next, I called out "Attachment!" And then I called out "Motherly love!" But those plants refused to budge. So I struggled hard, using all my weight and strength to uproot my deepest sins. Finally, when the entire field lay void of corn, I collapsed on a pile of dead plants. My effort to 'clean up Flo's garden' had been an incredible spiritual workout as well.

A few days later, Richard's younger brother Juan came to stay with Flo and overheard Richard saying to me that he guessed we weren't meant to spend the winter in Hawaii. Then Juan turned to us and said, "Hawaii sounds great. If you want to come with me, I'll treat you both to airfare."

"Right on, brother, we'll come," Richard replied. We were both elated.

On our way to the airport in Eureka, Flo was unusually quiet. "You know that you are welcome to come along with us, Ma," Juan told her.

"No, you kids go ahead, I don't like the idea of flying in the sky in a large piece of metal," she answered.

"Oh, come on; are you still afraid of flying? You know it isn't much different than driving a car," he said coaxingly, but it was no use. Flo would not change her mind.

I was excited, as memories of my trip to Jamaica during my last year of high school, came to mind. It had been wonderful, the air sweet smelling, the warm sea breeze, the white sand beaches and that glorious sun which you could almost always count on to be shining. Islands were incredible. There was so much diversity in such a small area. God is so good, I thought. Just when we were about to forget our wish to go to Hawaii, presto . . . He manifests it. I thought about Aunt Terry and how she had dreamed to go for years. Now, that dream is becoming a reality for me, I thought, as the car pulled up to the airport.

At the ticket office, a tall thin man with a pinched look to his face and large, thick, black-framed glasses gave Richard and I the old twice-over and, resting his eyes on our feet, said, "You can't board the plane barefoot, it's against the rules."

"That's right, I forgot about that," Juan said. "Where is the nearest shoe store?" "About ten miles into town, but there is a grocery store across the highway, you better hurry, the plane departs in a half an hour."

So Flo gave Richard a twenty-dollar bill and we both ran out the door. I wondered what he would find. But, when we reached the supermarket's small running shoe area, he quickly picked out a pair of white sneakers with a blue stripe for me and they fit. It wasn't so easy for him, though. Richard's feet were king-sized. I never really knew how big they were until he put on the largest pair in the store and his toes still curled in them. He took them anyhow. I couldn't contain my laughter. He reminded me of "Bozo" the clown, with his long reddish beard, balding head, long white robe and size fifteen sneakers sticking out beneath his robe. We both looked ridiculous. Biblical mysticism completely adulterated by the 'New Age' running shoe. They sure helped us run back to the airport in a hurry, though. We arrived just in time to say our farewells to Flo.

"I love you, Flo. Praise God for all your gifts," I told her. She embraced me, crying and said, "You're such a good girl, take care of my Sonny and please come back to see me soon."

She held on to Richard as though she wanted never to let go. There wasn't as much intensity with Juan, but I guess she knew she would be seeing him again soon. "Come anytime . . ." Her voice faded as we hurried down the hall.

❋ CHAPTER SIXTEEN ❋

We were seated in one of the largest jets I had ever seen, with three separate sections across its width. There was a large screen in our section and the stewardess gave us ear phones to listen to the movie that played. Juan sat in the same row as us, but across the aisle. He drank too much alcohol and flirted with the stewardesses. This made Richard angry with him. Although he never showed it, I just could feel him burning on the 'inside.'

During the long ride, I thought about why we had bent the rules and worn shoes for the flight. I felt a little funny about this, but didn't feel free to question my brother. That would mean I didn't trust him and trust was a large part of our relationship. A sister followed her brother and didn't question, just obeyed, I reminded myself. The fact that we had no return tickets, didn't bother me in the least. I could see us preaching on the islands for years. Soon after this, the two Dramamine pills I had been given started to work and I fell into semi-consciousness.

The next thing I knew, our 747 was landing on the big island of Hawaii. The pungent scent of flower blossoms, mixed with salt spray, hit me immediately and I took a few deep breaths, practically sucking the nectar out of the air. Oh, the smell of perpetual spring. I adored this smell in this dreamlike place. Even the airport was wonderful. It seemed to have a roof, but there were large areas with no walls at all. Plants and trees and birds were everywhere. The sun had just set, casting fantasy colors and shadows over everything.

In the airport, a woman with a young child who had also been on the plane, came to us and asked where we were going to rest for the night and if she could tag along. Of course we accepted her. She seemed to belong to some eastern religion by the way she was talking. Richard told her all about what we were doing and she seemed intrigued, yet held onto her own beliefs. Together, we walked down the quiet highway in the dark. We didn't know where we were going, we just walked. All the while I kept breathing deeply, feeling high from the heavenly scents. Finally, a car pulled up to our jet-lagged crew and the driver gave us a ride to a park by the ocean.

We made our bed on the sandy beach, listening to the ocean envelope the shore. I was surprised to find 'M's' (mosquitoes) buzzing around my head. I had also thought Hawaii would be a lot hotter, but the breeze off the ocean was cool enough for me to put my head under my bedroll for refuge from the 'M's.' That night, I had a strong feeling we would be meeting other Christ Brothers soon. I thought I saw someone in a white robe go into the park restroom, but when I went to follow I discovered it was a woman in a white dress and boots.

As usual, Richard was awake before me. He was always awake when I 'blinked in.' He loved watching the sunrises. I appreciated that he let me rest and very seldom woke me up. He had great patience. Some mornings he would say, "Good morning, sleepy head, I've been awake for hours." I guess I was catching up on years of no sleep after caring for two small children who woke me up throughout the night. Richard handed me a lit Bugler. Gesturing at the surroundings, he said, "Welcome to paradise sister."

The ocean was a green blue and very calm. It went on for infinity. The air was moist and warm. As we sat there praising God, I caught sight of a splash of white moving in our direction. As it came near, Richard recognized another brother and went to greet him. It was a brother called Italian Richard, to save confusion with Richard himself. He told us there was a group of brothers camping close by in the same camp site and brought us there. Calvin and Jan being the longest in this group seemed to be its leaders. The others were Patrick, Robert, Rick (Italian Richard) and Cynthia. It was great to meet them all, but as always, I felt especially on guard to make sure I acted and spoke righteously. We shared a meal of avocados and rice, sitting in a circle near the ocean. Juan seemed uneasy in the silence. I was hoping that meeting the others would convince him to join the 'Family,' but shortly after the meal he went his way and we never met up with him again.

After he had left, Richard and I took a long walk, exploring the island. It was the closest place on earth to the Garden of Eden that I'd ever been. The lush tropical forests were spectacular. Splashes of vivid colors broke up endless shades of green and banana, bread fruit, avocado, coconut, kiwi and passion fruit grew wild along some of the roads.

When we returned to the campsite, everyone was getting ready to 'hit the wind.' "It's time for some site-seeing," Calvin said with a grin. Two vehicles had been given to the brothers; a blue Chevy truck which Rick drove and a 1958 Willys Jeep which Calvin and Jan drove. Richard and I rode in the jeep as we started our tour of the island, noticing the many different landscape changes in one small area. We went from a fine sand beach to a rocky, volcanic shore in the space of twenty miles. I was shocked to discover that there are snow-peaked mountains on Hawaii. We went to every tourist attraction concerning the history and people of the place and I really enjoyed it all. We spent a lot of time having picnics on the beach and preaching to the people. Walking on the scorching volcanic rock was difficult to get used to, though; even the sidewalks were always frying hot.

When we arrived on the Kona side of the Island, we made a rundown old shack our domain for a while. It was situated a little way off the highway, on a ridge a mile or so up from the ocean. We converted this one-room shack to our kitchen, where we stored a common stove, bowls, pots and food. The open porch had a roof and this was our resting and eating area. The jungle around us provided us with most of our food. Banana, avocado, mango, papaya and many more types of fruit trees were growing all around us; in fact, we had more bananas and avocados than we could eat. I had been calling out for fresh fruit and here it was. There is a really different taste and feeling involved in picking fruit off the trees. It was heavenly. The weather was warmer on the Kona side, but it did rain a bit.

After a while here, I noticed that the brothers were collecting food stamps, which provided tobacco, beans, rice, corn and parts for the trucks. This didn't sit right with me. For one thing, in order to obtain them, we had to give our social security numbers and I had been told that this was 'the mark of the beast' spoken of in the Book of Revelation. My number wouldn't have done them any good because I was a Canadian. Also, you had to tell the authorities you were living at such and such an address and this seemed like lying to me. I preferred to be on the road and have God provide for me through the free gifts of love, from others.

As one of the leaders of our small group, Jan, had the organizational skills that were needed to take care of our money and groceries. I gave her the respect due to an older sister and we got along well. I guessed we were around the same age. Her face, still childlike, was tiny and cute, crowned with straight, dirty blonde hair. She was shorter and thinner than me and like most of the others, spoke with a noticeable American accent.

It was nice to be with sisters again. Cynthia reminded me of a cherub with her plump rosy cheeks, tiny pink mouth and large light blue, innocent eyes. Her curly blonde hair was so fine; it fell to her shoulders, like threads of gold. She is such a beautiful sister, I thought. I could feel the love emanating from her as I watched her over the next few days. She was one of the first up in the morning, bringing toast and coffee to sleeping angels. She was always serving; totally 'blissed out' to be serving. I learned some lessons about unselfishness through her.

Robert did a lot of the cooking. He was an extremely gentle, quiet brother. His grey hair and beard and weathered face revealed he was our senior physically, but 'the spirit' was what was real.

One day while in a grocery store, we connected with Sister Rose. She had dark eyes and hair, looked to be in her thirties and was an unusual sister, as I sensed right from the start. She was like the Christ Family's version of a women's libber. She was loud, strong-willed and clearly stated her aversion to the whole 'spiritual mate trip.' She didn't follow a brother and wasn't afraid to make herself heard. Jan told me later that Rose was her earth mother and that she had two other daughters in the 'Family,' as well. Sister Rose came right up to us in that grocery store as if she had known we would be there and said, "Hey, I've just got out of jail; nice hotel stay, warm bed, shower and room service. Not too much righteous food to eat, though. Good to see you, guys. Hawaii is great. Praise God!"

"What were you arrested for, Rose?" Calvin asked.

"A sister of the world wanted to 'transform' so we took her car and 'hit the wind.' Her parents flipped out and had me arrested for kidnapping and stealing a car. The sister crumbled when it came down to the crunch and went back to the world; no backbone; wouldn't have survived this lifestyle anyway."

She would have made a good army lieutenant, I thought to myself. I wondered why she was allowed to break the sister mould and still be regarded as a respected 'older sister.'

One day in camp, we awoke to find that an avocado tree had fallen down. These trees grew everywhere, in Hawaii. The winds had been wild the night before and the tree must have come down in the storm. So we all gathered up the fruit into a few basket containers we found in the shack. Calvin and Jan took over half the avocados to a local health food store and sold them. Again, I was taken off guard. I thought we were not supposed to buy, or sell God's free gifts. Why not just give them away?

After a few days, Richard and I both got itchy feet and we 'hit the wind.' It was such a wonderful feeling, walking down the tropical highway going nowhere and feeling so high. I walked praising God with my entire being. I loved everything around me with a passion. A hibiscus flower caught my eye and being slow enough with my thought, I was able to crawl right 'inside' and merge with it. It is so hard to describe this feeling; mere words fall short. No thoughts distracted me from this 'communion.' It happened with flies, trees, birds, animals and especially with my brother. Richard and I would sometimes seem to merge into one being, mostly at night while gazing at the infinite sky.

I consciously practiced being tuned in to my brother's needs and thoughts. This involved shutting off my thinking mind to allow myself to be open to his. Many times I knew what he was about to say before he said it, as if I had heard his thoughts first. When we walked, I concentrated on keeping in perfect step; no easy feat since he was about six foot four. When he preached, I heard his words in my head, moments before he was saying them.

One day as we were walking, there was a banana tree a little way off the road. Richard howled like a monkey and ran up to it, climbed the trunk with his legs wrapped around it and broke off the ripest bunch of bananas. On his way back to the road he found a coconut which had fallen to the ground and with arms full and face beaming he walked toward me with nature's free gifts. Everything we called out for was given: *". . . Ask and you shall receive . . . ." (John 14:13)* The miracles that took place in our lives every day astounded me. I knew that God was taking care of us. We sat down by the side of this tropical road and had a picnic. The bananas were fantastic. There just isn't anything that beats the taste of fresh fruit from the tree; no chemicals, no adulteration by the hand of man and no price tag on God's free gifts. The coconut wasn't easy to eat because the shell was so hard to break. Richard ended up doing it, though, using a huge rock. Everything was so simple and basic. I loved it.

Soon afterwards, a bright blue sports car passed us by and then stopped, with brakes squealing. A young man stuck his head out the window. "Hey, you guys want a ride somewhere?"

"Right on, brother," Richard said as we gathered our bedrolls and climbed in.

"So what's with the funny clothes?" The driver asked.

"You're the one wearing funny clothes," Richard answered and we all laughed.

"Do you people smoke pakalola?" He asked.

"We sure do, brother." Richard told him.

"Well, I just happen to have some really good stuff. I'll give you a couple of joints for later on, when you don't have to move, or do anything," he told us with a grin. Sure enough, when he let us off he gave Richard two fat joints. Richard was like a child who has just received a wonderful gift. I didn't care either way, although lately I had been learning not to fight it as much and was almost enjoying it.

We walked a short way before the heat of the day brought perspiration and exhaustion. The plastic water bottle that I carried with me was empty and I had such an unbearable thirst. That was one thing I couldn't stand. I could go without food, but to go without water was so hard. I looked out over the ocean and wished that I could go swimming without my robe; wished the ocean was full of fresh, clean water.

We took refuge from the sun under a massive tree. "We are sitting under a macadamia tree!" Richard informed me, as he looked up. We sat there, eagerly cracking the hard-shelled nuts with rocks. The task was tedious, but well worth it.

As usual, we were stared at by the people in passing cars. At one point, a whole parade of police cars drove past us. Then after a while a red truck pulled up and the driver offered us a ride. "So what are you people all about?" He asked.

"We're just working for the Lord, brother, living 'the truth' and spreading the word." Richard told him.

"Oh yeah, well, what's 'the truth'?"

"There are three keys which we live by. They are the keys to heaven which unlock the doors that keep us out. Killing, sex and materialism keep us from true sight; from heaven. You see, heaven is right here, we choose it. It's in our hearts; a state of being."

"So what do you call yourselves?"

"We are the Christ Family. We follow Jesus Christ who is walking the earth right now in a physical form," Richard went on.

A short time later the truck rolled to a stop. "This is as far as I go. Would you happen to have a joint I could buy from you?"

"We don't have one for sale, brother, but I just happen to have received two from the brother who gave us our last ride, so I'll give you one of them. Sister?" Richard motioned to me to get the joint out of my tote sack; so I handed it to him and he handed it to the brother. The man seemed uptight all of a sudden and his facial expression changed. He jumped out of the truck, came over to my side and pulled me violently out and handcuffed me. Just as he did this, two other cars screeched to a halt behind us and two men rushed over and handcuffed Richard to a police officer. "Anything you say can and will be held against you," we were told.

For a moment I thought I was dreaming, or that it was all a big joke, or something. It didn't seem real. In this situation most people would feel fear. My physical freedom was being taken from me. Richard and I had been separated. But, I knew I was exactly where I was supposed to be. I was being taken to jail for a reason that only God knew. I felt secure in knowing that God was in charge of writing this movie and that He wouldn't put me through anything I couldn't handle.

"So, how do you feel towards me now, little Christ?" The officer asked me as we pulled away in his red truck. He had a sinister grin on his face. He was so proud of his scam.

"I still love you, brother and pity you, too. You think you are in control, but you are in the same boat as I am. God is running this movie. You're just playing your role."

He seemed disappointed that I wasn't afraid, or nervous. "We'll see how calm you are when you're locked up and you're going to be there for a long time. We know more about you than you think. There are more charges than just one." I wondered what on earth he was talking about. I had never been arrested before.

When we arrived at the jail, he made a big show of power tripping by pulling me into the building by my long braids and saying loudly, "Come on, little Christ, let's see God save you now."

All the officers laughed mockingly. But, I thought about Jesus when He was brought to trial, it actually felt good to be persecuted for Him. Then he threw me into a putrid smelling cell and slammed the door. I landed on the dirty floor. I had never seen such a gross place. The worst was a urinal that had every type of human excrement all over it and the surrounding floor around. I stood up and walked over to the old cot. Its springs were broken and there was a dirty, stinky grey blanket covering it. I sat at the edge of the cot, closed my eyes and prayed for strength and endurance. I visualized beauty, nature, walking through the Hawaiian forests, anything to take me away from this place.

After a few hours, another officer took me to a room where they took my fingerprints and mug shots. Then the chief came in for questioning. There was some misunderstanding. They thought I was someone else. As I had no passport, I had to give them my parent's phone number for proof of who I was.

"Where is my brother?" I asked.

"Don't you worry about him, we're taking care of him," he said. I didn't like the sound of that. When I returned to my cell I heard Richard's voice.

"Sister, are you O.K.?"

"Richard, where are you?" I was so glad to hear him.

"I'm in the next cell. I saw them bringing you back in." Don't space on anything. Just 'kick back' and 'watch the movie.'

His words were interrupted by a harsh voice barking at us. "No talking."

That's O.K. with us, I thought, we don't 'need' words. The illusion would have us believe we are in separate cells. In reality we are one.

Hours later we were brought out, handcuffed again and taken into the dark night in two separate police cars. "We are transporting you to the state prison in Hilo," the officer driving my car informed me. Another officer sat beside me. We drove about fifteen miles to the next county line and there waiting for us were two more police cars and four officers. They switched handcuffs on us and transferred us into new cars. Richard winked at me with child-like humor as he was crammed into the police car. I preached to the officers all the way to the next county line, where we played the little charade again. I was amused at the irony of being treated like highly dangerous criminals when in reality we literally wouldn't hurt a fly. At the fourth switch-over, the last officer couldn't find his keys to my handcuffs, so I just slipped them off my tiny wrists and handed them to him. The shocked look on all of their faces was hilarious!

We reached the prison late at night. A matron took me to my cell, went through my tote sack and took away the Bugler tobacco. The room was clean with white walls, a sink, toilet and a decent bed. It looked like a motel room. I remembered how Rose had described jail and smiled to myself. I lay on the bed wishing I could have a Bugler and drifted off . . . .

Next morning, the matron was indifferent and cold, but she was not cruel. First I was instructed on how to keep the cell clean. She then took my robe for washing and accompanied me to the shower. The shower felt fabulous. It had been a while since I had one. Refreshed, I was escorted back to my cell.

One of the guards was drawn to me. He asked me all sorts of questions and we had the most peculiar preaching sessions through the little slot where the food came through. He agreed with most of our beliefs and looked at me with a sense of respect and reverence. "This is why I am here," I thought to myself. For the rest of my stay, every time he passed by my door on his rounds he would throw a cigarette under it and I would smile at him. It felt good to have a buddy at this time, although I wondered where Richard was and what he was doing. It felt strange to be away from him.

There was a Bible in my room and I spent much of my day reading it. I also had the time to contemplate, so I thought about all the lessons that God had been teaching me. I was learning the gift of patience, sitting in jail, or on the freeway for hours that turned to days, knowing that I was right where God wanted me to be. I thought about the times we had walked for long distances in cold, rainy weather without food and the faith it took to remain high and above the negative state of mind. I reflected on the patience and understanding that were needed to take a new brother and sister down the road and 'take a dive' into their space.

Another lesson was learning to turn the other cheek. This was something that was done inwardly, with your heart. I was learning to see God in everyone and let His light overcome the darkness. I didn't feel angry towards the police brother who had arrested us. Even when he had mocked me, I still felt love for him. I saw him as more of a victim than myself, because I knew God was running the whole show and he didn't.

The role of the servant is truly the role of the king. I was beginning to see what Jesus had meant by *". . . the first will be last and the last first . . . ." (Matthew 19:30)*. To serve and give freely without any thought of self creates an uplifting feeling. The irony of it all is that although you are exalting another by serving them, you in turn are also exalted. We reap what we sow It's a universal law that when you give, you receive. I was learning this on so many levels and also the depths of true giving, where thoughts of rewards disappear into the infinite vastness of 'the spirit.'

One day, I heard footsteps outside the room and they stopped at my door. Then a cigarette rolled under the door and I got out of bed to get it. I peeked through the food slot and saw the legs of my 'connection,' Peter, walking away. He usually stopped to talk in the evening when everything was quiet. I knew I could go for days without a smoke, but why did I feel excited to have one? We weren't supposed to be addicted to anything but love.

Later, I pondered on the lessons I was being taught about physical pain. A large part of pain involves focusing your energy on it, or thinking about it. If you direct your energy from the pain source, you don't think about it and don't feel it as much. Giving in to pain is allowing yourself to dwell on its negativity, reinforcing it. I also realized that the power of positive thinking can be used to convert pain into joy. My imaginary converter button allowed me to convert everything into good. If the button was shut off, if my awareness level dropped, I would push it back on and watch. Therefore, outside worldly influences were shut down to a minimum.

I was learning to dwell in the here and now, leaving the past and learning the true meaning of forgiving. This involved letting go of any bad memories, or feelings, in order to empty myself so that I could be free to be filled with God's love and awareness in the moment. I was learning that reality is only what happens in the moment and how we take away from it by hanging onto the past, or projecting into the future. When one lives in the past, or the future, he is robbing the present moment of its reality.

I was also seeing the importance of 'dying to one's self.' There are so many habits and ways of thinking that we are programmed into from early childhood. Influences fly at us from all directions, so that a child, being like a large sponge, absorbs it all and makes his evaluations of what reality is. I had picked up a lot of undesirable habits, or personality traits that I was now leaving behind, as I plunged into the Christ consciousness of truth and true love. Jealousy, envy, covetousness, adorning the flesh, depression, anger, hatred, false ego, pride, ambition, most emotions on various levels and many more human attributes, I now saw as unholy. There was so much going on inside of me that could not be seen. I was going through so many levels of 'mind' and 'the higher self' which we called the 'Christ mind.' There was a constant battle between these two minds and as the old, or lower self was conquered, I was able to see things that I couldn't see before. Each day was patterned to teach lessons and bring revelations. There was so much depth to the little truth the Lord was teaching me. Some of these lessons had to be learned over and over until they became a part of me. The most important one seemed to be the constant dying to my 'old self,' to allow God's Spirit to direct me, "... *to love God with your whole heart soul and mind* ....." *(Mathew 22:37)* Another one that kept coming up was to look for God in everyone and realize that we are all connected and part of each other, "... *to love your neighbor as yourself* ...." *(Mathew 22:39)*

I didn't feel locked up and frightened. I knew I was right where I was supposed to be and I praised God for all of the gifts he was showering me with.

Soon, Peter was convinced that vegetarianism was the way for him. The Lord sets up many situations to bring His word to all sorts of places. Our trial came up, after three days of prayer and fasting because the food they brought me was poisoned with flesh and dairy products. The matron brought me to the courthouse and in the hallway I met Richard. Richard was handcuffed and wore blue jeans and a jailbird shirt. His eyes were the same, though. They sparkled with light and a peace that outside influences could not disturb.

The judge sat high on his pedestal, his gavel gripped tightly in his right hand. An air of worldly power surrounded him. I felt as though we were back in the time of Jesus, two thousand years ago. It was a closed court; only a few officers and guards sat in on it. Then the lawyer called Richard to the stand and the judge asked him to swear on the Bible to tell 'the truth.'

The court was ghostly quiet. The judge cleared his throat and said, "What do you plead to the crime of pushing drugs on a police officer?"

Richard turned to him and said, "Brother, God is my judge. He knows what happened. He knows the hearts of men. I don't plead.

The judge didn't know what to do with us. I could see the lines of confusion lying heavily on his face. Finally he said, "In this case I shall let the prosecuted chose their penalty. You may pay a fine of five hundred dollars, thirty days in jail, or pick up rubbish in a city park for three days." I couldn't help but compare him to Pilate, who washed his hands of the responsibility of sentencing Jesus.

The sweet smell of nectar filled the air and the brilliance of the sun surrounded us as we walked out of the prison doors. A deep sense of relief filled me as my whole body relaxed. I hadn't realized that I was so uptight. I sure felt thankful to be out of physical confinement. It was great to be 'in the wind' with my brother again. We both hadn't eaten in days so we went to a church nearby and the caretaker gave freely of peanut butter sandwiches. I don't ever remember sandwiches tasting so great. We walked down to the beach and had a picnic there, watching life in the tropics from the 'outside.' It was wonderful.

We slept on the beach near the park, our bodies facing east so the sun would wake us in the morning. We had to report to the park caretaker by seven a.m. and since we didn't wear watches and were not aware of time, we had to depend on 'Mother Nature.' It sure felt great to be in touch with her again.

By the time we had paid our dues, we were ready for a change of scenery. So we traveled around the island, resting on the beaches, preaching to the natives and tourists, and enjoying the wonders that fed our eye and souls. We sat by the ocean and watched a family of whales go by, their spouts rising as they went under the water and came out again and again. We met a guy on the beach whom Richard preached to and he asked Richard if I was a deaf mute, because I was silent. This made me feel good. I liked this new image of myself being quiet.

We made a 'connection' with a man who brought us to a macadamia nut factory and gave us more nuts than we could carry. Much to Richard's delight, there were many pakalola 'connections.' It was prevalent on the island.

When we sat on the beaches, I wished I could wear a bathing suit and swim in the ocean. I felt very hot in my long robe and wanted to rip it off and let the sun and ocean devour me. Christ Sisters weren't allowed to show their legs in case it took their brother's eyes off God. I never agreed with that, because if sex is not in your space, it's not in your space. I didn't think it was fair that brothers were allowed to swim in their boxer shorts and let the sisters see their legs and chests when we weren't. I think I only went in the water once. It felt uncomfortable when I came out, with my robes twisted and soaked and sticking to my body like wet toilet paper.

At last Richard and I ended up back at the old shack where the other brothers and sisters were still hanging out. They were all gathered in a circle on the front porch.

"You're just in time to hear some news from the mainland," a sister told us. I wondered how anyone knew we were all here and found it strange that she would be getting mail. "There is going to be a 'Family' gathering in Washington, D.C. in the first week of May," she read aloud. "All of the 'Family' will be there. There has never been a gathering like this one. Quickly get off the island and come to the gathering of the saints."

We were excited. Was this the 'blink out' we had been told of? The end of the physical world was always in the back of our minds. We knew it could happen at any time. I was eager for it at times, looking forward to shedding my skin and flying. Perhaps the time was now at hand.

That evening, a group of red-neck, bikers rode up to the cabin on motorcycles. They were decked out in black leather, chains, tattoos, knives; the works. One of them spoke to us as the others stared, exuding hate vibes and trying to scare us. "You weirdoes better split." He stopped to spit. "We found this place first and we claim it as ours. If you're not out of here by morning we'll have to blow you out." All seven of us just looked at him and didn't say a word. "I mean what I say, don't fool around with us. You'll be sorry," he yelled over the noise of the bike engines.

"No killing, no sex and no materialism, brother!" Calvin shouted as they pulled away.

I wondered if they heard. I wondered if it really would do any good. These guys must have been part of Satan's Choice, or Hell's Angels. They were on the opposite side of the fence, for sure. Were we going to let them kick us out? I was watching a suspense movie this time. I'd heard of many miracles that had happened to Christ Brothers in situations like this. God always pulled through, protecting the brothers and teaching the others a lesson. I believed that we couldn't die. We had already died and gone to heaven, so even if a bullet did hit me, I was sure God would protect me with some sort of miracle, such as the bullet bouncing off me and hitting the oppressor.

No preparations were made to move on. We slept there, sheltered from the rain by an old, leaky overhang. The sound of the rain was magnified by the tin roof and the air was so wonderfully sweet. I lay there breathing deeply, praising God.

The sounds of loud engines, accompanied by the shots of rifles, drowned out the bird's songs next morning. For the first time, I witnessed panic in a group of Christ Brothers as Calvin yelled for everyone to run into the bush. Richard grabbed my hand and started running through tall grass in the back of the cabin. I was laughing. I didn't really know why, but I found it funny. I didn't understand the fear. We can't die; we are God's people, I reasoned. We have a shield of white light around us. So why are we running for our lives?

A good distance away, we stopped and hid in the bushes and trees. My bare feet were cut and bruised, my long hair matted with twigs. If it had been up to me, I would have faced those devils. I knew God would protect me. "Why did we run, brother?" I asked Richard.

"God told us to, sister. Every situation is different. 'The spirit' directed Brother Calvin to do this and here we are. Those 'bastards' are not only ruthless, they are evil. They all had rifles!"

"I know, but God would have protected us, wouldn't He?" I asked, still confused.

"He has sister; He has." Richard told me. I still didn't understand, but I let it go. Believe, just believe, I told myself. So we stood there, hiding in the woods.

I still didn't understand why we were doing this, but to question was to doubt and to doubt was to allow Satan to overpower my mind. So I put aside all thought and just stood there and 'watched the movie' as we hid quietly among the fruit trees and tall grasses. No one said anything.

After what seemed like hours, we heard the engines of the bikes rev up and then take off. Calvin stood up. "Well, was that supposed to be a little push from Papa to get us moving; to leave the island?" He asked with a chuckle.

"Right on, brother," Patrick replied.

"I have a feeling this gathering, this Washington campaign, is the end of the world party that we've all been waiting for," Calvin continued. "I know that for me, I've been going through more lessons on killing, sex and materialism than ever. Everything seems to be quickened. The vibration of the world is getting denser and denser. The more saints that are being pulled out of it, the more evil it becomes. I sure have been feeling the battle scars from this war, man."

I looked at Calvin as he spoke, his deep brown eyes so filled with light. His face gave evidence of a hard, former life, but its new found softness overwhelmed the harshness. His hair, full and thick, was French-braided down the back. Like most of the brothers he was thin; his height I guessed at about five foot ten. He told us once that he had been a professional thief before he joined the group. He drove getaway cars, climbed towering buildings in a black suit, stole jewelry and valuables from the rich and helped out the poor; a modern day Robin Hood. I really liked Calvin.

"Well, let's get our gear and 'hit the wind'," he told us as we walked back to the shack. Richard and I went in the jeep with Calvin and Jan. The other Richard and Patrick took the truck.

For the next few days, our 'connections' were mainly in the car sales department, as we went from car lot, to car lot, trying to sell the vehicles. One evening while Jan and Calvin bought some food, Richard and I stood outside the grocery store handing out declarations. A tall, slightly husky woman came up to us. Her eyes were clear and as blue as the sea and I knew she would be a 'primo connection.' Like a sponge, she absorbed all that Richard had to say and still it wasn't enough. "You are all welcome to spend the night at my house," she told us. "Please do, I must talk to you more."

We followed her to a beautiful home up on a hill overlooking the ocean. A large picture window gave us a full view of the sea and shore. The T.V. held captive two young teenaged boys, who balked at their mother's command to shut it off. They both stared at all of us as if their house was being invaded by beings from another planet and then they disappeared. After they left, we all sat around in a circle on the living room floor and Richard carried on with the preaching.

It didn't take much for Joan to see the need for no killing. Already partly vegetarian, she still ate fish and dairy products. She could see the sense in it when the 'prop' was removed and we brought it down to energy. She could see that eating something that had been killed was a negative form of energy. She told us that she was a psychic and always interested in going against the 'norm.' She also knew that the end of the physical world was at hand. I guessed that she was in her late thirties and separated from her husband, supporting her two sons. Her heart was open and kind.

The next day, we cleaned out all the unrighteous food from her cupboards and all leather products. Her sons were opposed to this and also to our intrusion into their space. They never once ate with us while we were there and there was some mention of them going to MacDonald's for a 'flesh fix.' I could see the discord we caused in her family, as our one-night stay turned into two weeks.

Joan shared her home, food and shower with the six of us: Richard and I, Calvin and Jan, Patrick and Rick. Cynthia had left with Rose while Richard and I were traveling around the island and Robert had 'hit the wind' after the biker episode. Joan went to work each day and left us in her home while we cooked and cleaned for her. She confirmed to us that she believed we were who we said we were and that she believed in the second key as well. She took an oath of celibacy. However, she wasn't yet ready to 'hit the wind' with us. "God gave me these two boys to guide for a while. That's my duty. It's not right to drop my responsibility on someone else," she said.

174

Richard and I took long walks during our stay. One time, we were so full of joy and happiness that we skipped down a dirt road, going downhill and singing "Zippidy-doo-dah" all the way. The small rocks didn't hurt my feet as I pushed them along. We felt like little children, carefree and full of passion for life. I didn't want to leave the island. The others had been there for a lot longer and were ready for a change in scenery, but it seemed as if Richard and I had just got there. If there hadn't been such urgency about going to Washington, we would have stayed much longer. The trucks were sold now; the airplane tickets bought. We were leaving in a few days. We made cardboard and cotton sandals to be able to board the plane.

Joan drove us to the airport and with a sense of hesitation, bade us farewell with tear-filled eyes. "She's a sister," Calvin said as we climbed the stairs. "Has more karma to burn off yet, but definitely a sister." The plane glided off the ground as I gazed at the swaying palms and the green-blue water. I couldn't help it, I knew it wasn't cool, but I felt blue. I wanted to stay in Paradise.

❊ CHAPTER SEVENTEEN ❊

We landed in the city of the angels (L.A.) on a cold, dark, foggy, rainy day. What a contrast to Hawaii. Everyone felt as heavy as the weather. I could see it in their faces. Richard and I sat in a restaurant with Patrick and Italian Richard, while Calvin and Jan went to make a car 'connection.'

Rick's long thick, wavy, black hair flowed over his muscular body. His black eyes seemed to dance with excitement most of the time and he almost always had a smile on his face.

Patrick, lean and wiry, stood close to six feet. His long, dark brown hair hung straight down his back, usually tied in a pony tail. His hazel eyes had coolness about them, as though childhood hurts were storming behind them, waiting to be released. His narrow face was marked with the battle scars of adolescence. He didn't seem to like sisters, for some reason. I got the distinct feeling that he was just barely tolerating me.

We sat there in the restaurant, sipping coffee and smoking Buglers. I watched through the window as the rain slanted down into the traffic-laden streets. Was the Washington gathering really the big 'blink out?' Was I ready, worthy to be transformed into light? I still had so much to learn, I thought.

Calvin and Jan ran past the window, their robes soaked and their hair dripping water onto their faces. A few seconds later, they joined us where we were sitting. "We've got a car 'connection'," Calvin told us. "The deal is to drive this car cross country and deliver it to its owner in West Palm. You have to see this car, it's great."

Calvin's words faded as my thoughts overpowered them. I wondered where Ariss and Sol were right now. Were they happy? Did they miss me? I wondered why I still missed them, after all the battles of the mind I'd fought and continued to fight. If this was God's will, then why was it so hard for me? "Get behind me, Satan!" I ordered my 'finite mind.'

We left the fog and smog of L.A. in a white, four-seater, sports car. We were quiet. I felt like it was an uncomfortable silence and I wondered why.

We stopped to refuel somewhere near Yuma. There was a variety store at the gas station and Richard went in to pay for the gas. The rest of us sat in the car waiting for him. He was talking to two rowdy-looking cowboys, who followed him out of the store and to the car. We could hear the conversation now, through the open windows.

"Come on, have a beer," one of them said as he handed Richard a can of beer. I could smell the reek of alcohol coming from them.

"No, brother, we don't drink 'rotten grain,' but if you want to buy me something I'll have a pop," Richard answered kindly.

So he went inside the store to buy Richard a pop and the other man came to the window, peeked his head in and said, "Howdy you-all," oozing alcoholic breath as he spoke. "So where do you dudes work?" He asked Calvin.

"We don't work for man, or money brother. We work for God," Calvin answered him. But, the cowboy didn't understand and the effect of too many beers showed in his stupefied facial expression.

"I don't see how you can live without working." He spoke with a slurred, heavy, southern drawl.

"We don't have to work, brother; we have suckers like you who do that for us." Calvin had said the wrong thing. I saw fire rise up in that cowboy's eyes. Then Richard got in the car just as Calvin rolled up his window and squealed out of there. I had been shocked at his words. Brothers don't talk that way. He must be 'taking a dive,' I thought. A moment later we felt a bump from behind and sure enough, the two cowboys were ramming us with a huge, high-wheeled truck.

Calvin put his foot on the gas all the way until the speedometer needle disappeared. I could smell exhaust from the over-worked engine and hear the squealing of the truck gaining on us. This time they appeared beside us, heaving into us from the side, trying to push us off the road. The small car jolted with each push. I was sitting on the centre bump in the back, getting banged around.

What an incredible movie I'm watching, an action-packed, thriller-adventure, I thought. Fear forced its way into my mind as our car weaved again under the pressure from these brutes. We were traveling at an incredible speed, yet Calvin seemed to have total control. Calvin turned into a gas station, made a U-turn, jumped over the divider and charged out onto the dark highway. His stunt worked. It allowed us to gain some ground, but when I turned around, I saw those glaring high beams on our tail again within minutes. There were very few cars on the highway. It was a black starless night. Then I noticed an island, separating us from the oncoming traffic. Just as the truck inched its way beside us again, Calvin whipped the car around, jumped over the concrete island to the other side and bolted into the dark night. The cowboys never caught up with us after that. We all let out a laugh, but I wondered how everyone 'really' felt.

This trip was an incredible test of endurance for me. The long hours of driving in the smoke-filled, compact car with my body parts strained, cramped and aching. The battle with motion sickness was bad enough, but the strange vibrations and moods that everyone was going through were downright freaky. It was as if we truly had left paradise when we left Hawaii. Peace was swept away. Calvin and Jan were bickering like a married couple. Patrick's sour face gave evidence of turmoil brewing.

"I've got a message from 'the spirit' brothers. It's time to get back to the old way of things," he announced firmly. "This be nice, rejoice and enjoy and the 'spiritual mate' space have brought too many weird trips. Look at those two, arguing like a worldly couple. It's wrong. Touching one another is wrong! No massaging, no hair combing, no touching at all. The more energy we give the flesh, the more we are of it!"

"Right on, brother," Rick agreed. "If this gathering is the end of the world party, then we have a lot of cleansing to go through. Sounds like a good place to start."

I didn't know what to think. All I knew was that I was sitting in between Patrick, Rick and Richard and I wasn't supposed to "touch" them. Now how do you suppose four full-grown humans, three of them large men, could travel in a back seat meant for two people without touching? Patrick kept pulling away from me as if my body were poison. Even when I rolled him a Bugler and handed it to him, if my fingers touched his, he would frown and pull away. I had to make sure to be careful not to touch him in any way. It was crazy! To add fuel to the fire, Richard became increasingly quiet and withdrawn. I would look to him for stability and assurance in this insanity and receive a blank stare. This brother, who was my emotional backboard, my rock, was changing somehow and it scared me. I no longer heard his thoughts, felt his spirit dance with mine. When I looked into his eyes he looked different, as if he was gone! I sat there cramped, with bodies crowding me, but I was alone. I felt as if we were in a pressure cooker that was ready to explode. There were vibrations around that were not from God. What was going on? Was this hell, so that from it, we would spring that much farther into heaven? I was confused! At the same time, beyond all the craziness, I found an inner strength that I had not experienced since the Peru trip. It was the strength of my will to survive. This time it was turned inward, survival of 'the spirit.'

We slept in campgrounds along the southern highway heading east. The nights were still cold and I found it hard to sleep. Everyone seemed restless. Uneasiness encompassed us. Somewhere near New Mexico, Richard spoke to me for the first time in days. We had paused at a rest stop for a meal. He was not joining us for meals; had not eaten in days. I, too, felt anything but ravenous, but consumed enough to keep my strength up.

"Sister!" He beckoned to me from where he was standing by the car. I came over to him, hoping he had finally gotten over whatever was eating away at him and that things would go back to the way they were. But, as I approached him and saw those strange eyes, my heart sank. "I have been wrong in the way I've been attached to you," he said. "I think I am in love with you the way worldly people are in love. This is wrong. I don't know where I have gone wrong, but I missed the boat somewhere along the way. I am not worthy to live this life." He spoke in a monotone.

"Brother, come on; don't you think God has forgiven you? You have seen something unrighteous in yourself. Now you're repenting for it. Forgiveness means 'don't dwell.' Give it up; let go. You must forgive yourself." My words seemed to fall on deaf ears. I'm not sure if he even heard me. I wanted to hold him tightly and tell him everything was O.K. I wanted to take his confusion and pain away, even if I had to bear them for him. Yet I couldn't do either. The other brothers and sisters wouldn't approve if I hugged him. We were under the strict code of 'no touch' now. I also felt guilt. Had I caused this strong brother to fall?

As the days swept by, my heart was being torn apart as I watched my strong, righteous brother go deeper and deeper into regret and guilt. I had to be strong for him. This was one road I couldn't follow him down.

The scenery and outside world were like a dream to me. So much was happening on the 'inside,' I didn't enjoy the trip. I was battling the part of me that wanted to follow Richard into his pit of confusion. I could sense that the other brothers and sisters blamed me for his state, which created a vacuum in me, pulling me straight to God. There surely wasn't any support system on the outside. As for Richard, everyone ignored him as if nothing was happening. There was no talking about feelings, or even a desire to understand. He kept everything inside and it was eating away at him like acid on flesh. I was torn between upholding a strong Christ Sister image and wanting to take Richard out of there and talk to him in an attempt to try to help him. But, if I was the main cause of his problem, would I only make it worse? Was I the one who should comfort him, or should I stay away until he worked it out? I was hoping Calvin would help, but it seemed that everyone was going through their own trips and battles. This seemed ironic to me. I thought we were supposed to be the 'saints,' the ones with the hearts. I understood our belief in not feeding a negative space, or succumbing to the flesh, but this was a situation where a brother's state of mind was in jeopardy. I was tormented. I didn't know what to do. All I knew was that I had to be strong for him. I thought about all the times he had been strong for me. When I was missing the kids, when I doubted this whole thing, he pulled through for me. I prayed for Richard almost unceasingly. My own physical discomfort now seemed far away.

Was this 'storm' we were all going through just Satan trying to pull us all back from God because the end of the world was so close? Or, was it God's way of molding us into the best possible state in which to meet Him?

By the time we reached Florida, Richard had become an empty shell. His eyes were void of light and love and it seemed as if his gentle spirit was somewhere else. How I wished we would have stayed in Hawaii.

After delivering the car to its owner, we marched at a fast pace over sand spurs for hours. No one said a word. I emptied my mind chanting, "no killing, no sex and no materialism" over and over, and my aching, spur-filled feet seemed to drift farther and farther away. We walked this way, non-stop, into the night. The dark sky surrendered its rain as we kept walking. When is Calvin going to stop? I began to wonder. Eventually he turned off the road and led us down a dirt driveway to a building site where the shell of a house stood. The roof and outside walls were up, inside were plywood floors and stud walls. We rolled out our bedrolls on the cool, damp floor and Richard quietly snuggled into his bag beside me. I smiled at him, but received only that haunted empty stare in return.

In the middle of the night, I heard Richard scream. "Sister, Oh God, where am I? Who am I?" He was fumbling around in the dark. I heard him bump into a beam. "Sister, where are you?"

I jumped out of my bedroll to run to him, when a hand grabbed me and one of the brothers whispered a command, "Let him be, sister!"

My mind was racing. I wanted to comfort him like a mother would comfort a child. I wanted to hold him and tell him that everything was all right. Yet, I had to obey my brother. I had to be emotionless, to be strong. I lay there listening to him scream out in the darkness of his mind, so alone and so lost.

Again he cried out in anguish. "I'm lost! Where are you, God? Where are you sister?"

This was my brother, the closest being on earth to me. I had to help him. I needed to comfort him. "Come back to your bedroll, brother. You need to rest," I called to him, my voice nearly cracking and my guard on my emotions slowly losing its grip.

"I can't see, I don't know where to go," he called out pathetically.

"Follow my voice, Richard, follow your heart," I told him.

The other brothers said nothing. I felt Richard coming towards me and sat up in my bedroll, reaching out my hand to him. He gripped it desperately for a moment and then let it go. I felt better with him resting beside me again, but still could not feel the connection on the 'inside' that we had once had.

In the morning, sunbeams shot prisms of light through the open doorway. I looked over beside me. Richard was gone! I ran through the empty shell of the house, but I couldn't see him anywhere. I ran outside and found his white robe thrown on the gravel. It was wet and dirty, but I held it to my heart and looked to the horizon as tears filled my eyes.

No one mentioned Richard. Everyone just carried on as though nothing had happened. Guilt tried to creep up on me like a serpent slithering its way through my defenses. "You are to blame for this," it said. "No, I won't allow you to penetrate," I thought. God forgives instantly so I must, too. Guilt was Richard's downfall. I have to be strong and wise.

We drove to a Laundromat to wash our robes and while waiting for our army blankets to be cleaned, we sat outside. A police car pulled up beside us and there was Richard, sitting in his underwear. "Does he belong with you guys?" The officer asked.

"Yes, brother, he does," Calvin answered.

"No, I don't want to go with them! Take me to the hospital." Richard intervened, shaking his head. Was he asking to be brought to a mental hospital? Had he really lost his mind? "We'll take care of him, brother," Calvin told the policeman. Richard got out of the car and walked past us to the other side of the small mall. None of us knew what to do.

"Can I go to him, brother?" I asked Calvin.

"Yes, you have something to do with this, sister. Go to him," Calvin answered.

I got up and walked to my brother. He sat all curled up, hands wrapped tightly around his knees, head down and nothing on but his boxer shorts. "Brother, what can I do for you?" I asked him. "Tell me, what do you want me to do?"

"I want you to follow your brother, sister. Just follow me," he answered. Was this what it was all about? Did he feel that I didn't want to travel with him anymore? I clung to a small ray of hope that this was all it was about.

"I'll follow you, brother," I told him. He smiled at me. He actually smiled. Things were looking up. Then he got up and started walking around to the back of the mall and I followed him. Around and around he went, in a circle around the mall, past the others, over and over. I just followed him, not knowing what was going on. Maybe he was testing me? It must have looked weird, this long-haired, bearded, tall, middle-aged man in white boxer shorts, leading this woman in a white robe, around a building, twenty times.

Calvin finally stopped the nonsense by throwing Richard his clean robe and saying, "Let's 'hit the wind.'"

As we walked, Richard asked me for one of the declaration pamphlets that I carried and I gave him one. The next minute he handed it back to me and then asked for it again. Then, when we got a ride in the back of a pick-up, he asked me for a hair tie. I gave it to him and he tied his hair in a pony tail. A few minutes later he handed it back to me and then asked for it again. Was he testing me, or was he out of his mind? These things went on until the next day.

It was Palm Sunday and we were asked into a church basement to share the Palm Sunday meal. There was a huge gathering and lots of food. Richard was totally dazed by this time and I had to get his food for him and feed him. When I lit him a smoke, he put the wrong end in his mouth and burned himself.

"I just have to follow you, sister, right?" He said to me as he got up and went outside. When I went out to see where he had gone, he had disappeared.

I was so confused. Who do I follow? I wondered. I thought about leaving the others, but I remembered that Lightning didn't want us to travel solo anymore. Would I ever see Richard again? Would he ever be well again? Would I ever feel peace again?

❋ CHAPTER EIGHTEEN ❋

O ver the next few days I plodded along the sidewalk behind Jan and the others, on 'cruise control,' 'automatic trucking.' Richard never left my thoughts. A part of me had disappeared with him that day . . .

Once again, the others never spoke of him, or what had transpired. Why? Could what happened to Richard not be explained, was it not part of the program? My thoughts were interrupted by a man who came running out after us as we passed his house.

"Brothers, wait. I have been praying for you to come. I met some brothers a few months ago. I wasn't ready to join then, but I am now. Come on into my home and get cleaned up," he said excitedly. He was a young man in his early twenties, I guessed; tall and wiry with green eyes encased in long lashes. We stayed at his small house for a few days, 'liquidating' his material possessions. I learned that now, when a new member joined, his possessions were sold and the money placed in the Christ Family bank account. This seemed strange to me. I thought we were supposed to give our possessions to the poor. Why did we need a bank account? I asked Calvin about it.

"We don't want to give it to Satan anymore, sister. This is a war we are fighting. Anyone who is not with us, is against us," he answered me.

The new brother, Ted, had a red Volkswagen travel van. Calvin and Jan became caretakers of it. We met a large group of Christ Brothers in a park. We slept all together that night, under the stars. I had hoped that Richard would be one of them, but he wasn't there. It felt strange to roll out without him by my side.

The next day, after a breakfast of coffee and bread, we were told that it would be too hard to travel in such a large group so we were sent out in twos and threes and told of a rendezvous spot; some park in Jacksonville. Patrick was appointed to travel with me and he wasn't at all pleased. He didn't like traveling with sisters, let alone one who he thought had caused the downfall of a brother.

"Well, let's 'hit the wind'," he groaned to me as I picked up my bedroll and ran to catch up to him. He was trucking at an incredibly fast pace on the shoulder of the highway. The Florida noon sun was melting me; perspiration covered my body. I had been experiencing some sort of flu and today it was bad. Sandspurs stuck to the bottom of my feet as we marched in that desert-like heat.

"Can we stop and rest a bit brother?" I humbly asked, after what seemed like hours.

"No! Get out of 'your horse,' sister. If you're not strong enough to be in the Lord's Army than get out," he bitterly answered me. I chanted the three keys in an attempt to keep centered, concentrating on keeping up with my brother, until my head became dizzy and I collapsed by the side of the road. Then I realized that I had the Bugler can, so I pulled it out of my tote sack and called, "Brother!" Holding the can out to him. He whipped around, snatched the can from me and left me in the dust!

I lay there alone, head spinning, body too weak to get up. My physical body always seemed to get in the way of things. I'd been experiencing so many 'creature features' on the road and I was getting really tired of it. Thoughts of Richard, the children and my parents bombarded my mind as I dove into the realm of self-pity. Where had that crystal-clear perception gone? Where was I? I had no idea where the gathering place was in Jacksonville.

The thought of going home flashed across my mind just as a red pickup pulled up beside me and stopped. A man got out and asked me if I was O.K. "Do you need a ride? I suddenly became aware of the reality of rape. But, then I heard a voice inside say, "Where is your faith." I was able to shut out any more negative thoughts. I preached to this man as we drove, which helped me to feel more centered and strong. I asked him to keep his eyes open for Patrick and I watched the road too, looking for him. I hoped that we would pick him up, but he must have gotten another ride because we never saw him.

I was dropped off in the rain by a small store on the outskirts of Jacksonville. So, I went in and asked the man where the closest church was. He told me it was a few miles down the road beside the store and gave me a soda which seemed to help calm my stomach. Walking down that winding road, I felt stronger. Now I was going to have the opportunity to communicate with the Holy Spirit without the middleman of a brother. It was safer to travel with a brother, but I was going to have to get used to it and exercise faith as I never had before. Something inside of me smiled at this thought. Yet as I walked, I couldn't stop my mind from focusing on Ariss and Sol again. I missed them so. I wondered how they were adjusting to their new life and if they remembered me. I sang Christ Family songs to fight the thoughts that were sure to drag me into untruths.

There was no one at the small wooden church. I was almost completely soaked by now since it had been raining for a while. Wondering where to go, I scanned a group of mobile homes near the church and felt a 'pull' to one of them. I walked over to it and knocked on the door. A young, overweight woman with shining blue eyes flung the door open and gasped, covering her mouth with her hand as she drew back.

"Don't be frightened, I'm just a traveling Christian in need of a meal and a place to rest for the night. I went to the church, but no one was there. I thought perhaps you could help me," I told her.

"Oh, excuse me. You startled me. I thought you were an angel for a moment. The Pastor is out of town. I'm Kate. Come in before you get your death of cold; come in."

The trailer was cluttered with kids toys, and magazines, and unwashed dishes. She moved some dirty laundry from the couch, making me a spot to sit. "Would you like a glass of lemonade?" she asked.

"Praise God for your love," I nodded affirmatively. Just then a little girl came running into the room with a book in her hand. She was beautiful, with curly blonde hair, deep blue eyes and a pug nose. "What's your name?" I asked her.

"Sally," she said, a little shy. "I have a baby sister whose name is Trixie, I'm three and she is one. Will you read this to me?" She handed me the book. As I read it, the words didn't register because I was thinking about Ariss and Sol. They were the exact age that these children were. Sally even looked like Ariss. She must be talking now; Sol must be walking. I praised God for sending me here to be able to love these children as my own for a while. I would go through times when I needed to hold a baby so badly. This was one of them and He pulled through for me again.

Kate offered to wash my robe and said I was free to have a bath. What a treat. It had been a while and although I washed the best I could at restrooms, it never compared to a nice long soak. When I got out, I washed all the dirty dishes and cleaned up the kitchen for her. She protested at first, but was very pleased when the job was finally done. "Frank is going to wonder what happened today. He's going to want to keep you around for a while," she winked at me.

"Well, sister, just returning the kindness you've shown me." I had always believed in cleanliness and order and so did the Christ Family. If my space was clean around me, I felt clean inside. Whenever we were invited into a home, I always 'zenned' (cleaned) the place if the owners allowed me to.

I enjoyed playing with the kids. Kate didn't seem to receive much of what I preached, so I just left it at that. There are times when actions speak louder than words. Although she thought my diet was peculiar, she made something righteous for me to eat. She and her husband let me spend the night and offered me a ride into Jacksonville in the morning. Since I had given the Bugler to Patrick I was glad that these people smoked and shared their smokes with me. That night, I rested on their couch.

In the morning Frank and I looked at a map of the city, trying to locate the park where I would meet the others, but I had no idea where it was. So Frank picked out a park that would be likely, one of the largest in the city and they drove me there. They had made me a lunch of peanut butter and jelly sandwiches and some fruit. There was a large gospel gathering in this park, but no white robes in sight. I roamed around for hours, eyes drawn to white clothing, but the brothers weren't there. I wondered where I should go from here. I asked someone where the highway heading north was and they told me it was way over on the other side of town.

A man stared at me when I sat down. His clothes were tattered and his face unshaven and dirty. He sat across from me and watched me take out my lunch and eat a sandwich. I walked over to him and gave him the other one and my apple. "Thanks," he said, and started eating it ravenously.

Finally I left the park and headed to the north end of town. Hours later, the sun was setting and my feet were tired. I found shelter that evening by a grand oak tree in a school yard. Its ancient branches spread over me like an umbrella. The birds that made it their home sang their sunset songs. My stomach growled as I thought of the sandwich I had given away. I felt strange here out in the open, all alone. I missed Richard, I missed my children, I missed my parents, Don, Ed, Will, Judy . . . . "Stop it," my 'Christ mind' ordered. "Self-pity is of Satan."

Again, I battled my mind's fear of rape. I had to trust God fully to protect me and convince myself that if something hurtful happened, it would be for a reason. This was truly a test in overcoming fear.

The streets were quiet when I walked through them that morning. The sun spread beams of soft light, creating a dreamlike atmosphere. The birds were chirping from all directions, actually harmonizing. I felt great! The fact that I hadn't had a smoke, or eaten, seemed far beyond me somehow. But, I wondered why the streets were so deserted. Up ahead, I saw the steeples of a group of churches and headed in their direction. It was part of our job to 'test' the churches. We were to see how giving these people who claimed to know Jesus and have a handle on truth, truly were. Then I saw someone walking towards me. We were the only two people on the street. As she passed me we exchanged smiles. "Happy Easter," she said with a warm smile.

"And to you sister, praise God." I replied. So it was Easter, I had had no idea. Surely one of the churches will give freely of a meal in the name of Christ, I thought. Sometime later, the fourth church door was slammed in my face. Not one of them! 'Pharisees,' hypocrites! I felt anger; like the righteous anger that Jesus felt towards the 'Pharisees.' They preach about love, but their actions are without love, I fumed to myself. They make a show of holiness in front of men, but inside they are like serpents ready to bite. There were times when we did find hearts in the churches. Many of the priests and preachers were genuinely giving, showing true Christianity, but here in Jacksonville, on Easter Sunday, I found no heart.

As I made my way out of town, a bright orange sports car pulled up beside me and a man with long, light brown hair got out. His eyes sparkled as he beckoned to me.

"Hi! What's the sack cloth for? What do you believe in?"

"That's a loaded question, brother, do you have all day?"

"Sure do!" He replied with a grin.

"Well, I have died to the world and myself; my robe is my white flag of surrender. I've surrendered my will to God and He uses me now and directs my life. I have forsaken all for Him; all desire, all attachment, all of me. You see, it's the end of the world party, brother, Jesus Christ is back on earth and we are His followers, proclaiming 'the truth.'"

He sat there gazing at me, with awe and respect reflected in his clear eyes. "Will you come home with me and tell me more? I can cook a meal for you and give you what you need."

"That would be right on, brother, but there is one thing I must clear with you first. I am celibate. We believe sex is a sin, the downfall of man. That is the second key to heaven, no sex. So if you will respect that, I will come."

"Yes, I can understand you more than you know," he said with a smile. He couldn't stop asking me questions. "You mentioned something about no sex being the second key, what are the others?"

"No killing is the first key to heaven consciousness. On the physical level it means not taking any life. We don't kill bugs, birds, or animals. We don't pay a hit man to do it, either, which means we are strict vegetarians; no leather, no dead flesh, no eggs, cheese, milk or honey. If you give life and freedom you will receive life and freedom. You reap what you sow."

He sat there, listening with open ears and heart as I continued. "On the ethereal level, no killing goes very deep. I'm still learning lessons about it. It is awareness to not have one bad feeling about your brother, to stop the constant judgment. It also means to stop the carnal-thought life and rise above your 'finite mind' where hate, jealousy and envy live; to die to that mind and let God fill it with new and holy thoughts. We call that new mind the 'Christ mind.' It has the ability to convert negative to positive. It is able to love truly the way God wants us to love, without thought of self, giving whole-heartedly. To die to your earthly ego and be given a new ego that is totally the opposite of the old one. Instead of everything being taken inward greedily, for self, it's given to everyone around you. These ideas are the wings that enable us to fly above this earthly plane and dwell in a heavenly one. You see, we don't have to wait until our physical forms die and change in order to go to heaven. Heaven is within us. Heaven is right now, for those of us who chose it."

"Do you have a name, you angel from God?" He asked me.

"My 'handle' is Maureen, Maureen Christ."

"Mine is Greg and I am so happy to meet you, Maureen. Everything that you have told me sounds right to me. The only thing I question is the eating of dairy products. You see, I've been a vegetarian for years also, but I eat milk and yogurt. What's wrong with it, we aren't hurting the animals by using their by-products, are we?"

"We are hurting them by abusing them," I answered. "Cows are no longer cows, they are milking machines. They are artificially inseminated and then when they give birth, the baby is snatched away and not allowed to nurse because man wants the milk. The mother doesn't get the satisfaction of seeing, or being with her child. It is fed soy milk, which man should be drinking, if he really thinks he needs milk, but man is the only species that never weans off milk. He just thinks he needs it. Cow's milk is for cows, cat's milk for cats, goat's milk for goats, dog's milk for dogs and breast milk for humans. It's simple; it is only natural. Chickens are also abused and not allowed even to sit on their eggs until they hatch. They are all crammed together and given hormone shots for bigger eggs. They have no freedom anymore. They've been adulterated for the dollar bill and our demand for their products. There is nothing natural left in the raising of animals. They are used and abused and I don't want to support that system of greed and cruelty," I told him.

"I see where you are coming from," he said still deep in thought, absorbing it all. "Here we are; I've been driving in circles for a while not wanting to disturb the flow with a change in scenery." We both laughed.

I felt comfortable with him, as if he was a brother. Some day I will see him in a robe, I thought. He got out a can of Drum tobacco and rolled himself a smoke before getting out of the car. "Far out, brother, you smoke roll-your-owns, too; and Drum is from Canada."

He looked over at me, surprised. "You smoke? I never thought you would. I've wanted one for a while now, but thought you wouldn't like smoke blowing in your face. You want one?" I nodded, "Yes" and smiled. "Let me roll them brother." Amused with me, he grinned and handed me the can. I hadn't noticed how much I enjoyed rolling until then.

His house was one of those huge, old brick ones with lots of character; round dormers, stained glass windows, just downright grand. Greg rented an apartment on the main floor. Inside were hardwood floors, window and door frames. In the middle of the living room, a life-sized poster of a swami sitting cross-legged stared back at me. There was a hint of incense hanging in the air. The apartment was clean and tidy. The living room and kitchen were huge and there were two bedrooms. One was Greg's and the other was an empty room, where he told me that I could put my stuff, so I rolled out my bedroll on top of my army blanket. Greg even handed me a pillow. What a treat! I had slept without a pillow for so long now, but I really preferred one. I felt comfortable in his home. It reminded me of my own former home, it had the same feeling.

"How about a meal of fried rice and vegetables?" Greg suggested.

"Right on. The body hasn't seen food for a while. I'll help you."

We flowed in the kitchen, the way Don and I used to. I chopped the vegetables and he cooked the rice and did the frying. I had the distinct feeling that I knew him from somewhere; another lifetime, perhaps? When he got out the wooden bowls and chopsticks, I knew this was a definite setup from God and I thanked Him. I loved eating with chopsticks and wooden bowls; not too many people in our culture do.

To eat, we sat on the living room floor on one of those eastern-type area rugs, cross-legged. Greg put on some quiet music and we ate by candle-light. I guess I hadn't known how lonely I'd been for an understanding spirit until now. We shared a wonderful meal; the energy was high.

"I have traveled to India in search of some meaning to life and my purpose here," he told me. "I found many pearls of wisdom in my travels. Much of what you believe in, I have heard before, but I have never met anyone like you. You amaze me. You are truly 'living' it. I feel so much respect for you," he told me.

"You can live it too, brother. God has sent me here to show you how," I said. "No killing, no sex and no materialism are the keys that open up the door to truth and spirit. They are just the beginning of a totally different life. They strip you of so many distractions that come between you and God. The answers unfold as you live this life."

"I just can't see myself living without sex. Don't get me wrong; although I would love to share that with you, I respect your choice. I just don't think I'm ready to give up my sexual nature, or my physical comforts yet. I know you're right. I admire you for having enough strength to do it," he said.

I looked at him, his eyes so sincere and his brown hair falling to his shoulders in a gentle wave. He was good-looking, about six feet tall, lean yet strong. I guessed he was in his late twenties. After our meal we lay on the floor and listened to a tape of a Guru telling parables. It was great. A lot of our beliefs were the same and I now knew why Greg understood me. How I wished he would follow me down the road.

He had a party the next day, out in the back yard, and I got the opportunity to preach to a lot of people. They were playing music, drinking, playing badminton, having fun. A part of me looked at that carnal fun and yearned for it. I knew too much to be able to be amused in such a worldly way, but there was a small part of me that seemed to miss it, somehow. It wasn't easy being the outsider; the strange one.

Greg took me to all the parks in town, searching for the brothers. I stuck my head out his sun window on the roof of the car and scanned each park for white robes. They were none in sight. So I decided that I wasn't supposed to meet them; besides, I was doing just fine, trucking solo. He also took me on one of his weekly adventures of going through the rich section of town on garbage day and going through the garbage.

"You know the old saying; 'one man's garbage is another's treasure.' You should see some of the stuff these people throw out," he told me with that grin of his. We got back to his pad with a car-full: roller skates, a T.V., a frying pan, an old trunk.

For the next few days, Greg went to work and I stayed at his home and had a hot meal ready for him when he returned. But, I was getting too comfortable and knew that it was time to 'hit the wind.'

I caught a ride with him one morning to the university where he taught art and we said our farewells. "Praise God for all your love, brother, I really enjoyed myself. I'll see you 'in the wind' some day," I told him.

"I will never forget you, Maureen." His hazel eyes gave a hint of sorrow as we parted.

Walking through the city towards the freeway, I was feeling great. I felt secure in my faith in God to take care of me and guide me. The fact that it could be months before I connected with another brother or sister didn't bother me anymore. I had my 'shield of faith,' my 'helmet of salvation,' my 'breastplate of righteousness' and my 'sword of truth.' Satan could try to defeat me, but I knew that I had already won. I was with Jesus; the light of the world.

After a few hours, I passed by a small park on the other side of the road and saw a circle of white monuments in it. I was interested to see what the statues looked like, but not wearing glasses and being nearsighted, I couldn't see far. I headed across the road towards the park. As I approached them, the statues turned into two Christ Sisters and a Brother! I could feel my heart beating faster with excitement. "Howdy, sister," one of them called to me. "Are you with anyone?"

"Yes, brother, with God," I replied. We all laughed. Two of them looked familiar; I had seen them in camp. They weren't part of the group that was meeting here, but they were the ones I was supposed to meet. Here, once again, I witnessed proof of the theory, 'give it up and you get it back.' I had finally given up on finding the brothers and settled into trucking solo and God gave it back.

"Where were you heading, sister?" Brother Tom asked.

"To the freeway heading north; to the Washington campaign, God willing," I answered. "Mind if we join you?" He asked, grinning a bit sarcastically.

"Right on, brother; would be honored."

So now the four of us were heading out of town when a dark-skinned woman in her late twenties came running up to us. "I've met you people before," she said. "You're part of the Christ Family, the vegetarians? Please come home with me and talk to my husband. I have told him all about you people, but he doesn't believe it, coming from me. I mean that Jesus is back and all that." She spoke excitedly, her black eyes gleaming. We followed her to her townhouse in one of the residential areas not far away.

Dana's husband was sitting in the living room, hypnotized by the 'boob-tube.' The room was dark; all the curtains were drawn to keep the sunlight out. He was so engrossed in the program that he didn't hear, or see us walk in and when he looked up, there we were, sitting on the couch next to his chair. His face dropped in fear and surprise, his body jerked. He looked over to his wife with questioning black eyes.

"These are the people I was telling you about, Bill, the ones that are following Jesus," she reassured him. Brother Tom spoke next.

"God has brought us here for you and the sister, brother. He's the 'Conductor' of this grand orchestra; we are just the instruments from which His will is made into music. We have emptied our minds of the trivialities of this world, from all the garbage that keeps the voice of the Lord buried deep inside. We have died to ourselves and this world and now have received the gift of being the vessel of the Holy Spirit, messengers of the Lord. You see, the world, the way it is, has very little time. Jesus is already here. The Second Coming has come. We are living in the end times . . ."

Tom and Bill talked for hours. We just sat there, eating every word as if it was our spiritual food, for truly it was. Watching the beginning of a 'transformation' was incredible. You could actually see the 'finite mind' freak out and then succumb to 'the truth.' It was great to see the Christ Brother handle every question and opposing concept with ease and certainty. It really was something to watch. We not only sat

190

quietly observing, we also played our part by praying for the brother on the 'inside,' giving all our energy to him and the people receiving 'the truth.'

Bill and Dana decided to go for 'the truth,' so for the next few days we were 'zenning' their home of unrighteous food and other products. All labels had to be read carefully; shampoo, soap, everything. They had a three-year old son who opposed our invasion with a passion. He was uncontrollable. One of the sisters thought he was possessed and laid her hands on him, calling out the demons. I had never seen that done before and it seemed to work, but was strange.

A few days later, a large group of brothers and sisters connected with us. They were the group I'd been looking for and we all camped out in Bill and Dana's backyard. One was a tall, lanky, dark-skinned brother. I believe his name was Matthew. He seemed to be the leader of the group. He was so full of positive energy that it overflowed from him. He sang Christ Family songs a lot, in the most angelic voice I have ever heard. He was a shining example of a true brother. Brother Peter was also there. I was intrigued by him, as well, but he kept mostly to himself. Patrick and Rick were there, but Calvin and Jan weren't. I remember there being some discord and confusion after a week or two and I didn't like it. I had been through too much of that this spring already.

In a dream one night, 'the spirit' told me to leave. It was very clear. I never doubted that message. I awoke before the others, just as the sky was getting ready to birth the sun. As I walked into the kitchen, I met Patrick there, drinking coffee and making toast. He looked up at me, a bit surprised. "'The spirit' has told me to 'hit the wind brother'," I said to him.

"I'm leaving too; the space feels unclear here. If these people really wanted to go they would be ready to leave by now," he said, displeased.

"Well, brother, I believe the hold up is that they are trying to sell the house first to clear up their debts and then give the rest of the 'coin' to the 'Family'," I said.

"Yeah, I know things aren't the way they used to be," he said. He handed me a slice of toast.

"If you want someone to 'hit the wind' with, I'll try and keep up with you this time, brother," I said to him. His face looked shocked as if he thought I had never forgiven him for his ruthlessness that day when he left me by the side of the road. Then it spread into a smile and he said, "I'd be honored, sister. There's one thing I'd like to know, though, why didn't you stop to pick me up when you got a ride in that red truck?"

"You saw us pass by? I was looking for you, brother and so was the driver. We never saw you. I thought you must have gotten a ride." Patrick just looked at me, "Well, come on, let's 'hit the wind'."

As we walked out onto the street, Peter met us. All three of us were on the same wavelength. I felt honored to travel with him. He was a highly respected brother.

We walked through the quiet streets and it wasn't too long before we heard a voice calling us, "Hey, if you guys are the saints, hop in." We turned around and spotted a red Volkswagen van in a parking lot under a weeping willow tree. Calvin's face was sticking out of the window smiling at us. We boarded the van and in no time found ourselves on the highway heading north. What a 'set up!' I was so glad that I had listened to 'the spirit.' It was great to be 'in the wind' again. Everyone seemed to be in a space that was a bit lighter, although Peter spent most of the trip curled up in the crawlspace at the back. He seemed to be in pain and was disturbingly quiet.

Passing through Georgia, South Carolina, North Carolina, Virginia and then Washington, we experienced many 'connections' and miracles. Most of the churches we knocked on were giving. One in particular let us rest in the hall basement and use whatever food we wished from the huge kitchen. We went mad with cooking. We cooked beans, baked potatoes, blueberry pies, cakes . . . enough food for leftovers for a week. There was a fireplace in this church and we spent a wonderful time sharing the warmth and wonder of it all.

Peter and I touched hearts now and then. I felt close to him and wondered if we had been together in another lifetime. One night in another church basement, he opened up a little. "These 'trips' of who we were in another lifetime are really getting to me. Everyone looks up to me because I've been labeled 'Peter.' I'm just the same as everyone else, sister; probably worse. My body is always failing me, I have headaches and chest pains, I think about my daughter and miss her. I'm tired of upholding an image."

"I know how it is, brother," I said. "I'm always going through some kind of trip with my health, too. I have two 'hobbits' that I had to leave behind; they are just babies. Sometimes the pain is unbearable. When will I finally let go of that attachment?"

He just looked at me. We had already gone over the border of what we were supposed to talk about. We weren't supposed to be feeding any energy into doubts, or complaints.

From then on, whenever I felt Peter in pain, I would try to take some of it away and bear it for him. At times, I would feel an intense headache and I would then thank God for allowing me to help him. 'The truth' that we are all equal in the eyes of God became more real for me after talking to Peter. I had always looked up to older brothers and sisters with awe and respect, as though they were above me. Although a pecking order existed in the 'Family,' I knew in truth that we were all the same: *". . . The first shall be last and the last first . . . ." (Mathew 19:30)*

We crossed the bridge into Washington, D.C. in the early morning mist, with great anticipation. I was looking forward to seeing my brothers and sisters from Canada. I hoped that Richard would be there. I was looking forward to seeing Lightning Amen again, to hear him preach, just to be in his physical presence. If this was 'blink out,' then what better way to disappear from the face of the earth than with all of your brothers and sisters? I was so excited.

At the rally spot, instead of thousands of white-robed angels, we found an empty field. Desolate! Where was everyone? Calvin asked a person if he had seen any white robes around. "There was a whole mess of them here a few days ago," he answered.

192

Had they all 'blinked out' without us? Were we not worthy of it, not high enough? I was devastated.

Calvin turned to us, "Well, it's all in the Father's will. Praise God for everything. We are right where we are supposed to be."

My mind was buzzing with the events of the past few days. I had felt an urge to travel faster, impatient with the slow and easy pace that my brothers were traveling at. I remembered fighting the feeling off and thinking of getting out and catching a ride with someone who wouldn't stop so much. What if God was teaching me patience through this? Now what was He teaching me? That my feeling had been right?

We ate a meal of sandwiches and fruit in a nearby park, where two brothers came and joined us. "Is this it?" someone asked.

"No, brother, seems like we missed the party. Someone saw a large group here a few days ago," Calvin answered. "Good to see you, though; want a sandwich?"

He introduced them as Brother Francis, who was the reincarnation of Francis of Assisi, and also Peter's physical brother and Brother Gary. They both had an air of being well-seasoned brothers who had seen a lot of wind. Gary had long, straight black hair and dark, sparkling eyes. He was a small-structured man about the same height as me. Francis was tall, blonde and blue-eyed. He sat beside me, staring at me and then when he sensed I was uncomfortable, roared with laughter. He reminded me of Les, who also liked to play games with people and see their reactions. He was our comedian, always pulling 'high ones' and keeping the space light. We had good times together, just blowing 'in the wind' with no destination.

Some time later, we connected with another group. Moses and St. Nicholas were amongst them. He was a tall, broad man with curly red hair and beard and rosy cheeks. He was originally from Wales and had a heavy accent. Moses was young, tall and had light brown hair. He didn't fit his role quite as well as Nicholas, but he was Moses. Both of these brothers were a riot to be with. There was some helium gas in one of the church basements and Moses sucked some into his lungs and said, "No killing, no sex, no materialism in a Mickey Mouse voice. Soon all of us were giddy and talking like cartoons, our laughter echoing off the walls. Nicholas and Moses loved to cook and they made the most delicious vegetarian pizza that I ever tasted. It had some weird concoctions on it, like instant mashed potatoes and nutritional yeast, but it was great.

After a while, Peter, Francis and Patrick 'hit the wind.' Part of me wanted to go with them. I don't know if I was waiting to be invited, or what, but I didn't go. Then we picked up Bill, a hitchhiker who converted and turned his life around. Calvin felt there were now too many of us traveling together, so he appointed small groups to 'hit the wind.' So Gary, the new brother, Bill, and I walked down the road together, off on a new adventure in the life of Christ.

❊ CHAPTER NINETEEN ❊

O ur new group made 'connections' with all sorts of people, one after another. I enjoyed listening to Gary preach. He had a style all his own. He seemed to reach the people on their own particular level without making himself seem higher. Clarity and kindness emanated from him. I knew I would enjoy following this brother.

Traveling through the States, walking through all the different cities and country sides that I had watched on T.V. as a child, was grand. The various accents the people used through the regions of North America were so diverse. I was amazed that most places did not have public sauna houses, as we did in Thunder Bay, and that there were no restaurants that sold perogies. Two things I particularly missed were McIntosh apples and birch trees.

'The spirit' led us north to New York State and just a few miles outside of New York City, we had a run-in with a policeman. He stopped us for walking on the freeway and asked us our names and earthly information. Bill, being a new fledgling and all, got the policeman all riled up by not giving him any name, but "Bill Christ" and for his address, 'in the wind,' in the 'state of bliss.'"

"All right, wise guys into the cruiser. You're charged with walking on the freeway, vagrancy and lying to a police officer," the cop said angrily.

Gary never said a word, but the policeman seemed to have it in for him. We believed when the evil in someone saw an angel, he felt violent hate towards them. Since Gary was a reflection of truth and light, the darkness within the officer reacted to the light with hate and violence. When we arrived at the police station, the cop took us to the office, and leaving Bill and I there, he pulled Gary by his hair into another room. Were they beating him? I heard that many brothers were abused by policemen. I sat quietly and prayed for Gary, "... *Behold, I send you forth as sheep in the midst of wolves: Be therefore as wise as serpents and harmless as doves. Be aware of men, for they will deliver you up to the councils and they will scourge you in their synagogues. And you shall be brought before governors and kings for my name's sake ....*" (Matthew 10:16-18).

Two officers questioned Bill and I. I gave them my age and earth name, but let them know that it wasn't real, that who I really was, was Maureen Christ.

"Do you know what the New York women's prison is like, girl? Those cats will tear you apart. That's where you are heading, you know," one of them sneered at me, trying to promote fear.

I just smiled and said, "Praise God, brother. If that is where He wants me to be, then that is where I shall go."

"No, you don't understand those women are tough and pitiless. You have no idea what they will do to you." He looked surprised at my calmness.

"They can't touch 'me,' brother. Who I really am is 'the spirit' inside this flesh. God isn't going to allow anything to happen that He doesn't will. There is no room for fear when you have faith in God." They both looked at me in disbelief. We sat in silence for about an hour. They seemed to be uncomfortable in our presence. One of the officers had tears in his eyes. "When I look at you, I see Mother Mary looking at me; those big eyes of yours are so beautiful and full of light. It's as if you are looking right through me, it gives me the shivers," he said. "Please, just go. I don't know who you are, but if you are from God then I don't want your blood on my hands; just leave, all of you. Watch your step around here, this is a tough area." Gary came out of the back room just as we were walking out the door. "Praise God," I said. "It's a beautiful day."

As we walked, I thought about what the officer had said about me looking like Mother Mary. That was every sister's goal, to be as loving and holy as she. Cher was the closest person to Lightning; she walked right beside him, understood him. She was the sister's example, as Lightning was the brother's. I was starting to feel a real closeness to her; not that I worshipped her instead of God; just the closeness of a woman spirit. I was pleased that the policeman had seen her in me.

After a while, we came to a small pizza place. The Italian family who owned it invited us in warmly and made us a special vegetarian pizza. It was wonderful! They offered us rest in the garage for the night and we accepted with thankful hearts. "God has blessed you all," Gary told them as we left in the morning.

We walked the remainder of the way to New York City that day. The sun was about to set in the western sky as we reached the Brooklyn Bridge. It was amazing. I had never seen so many lights. We stopped at the top for a Bugler and just gazed at the miles and miles of concrete jungle. Millions of human beings, all crammed into this one place.

It was dark by the time we got to the other side. It must have taken us a few hours to walk over that bridge. It wasn't meant for pedestrians; the hordes of cars drove very close by us. My body was rigid from the tension and I was so glad to be off it.

Finding a safe resting spot in New York was no easy feat. We walked to a few youth hostels, but they were all filled up. We went to a few jails, but they, too, were filled. So, we roamed about the streets for hours.

Loud voices came up from behind us. Someone jumped Gary and another grabbed Bill. "What's the funny dress for, man? Are you a fag, or some kind of holy man?" A mocking voice asked Gary. Another guy grabbed me and tugged harshly at my arms as he pulled them behind my back. One of them pulled out a shiny steel switchblade and teasingly ran it under our noses.

"We are followers of Jesus Christ, brother. He's here on earth again. We are peaceful people. We won't give you any fun," Gary said, almost too coolly. I chanted the three keys in my head and prayed for protection in an attempt to fight the rising emotion of fear.

"Don't you know you are in the Bronx, man. And, this sidewalk you are walking on just happens to belong to us," the one with the knife said. "So walk on the other side, man. Let them go," he ordered the others.

All of them were wearing chains and black leather. We never said a word and quickly crossed the street, unhurt.

The sky hung heavy, threatening rain. Gary led Bill and I to a baseball field and we rolled out in the dugout. It was old, the paint chipping, graffiti everywhere and the smell of urine was strong. *". . . Foxes have holes and birds of the air have nests; but the son of man has no where to lay his head . . . ." (Matthew 8:20).*

The vibrations of that city were incredible. It took so much energy out of me. We didn't stand out in the crowd as we did in smaller cities. No one even noticed us. People raced through the streets in herds, all in their own individual worlds. They seemed oblivious of one another. We sat in the centre of one part of the city, one day, preaching the keys to the passers-by. Most people didn't even hear us.

The streets of New York were dirty and broken bottles lay everywhere, at least the part of town we were in was like this. Anyway, it sure isn't a good place to walk barefoot. Our feet were full of slivers of glass. I was becoming a pro at picking slivers out of my feet, but I just couldn't keep up with it here. After a while the glass in my feet became infected and the infection made me ill. I was weak with fever and dizziness. Gary asked around if there was a free hospital and we found one. The nurses were appalled when they looked at my feet. "There's so much glass I can't hardly see skin!" One of them exclaimed. "Why don't you wear shoes, honey? You're crazy girl!"

It hurt when they took out the glass; especially from the infected places. But, I didn't move, or flinch. I was a Christ Sister. I had risen above feeling every little bodily pain. I told myself this, but I knew darn well I still felt pain.

The nurses gave me penicillin and funny-looking paper slippers to wear. "You must rest for a few days and keep your feet protected," one of them told me. Outside I kept the slippers on for a while, until Gary turned to me. "Take those off, sister," he ordered. I slipped them off almost embarrassed that I had to be told and put them in my tote sack.

We walked to some of the churches, but most of them were impossible to get into. They were surrounded by huge iron fences with spiked tops, forbidding entry. Big, black and foreboding, cold metal with padlocks and chains bolted the gates. Finally, at the last church we tried, we caught the preacher going in and he opened his doors to us. We had a long and interesting 'rap' with him. He gave us a ticket for a motel for the night and a bit of 'coin' for food. That evening, while lying on my bedroll, I saw two angels flickering around the room. They were in the form of lights, like Tinker Bell in the story of Peter Pan. There was a loud buzzing in my ears and I felt high as I watched the lights dance around the room.

Next day, as we walked through the city, we found crates of fruits and vegetables that were being thrown out by a small supermarket. It was strange to see the garbage brought to the front instead of the back. We filled our sacks with avocados, oranges, grapes, apples, potatoes, squash . . . what a fine gift. It seemed to be brought out just for us. We caused a stir on the street and soon others were filling their bags with stuff, too. Everyone was smiling. It was a great feeling. This is the way it was meant to be, in the Garden of Eden food was a free gift to man, I thought.

Close to the outskirts of town, we found a nice spot by the river to camp for a few days. Gary carried a piece of plastic rolled up in his bedroll and with sticks for poles; we made a plastic tent over our resting place. We took all the big rocks out of the area and made a trench on either side for the water to run down. It was on a slight slant, running downhill to the river bank. With the stones, we made a fireplace for cooking. We had been given an old frying pan, a pot and a few dried goods by an old preacher on our way out of town. We weren't totally out of town yet; New York goes on forever. We cooked beans, soups and pan breads. It was a glorious spot there in the woods, so close to, yet, so far away from the congestion of the city. We used the river water for cooking and even drank it if we needed to. It wasn't clean, but it was water.

There was a thunderstorm one night, as Gary had predicted. The lightning was luminous, the thunder earthshaking. The three of us sat under our thin piece of plastic and watched the show. A bit of the rain slanted in at us through the sides, but our bedrolls remained dry, the plastic intact and the water rushed through our hand-dug trenches. It was a great feeling to be out there experiencing the storm.

Gary went on some pizza and bagel runs and all were successful. We ate heartily while we camped there, but I wondered why I was still experiencing bodily illnesses. Why had I not risen above them like other brothers and sisters? I was conscious of having misled people at times, regarding the flesh. When someone would ask me if I was cold, I would answer, "No, I'm not this physical body." All the while I shivered. I really didn't want to feel the cold, but I did. I let on as if I was high all the time, telling people that I was in heaven. I knew I was supposed to feel that way, but sometimes I was miserable, dirty, hungry and confused. I had an image to live up to and it was a constant battle to live up to what you let people think you are. It was the old carrot dangling inches in front of me, perfection always in sight, but out of reach. I knew all my negative thoughts and feelings were from the 'finite mind,' Satan.

To rise above that mind was the key to bliss. To be like a little child, full of awe, trust and innocence, yet wise and prudent was a difficult balance to maintain. If it was a gift from God, then why did I have to try so hard? I had aligned my will with God's.

Everything I thought, or did was now His will. Why did I still feel so earthbound and human?

After about four days or so, of resting and taking penicillin, I felt strong and ready to 'hit the wind.' As we traveled on, we found that some cities on the east coast blended into one another, with no rural areas between them. At times, this posed a problem for Gary whose body lacked an early warning system when it came to bowel movements.

In one particular city, we were passing through a rundown district of town when Gary got that frantic look on his face. With knitted eyebrows, he scanned the endless rows of town houses for somewhere to go. There were no trees, bushes, or gas stations in sight. Just house after house, their roof tops touching . . . then, "Wait here," Gary told us as he darted across the street to an older, two-storey brick home, up the steps two at a time and in through the front door.

Bill and I waited until he reappeared. The look of relief his face told us everything had gone smoothly in there, but he never said a word and just continued 'trucking.'

As I followed my brothers, I laughed to myself as I conjured up what might have transpired inside and the shocked look on the faces of the inhabitants as a madman in a white dress burst into their home and ran to the bathroom. I wondered if incidents like these had anything to do with the fact that Gary preferred traveling down county roads and small towns.

Gary and I were pulling for the new brother, Bill. A lot of our energy was focused on him. He was a sincere and searching soul, wanting to change and conform to our lifestyle. We saw and felt him struggle and Gary was very patient with him. There were stretches where we would walk twenty to thirty miles a day. My body ached and my feet burned all night, so I could imagine how Bill's felt. One such night, we were walking down a dirt road, in the dark, searching for a resting place. The rocks were sharp like ballast. It was too dark to see. Gradually, Bill began to lag farther and farther behind. Gary, feeling compassion, stopped and waited for him to catch up instead of firing on him. I admired that quality in Gary. I knew in my heart that Jesus was the ultimate example of compassion, so it felt good to wait for our brother.

Sleeping in the woods in our bed of moss and dried leaves with the sound of water running over rocks and the crickets calling their mates was so wonderful. The stars, always brighter away from the neon lights of the city, never bored me. The sound of the leaves, moving in the wind, was soothing. Then sunlight and the chirping of birds in the morning would welcome us to another day in the life of Christ.

Ever since I can remember, being surrounded by nature has always been a sort of sanctuary for me, like being in a church where God is magnified. Now, more than ever, I felt this. It was wonderful to walk through the woods barefoot, gently 'communing' with the earth, experiencing the different textures under my feet. Moss was my favorite, more luxurious than any plush carpet.

We left food out for our animal friends and squirrels, chipmunks and various birds came near us. A few times we got close to deer, but the fear of man made them run away.

Once again, I imagined how it would be in the Garden of Eden, when man and beast would live harmoniously, in true peace the way we were meant to; in a world without fear and killing. I was anxious for the cleansing of the earth and to see this restoration come into play.

At this time, we were more, or less heading towards Boston. We had heard that a lot of brothers were marching on the city. After we'd walked a few miles on the freeway, a car stopped. "Hey, you people look really interesting. Want to keep me company for a while?" The driver asked.

"Right on, brother," Gary answered, and Bill and I climbed in the back seat.

"My name is Ted. What are the costumes for?"

"We are disciples of Jesus, Brother Ted. My 'handle' is Brother Gary, and this is Brother Bill, and Sister Maureen."

"Oh, Jesus freaks. Well, He's a good person to get freaked over, I suppose."

"He's the one and only, brother. He's our example of how to live 'the truth' in this world of illusions. You see, there isn't much time left; all the signs are here. The Book of Revelation in the Bible talks about us. We are the one hundred and forty-four thousand chosen ones who wear white raiment and are celibate. We are gathering God's people while the angels hold back the four winds . . ."

This brother was so interested in what Gary had to say that instead of letting us off at the fork in the road that went to Boston, he drove us on to New Hampshire. There he took us to a little town in the mountains and let us rest in his backyard. He offered us some floor space in the house, but Gary preferred to be outdoors, even though it was cold.

In New Hampshire, we walked many miles down country roads. The nights were still cold and a few mornings I woke up with frost covering my bedroll and joints too stiff to move, at first. I had always disliked the cold and could handle being hot much more easily. These nights were an incredible test for me; a test in obedience, in patience and in denying the flesh and not focusing so much energy on it.

One night we made our bed out of old autumn leaves in the woods a little way off a country road. The night was clear and not as cold as it had been for the last while. From my bed I gazed up at the stars and spotted 'the Christ C.' This was a constellation of seven stars that formed a letter "C." We had been told that this had just appeared in the sky at the moment when Lightning awoke to his true identity and started living this life and that all the scientists were baffled as to where it had come from. I made a little ritual of finding 'the Christ C' every night.

It took a few minutes for the mosquitoes to smell us, but when they did, they brought all their family and friends along for the feast. This part of the country reminded me more and more of Canada, with the evergreens, poplars and other greenery, wild flowers, and of course, the mosquitoes. We were non-violent so we couldn't swat them and had to keep that old habit and very natural response under control. Even with our heads under the shelter of our bedrolls those little beasts bit through somehow, for we awoke with eruptions on our heads and faces.

Gary carried a map with him and after consulting it, told us we were in the White Mountains and that there was a town about fifteen miles away. The walk there was spectacular, as the rolling hills folded into glorious peaks. From certain points it seemed we could see forever. The forest turned into farmland as we approached the town. We saw sheep, pigs, cows, horses, ducks and geese and stopped to watch them for a while. How man could slaughter these peaceful creatures that trusted him was beyond me. Looking into the deep dark eyes of a cow, I saw that the life-force within her was the same one as within me. She was nature's lawn-mower. Then I thought about lambs and how they are the only animal that doesn't cry when they are killed. Jesus compared Himself to the lamb and allowed himself to be killed. He said He would be the last blood sacrifice; but man, in his ignorance and lust for killing, is still killing Jesus every time he kills an animal. I envisioned the days to come when the lion would lie down with the lamb and all creatures and man would live in peace.

We walked through the White Mountains, preaching in the small, backwoods towns. These towns seemed oblivious to large cities; the prices of food and tobacco were years behind and some labels were ancient. We were invited into homes and had many fine 'connections' and much sharing.

In the State of Maine, we reached a small community just as the sun cast its last bit of light. We had walked well over twenty miles that day and had not eaten. There was a light on in a small white church and as we approached it, we heard voices. All eyes were on us as we stood at the back of the room observing. Bible passages were read, people were sharing and confessing and they also got caught up in speaking in tongues and such. After it was over, a few people came to talk to us. From most we felt judgment.

One woman was totally intrigued and she took us with her that night to a hand-built, log home a few miles north of town. She lived with her daughter and son-in-law and two young grandchildren.

I slept beside Grace that night, downstairs in her suite. She wanted to sleep in a sleeping bag on the floor next to me. We talked about God and truth all night long. "I wish I could come with you and live the life of Christ, but my body is too old to travel around the world preaching," she said.

"You're not too old; there are brothers and sisters in the 'Family' who are older. There is this one sister who is in her fifties and has bad arthritis, but she's still trucking."

"You don't understand. I have cancer and my body is going to leave this world soon," she told me. "If only I had known earlier."

"God knows your heart, sister; you are doing His will right where you are. I love you, Grace. I feel so close to you, like I have known you before."

"I feel the same way, child. Praise God for sending you to me." She rolled over and gave me a big hug.

We stayed with her for a few days and then said our farewells. There was still frost on the ground when we left. She had given us as much food as we could carry. She stood at the end of the driveway waving to us until we were out of sight.

The streams we drank from were cold and clean. I had a plastic water jug that I carried with me. I found it difficult to go too long without drinking and the Lord, knowing this, always kept my water jug filled. It was a symbol to me, how He always filled my heart when I was spiritually thirsty.

The next few days were the most trying days I had experienced since joining the Christ Family. We were still in the mountains, walking all day long except for the occasional ride. By now, it was May, the black flies were wild. All day long they hovered about us in massive swarms, ruthlessly biting chunks of flesh off our bodies, flying into our ears, eyes, mouths and noses. There was no escape from these vicious little creatures that we were supposed to love. We couldn't even sit down for a smoke! So we rolled them, smoked and even ate while we walked; all at high speed. Besides being exhausting and frustrating, it was a test far beyond what I thought I could handle. At one point I started to cry. I wanted to kill them all and felt guilty for wanting to! I felt as if I was losing my mind; there was nowhere to hide. Even the night brought no solace, for then the mosquitoes came out, humming their war song.

After what seemed like months, we were in Portland, Maine, away from the bugs. I never was so relieved to smell the polluted air and hear the sweet sound of traffic and noise. A young woman followed us for a few days, but didn't 'transform.' A man who owned a pizza place gave us free pizzas whenever we wanted them. There were so many people we touched hearts with and seeds were sown.

One night we slept in a boxcar in the railway yard. Gary had chosen a shelter because it was raining. In the early morning we awoke to the sounds of our door being slammed shut and some voices on the other side. In the darkness, Gary ran over to the door and yelled, "Hey, we're in here, let us out!" No one seemed to hear and the car jostled about as they hooked it to the train. Again we heard a voice and Gary yelled again. This time he was heard and the door opened. Light poured in, scattering the darkness. The husky fellow on the other side stared at us with a stunned look on his face, as if he wasn't sure we were real. "Get out of there. What are you doing in there? Who are you guys?" He demanded.

"Traveling Christians, brother, we are followers of Jesus," Gary answered him.

"Well, on your way, now."

A few days later, we ended up taking a freight train out of Portland. We didn't know where it was heading, but we made ourselves comfortable in the open boxcar and just 'watched the movie.' We rode throughout the night, stopped in the early dawn and got off, and walked through the town of who knows where? It was interesting not to know where we were. My 'finite mind' so badly wanted to have a handle on it that I asked a woman in the coffee shop. When she told me, it didn't do any good because I didn't recognize the name, or even what state we were in. I took it as a message from God, telling me to not worry about it. We were wherever He wanted us to be.

There were many times when my 'old mind' would reach out for familiar things, like remembering how many birthdays had passed, or what month it was, or how old the children would be now. Yet my 'old mind' was slowly dying as my new mind (which we called the "Christ mind") grew stronger every day. It thought only positive thoughts, converting negatives into positives in a wonderful victory for righteousness. The 'Christ mind' did not dwell in the past, or future. It praised God for everything every moment of every day. It knew and felt its connection with every living thing and was conscious of the presence of God at all times. With no boundaries, or limitations, it dwelt in the eternal growth and love of God. Through this new mind, God was teaching me how to love, revealing truths so deep that the old 'finite mind' could never have grasped them.

There were times when I felt at one with the life-force within all living things. My mind, void of thoughts, was clear and open and extremely aware. I felt the cord that ties all life together; I felt the connection so clearly. It was as though I was seeing a tree, or a bug, or flower with totally different eyes. The wonders all around kept me in awe and ever conscious of the definite presence of God. At these times I wanted to hold onto my experiences forever. Though I could not, the nectar that I tasted remained on my tongue through the 'storms' giving me strength to fight the battles that were necessary to reach new ground. Each time a battle was won, I was able to climb higher, see more clearly and experience revelations beyond my own understanding.

That night a rocky shore by a river was our bed. Ironically, it was one of the most comfortable resting spots in a while. The rocks were smooth and round and they molded to each of our particular body shapes. Closer to the shore were large, flat slabs that we used to make an oven and a fireplace. There we baked two loaves of bread and boiled beans in a old coffee can. There is something really special about using the tools that nature provides. I felt so close to the earth; I was flowing with her instead of against her. I washed our wooden bowls and spoons in the river with sand; nature's natural cleanser. It was great not to take part in polluting her.

Afterwards the three of us sat around the glow of the fire in silence. "Tell us a story again tonight, sister." Bill asked. 'The spirit' gave me stories to share. I never knew what was going to come next, or how it would end; it was as though I was listening to them, too. That is why I say 'the spirit' gave them to me, they were an inspiration. Many times they would be inspired by something I'd see, like a leaf floating on a current of a stream, or a pebble on the beach, or a rose bush in a field of poison oak. Other times they'd be inspired by stories I had heard, or read.

"Once upon a time," I began, "there was a young sister who lived on a bay in a small town. For as long as she could remember, she loved to go down to the beach, sit on the docks and watch the sailboats winging across the bay. How she wanted to sail.

One day, her father gave her a sailboat. What a 'far out' gift. It was light blue with white trim and a white sail. Every day she'd get on the boat, which was tied to the pier, unfold the sail and sit there imagining herself sailing across the harbor with the others. Little by little, her father and the other sailors taught her tips on how to tack and set her sails, how to go upwind and down wind and other tricks of the art. Soon she was sailing around the bay with all the others, gliding in the warm summer breeze.

Now, all the sailors warned her not to go near Logic Point, because beyond Logic Point was the Dark Sea. The sea was unpredictably dangerous, she was told. No one had either come from beyond, or gone past Logic Point. She was really curious the first time she saw the point and as she sailed near it, she noticed that the Dark Sea beyond was anything but dark; in fact, the bluish-green water seemed to sparkle and bounce with joy. As she gazed at it, the sister felt a sense of peace come over her and a strange desire to go beyond the forbidden point. As she was tying up her boat that evening, she asked one of the older sailors, "Why do they call it Logic Point?"

He looked at her, his face grave with seriousness. "Well, honey, it's because anyone who dares to go beyond it would have to be illogical, crazy, not in their right mind. The sea beyond the point is wild and mysterious." He continued, gruffly, "The waters are unknown. Years ago, I watched a young lad venture past there in a small boat. He never returned." A sense of sadness was evident in his voice now. "Just be happy here," he warned her.

For quite a while, she felt happy to sail around the harbor with all the others, but as time wore on she became increasingly aware of her discontent. There has to be more to sailing than this, she thought. Her heart reached out for truth.

Every day she found herself drawn to Logic Point from where she would look out over the sea, searching for something. What "WAS" that something that lured her here? She wanted to let her boat go beyond the point and sail far out to sea, but the stories the other sailors told her haunted her mind.

One evening, as she tied her boat to the dock, she gazed out over the bay to the point and caught sight of a speck of white moving towards it from the sea. She squinted her eyes and watched the object come closer. What was it? As it approached, she couldn't believe what she saw; a pure white sailboat, effortlessly gliding into the bay toward the docks. People gathered around her now, astonished as she. No one had ever come in from the Dark Sea.

The sails, luminous white, shone in the twilight. The man sailing the boat was clothed in white raiment. With skilled hands, the stranger docked his boat with hardly a bump, or sound. There was no doubt in her mind that he was truly a seasoned sailor. He moved with graceful confidence and no wasted energy. His face was bronzed and weathered. His golden hair cascaded down past his shoulders; his beard was unshaven. His eyes were blue-green like the sea with a shine in them like the sun on the waves; incredible, strange, yet knowing eyes. When he looked at her she felt totally exposed, frightened by, yet attracted to this stranger. He was beside her now on the dock as the frightened crowd dispersed; yet she remained. She looked down at his feet and noticed he was barefoot. The moonlight reflected on his face, now. Such an ageless face, she thought. Being in his presence made her feel calm and relaxed.

Peace emanated from him. Who is he? She wondered.

"Why did you come?" She asked.

"Why did you call?" He answered.

"I didn't call. I don't even know you," she told him.

"Every time you sailed to Logic Point and yearned to go beyond, you were praying, calling me. You are not content to sail around in circles in the sheltered bay like the others. You seek truth, far beyond logic. You desire to understand mystery, even the unknowable Dark Sea. Come with me and I will show you that the stories you've been told are all lies. You will not die, you will learn to truly live," he said.

"No one saw the two sails as they rounded the point just before the break of day. No doubt, she had many adventures on the high seas, but that'll be tomorrow night's bedtime sequel," I told my brothers.

"Right on, sister," Gary smiled at me and handed me a Bugler. "Praise God, what a great story. I can hardly wait 'til 'manana' (tomorrow in Spanish).

"There's a shooting star," Bill said as he pointed to the sky.

"Did you know that when we see a shooting star, it means that a new brother or sister has 'transformed'?" Gary asked Bill.

"Right on!" We lay back in our bedrolls, gazing at the infinite sky. I felt secure wrapped up in the love of God and my brothers. "See you in the 'ethers,' brothers," I said to them. "I love you guys."

We believed that we also preached at night, traveling around in our light body to wherever God wanted us to go. The 'Christ mind' never sleeps; that is why we called it "rest," never sleep."

❊ CHAPTER TWENTY ❊

The city of Boston reminded me of New York, in the seriousness of people, rushing everywhere, another day, another dollar, another thing to buy.

The rain slashed down on us that night as we roamed the city in search of a resting place, but there was none to be found. We made a few 'connections' with some night people, but no one took us home. Hungry, we went into an all-night Chinese restaurant and the cook gave freely of a meal of rice. As night birthed the dawn, we followed the quiet streets to a park, laid our bedrolls down on the damp ground and crawled in. I was so tired that I didn't care about getting wet; I just wanted to lay my weary body down. I 'blinked out' immediately.

All of a sudden, I heard the muffled sounds of someone shouting, as if from far away. My body fought waking up, but the voice became clearer, the nearer I came to consciousness and I suddenly realized that someone was poking me with a sharp object.

I poked my head out from under the bedroll and there was a Roman Centurion on a black horse, poking me with a dagger and shouting, "Get out of here, you can't sleep here."

I had to blink my eyes; was I dreaming? Was I recalling something from the past, from when I was a new Christian in another lifetime? What was going on?

"Come, on sister, let's 'hit the wind'!" I saw Gary rolling up his bedroll and Bill already prepared to go. This was real? I looked back over to our oppressor and realized that she was a police officer, riding a horse and holding a poker. She looked so much like a Roman from the past. I had never seen anything like this before. Still dazed, I let Gary help me roll up as she sat on her high horse, waiting until we left the park. There was nowhere to sleep in Boston, night or day. "Let's shake the dust off our feet, from this town," Gary said as we trucked on out. *". . . Neither take no shoes, no two coats, nor script for your journey, a workman is worthy of his meat. And into whatsoever city or town you enter, inquire who in it is worthy and there abide 'til you go from there. And when you come into a house, salute it, and if the house is worthy let your peace come upon it, but if it is not, let your peace return to you. And whosoever will not receive you or hear your words when you depart out of that house or city, shake the dust off your feet . . . ." (Matthew 10:10-14).*

Gary liked to travel off the beaten path. He felt 'the spirit' was guiding him to little towns which had never seen a Christ Brother. We went through stretches on these roads with little food or water, but God always picked us up when we thought we couldn't go anymore. There were days when we lived on wild berries. I always had a passion for berries.

In the mountains of Pennsylvania, we met people who lived in rundown little houses and lived primarily on beans. They were Hillbillies. Dressed in rags, barefoot and dirty, they wore smiles on their faces and there was no trace of the frantic lifestyles we'd encountered in the big cities. These people were laid back! One man gave us a container full of berries and fresh beans from his garden. We walked many miles up in those hills.

In a small town inhabited primarily by Pennsylvanian-Dutch folk, we rested for a few days. These people dressed in black; the women in long dresses and bonnets and the men in black suits and hats. They kept to themselves and seemed fearful and reserved about the world.

One evening, I was craving popcorn. We were sitting on the street, Gary was preaching to a few of the street people. I told him I had a 'connection' to make and started heading somewhere. I was led to a movie theatre, so I walked in and asked the manager if he would give freely of some popcorn in the name of Christ. "I sure will," he said with a smile and handed me the largest bag of popcorn I had ever seen. It seemed as if the manager had been waiting for me. What a 'set up.' I stayed and preached to him a bit and then headed back to where the brothers were, excited about the popcorn 'connection.' Gary and Bill were laughing at my struggles to keep the huge plastic bag from dragging on the sidewalk. We sat on the street corner, sharing popcorn and 'the truth.' We made a sign that said "Free Popcorn!" The popcorn was a 'prop.'

In our travels, we met people whom we knew would some day be walking barefoot and in a robe. There were others who seemed to have already let Satan have their souls. We knew this, of course, because we were the walking judgment of the world. We judged people by their reaction to us. At times, it seemed we were given something like 'x-ray vision' to see into the hearts of men. Our whole purpose was to preach truth to all men and allow them to choose to follow, or reject it. We had sacrificed our lives for the whole world, for our mission had no self gain. I no longer thought in terms of 'what I wanted to do.' I had given up playing the piano, my artwork and my dreams of raising a family in a solar dome in the country. Everything had been given up. I only wanted to be a righteous reflection of Jesus Christ and live in the Father's will. I felt alienated from the world; in it, but not of it. There were times I was so high, so full of joy that I could barely contain myself. I had been selected as one of God's chosen.

In the city of Philadelphia, we took a subway train to the area of town where Gary's parents lived. The tension on the train was intense. People looked unhealthy, tired and burned out. Unhappiness is not knowing what you want and killing yourself to get it, I thought.

On our walk we passed by a park in which there was a tree with purple and white mulberries hanging heavily on its branches. I had never seen this type of berry before. I'd heard of it in the nursery rhyme as a child: "Here we go round the mulberry bush . . ." I started singing and grabbed both my brother's hands as we circled around the white and purple tree, skipping and singing like children. I had experienced 'light times' like this before, when we wiped away our concepts of 'adult behavior' and were free to be happy and childish. I loved it. "Peter Pan" being one of my childhood idols, I had never wanted to grow up. So the three big 'little' people sat under the mulberry bush and feasted on the juicy berries.

Soon afterwards, we arrived at a large brick townhouse. Gary stopped on the sidewalk in front and gazed at the house. "This is where my earth parents live, my old stomping grounds as a child," he said. He walked up the front steps and knocked on the door. A black-haired woman with kind eyes answered, her face showing a mixture of delight and surprise.

"Oh my God, Gary!" She exclaimed. "It's been so long. I'm so happy to see you. I've been worried sick over you. Where have you been? Oh come in, come in!" She looked over to Bill and I and gestured for us to follow. As we walked through the living room, I glanced around. The home was warm and homey, decorated with a touch of class. She took us down to the basement, to the guest room. We left our bedrolls and tote sacks there and followed her back up to the kitchen. "I'll make you something to eat, what would you like?" She asked.

I watched carefully the interaction between Gary and his mother. He called her "sister" and held back any natural special feelings for her. His mom was elated to see him and tried hard to contain her hurt. He had not contacted her in years, in fact, not since he had joined the 'Family.' His parents hadn't even known if he was still alive, or what had happened to him. When Gary's dad came home, I felt the friction. He couldn't understand what his son was doing and felt only the hurt that Gary had caused him and his wife.

We had some heated discussions about who we were and about Jesus and 'the truth.' Being of the Jewish faith, his parents found it very hard to accept the fact that their son believed in the Second Coming of Christ, since they were still waiting for the first. All in all, however, they made us feel welcome even though they disliked what we were doing.

Eva, his mom, was a talented dressmaker and one day she took me to her shop and showed me some of her work. She was working on a wedding dress, a very intricate design. She was good at what she did. I found it hard to relate to, though, because we in the Christ Family didn't believe in worldly marriage, or fashion. Then somehow we got onto the topic of children. "You'll never be able to have children and fulfill the destiny of your womb, Maureen," she said. "You are young; this way you are living is robbing you of so much. It's wrong. Can't you see that they have control over you, of your mind? You "AREN'T" free as you claim to be. You are bound by heavier chains than we 'earthlings,' as you call us," she added. Somehow, I felt that I would be lying if I just left it at that and never told her about Ariss and Sol, so I did. This was the wrong move. She was appalled at me for leaving them and more than ever tried to talk me out of 'the truth.'

Many of the things that Eva said seemed to bite away at me for days after we left. I felt the force of her words on my heart and I went into another 'dive' of missing the kids and feeling a great loss. All of this was on the 'inside.' I didn't know if my brothers could feel it, or not, but I had a feeling Gary did. In one of the homes we were welcomed into I picked up the Bible and read this: *". . . Verily I say unto you, there is no man that has left house, or parents or brethren, or wife, or children for the kingdom of God's sake, who shall not receive manifold more in this present time and in the world to come, life everlasting . . . ." (Luke 18:29-30).*

This did not completely erase all my misgivings, but it did help me to feel that my decision to give up everything for God had been justified.

In Maryland, Bill decided he wanted to 'truck solo.' He was a strong fledgling by now, ready to leave the nest and check out his wings. In a strange way I felt as though we were his parents, for we had taught him how to live this way and prayed for him on the 'inside' relentlessly. I felt an attachment for Bill that I had never known was there until he walked down that road without us. "It's time for him to put in his 10,000 miles," Gary said.

Gary and I walked on in silence into the night. I followed him up a little hill in an open field and we rolled out in a valley in between a few small dips of rolling grass. It felt so good to crawl inside my bedroll. But, just as I was about to blink out, I felt some raindrops on my face. I looked over at Gary, but he just pulled his bedroll over his face and snuggled deeper into it. This surprised me because Richard had always gotten up and searched for a dry place if it started to rain; he didn't like getting wet. I put my head under my sleeping bag just as thunder shook the earth and the rain slashed down. After a moment I peeked out from under my bedroll at Gary, but he didn't move. He was resting through it all. It rained hard all night and soon our little valley was flooded. I lay there in a huge puddle, waiting patiently for morning, or when my brother would move, whichever came first. The morning did. Gary looked well rested, but soaked. Our robes and blankets and bedrolls were heavy with water. So we walked to a Laundromat and dried our stuff. It was still raining and it kept up all day.

In the Laundromat we met a salesman who was interested in us and we ended up spending that night in his hotel room with him. He ordered a veggie pizza for us. The next day, he gave us a ride to a town in Ohio somewhere. We drove all day and he dropped us off at dusk. We found a quiet park and rolled out.

I awoke before Gary and the first thing I saw was a fat, juicy raspberry, hanging a foot away from my face. I reached up and plucked it and popped it into my mouth, my favorite berry. Sitting up now, as far as I could see, there were fruit-laden raspberry bushes. I got out of my bedroll and walked around the desolate park in amazement. There were raspberry bushes everywhere. I wondered if I was still dreaming. This was like a part of the Garden of Eden. In my inner vision, the raspberries no longer had thorns and each berry was the size of a pear. Often I would visualize and create different scenes in my mind, such as the animals and man living in harmony, mosquitoes sucking on grapes instead of blood, the sun always shining and mist every morning to give moisture to vegetation instead of rain. In my visions I was able to fly and was given the gift of creating little scenes at will. They went on and on, the daydreams that I would have.

After eating as many berries as my stomach could hold, I went back to get my wooden bowl. Gary was still resting. It didn't take long to fill the bowl and I brought the gift to him, gently waking him up. "Far out, breakfast in bed, Praise God," he said with that smile of his.

We stayed in our little Garden of Eden that day, watching joggers, people and their dogs and Frisbee players. Christ Brothers and Sisters were observers and at times the reactions we would receive from people were amusing. All we were doing was being, but just our existence would offend some and create fear in others. Then there were the ones who were drawn to us as if by some magnetic force they couldn't explain. Like the man that came riding by on a bike and nearly smashed into a tree when he saw us. He came towards us with long strides of determination; his deep brown eyes seemed to look right through us. "You have been sent by God, haven't you?" He asked.

"Yepper, brother. We are here for you," Gary answered.

The young man had tears in his eyes as he explained to us, "I have been praying to God to show me the way, to give me a sign, to direct me to where He wants me to be and here you are. What is the message?"

"God is calling you to come out from the world and its ways and be born again into 'the truth.' We have been transformed into perfect reflections of Christ. Everyone has the choice, but you have to want truth more than anything. You have to give up your will, your mind, your heart, everything and stand naked before the Lord," Gary told him. His eyes grew bigger as he listened. I sat quietly, tuning into 'the spirit' speaking through Gary.

"What must I do to serve God?" Ray asked, his body twitching with nervous excitement.

"... *You must pick up your cross and follow me . . . ,*" *(Mathew 16:24)* Gary quoted from the Bible. "You must forsake all, including yourself and start your pilgrimage in blind faith."

"But, what do you mean. What are your beliefs?" Ray wanted to know everything right now. How I could relate to this yearning spirit. "We are disciples of Jesus Christ. We are gathering the chosen ones. You see, we are living in the last days. The signs are all around for those who have eyes to see them. People don't care; they carry on, the blind leading the blind, marrying and partying just like in the days of Noah. Only this time, there will be fire falling from the sky, not rain. Look at the world: pollution, havoc, nuclear wars. The system that people worship and can't live without is the beast. Jesus has already returned and only a few believe it."

"What! You're telling me that the Second Coming of Christ has already taken place?" Ray was shocked.

"That's right, brother, Jesus Christ is walking barefoot on the earth, dressed in a white robe just like us."

The conversation went on for hours as I rolled Buglers and listened. Gary had a good answer for every question that Ray asked. 'The truth' had an all encompassing, circular logic. There seemed to be an answer for every possible question. We even knew the answer to every world crisis. The reason why a small, innocent child was starving in the third world was because in his last life he had been a cruel murderer and this life was his karmic penance. Also, if people stopped having sex, there wouldn't be so many mouths to feed. And if they stopped eating cows, there would be enough grain to feed the whole world. There was an immense amount of security in being able to explain everything and it all boiled down to the fact that if everyone lived like us, the world's problems wouldn't exist. The world would be a Garden of Eden where peace and harmony prevailed. Then we could use our gifts as procreators to create beautiful things. We would still grow and learn, for perfection is not stagnant. But, this growing would be different from our present earthly battles against evil, for when good triumphs over evil, how much stronger that good becomes than if it was only, always good.

Ray invited Gary and I to his small apartment. We talked all night, trying to help him let go of the ideas that held him captive. In the morning, he took the sheet off his bed and asked us to sew him a robe. "I'm going to say goodbye to my girlfriend. I'll be back soon," he told us.

Gary didn't like that idea. "I don't feel you are strong enough for that tense an ordeal yet, brother," he told Ray. "The best thing to do is leave now; ". . . *Let the dead bury the dead . . . ." (Mathew 8:22)* But, Ray went anyway.

As Gary had suspected, Ray returned with doubts. It seemed that all the understanding he had gained the night before was lost. We went ahead and finished his robe late that evening, but in the morning, Ray was full of fear and anxiety again. He kept 'flip-flopping,' from wanting to come, to not wanting to. "You must have blind faith, brother. How would you know what a peach tastes like if you had never tasted it? To let go of everything means cutting your strings of attachment. You have to let go," Gary told him.

"I know you are right, but I just don't feel I have the faith. I want it, but I'm just not there yet," Ray answered, with tears in his eyes.

"Well, brother, your robe is made for you and you know the foundation. Live the keys and learn and grow in 'the spirit.' Call out in your heart for God to send you another brother who will take you down the road. ". . . *Ask in My name and you shall receive . . . ," (John 14:13)* Gary told him. Then he and I walked out of the building, leaving Ray in a torment of guilt and self-pity. I prayed for him for days. "We'll see him 'in the wind' some day soon, sister," Gary assured me.

Later that week, I followed Gary through a small town. We had walked about twenty-five miles that day and my burning feet ached to be still, my stomach to be fed. He stopped at a good-sized brick church and knocked on the door of the registry. A woman came to the door; probably the housekeeper. "Yes?" She said as she looked us up and down. "What do you want here?" Now her voice was a bit frightened.

"We are traveling Christians, sister; fear not. We are brothers of Jesus Christ in need of a meal and a place to rest. Can we speak to the priest?" Gary asked her.

Her face seemed to relax a bit, though her eyes remained squinted with suspicion and mistrust. She opened the door wider. "Follow me, then," she said. "I'll bring you to Father Denly."

We walked down a plush carpeted hall, which felt great under my tired 'pads,' and stopped in front of a wonderfully carved oak door with a crystal door knob and a brass knocker. She knocked on it three times.

"Come in," said a deep voice from behind it. Father Denly sat behind a huge oak desk, absorbed in some sort of paper work. "What would you like, Martha?" He asked her, without even looking up.

"There are two people here to see you, Father," she answered and motioned for us to step into the room.

When he looked up at us his face turned a ghostly white, like he was hit with a lightning bolt somewhere deep within him. We both saw it. His initial shock was quickly masked with arrogance. "Who do you think you are?" He said rudely.

"We are the saints, brother, don't you recognize us?"

This answer perturbed him even more. "God has sent us here to see if you are truly doing his work," Gary went on confidently. "We are weary from traveling and are in need of a meal, a shower and a place to rest."

"Wait a minute, now, just who do you think you are, anyway?" Now this priest was getting really angry.

"I told you, brother, we are the saints, disciples of Jesus Christ. We have forsaken everything of the world and ourselves to follow Jesus one hundred percent," Gary told him.

Fear and anger spread across his face. He grabbed the black phone on his desk and called the police. He was dressed in a black suit with a hint of white on his collar, near his vocal cords, as if his purity was in word, alone. He was so uptight, so beyond the love of Christ, yet supposedly he was a representative of Jesus. Hordes of people respected and looked to him for spiritual guidance. Yet, here we are, the true followers of Christ, asking in His name for our needs to carry on His mission and instead we were being thrown out.

Within minutes two police officers were by our sides, escorting us into their car. "We didn't do anything, brothers," Gary told them.

"We have our orders, we have to take you to the county line," one said.

"We haven't had a meal yet today, could you give freely of some 'coin' for a loaf of bread and some peanut butter?" I asked them.

So the driver stopped at a store and we all went in and got some juice, bread, peanut butter, jam and chips.

"We really appreciate your love brothers," I told them when we got back into the car.

"What are you doing around here anyway?" The driver asked. "There are lots of rednecks in this town, you know. It's probably best that we're driving you out of here."

"We are disciples of Jesus Christ brother. We travel around preaching His word to all," I explained. "You see, there is a lot more going on than the human eye can see. Spiritual warfare is everywhere, but we've already won. So we are just 'watching the movie,' playing the role, working for God. He sets everything up, we just follow the Holy Spirit 'inside' which leads us to where we are supposed to be. Like that movie with the priest; it was all 'set up,' not only for his benefit, but for you guys, too. God always has us exactly where He wants us."

"Well, I don't know anything about that kin'a stuff, but you two seem like pretty harmless folk to me," one of them said. "Here we are, take care of yourselves now." Then they dropped us off and drove away. The country road was quiet; the night, black. I followed my brother, walking on the rocks on the shoulder of the road. It was so dark, I could barely see in front of me. We passed by a few fields, but when we walked closer to them we saw that they all had barbed wire fences protecting them. We moved to the other side of the road, but found the same thing. There was just nowhere to rest.

My body, so exhausted, had to be pushed onwards. Suddenly, the blinding headlights of a car, speeding down the road towards us, invaded the darkness. Music and loud laughter spilled from its windows as it approached us. The car slowed down as someone from within threw a beer bottle at us and then screeched away; its occupants roaring with laughter. The bottle just missed my head and skinned the side of Gary's.

We never spoke. I was fighting negativity. I had wanted to shout at those 'bastards.' Hungry, tired and downright stretched too thin, I could feel the vibrations of the world creeping more easily into my space. I prayed for strength and guidance to endure this little 'storm' with strong sails.

Finally, we came to a stretch of land; a little hill off to our right that wasn't fenced. I followed Gary up the hill to a fairly flat spot on the far side, protected from the road by the hill. A resting spot. "Praise God," I said as we unrolled our bedrolls. Then I made us sandwiches. Everything tasted so great.

"What a feast," Gary said. I could see his white teeth when he smiled. The crickets sang through the forest. This had been a test in following our feelings, instead of our eyes. I never did like walking in the dark. Had this movie been 'set up' for me? Was it time for me to let go of another 'old tape' and trust God to see for me?

❀ CHAPTER TWENTY-ONE ❀

A few days later, we sat by the freeway for hours in the heat, watching the cars pass. "Billboard service," said Gary, breaking the silence. "It sure develops patience."

"Yepper, brother, it does," I said.

After hours, our 'connection' slammed on his brakes and backed up. "Come on in," he said, opening the passenger door to his truck. "Where are you heading?" He asked, once we were inside.

"We are just 'in the wind' brother, we'll go as far as you wish to take us," Gary said.

"No destination? That's strange. What are you guys, anyway, Hare Krishna or something?"

Gary laughed. "No, brother, we follow Jesus Christ and we don't have a destination because we are already there. We are living in heaven in our hearts, so it really doesn't matter where we go physically. There are times when we feel definite 'pulls' to a certain place, but right now we're just going with the flow," he told him.

This man took us onto a road called the "Blue Ridge Mountain Parkway." It was a long sight-seeing road off the main highway, running through the Blue Ridge Mountains and passing through quite a few states. We were dropped off up north and walked south, passing through Virginia, West Virginia, Kentucky and Tennessee. There were lookout points every so often where we could see for miles. I felt so small at these times, compared to the magnitude of the splendor surrounding me. Gary and I walked much, ate little and praised God through it all. It's hard to say how long this took for we didn't keep track of time, but I guessed three or four weeks. There were nature trails off into the woods and we went exploring, catching glimpses of wildlife; squirrels, birds, moles, snakes, rabbits and bears. For the first while, at night, we would tie our tote sacks up in a tree because someone gave us a whole bag of Pecan Sandy cookies and bears love cookies.

One evening, while resting in the woods on a dark, wet night, I heard the rustling of leaves and branches being crushed underfoot by a large animal. The sound was so close to us that it woke me right up. Opening my eyes brought no solace, for the night was black, as black as when my eyes were closed. The sound of heavy breathing came closer; the animal was so close that I could feel its breath on my face. Gary was oblivious to it all and fears' icy claws grabbed hold of my throat. I couldn't utter a sound. Was this a childhood fear about to be played out? Visions of mountain lions and bears with dagger sharp fangs, ready to rip a hunk of my flesh, flashed through my mind. My body instinctively cut back on breathing as my 'Christ mind' came into play to calm the 'finite mind.' Animals can smell fear. I knew the chemistry behind that. So here, in complete darkness in the woods, I lay frozen with a large, unknown animal breathing down on me! "Let's see how her faith holds up here," I imagined an angel saying, "no killing and no fear." I told myself over and over and felt a calming wave wash through me. It's all in the Father's will. I have no idea how long I lay there with the mystery creature, but after some time I felt and heard it walk away, the sound of twigs breaking beneath its heavy weight.

There were few towns along the parkway, so after our food stash was depleted we ate mainly berries. The blueberries in one place grew on such high bushes that they looked like trees. They were plentiful and easy to pick.

The few people we met along the way all warned us of the rattlesnakes that were abundant. They also told us the bears were not too friendly, either, and thought we were crazy to be sleeping in the woods. We walked and climbed about twenty miles a day. When we laid our bodies down my feet were on fire. "Reflexology to the max," I thought.

One day as we were walking I felt so high, as if my feet weren't touching the ground, as if I was floating over it. I could see my body walking as I hovered above. We believed that our bodies were transforming into light as the vibration we lived in became higher. The physical plane was a dense vibration of a higher plane, which went beyond the astral plane to 'the spirit' world. So we believed that we weren't going to die a physical death, but instead transform into our light bodies when Jesus takes us up in the first resurrection. We called this 'blinking out.'

How I had always yearned to be able to fly, to be free from what held my spirit captive in this physical plane. God was raising me up for a short while, giving me a glimpse of what was to be. This would happen often, he would give me a revelation, or vision and I would feel so elated. Then he would put me through a tribulation and my awareness would drop. Two steps forward and one step back, on Jacob's ladder. Every time I went through a 'storm,' I came out of it with a little more wisdom and understanding of 'the truth.' The deeper I got into it, the deeper I could see. I began to realize that everything I went through was for the ultimate good and was learning to praise God through it all.

One day, Gary led me to a wondrous place in the woods. There was a clean, fast moving river running through this spot. It was a conservation area, somewhere in the hills in one of the states. The only state we tried to reach was 'the state of bliss,' so it really didn't matter to us. I think Gary knew where we were; he carried a map and looked at it now and again, but I didn't concern myself with the physical details as such. For a few days now, Gary had been feeling that he was getting the message from God that we should fast. So we set up camp by the river bed, on a flat piece of land. We laid out our bedrolls, with our army blankets on the bottom to soften our bed. We put the Bugler can at the head, in between us, and there it was; the official Christ Brother resting spot.

It had been quite a few days since we had bathed and the gurgling water seemed to be beckoning me. I went into the bushes, took off my robe and put my apron back on. It seemed ridiculous that I had to bathe with clothes on, but I had to be a righteous sister. I thought about Richard as I bathed in the river. What happened to him? Had it been my fault? I wasn't conscious of doing anything wrong. We never had sex again after that horrible time in the orchard. Did I cause him to fall in love with me, somehow? "God forgive me, if I am to blame for Richard losing his grip. I only want to serve you; I want to be a righteous, holy sister. I have given you my life, my whole heart, mind and soul. Fill me with your love," I prayed.

We fasted for three days by the river, the sun, wind and water healing us. Hours would pass without a word. The silence was totally comfortable with Gary. Being with him was almost like being alone. God sure did bless me, by setting Gary and I up to share this space together, I thought.

My stomach ached. Flashes of me starving up in the Peruvian mountains came to mind. I had to battle these ghosts of my past. My 'finite mind' and body did not like the feeling of being hungry at all.

This denial of the flesh brought me 'inside,' to depths of 'the spirit' that I had not yet touched. Revelations and realizations filled those three days. By the third day I was light-headed, mouth parched, yet so high–beyond hunger now. I could have fasted for much longer, just lying in the sun beside my brother, in this peaceful place.

In Tennessee we got off the trail and a good-hearted fellow took us to his country home for a few days, where we rested in the unfinished basement. There were two boys, and a girl, and a "Ma," and "Pa." The eldest child was close to our age. He took us for picnics. One night, we were riding down the road back to his home when he stopped the car on a bridge overlooking the mountains and a valley. "Look, isn't it amazing!" He pointed to a cluster of lights twinkling in the valley. We got out of the car to get a better look. "You see, there is no town there, no group of houses, no nothing. In the daytime people have gone down there to see where the lights are coming from, but they find nothing but trees and meadows. There's been scores of scientists come round here to check it out, but nobody knows anything about it," Dan said in his heavy Tennessee accent. We stood there in wonderment, gazing at those mystery lights that flickered reddish-pink against the darkening horizon.

Dan's parents were generous and comical, always joking around and I found it amusing that they addressed each other as "Ma" or "Pa." I helped Ma cook and clean. She was a sweetheart of a lady, fussing over Gary and I as though we were her own children. Next to where we rested in this house was a boat. I found Gary looking at it often with a thousand-mile stare. He also gazed at the pictures of sail boats that were plastered on the wall.

"Sister, how would you like to sail?" He said on one such occasion. "I feel that God is calling us to the sea, to preach the word to those who travel the waters. In the world, before I 'transformed,' I worked on the ships and sailed sailboats. I was living in Florida and was just about to complete building a sailboat that had taken me three years, when the brothers came to me. I never got the chance to sail it. I gave it up to God to live this life. For years now, sailing hasn't crossed my mind. I've prayed about this and God has told me it's O.K. to sail now. He's giving it back to me. I feel a 'pull' to the sea."

"Right on, brother, I'm beside you," I said, wondering how I would overcome my motion sickness in a sailboat.

And so to the sea we traveled. We reached the southeastern shore of South Carolina one warm night. Someone had given us some fresh peanuts. We actually pulled them out of the ground at this farm where we spent the night. I was amazed to see that peanuts grow like potatoes. We made a fire by the beach and using the salty water from the ocean and an old can, we boiled a big batch of peanuts and feasted on them. This was a dish common to the south called 'goober peas.' We ate the shells and all; they were softened by the salt water and tasted salty. Well, here we were, eating 'goober peas' and listening to the ocean tear away at the shore, smelling the ocean air and feeling so high . . . .

A short time later I came crashing back to earth with an insatiable itch that covered my body. I must have rubbed up against some poison oak in the woods, for I was covered with an unbearable, itchy rash. Night after night, day after day, I battled to keep my hands from tearing my flesh open, in an effort to stop the irritation. I tried rubbing alcohol, lemon juice, calamine lotion, but nothing soothed it. I battled between 'the flesh' and 'the spirit' for days, and in the end 'the spirit' won the battle. God was not going to give me more than I could endure.

Along the coast we traveled, checking out marinas in various ports in search of our sailboat 'connection.' We rested along the seashore. So did the sand fleas. The houses along the beach were built on stilts that rose to great heights. We watched the heaving water swelling and receding while gulls bobbed on the waves.

Brother Gary and I were becoming very close. We truly loved and trusted each other. As with Richard and I, we experienced telepathic communication. One day in particular, I remember it being very strong. We were 'catching some space' lying in a park in the afternoon. The vibration of love flowing between us was intense; we felt the merging of our spirits. The feeling was so wonderful that I wanted to ride it forever. Our telepathy was beyond words, or any scientific concept, so I can't adequately explain the feeling.

Afterwards, Gary spoke to me, "Sister, I have never felt so close to anyone. Sometimes I feel guilty about how much love we share and must remember to keep my focus on God, who's Spirit inside of us and is the source of that love."

"I understand what you mean, brother. At times I feel that I'm becoming attached to you and must constantly give it up to the Father. In giving it up it seems I receive more love and a higher understanding of true love," I told him.

Throughout my travels, along with all the other 'creature features' I had to deal with, I had wisdom teeth that would go up and down. For weeks, the pain of teeth, trying to break the hard flesh of gums, gave me headaches and 'jammed my space' constantly. A few times a tooth would become impacted and infected, releasing its poison through my whole body. A woman we shared lemonade with on the large veranda of her country home gave me some clove oil and aspirins. Eventually, one tooth got so bad that we sought out a dentist in the next town. He cut my gum open to let out the pus and enable the tooth to finish emerging.

I looked at the whole 'wisdom tooth trip' on a spiritual level. True wisdom was trying to push its way through the hard skin of my 'finite mind.' At times it would almost make it through, but then it would be hung up and infected by some trip of the mind. The dentist cutting my gum was like the hand of God, searing my mind to help it find true wisdom. The interesting thing is that all of my wisdom teeth did come in during my travels.

One evening, the gravel behind a theatre in a small town was our roll-out spot. Gary and I were resting head to head, making a straight line with our bodies because of the levelness of the spot. Instead of 'blinking out' this night, it seemed that I was caught in between the conscious and unconscious, in a weird realm. I was aware of the heaviness of my body. It felt as though an invisible force had me pinned down, as if someone, or something was lying on my body. I heard voices and noises. Some of the voices sounded familiar and I thought I heard Gary calling me. I tried to turn around to see him, but I couldn't move. There seemed to be a definite presence of evil, although I could have interpreted it as evil because it was the unknown. Many times I tried to move, but I couldn't move, or speak, for when I tried to yell, my voice failed. I chanted the keys in my mind, but the voices tried to overpower them, all talking at once.

Wherever I was, I didn't like it; I either wanted to wake up, or go to sleep. I couldn't even open my eyes, for the strange force had taken control over my entire body and was trying for my mind as well. After what seemed like an eternity I finally pulled loose and, turning over onto my stomach, reached out my hand and yelled, "BROTHER!"

As soon as this took place, my body seemed to be swept away into space at an incredible speed with Gary getting smaller and smaller until he and the world were no longer visible. I have no idea what took place, or how long I was there, or even where 'there' was; but at last I found myself back in my bedroll, the force gone and my body and mind feeling normal once more. I woke Gary and shared my experience with him, quite shaken by it all.

"We are being attacked by demons because we are with God and pose a threat to Satan," Gary decided. "There's also a lesson here for you, sister. Instead of calling out to me, you should have called out to God. He should be your security, not me." Gary's words hit me hard.

That experience was one of a few that Gary and I both had with the definite presence of a powerful evil spirit. Another time, we were resting in a churchyard side by side. The night was clear and still. Then all of a sudden, the wind was so strong that it actually picked me up and blew me on top of Gary! There was that invisible presence again, that same feeling of hovering beings surrounding us. Gary and I both awoke and sat up in our bedrolls. I looked at the trees to see if a physical wind was blowing, but they remained still. "Can you feel it, brother? I asked. That is the same spirit that kept me captive the other night."

"I feel it, sister, it's strong. It is playing on our sexual nature tonight. It is a sex demon, that's why it blew you onto me. We must stay alert all night," was Gary's explanation. We sat up all night, chanting, "No Killing, No Sex, No Materialism; Jesus Christ Lightning Amen." He had decided that since the love between us was pure, Satan wanted to taint it with lust. We were victorious in our battle and the presence left by morning.

Focusing my attention on God and 'the truth' every moment was a goal that was becoming more real as time passed. I also noticed a merging in my mind of Lightning Amen with Jesus and God. I had a hard time with this at first, but now their unity was unfolding.

One of Gary's favorite treats was potato chips. On many occasions we would hit up a potato chip truck delivering to a store and we were given many bags of chips. I didn't particularly like chips. They were 'junk food' to me. I began to wonder if God had set me up with this brother to end my hang up and 'old tapes' about preferring healthy foods. Lately I had been feeling a desire for fruit, almond butter, miso soup, figs, almonds and cashews. Could all these potato chips be a lesson in placing less importance on physical food?

We had just spent a few days at the home of a really good 'connection.' The woman wanted us to stay longer and loved to listen to Gary preach. She gave me a twenty-dollar bill when we left. "Buy some good food with it," she said. I thought about the things I'd been craving and battled with this thought the whole day, wondering if I had the right to mention it to Gary. As soon as I was able to shoot it out of my thoughts, it would come back. Finally, I got up enough nerve. "Brother, I've been battling the desire for some health food," I said. "In the world I was extremely health-conscious; at one point I only ate fruit. I feel a need to indulge in some good foods once again, in order to burn out on it and get it out of my space," I confessed.

"Right on, sister, can do," Gary told me.

He asked a man on the street if he knew where there was a health food store and it so happened that there was one right around the corner from where we were. The scent of herbs and flower oils filled the air of the store. I took a deep breath of the old familiar smell. "Whatever you want, sister," Gary said with a smile, "we have twenty dollars to spend."

This immediately put me into doubt and guilt. Twenty dollars was a lot of money to us. It would last us a week on the road. He just said it was O.K. to blow it all in one place? I went over to the bins of food. I scooped up a bag of cashew nuts, almonds and figs. Then I proceeded to the peanut butter maker and filled a container with freshly ground peanut butter. Next, a jar of coconut milk and some organic pears and peaches, then I topped it all off with a jar of almond butter. Gary just smiled that wonderful smile of his as we carried the two full bags of food to the park.

Everything tasted fantastic. "Good stuff," Gary said as we ate. "It should last us quite a while, too." He was being supportive of this struggle for me. I still didn't fully understand why we shouldn't take care of our bodies while we were still using them for God's work.

We were nearly given a little sailboat, but it never materialized. Gary and I walked many miles along the beach, heading north. In North Carolina we connected with a man who gave us a ride to Norfolk, Virginia. Robert was on his way to visit his Grandma. He was very responsive to Gary's preaching, soaking it up like a sponge. When it came time for us to leave he begged us to stay with him for a few more days.

Somewhere along the Virginia coast there is a town that contains a building that is a monument to Edgar Cayce. We roamed about the place, watched a few films about Edgar and met quite a few open people there.

We traveled on up to Chesapeake Bay with Robert. It was there that he asked to put on a robe. While walking through the city streets, Gary led us into a fabric store. "Time for new robes," he stated with a smile. We walked over to the cotton section and picked out some heavy white denim. "This looks good and strong, it should last quite a while," Gary said.

Sewing a new robe was always a special treat. In this case it was a special blessing; brand new heavy cotton instead of used sheets.

Each Christ Family robe was hand-stitched. Cutting the material out, the length of the thread on the needle, the tightness of the stitches, the spacing of the stitches; each was symbolic. Each taught some revelation, or deep meaning. I learned that trying to save steps, or time, by putting a long thread on the needle only led to tangles in the thread. This tangling taught me much about expecting things to work out too soon and having patience. There were moments when the sewing felt like work, when I grew impatient to have the robe completed. It was through these moments that God taught me more about enjoying each moment to the fullest. The only time a job feels like work is when I'd rather be doing something else. Wiping every thought out of the mind and just sewing was another form of meditation.

Eventually, I got to the point where no matter whose robe I was stitching, I treated it as if it was for Jesus Himself. Every single stitch was pulled through with the positive energy of love. Gary and I helped Robert learn the art of hand-stitching. He was clumsy with the needle at first, but by the second day showed a definite ease with the project. Gary and I sewed most of it for him. At this point, Gary gave up all efforts towards a boat 'connection' and sailing south. God had sent us a new brother to guide and teach.

Robert was an architect and found it extremely hard to recondition himself not to gaze at buildings and admire them. Gary had to remind him constantly to look at nature, things that God had made and give glory to Him, not man. There were many things Robert had to let go of in order to live the life of Christ and it was our job to make him aware of what had to go. The struggles and battles within a new brother were intense and much doubt and fear still remained in him. The clear, high vibration that Gary and I had traveled in no longer existed. Because of our genuine love for him we climbed down the ladder in order to reach our hands out to Robert and pull him up. The 'transformation' of Robert was also a hard time for me. The things that he was being hit with, hit me too, but on a much deeper level than when I had 'transformed.' I realized that I still had much of the world and its ways inside me. I was being hit in the deepest depths of my being as revelations and realizations came to me one after another like rolling stones; crushing images and ego. My eyes were opened to see as I had never seen before. The pain felt good and I wondered if Gary was going through this too.

I felt so insignificant and small compared to the universe and God's plan. I was very quiet and still. I felt shame because I had thought I was beyond some of the things that were still in me. Perhaps I was seeing myself in this light in order to be able to relate to Robert, better.

Robert's robe looked dazzling on him. He definitely had that 'new brother look,' though; white skin, short hair, no beard or moustache, a little overweight and tender-footed. A seasoned brother, on the other hand, carried himself with an air of confidence and righteous pride. He walked erect, with a lean, tanned body. The soles of his feet were tough, his hair and beard long, his eyes clear and magnetic.

The three of us traveled inland down county roads. We stayed at a campground for a few days, sewing new robes for Gary and me, too. It was a wonderful spot by a river.

This time we sewed our own robes; most other times we sewed each other's. Gary and I both agreed on making the A-frame design, in which the arm seams were made at the shoulder and the material was cut on an angle, so there was less of it on the top and flaring at the bottom. The other style was a rectangle cut, more of a square, with the arms attached at the elbows. This style had a lot of excess material. There were disagreements in the 'Family' regarding which style was acceptable. I didn't see why we just couldn't make the one we preferred and that's exactly what Gary and I did. I was relieved that he wasn't hung up on the issue.

In this campground, the water seemed to laugh with pleasure, while running over the smooth rocks in the stream. There was a small, sandy beach where we sat to sew our robes. The river was clear and full of rapids and small swimming holes. Most of the time we used sand to clean our bowls and bodies. This time I had been given a bottle of pure, vegetarian, biodegradable, mint-flavored soap. It was called Dr. Brenner's pure Castile soap and could be used as a shampoo, body soap, laundry soap, toothpaste; you name it. It was the sort of soap found in your local health food store. The label was covered in writing, some of which were spiritual messages such as "Health is our great wealth," and "Absolute cleanliness is Godliness," and even, "Love can strike like greased lightning sent by God to spark mere dust to intense blazing fire and create new love-faith-hope-guts-will-strength as only God inspires!"

One thing that Robert asked many times was: "When will the sisters be equal to the brothers?" He saw our definitely subservient role and didn't like it.

"The sisters are equal to the brothers, we both have our roles to play in 'the movie'," Gary told him. "The brother creates the space and the sister fills it with love. It's the natural order of things, first came Adam, then God created Eve from his rib to be a helpmate. Since Eve led Adam out of the Garden of Eden, she must follow him back in."

Robert wasn't very satisfied with that answer. I could see the discontent in his eyes.

"Don't worry about me, brother, I'm happy with my position in the Lord's Army." I told him. We were all sitting around the camp fire and I started singing a song that one of the sisters had composed. "Look above. You can see his crown in the heavens. Lightning's come and he's brought his reward with him. Are you prepared to fly and enter in the kingdom? In the song, the rhythm of creation, in the flow, forget yourself, seeing God in all things. Don't be caught behind, climb on board the A train . . ."

One morning a barrage of trucks and cars carrying men with rifles invaded our serene campsite and the peaceful vibrations changed to uneasiness. Without a word, we packed up and as we were leaving, I heard someone mention it was the first day of squirrel hunting. I felt angry as we drove down that dirt road. Those same squirrels, who were our friends and whom we fed and played with were now in great danger of losing their lives. When would the slaughter of innocent creatures end?

Gary didn't like driving in a 'spaceship' (car). He preferred to walk and so did I. Our plan was to sell Robert's car and bring the money to the Christ Family's desert camp. In one of the larger cities, we sold it to a used car dealer for three hundred dollars. It was worth much more, but we didn't really care, we were happy to be free of it.

As we walked through the slum area of town, a young man came running over to us. "Wait! Wait, I want to come with you guys. You are angels, aren't you?"

"Yes, we are, brother, sent from the Most High; a special delivery for you. Take off your shoes and follow us," Gary said to him.

Without a word, he took off his worn out leather shoes and left them in the street. We walked in silence for about a mile and when we reached a park we all sat down under the shade of a grand old tree. "My name is Dave," said the youth looking over at Gary with searching blue eyes. "What must I do to live as you do?"

Gary looked over at Robert and putting his hand out to him, said, "Tell him the truth, brother."

Robert was stunned. "Well, br-brother," he stuttered, "the Kingdom of Heaven is at hand. It is now time for man to open his eyes to the illusions of this evil world and turn his back on it. Jesus told us there would be wars and rumors of wars, son against father and mother against daughter. All of these signs are happening now. The greatest sign of all is that Jesus is back, the Second Coming is here. He's living as we do, wearing a white robe . . ." Once Robert got going, 'the spirit' flowed from his lips. Gary and I looked at each other with the sort of pride that parents have for their child.

Dave went to his room at the Y.M.C.A. and took the sheet off his bed. He had little of anything. We were invited to spend the night at some people's home and there we sewed Dave a robe. Being a child of the ghetto, his feet and body were already pretty tough. He kept right up with us without a single complaint about sore feet. Two by two, we walked out of town.

Days later, Robert asked Gary if it would be all right if he took the new brother on his pilgrimage. Robert was always sorry, unusually polite and we teased him about it often. Gary laughed, "Follow your heart, brother. If that's where God is leading you, it must be all right." Then he and I watched as our baby brothers took their first steps away from us. "They'll make it, sister, so just put that mother bear instinct up on a shelf somewhere and leave them in the hands of the Father." Gary had read my thoughts. Yet, I had a strong feeling that both of them were going back to the ways of the world.

I smiled at him, masking my doubts. "Right on, brother, let's do some cruising."

"How about checking that Pizza Hut out for a salad?" He asked.

"Sounds good, let's boogie." We walked into the restaurant and I asked to speak to the manager. "We are traveling Christians, brother. Can you find it in your heart to give freely of a salad in the name of Christ?" I looked at him, my eyes never wavering from his. He glanced away in a bit of discomfort, breaking the stare.

"How about a pizza, too?" He answered.

We all broke out in smiles. "Right on, brother, we appreciate your kindness. Can you make it without cheese, only vegetables on it?" I asked.

"A pizza without cheese? Why?" He asked.

"Well, brother, we don't eat animals, or their products. We are strict vegetarians for love of God's creation."

"A pizza without cheese coming right up. Help yourself to the salad bar in the meantime."

We knew the food was just a 'prop' to inform the manager about being vegetarian, but that 'prop' sure did taste great.

The hills of West Virginia flowed into misty Blue Mountains. I'd never seen mountains that color before. The forests were starting to change into their costumes of many colors. It must have been autumn. Pear and apple trees, pregnant with fruit, grew wild along the dirt road, offering gifts to us.

The crisp air, carried by strong winds, let me know deep inside that changes were right around the corner. Throughout my life, most of my inner changes had taken place in the spring, or fall when the earth was changing.

By now, my feet were used to walking without shoes and I enjoyed it so much that I doubted I'd be able to stand the confinement of shoes anymore. 'Free toes' is where it was at. I was much more aware of how and where I stepped now. Walking through the forest, I now avoided crushing wild flowers, whereas when I wore shoes I wasn't even looking where I walked half the time. Walking over moss was my favorite. In my visions of the Garden of Eden, the perfection we would soon return to, the ground was covered in moss. I was looking forward to that day with an ever-growing passion. Although I loved the earth, I didn't like what man had done to her and it was too late to turn back now; too much damage was already done. I praised God for all the wonders that surrounded me, but I was learning to detach myself from it all.

We were being mentally trained to walk through the coming deluge and not be affected by any of it. At times I would imagine it happening; bloody bodies screaming and laying everywhere, buildings destroyed, cities devastated and the entire system overthrown. And I would just keep walking, in the world, but not of it, understanding that what I was seeing had to be. The physical was just an illusion anyway; 'the spirit' in those bodies would live forever and 'the spirit' was what was real. The greatest test for me was to imagine witnessing people I loved, being among those bodies and still be able to walk through it without emotion. At this point in my journey I thought I was almost there. I no longer had doubts about the life I was living. My perception was clear and I felt honored to be a servant of the Most High and to know without a doubt that I was in the light of 'the truth.' Everyday I 'copped space' (understood more). My awareness was unfolding at an incredible rate.

Gary was such a wonderful being to 'share space' with. He had gentleness that shone through him like a luminous aura. I loved following him, listening to him preach, resting beside him. I truly felt as though I were his sister. We were like little children, blindly holding onto the hands of our Father, allowing Him to lead us. It was such a freeing feeling to not worry where I was going, where I would sleep, what I would eat. We gave everything up to the Father who led us and truly took care of us.

At times I would catch glimpses of the divine plan of God; of how He sets up so many people to be part of the whole movie, each one benefiting and learning a different lesson. The wonders of our God and the infinite wisdom and love that He offers so freely are extraordinary. I praised God for giving me this sight, but as soon as I held onto it, wanting to see more, it was taken away. Just like that. This taught me many lessons; one being not to hold onto anything, even spiritual sight. Everything is a gift from God, to be given, or taken away at any moment. God knew my heart. He wanted me to go with the flow and just be an open vessel for His love to flow through. I was learning.

Riding in an old pickup truck with Jim, a 'primo connection,' we started up a rough muddy, dirt road that sloped steeply. Thick forest lined both sides of the narrow road. I hoped there wouldn't be a car coming from the other direction, for there was barely enough room for us. The truck sputtered as the driver put it in over-drive and flew over the potholes, knocking us all over the place. I thought about my life as we struggled along and compared it to that road. How many times had I struggled in the thick muck and had to ride over huge potholes?

The climax unfolded as mist rolled across the enchanting farm, where thick forest opened into rolling green-blue grass, a huge garden and an ancient, classic farmhouse. White pillars supported the large porch. Mountains soared behind and all around the house; the view went on for miles. "Here we are; home sweet home," Jim said with a sigh of relief. "It's a hard ride getting here, but once you're up here it sure is worth it. We're on top of Peter's Mountain," he informed us.

"The air is so fresh and clean up here, it's a wonderful place." I said. Gold and orange leaves added to its beauty as the last rays of sunlight sparkled on them. We walked around the yard a bit. There were two pear-apple trees bearing fruit in the front yard. In the back was a small orchard of apple trees.

As we walked into the house, I felt at home right away. The air gave a hint of incense. An old tapestry rug lay in the centre of a living room that was large, old fashioned and homey. In the kitchen, Jim had glass jars filled with dried beans, rice, nuts and dried fruit. It looked a lot like the kitchen I once had. There were even biodegradable soap and shampoo in the bathroom. Jim told us there was something wrong with the plumbing in the house and that we had to use the outhouse because there was no running water right now. He collected rain water in big buckets. It felt so good to be there with this very sensitive person who was receiving 'the truth' as if it were a natural thing for him. Jim was already mostly vegetarian except for bits of dairy products and for the right reasons, too. He reminded me of my physical brother, Ed, in his outward appearance and mannerisms. He was tall and slender, with brown hair that hung past his shoulders and a long beard. His hazel-green eyes were kind. He could have put the robe on right there and have looked like a well-seasoned brother right away.

That night, Gary and I rested on the porch with Jim's dog, Ben. Ben was a large black Lab with a loving and mellow nature. I was elated to have a dog friend again. The stars looked so close. It was a magical night. But, in the morning, we were wet from the mist and it was cold. So for the remainder of our stay we rested up in the attic.

I did a lot of cooking there. Jim showed me how to make tofu and we made apple jelly, apple juice and dried apples.

Every day, Jim seemed to come closer to accepting 'the truth.' He already seemed like a brother to me; there was no spiritual warfare, no conflicts. Every night we shared a meal by candlelight and talked about truth.

"You people have so much courage, to live the way you do. No home, no possessions, no dreams, or desires of this world . . ." Jim said, admiration evident in his voice.

"It's not really a matter of courage, brother, it's faith," Gary answered. "You see, we really don't want any credit. Give all praise and glory to God. He is the one who changed us. He is the One who is leading us, taking care of us, setting us up with you and other 'connections.' You see, it's like we are just actors in a movie. The difference is, we don't know the script until the moment we are to speak. It then is given to us, spoken through us. It's quite amazing."

"Yes, it is amazing. You people are so free. You are totally open and honest and so pure. You aren't just talking about abstract truth, you are downright living it!" Jim said.

"You can too, brother. That is why we have been led here to you. God knows your heart. He knows you desire truth more than anything," I told him.

"I know, but there are still a few things that don't seem right to me. I believe spiritual enlightenment is a very individual, personal journey. The idea of having to follow the rules of a group doesn't seem right to me. I don't want anyone to be a middleman between God and me. I don't want to have to live up to anyone else's interpretation of truth." He was so close to accepting 'the truth' and putting on a robe, but I could feel the apprehension in him. You had to snap the last string of attachment in order to take that first step. Like a babe learning how to walk, you had to humble yourself before God, be stripped of your false ego and admit that you know nothing. From there, the Lord could teach you how to be a new shining being, but you had to give up the old in order to receive the new.

One day we went down the road to a nearby farm, where a friend of Jim, lived. "Jake is an interesting guy," he told us on our way there. "He lets me take showers at his place and I'm sure he'd welcome you, too."

"Right on, brother, a shower sounds great."

Three dogs came out to greet us with long, wet tongues and wagging tails. Open fields bordered by forests and rolling hills surrounded the house. A tall, thin man with a sinister grin and blue eyes greeted us. The lines on his face gave evidence of much laughter. "Good to see you, Jim. Well, well, what have we here? Hare Krishna, or the Ku Klux Klan?" He asked with a laugh.

"We are children of God, brother, followers of Christ," Gary informed him.

"Well, how do you do, children of Christ?" He put out his hand for a handshake.

"The handshake is in the heart, brother," said Gary, refusing to shake his hand.

"Well, everybody, come on in, I've just made some coffee," said Jake, motioning to us to follow. His home was new and still in need of some finishing touches. The kitchen was large and bright, with a glass wall that overlooked meadows and mountains. We sat at a huge wooden table. Then Jake took out a Bugler can and started rolling himself a Bugler. I had never seen an 'earthling' smoke Bugler tobacco before. So I took out our Bugler can and started rolling smokes, too. We all laughed. Although this brother seemed a bit 'bogus' and mocking, here was our common ground.

"Now that's some good tobacco, ain't it? Jake said. "So here we have Brother Gary and Sister Maureen way up in the hills of West Virginia. What's brought you two here," he asked?

"We just blow 'in the wind,' brother. We are in the will of the Creator and He wants us here right now," Gary told him.

"Where do your food and clothing come from?" He asked.

226

"We have faith in God that He'll provide those material things for us and He does. We just concern ourselves with the things of 'the spirit' and our physical needs are taken care of," Gary explained.

Jake looked long and hard at us and then took a plastic bag from his pocket and rolled the biggest joint I have ever seen. It was cigar-sized, at least. He fired it up and took several long tokes before passing it around. Then he cracked a Cheshire cat grin and said, "Well, what about plutonium?"

I looked at him, not sure what he was talking about. He was a hard character to figure out. At times he seemed sincerely interested in what we had to say, but other times he mocked us. For example, when we explained that we didn't believe in sex, he looked pityingly at me and said, "Oh sister, what a waste, you are such a beautiful, delectable creature."

When Jake wasn't rolling a Bugler, he was rolling a joint. It amazed me that he could still function. He had two workers who lived in a little guest house whom we met and had the opportunity to preach to. We visited the farm a few times before we left Peter's Mountain.

Back up at Jim's place, the energy was such a contrast to where we had just been. Again, it was symbolic to me that Jake lived at the bottom of the mountain and Jim at the top. Jim was much higher in spiritual awareness. The three of us flowed. "I'm really enjoying your company, he said to us one night, breaking the silence. I've grown quite accustomed to having you two here. Stay as long as you wish."

"Brother, we feel the same way. You feel like a brother to us. But, there are many people out there who are calling out for truth. We have a mission; we must continue to travel and tune people in to 'channel seven.' You are being called to come with us, Jim," Gary told him.

"I knew the time was coming soon. A part of me wants to come. All that you have talked to me about seems true in my heart, yet there is something that doesn't seem to fit. I can't put my finger on it, but it's there. I can't go until I find that missing piece of the puzzle," Jim explained.

"Perhaps that piece is a part of you that is afraid to go for it, one hundred percent, brother," I said to him. "Taking the first step is like walking off a cliff in the darkness. To begin, you have to let go of the world and the program."

Jim drove us down the mountain to a small town. There was silence all the way. I felt his turmoil. "I just can't come right now," he told us as we got out of the truck.

"Just keep living the keys and everything will fall into place," Gary assured him. "'In the wind,' brother," we both told him.

"'In the wind'," he echoed. Emotion knocked on the door of my heart, but I refused to answer it.

❊ CHAPTER TWENTY-TWO ❊

The cool winds were becoming more bitter each day and resting outside was uncomfortable, so we walked south, towards Tennessee. As we sat by the side of the road for a smoke break one day, a dark car passed us, then slammed on its brakes and backed up, "Do you kids want a ride? I'm going as far as Princeton," a man's voice called to us.

"Right on, brother," Gary said as we got into the car.

"You people are peculiarly dressed," the driver continued as he started down the road. "Why the white robes?"

"They are our wedding dresses, brother, a symbol of our marriage to Jesus Christ," Gary answered. "They are also our white flags of surrender. We have surrendered our will to God and have given up the fight against Him."

"You say you have married Jesus? What do you mean by that?" The man asked earnestly.

"It means that we are living the same life as Him; no killing, no sex, and no materialism; peace, true love and harmony. Jesus is back on earth, riding in a flesh body. The Second Coming of Christ is already at hand. He's back and we are His followers. We have given up our old lives and ways to obey him. Our mission is to preach his word and gather the chosen ones from the four corners of the earth," Gary said.

"How do you know this guy really is Jesus? The Bible warns of many false prophets leading thousands astray by performing miracles and claiming to be Christ," the man asked.

Gary answered him without a doubt. "I know he is Jesus because of His fruits. This life has changed me into a loving and caring, unselfish being. I know because I called out for truth and wanted it more than anything in this world. Why would God deceive me?"

Next the man addressed me. "When was the last time you saw your parents?"

"We don't space on time much, brother," I told him. "Time is a man-made concept, a mere illusion. My parents are no more important to me than you, or anyone else. You see, true love leaves no room for favorites, we love everyone equally," I told him.

"I see." He paused for a few minutes. Then he started in again, "But, don't you think your parents are worried about you? I don't see that as being a good fruit."

"I have faith that God is looking after them, brother. Anything they go through will eventually teach them lessons that will bring them closer to God," I answered him. He seemed to be really interested in our cause.

"So where are you from?" He asked me.

"Well, brother, we are from God, but if you want to know where my physical body was born, it was Thunder Bay, Ontario, up in Canada." I don't know why I gave him that information; we usually didn't reveal such things.

"Canada!" He said excitedly. "I've always wanted to go there. I hear the fishing is great."

"We don't fish, brother. We let the fish be free. We are strict vegetarians for the love of the animals and to obey God's law of ". . . *You shall not kill* . . . ." *(Exodus 20:13)* You see it's time now to start walking back into the Garden of Eden, where the lion lies down with the lamb," I said.

"Yes, well, speaking of food, how about coming to my place for lunch? We'll be there soon," he offered.

Ken lived in a large brick home in Princeton, West Virginia. His wife came to the door to greet us. She was thin, blonde and wore glasses. Throughout lunch she seemed nervous and kept looking at us with a kind of pity. I didn't understand this.

Why was she feeling sorry for us? We were the saints. We were the lead actors in the only movie that was real. I sensed that she knew something about us that we didn't. It was strange. After lunch, Ken gave us a ride to the freeway where we walked until dark and then rolled out in the woods a little way off the highway.

For some time now, everyone we met had commented on how beautiful my long hair was. It hung below my waist by this time. I didn't feel comfortable with such comments about my physical body and usually ignored them or replied, "I'm not this physical body, don't dwell on it." Many men looked at me with admiration and would say I was beautiful. On guard with vanity, I constantly fought against it. This particular night in the woods, I felt an urge to cut off my long hair. Perhaps I was attached to it after all. I didn't want to take the chance of having my hair come between me and 'the truth.' So I looked through my sack for the little nail scissors I carried. Gary awoke and asked me what I was doing. "I have to cut off my hair brother. Too many people are distracted by it and sometimes I feel I'm attached to it," I told him.

"Calm down, sister. Just the fact that you were about to cut it off for God is enough. You've proved it to yourself and He already knew. You don't have to do it now. Everything is cool. God gave you a beautiful 'creature' to ride around in, don't feel bad about it and just give all praise and glory to God."

"Praise God for your wisdom, brother," I told him as I rolled two Buglers. I was somewhat relieved to not have to cut it. "You know, brother, I truly love you. I could cruise with you through this movie forever."

"Yepper, sister. I praise God every day for giving me such a beautiful spirit to travel with. You are quite an angel." Our words faded into the stillness of night as our spirits soared.

It was around this time that I began to feel we were being followed. I sensed a presence, always lurking just out of sight. One night we were given a hotel room in a town close to the Tennessee border. It felt great to have a shower and rest inside, away from the cold dampness. We rolled our bedrolls out on the floor. We were so used to resting on the ground that resting in a bed was foreign to us. We preferred the floor. The maid must have found it strange to see the beds untouched the next morning. We ate sandwiches and Gary's favorite, potato chips. Sometimes we made an entire meal of chips and V-8 juice. Nutritional yeast mixed with olive oil for a dip with bread was another favorite.

So here we were in this hotel room, eating chips and flicking the channels of the T.V. This was something we rarely, if ever did, but it wasn't forbidden, or anything. The opportunity just never presented itself. We watched a movie called "Charly," (1968) based on the novel "Flowers for Algernon." It was about a mentally handy-capped man, who became part of an experiment and with the aid of a miracle drug became a genius. Eventually the drug was discontinued and he returned to his original state. This painful transformation touched me somehow.

Sitting on the highway the next day, I again had that feeling of being watched. I told Gary about it and he sensed something, too. So I put my head down and closed my eyes for a while and a multi-colored van kept coming to mind. "I think we are going to be picked up by a colorful van, brother," I told Gary. "It's a strong feeling."

Within a short time a multi-colored van, the same one as in my vision, stopped in front of us. It was a very plush, camper-type van. I sat in the back while Gary preached to the young man in the front. He stopped at a grocery store and handing Gary two dollars, asked him to go in and buy some orange juice. Gary then handed me the money and I jumped out, because it was the sister's duty to buy the food and take care of the 'props.' When I returned to the van, the man started it slowly, pushed me down in the back and opened Gary's door, struggling to thrust him out! What was going on? This movie was getting crazy. He managed to throw Gary out and when I lurched up at him, he threw me back down again. Was this guy a pervert? I screamed "No sex!" I was able to get up again. As we struggled, Gary managed to open the door and began to climb in. The man then released his hold on me and pushed Gary out. The van was slowly moving forward and I jumped through his open window. I landed on the ground, on my side, but I didn't feel a thing. I was numb from the adrenalin rush. I heard Gary yelling to some people, "Help! Someone is kidnapping my sister!" The van pulled away with a screech. Gary, thinking that I was still inside, ran into the grocery store. I pushed myself up and walked to the store just as Gary came running out. I ran to meet him and we instinctively embraced.

"How did you get away?"

"I don't know, brother, it was a miracle; the angels helped me fly out the window." My voice was shaky, my body trembling. "Praise God!"

"I don't understand what he wanted," Gary said, puzzled.

"To rape me? I don't know."

"Well, let's leave that space now. It's gone, give it up," Gary said.

"He has all our stuff, our bedrolls, tote sack, money from Robert's car, our Bugler . . . I could sure use one of them right now," I said.

"I'm just glad that you're here, everything else doesn't amount to anything," he answered.

So we walked down the highway into Tennessee, feeling very light with just our robes and army blankets on, carrying nothing. I liked it. This was a real test in faith for me and I felt strong.

We stayed at a Salvation Army shelter for the night. It was far too cold to rest outdoors with no bedroll. Gary and I were separated for the night. Again, I could feel something in the airwaves. The winds of change were roaring and I felt a space change approaching me like the subtle tide of the ocean as it engulfs the shore. I fought feelings of uneasiness all night and prayed for the strength to endure all tests that would come my way.

Just as my body and mind eased into a restful state at last, a banging on the door brought me to. "Time to get up. It's six o'clock; check-out time." A voice on the other side of the door yelled. So Gary and I were given a bowl of oatmeal soup and sent out into the brisk, cold morning. It felt great to be walking beside my brother.

Three large men approached us on the sidewalk and stopped to ask us something. Suddenly, two of them grabbed Gary and the third man grabbed me. He threw me into a car that had just pulled up and someone in the car sat on me. We pulled away as I heard Gary scream, "Sister!" . . . Gary's voice faded and the hollowness in my gut told me that I wouldn't be hearing it for a long time.

My body ached under the weight of whoever was on top of me. I couldn't see anything; my face squashed into the cold vinyl seat of the car. Voices were speaking excitedly, but nothing they said registered. Everything was hazy, almost unreal. Finally the car stopped and two people pulled me out by my arms and legs and shoved me into another car. This time, I was allowed to sit up, with someone on each side of me. There were two men in the front as well. I didn't understand what was going on. What were they going to do with me? Where were they taking me? Meanwhile, a song on the radio was blaring, got to get away, got to get away now!" I looked out the window and saw the freeway exit and escape signs. Were these messages, telling me to get away somehow? My mind was freaking. It kept flashing through a whole barrage of possible ways to escape the scene.

All at once, I felt ashamed to be feeling confusion and fear, just because of what was happening on the outside. So I talked to God and asked Him for strength to stand on my foundation of truth and not let what was happening affect me, or alter my inner space and peace. True peace of Christ was a gift that did not falter when things weren't running smoothly. When Jesus was being tortured on the cross, he still remained true. I knew who I was and I would be strong for Jesus. These guys could do whatever they wished to my body, but they couldn't touch the 'real me.'

Now I felt invincible; I was being taken somewhere because my abductors needed to hear the word of God. Once I decided this, the natural impulse to escape mellowed and I sat back and 'watched the movie.'

"So, where are you taking me and why?" I asked the driver.

"I can't answer any questions. I'm just the driver."

"Do you realize that you are kidnapping me?" I said.

"Yes, but it is for your own good. Wait and see," he replied.

I looked at the man beside me and was taken aback to realize that 'he' was a she. She had a T-shirt on that said, "Almost Heaven, West Virginia." I looked at this hefty, short-haired woman and said with my holier-than-thou attitude, "You are almost in heaven sister, but I'm already there. The keys are right inside of you if you wish to open your eyes to them."

"No thanks," she replied. "I've already been to heaven and back and I like it better here."

They all laughed. These were the strangest 'connections' I've ever had. They weren't intrigued with my apparel, or unusual way of life. Who were these people? They seemed to know something about me that I wasn't aware of.

"Can you stop at this gas station?" I asked. "I have to go to the bathroom."

"No way, we aren't letting you out of our sight. You already got away on us once."

It was then that I recognized the voice. It was the guy in the multi-colored van that I'd escaped from days before. "What's going on? You brothers have been following us for days, haven't you?" I asked.

"Yep; we know everything you've done in the last five days," he said, confirming my feeling of being watched.

They drove down a country road, where the woman came with me into the bushes while the men scouted close by. "Don't worry," I told her. "I'm not going to run away. God has me right where I'm supposed to be and this movie is really intriguing. All I have to do is 'kick back' and watch," I told her.

When I finished my pee, they drove around in circles to try to confuse me, but all they accomplished was to make me carsick. We drove for hours down dirt roads in the hills of West Virginia before we reached our destination. It was a farm, with horses running in the field and a huge, ranch-style house with white stone and wooden pillars. It felt so good to get out of that car. A middle-aged, tiny woman with black hair came out to greet us. She held out her arms to hug me and said, "My name's Dee. Welcome, honey."

"Love without touch, sister," I told her as I stepped back from her embrace.

Her smile changed to pity. "You poor dear, come in and let me make you something to eat."

I followed her into a large kitchen and was allowed to choose from a variety of foods. I chose fruit and nuts.

"I would appreciate having my Bugler back," I told her and she gave it to me.

"Come with me into the living room, will you dear?"

It was a huge room decorated in autumn colors, with a fire burning in the fireplace. Soon a man came walking in with a Bible in his hand. He sat down and started drilling me with questions, reading quotes in an attempt to disprove my beliefs. We had a 'shoot out' (debate) that lasted for hours. I could feel my energy being drained so I went 'inside' myself and prayed, putting my head down on my knees. Immediately the image of Jesus, when He was on trial, came to my mind. He didn't waste His energy on trying to convince His accusers of who He was, because they had already condemned Him in their minds. So He stood there like an innocent lamb, saying nothing. When He was asked if He was the King of the Jews, He said, "*. . . Your words, not mine . . . .*" *(Luke 23:3)*. I felt very close to Jesus, so I asked Him for His strength at this time of my own trial. By this time, I had it pretty well figured out. I had heard a brother talk about deprogramming once, so I put all the pieces together and knew that this must be it. I knew God was allowing this to happen to make my faith stronger and strengthen me for more tribulations to come.

"So, you believe that Jesus Christ is walking on the earth again in a physical body, right?"

"Your words, not mine," I answered and put my head down.

That made him angry. "Look at me; can't you see I'm talking to you? Don't you know I'm trying to help you?" He asked.

He had more questions, but I didn't bother "*. . . throwing my pearls before swine . . . .*" *(Mathew 7:6)* I just hid behind my 'shield of truth' and chanted; "no killing, no sex and no materialism."

Hours later, he threw the Bible down. "Damn it! I can't get through to her. Find someone else to do it," he said. He was speaking to a second man who had just come into the room and who looked familiar. He was Ken, the man who had taken Gary and I to his home for lunch! Now everything was becoming clearer.

"Who has given you the right to kidnap me and keep me here against my will?" I asked him.

"Your parents have, Maureen. In fact, your father is on his way here right now."

Oh boy, are they ever playing dirty. They are bringing my 'earth dad' here to try to make me relate to my 'old self,' I thought.

"How long do you plan to keep me here?" I asked him.

"That's up to you. As long as it will take you to acknowledge the fact that you've been conned and are under mind-control.

"Well, it looks like you're going to see this face around here forever then, brother, because I won't ever denounce 'the truth,' or take my white robe off on the 'inside'," I told him boldly.

"Fine then; welcome home!" He said with a smirk.

234

Everywhere I went in that house, someone followed me. There was no privacy at all. I had to be aware of keeping centered constantly. It was like being attacked. I thought about how much I was going to grow spiritually through all this, about the stories I'd have to tell my brothers and sisters when I got out of there. I wondered how Gary was. I refused to share the evening meal with these evil people, so Dee brought me a righteous sandwich and sat with me while I ate.

That evening, the living room was full of people. I was introduced to them and told that they had all been in various cults and were now learning that mind-control is what kept them there. One by one, they shared their experiences with me. One woman was from "The Divine Light Mission," another from "The Moonies," others from "Hare Krishna" and other religious groups. I sat there and listened; all of them seemed sincere and to want truth more than anything. In fact, many of their miraculous experiences were similar to mine. They had all believed with their whole lives, just as I still did. I could see the loophole in each of their groups, though. They now called them "cults."

Then, all at once I realized these people had been led astray, just as the Bible warns and that God, knowing their hearts, had set this whole deprogramming movie up so that I would be here, to bring them all the real truth! Things were becoming clear now. I began to preach to them about Lightning, the keys and the brotherhood, feeling so high. I went on like this for a while until one sister interrupted me.

"You haven't heard a word we've said, have you?" She declared. "Don't you see we are all in the same boat? You don't have a handle on 'the truth' anymore than we did. Open your eyes! Open your mind! Look at it all objectively. Step off your high horse and take a good look around you, girl."

"What have you got to lose?" Someone else said. "If you have been deceived, then you will see it and if the Christ Family really is 'the truth,' then no one can take it away from you."

A dark, curly-haired man spoke next. "Maureen, all we want you to do is make sure you are following Jesus. Have you tested 'the spirits?' How do you know for sure?"

"I just believe it; faith in God, brother," I answered.

"But, God gave us a thinking mind, so that we could reason. He made each of us different and unique. He never made us to be clones."

I wasn't in the habit of thinking, or reasoning in that way. We had been warned not to doubt, not to use the thinking mind; it was Satan. I was used to fighting that mind each time it reared its head. My attitude was frustrating one of the women. She walked over to me with a mirror in her hand and told me sternly, "Look at yourself. Your pupils are dilated; you have no feeling, no emotion, no life. You look like a zombie!"

"That's just my physical body you are seeing, sister. That's not me," I told her, pushing the mirror away.

"Well, just look at you. You walk around in that white robe preaching so-called truth, begging for food, free as a bird, while someone else is burdened with bringing up the children that God gave 'you' to care for. You say the world is evil, yet you handed your own children over to Satan's domain. What kind of a mother are you? What kind of a saint? Who are you fooling?"

I was stunned for a moment, feeling a blow to the one open sore in my hard heart. Then, before I could answer her, my dad and Brian, who had let us stay in his house in Thunder Bay which we had called "Christ Corner" came into the room. Behind him, Sister Cheryl and Brother James followed, wearing blue jeans and sweatshirts! My mind was blown. My dad sat on one side of me and Cheryl on the other. I could find no words to say to them; instead I reached for the Bugler can, opened it and pulled out a rolling paper. Cheryl snatched the can from me and said, "This has to go, it has a significant relation to the cult." Then she handed me a Camel cigarette instead; strange.

"What's going on, sister? Why are you both dressed in funny clothes?" I asked, wondering if they were incognito in order to get me out of there. I was anxious to talk to them alone.

"That's just what we're here to explain to you, Maureen," she answered. "It's all a lie. Lightning Amen is not Jesus Christ and the Christ Family is not following 'the truth.' We have been taken for a ride. We've been deceived."

What was she saying? Was she serious? I watched carefully for any facial expressions hinting that she was just saying all this for the benefit of the others, but there was none. I had known Cheryl for a long time. She was serious! Confusion tried to eat its way into my mind, but I blocked it out. It's a trap. I thought. Perhaps I'm here to bring them back with me, because they have fallen away from 'the truth.' My mind was reaching for handles and holding onto 'the truth' with swiftly unraveling strings. "What do you mean it's a lie? What are you talking about?" I asked.

In reply, James pulled out some papers. They contained information on Lightning and he read me some of it. Lightning's real name was Charles McHugh, he had been married twice and had a couple kids. James told me they had obtained this information from the F.B.I. The papers also claimed that Cher was his second wife and that he was once a painter and part of a motorcycle gang. James words became a blur in my ears. They couldn't be real. I had experienced truth, spiritual enlightenment, so many miracles. These were lies, they had to be . . .

"Your mother, grandmother and sister told me to say 'Hi!' for them," said my dad, jarring me out of my dream-like state. Ariss told me to tell you she loves you. Here is a picture of the kids. They've grown lots since you saw them last."

I reached for the picture with trembling hands. The photo, like a hologram, was so clear that it was as if the children were right in front of me. Ariss' arm lovingly embraced her little brother. Her hair was darker and straighter than I remembered. Everything about her had grown, yet her face struck a familiar chord in me; the same chord that I had battled so often to silence. I stared at Sol. His timid expression, his pensive eyes, and long, wispy blonde hair were unrecognizable. This was my baby?

Their innocent faces reached inside me, through the thick, emotionless river of ice, deep down to the bottom of the river bed where the last trickle of mother instinct still flowed. The love in their eyes warmed that ice, melting it into tears and the cool, calm, restrained Christ Sister lost all control. Holding the picture to my breast, I buried my face on my knees. I felt so ashamed for not acting righteously. Yet at the same time, I felt so ashamed for having left my babies. Voices whispered all around me, but I felt as though I was not really there. My head was spinning, my mind racing. After all this time, after all the battles I'd won over my old mind and attachments, I still felt a hollow, unbearable, empty ache for my children. I wanted to gather them in my arms and never let them go. I wanted to love them as a mother. These beautiful, motherless children . . . I had missed them so much! I wasn't there when Sol took his first step, when he uttered his first word, when they hurt themselves and needed comforting, when they were sick, when they were happy . . . I never shared any of those times. Could I have given them up, given my entire life, to follow a false Christ? Was I deceived? I felt so confused; lost in an unbearable maze of pain.

That evening, Cheryl and I slept in bedrolls on the floor. Two other women were also in the room, on beds. There was a bed for us, but I refused to lay in it. I lay there, restlessly listening to the heavy breathing of sleep around me, my mind running wild in the dark night. Thoughts were coming faster than I could sort them out; confusion arched its bow and aimed straight for my heart. Was this real? How could the Christ Family be a lie? Why would God allow me to get into something false, when I had prayed to Him to tell me if it was true, or not? Did He allow me to experience it only to bring me to this point? Is He now telling me that it isn't true? But, if this isn't 'the truth,' then what is?

I got up and reached for the door. It was locked. I walked over to the window to open it for fresh air and to gaze at the stars. I found it barred. I was a prisoner! I panicked. Suddenly, all I could think of was escaping.

Cheryl awoke, saw me by the window and called out, "What's the matter, Mo?"

"They've locked me in here. You have to help me get away."

"I can't do that. It's for your own good. Believe me, you'll see."

"I'm confused Cheryl, if I'm not Maureen Christ, then who am I? This is my entire life we are talking about, not just a fragment of it. My whole heart, mind and soul are in it," I said.

"I know how hard it is, Mo. There's a lot to learn. Just try to rest now. Time will heal." Her words, intended to soothe, brought no solace. I was devastated.

As we lay there in the bleak silence of the night, I felt myself being thrown into a huge, black hole. I had no handles to hold onto, no concepts and no truths. I was empty, alone and afraid. In desperation I whispered, "If my life as Maureen Christ has been a lie, then I have nothing, I know nothing and I am nothing."

❋ CHAPTER TWENTY-THREE ❋

During the next few days, I was exposed to information that revealed a whole new side of 'the truth.' Words like "brain-washing" and "mind-control" and how the Christ Family used them to control people, were explained to me. It all seemed so bazaar. I was being told that the reality I believed in with my whole heart, soul and mind was not real.

I had been led astray, deceived. This was not easy to accept, because I had been trained to believe that anyone not in the Christ Family was a tool of Satan. How could I trust that these new people were right?

Ken's son Cage had been in the Unification Church cult, known as "the Moonies." He was one of three people who talked most to me, trying to convince me that I was in a cult. Cheryl and James dominated much of the conversations, constantly bringing up facts about the Christ Family.

James told me that Brother Francis had been killed by a car. This totally shocked me. He gave me proof in the form of a newspaper clipping. Tears stung my eyes as I read it. How could this be? We were told that we couldn't die. I truly believed it. We were the saints. We were going to turn into light. We didn't have to die a physical death, or reincarnate again. I felt a double whack when he told me that a sister had drowned in the Colorado River. The current swept her under as brothers watched on shore. Other issues were brought up, such as the 'Family' using food stamps and lying about living in one place. This had always bothered me. When I first joined the group, I was told that the social security number was 'the mark of the beast' and that we should rip it up and forget it. Yet, to obtain food stamps the number was required.

Later that day, Cheryl told me that Don, Les, Judy, Jerry and Tony were also not 'in the wind' anymore. She said that Don and Judy were in Minneapolis being rehabilitated right now. I looked at her in disbelief. Don, the brother who had brought me 'the truth,' was now turning his back on it? He had lived it with his whole heart and soul. I knew that he had been a strong believer. "I can't believe that Don is out of the robe, Cheryl. You're just telling me that to bring me out," I told her.

"Maureen, it's true, I even have a tape of his voice that he made for Judy when she was coming out. I'll play it for you. See for yourself."

I sat in amazement listening to Don's voice talking to Judy, yet he could easily have made the tape for me. He touched on exactly how I was feeling; my doubts and hesitations. "I never realized how narrow-minded I was; how I never allowed myself to see anyone else's point of view but my own." Don's voice was unmistakable. "It's scary because I know your whole heart is into the Christ Family just like mine was, but Judy, try to listen to what these people have to say. They aren't your enemies as you may think. They are there to help you. They are coming from a right-on-space. It's hard to believe, but try to understand it. We have been deceived. It is a cult . . ."

I was totally blown away! Seven brothers and sisters were all stepping out of the Christ Family realm. Why? And, why was I so afraid to?

That night, I lay awake in my bedroll, head buzzing. I now realized that I had been holding back from really listening to anyone here for fear of having 'the truth' taken away from me. I had been told that if I ever left the Christ Family, I would live in sheer hell. I would be doomed because I had seen the light and turned my back on it. Now it seemed to me that a tiny speck of light was shining from another perspective. How could truth be taken away from me when God Himself had given it to me? Only He could take it away. The fear that I was feeling was actually contradictory to our beliefs. Fear is not of God; fear comes from disobeying the first key of no killing. Then why was fear used as a tool to keep me in the group?

My head pounded with an intense ache. I wasn't used to thinking independently and it actually, really hurt. I decided that I would try to see what these people were talking about without completely divorcing myself from my beliefs. I thought about Don and Judy being out of the robe. I wished that I could be with them, talk to them. Was it possible that they were being brain-washed out of the Christ Family and I was being set up by God to be the strong one to take everyone back with me? My mind kept flipping back and forth between grasping what was being revealed to me and losing it all as Maureen Christ appeared. It was like seeing things from two totally different points of view at the exact same time.

Someone rang the dinner bell and we all gathered around a huge table. There were four or five other people there like me, as well as deprogrammers, security people, Dad, Brian, James, Cheryl, Dee the cook, Ken Junior; whom we called Cage and Ken, the head of the group. It was quite a mob and it was always changing, as new people were brought in. The smell of bacon and eggs sizzling on the burner disgusted me. I am supposed to trust and believe these barbarians who eat my brother animals? Confusion was everywhere . . . people being loud, joking, interrupting one another . . . I was so used to the Christ Family 'communions:' peaceful, orderly and silent, one person speaking at one time, all the same food, live food; not dead. I was so uncomfortable. I felt as though I had landed on a strange planet, totally unable to relate.

239

Cheryl came into the room and told me that Cage and James were waiting for me in the living room to talk with me about mind-control. I sat down close to the fireplace on the floor, cross-legged, pen in hand, my notebook close by. I wanted to learn and understand all of this. I had to know. Then I could either accept it, or reject it and find some way to 'hit the wind.'

"So what is mind-control?" I asked.

Cage looked at me, smiled and began his explanation. "Mind-control is a behavior modification of one's belief structure. It's a reshaping of a person's free will that manipulates individuals into single-minded devotion to a group and a leader. It is a coercion that forces your thinking to conform to their thinking, to fit their beliefs. To join the Christ Family, Maureen, you had to change yourself to fit into their structure. They wouldn't accept you the way you were. You had to change your language and your means of expressing yourself, to stifle your emotions, to give away material possessions, to turn your back on your family and friends, to give up your children, to give up yourself! In your willingness to change and give these things to God, you allowed yourself to be coerced and manipulated to the point where you couldn't even see it. You were not allowed to question, or doubt; therefore you gave up your thinking, reasoning mind and blindly followed."

I had a hard time absorbing all the information that was being revealed to me, but I wrote a lot down. I knew I would be given the fuller understanding when I was ready for it. I did see some of what he was saying, though, and couldn't deny it.

"What is a cult, then? I asked.

He went on. "A cult is a false religious group practicing mind-control techniques for the purpose of exploiting their members, usually for power and wealth."

"Well, I can see that in other groups, but I can't see it in the Christ Family. Lightning doesn't live in a mansion; he lives on the road like us."

"Charlie never walked on the road much since they fixed up the Royal Coach," Cheryl piped up. "His feet were more tender than a new brother's."

"Well, even if that's true, he put his miles in. He deserves it," I said, defending him.

"Some cults are more into money than others," resumed Cage. "It seems to me the Christ Family was more into power. Charlie had such a strong hold on you guys that you didn't have to all be together under the same roof. You traveled in twos, or alone and still were under a magnificent amount of control. That's a lot of power for one guy to have over so many people," Cage said.

"They never used to have a bank account, Mo, but now, instead of giving the new brother's possessions away, they sell them and put the money in the account. All members are encouraged to deposit any money they get given to them, but only Charlie, Cher and Martha can take money out!" James contributed.

"That's true, but the corruption level is nowhere near these other cults," I said.

"Yes, but one hole in the bucket drains all the water," Cage told me. "If there is one untruth, or deception, then it can't be 'the truth.' It's marred. So let's look at the Christ Family and see if we can see some hidden falsehoods. First of all, the leader's

240

name is Charles McHugh, so let's not call him Lightning any more. It's Charlie, O.K.? We have some information on his past. We contacted his mother and the garbage about his virgin birth and miracles as a child are 'B.S.' He's been divorced once, with two children from that marriage and married again to Cher, who also follows him. He was into bikes and he painted buildings for a living for a while. He went bankrupt just before he started living as Jesus Christ Lightning Amen."

It was hard for me to listen to all this about Lightning. I knew it could be true because when I first got into the 'Family,' Sister Margaret told me that he and Cher were married. This bothered me then, but it was just one of those things that I put on the back burner and didn't think about. But, to call him "Charlie" felt so strange. To think of him as just some "Joe Blow" who had made up the whole story was devastating. Yet I could see the possibility of it becoming a reality to me. All this was so hard for me because if Lightning really was Jesus and I was being talked out of believing in him, then I would be turning my back on my Lord Jesus. I couldn't help thinking of how Jesus was treated the first time He came to earth. This information could be untrue too.

That evening, while lying in my bedroll, I felt the strange emergence of a lost and forgotten Maureen. Feelings and memories that had long been locked up now broke their chains, as the battle between the 'old self' and the 'Christ mind' began to rage within me.

A movie came to my mind. Gary and I had watched it in the motel room a few days before. It was called "Charly" and was about a mentally disabled man. With the help of a drug which was first tested on his white mouse, he accelerated through school and became a genius within a short period of time. But, as a genius, Charly no longer had his childlike, joyful nature. He was thrust into the demands of modern life. Although extremely intelligent, he had lost something very special. By the end of the movie, the drug had to be discontinued to save his life, so Charly slowly lost his genius and reverted back to his former state. In one poignant scene, while still a genius, he was looking in the mirror and saw the reflection of his former dumb stare in a premonition of his future. He panicked and felt fear as the inevitability of his 'old self' taking over his new self again was revealed. His pain and horror were unbearable.

This was the scene of the movie that I was relating to. I was experiencing my two identities clashing. I couldn't help feeling that there was much to lose if I chose my 'old self.' This 'old self' I had fought so violently for two years was still alive and strong, awaiting a break in the thick, cold ice that covered my mind. This 'old self,' which I ignored, shot down, denied and battled with, that I believed was Satan, was revealing itself again.

The realization that my mind might have been under the group's control took away my blind trust in the Christ Family. The reasoning that had just been revealed to me could not be denied. Yet, I didn't agree with the world and its ways and couldn't see myself adapting to the 'normal' lifestyle, with a house, possessions and a job. 'Human' ways were foreign to me. Moreover, I didn't believe in the system of greed, nor did I wish to support it. Therefore, I had to make a choice between two worlds, neither of which I belonged in any longer. I felt alien, mixed up and very alone.

The morning sun shot prisms of light through the window, bringing day to a long restless night. I looked around at the three other women still in blissful slumber. They had all been through a similar experience and must have felt the pain I was feeling. This united us.

"Good morning." Cheryl greeted me with a smile. Here was a special friend. We had been through so much together. Three months ago, she had been deprogrammed by Ted Patrick up in Thunder Bay. Her agony must have been close to mine. For the first time, I looked outside myself and my world of pain and saw her. I realized how narrow-minded I was. Had the Christ Family life taught me to be like this?

"I appreciate you being here for me, Cher," I told her.

"I wouldn't want to be anywhere else, Mo," she replied. "You know, you're real lucky that you have so many of us who are out of the cult now: Don, Judy, Les, Tony, Jerry, James and me. There is a lot of support waiting at home for you," she smiled.

The fact that Don was out of the Christ Family had the biggest impact on me of anything, more than mind-control, more than the untruths and inconsistencies. I knew his heart and passion for God. He was a true and strong brother and I knew that if he was stepping out to take a look, then maybe it was a good idea. Cheryl told me about his deprogramming; how he was handcuffed to his older brother for days in a little trailer. How he called his parents "Satan," and how angry he was. Of course, this was 'righteous anger.' It took days before he would even listen to anyone. But, what made him listen? Why did he choose to leave the group?

It was baffling that eight of us were now out of the Christ Family, all at around the same time. Cheryl said it was a miracle. I supposed I could see it that way, too. The realization that so many had taken a close look at what we were into really helped me in my decision. If I had been the only one, I'm not sure I would ever have gotten out of the trap of circular logic.

Carol, one of the girls helping me, came into the room holding a pair of faded denim overalls. She handed them to me, saying, "Everyone would like to see you out of that robe. How about checking out some 'funny clothes?' I felt afraid at the prospect of taking off my robe, but fear was not of God and I pushed past it. "These are something I would have worn before," I said, taking them from her. My dad had brought me a white shirt of Ed's from South America and it completed the outfit. Taking off my robe felt strange. Was I doing the right thing? I managed to reassure myself by reasoning that no-one could take the robe from me 'on the inside.'

Going downstairs I met Brian, our friend from Thunder Bay. His warm embrace and smiling face let me know that he really cared. "We have been praying for you and this is an answered prayer, a miracle," he said.

Just then my dad walked in and smiled at my apparel. "You look great, daughter. It's so good to have you back again. Brian and I will be leaving tomorrow, but Cheryl and James will stay on. If you feel you need to stay longer than three weeks, then take more time. Don't worry about anything. You have a place in our home when you come back. Your mom and I have adopted the children you know, so Mom is their mom right now. But, we'll cross that bridge when we come to it. We love you, Maureen and love will overcome all." He leaned over to embrace me.

Boy, I've caused these people a lot of pain, I thought. I'm in debt up to my ears in that department. How will I ever get out? Then I said aloud, "Thank you, dad, for all you've done." I had said "thank you" for the first time in two years.

Next, Dee hustled us outside to take a picture. That felt strange, too. Then the idea of going home flashed through my congested brain. I knew it wasn't going to be easy. I didn't know how I was going to deal with my children, no longer being my children and not having a say in their lives. But, I guessed I didn't deserve them anyhow. I feared confrontations with my mother and didn't know how we could live harmoniously under such bizarre conditions. Yet I couldn't deal with the intangible future now. There was far too much in the 'here and now' to deal with.

That night, Dee tried to take my robe from me. "You really should throw it in the garbage, honey," she told me.

"No. I have something else in mind," I said as she followed me into the living room. Everyone clapped to make the point that they were pleased that I had taken off my robe."

"It's really best if you get rid of everything associated with the cult," Dee persisted.

I sat in front of the fire, watching the flicker of dancing light, holding my robe closely to my heart. I had given up my home, my possessions, my birthright and place, my dreams and creative aspirations, all the things that meant something to me . . . I had given up my old habits, my personality, my friends, parents, grandmother, siblings, my children and my mind! I had preached to hundreds of people and led them astray . . . I suffered emotionally, endured frigid temperatures, black flies and mosquitoes feasting on my flesh, the cold rain, all the weariness of the road, day after day, month after month . . . all the battles of the mind. Now I was overwhelmed with questions; questions I had never allowed to seep through the tiny cracks in the caked clay of my mind. If it is a lie, if it is really not 'the truth,' then what is it? If this movement is not led by Jesus Christ, then who is it led by? If it is not inspired by the Holy Spirit, then who is inspiring it? What is left for me now? What am I going to do with my life? This life I so freely handed over to this cause.

Stinging tears rolled down my cheeks. I felt used. I curled up my newly-made robe, hand-stitched with love and made from fine white cotton, opened up the doors and threw it into the fire! Relief and grief overcame me as I sat and watched my life and beliefs being engulfed by the roaring flames, those unforgiving flames which turned that pure white robe to black, violently consuming it, transforming it to ashes! "This is my life, burnt ashes!" I cried.

❋ CHAPTER TWENTY-FOUR ❋

Outside, the strong autumn winds howled as if feeling my pain, beckoning me outdoors. The wind blew through my long brown hair; the sun kissed my face. The hills and mountains were clothed in their autumn dress. I stood there for a moment, feeding my senses with all this beauty and once again felt that close connection with the earth. There was something I knew. I knew that I needed to feel close to nature. I needed to be away from manmade objects and intellectual conversations and just feel. I needed to just be a human being on the earth, nothing more and nothing less. Someone was always with me, in case I ran away. We walked down a pathway through the woods and I absorbed the treasures along the way. Moss-covered rocks, multi-colored mushrooms, tiny wild flowers all touched my heart. These little marvels of creation helped me to feel less important. As we stood on the top of a hill, the insignificance of my self and all my problems faded as I absorbed the serenity that surrounded me. Of course, this only lasted for a while; my 'deprogrammer' was standing by the window waiting for our return.

During the rest of the day I learned about mind-control. A man named Dr. Robert Lifton had written a book on mind-control techniques called "Thought Reform and the Psychology of Totalitarianism." He asserted that there were eight points which characterized any mind-control situation and which are used by all cults:

1. Environment Control
2. Mystical Manipulation
3. Demand for Purity
4. The Cult of Confession
5. Sacred Science
6. Loading the Language
7. Doctrine over Person
8. The Dispensing of Existence

Lifton studied Americans who were prisoners in the Korean War and subject to brainwashing. I found it interesting that these techniques were used in a military setting, yet they could be applied to every cult. I will go through the eight points and explain how they were used in the Christ Family.

1. *Environment Control:* The cult controls where you live, how you live, what you eat, what you wear, but also, what you hear. You have to leave your home, family and friends, your old environment and let the cult create a new one for you. It controls human communication both outside and inside the self. Within my self, I cut down my own thinking to prevent desire for anything outside the cult's rules. I could see this in the way I converted literally everything to the group's way of thought: music, billboard signs, what I read, what I saw. The Christ Family didn't need to be together in one place to be under control. The world couldn't touch us because we kept ourselves under control. Whatever information we absorbed, was transformed first. Also, everything was either black, or white, according to 'the truth' as defined by the Christ Family. I was told not to think, not to question, that my mind was Satan. Everything in the world was illusion. We were the only ones who were alive, in the world of the spiritually dead.

2. *Mystical Manipulation:* I believed I was an angel, a saint. I manifested the mystique that Lightning had created. Wearing white robes and walking barefoot gave us an aura of mysticism. The silence and order of mealtimes in camp, along with the sharing of food and the rolling of Buglers; how slow and peaceful it all seemed. These acts appeared spontaneous and were seen by us as proof of being tuned into the Holy Spirit, but we were trained, chastised and indoctrinated in how to act. To use a parallel example, let's say a child has just been brought out of the African jungle where he ran around naked all his life. He is brought to America and witnesses a schoolroom environment for the first time. He's amazed at the order of things. The bell rings, kids line up and walk to their rooms. Each child sits in a seat, without fighting over which seat he or she wants. There is such order. The African child is mystified by its apparent spontaneity. Yet in reality we all know the kids have been trained and programmed how to act. There is no mystique to their behavior at all. In my case, I had a mission to carry out and I was made to feel special, holy. This mission, or higher purpose, was above and beyond ordinary human decency. For example, I would walk on hot pavement until my blisters bled; the higher purpose impelled me to keep on going. 'The truth' was reality; my body was of little importance. Believing that we were the reincarnation of the saints was mystical, as were all the accounts of miracles we were told and stories such as the three keys being the original commandments that God gave to Moses. We believed them without questioning where they had come from, or how valid they were.

3. *The Demand for Purity:* This involves believing that perfection can be attained. Everything is judged as morally right, or wrong. All good is for the movement; all else is evil. We were all involved in a compelling fight to search out and eliminate negativity. For example: I would cut down thoughts about the children and suppress them. I consciously separated "me" from the "flesh body" saying, "I am perfect, but my flesh is not. I don't sin, but my flesh falls short of 'the truth.' This creates a narrow world of guilt and shame. You keep striving for perfection, but it's just out of reach. We could blame some of our impurities on the outside world and believe we were burning away its sins, but the cult constantly kept our sense of guilt and shame alive as a lever to control us. When I didn't meet the Christ Family's standards, I felt shame. I always felt I wasn't good enough, that everyone else was perfect, but I wasn't there yet. When I was hypocritical, telling people I was in heaven, or that I wasn't cold because I wasn't this body; I would actually be shivering and wondering why I was still cold. I felt guilty.

4. *The Cult of Confession:* Each cult member is required to confess his or her feelings, which are then exploited rather than comforted. The cult owns you! It is perfect and has received perfect enlightenment. So when you express guilt feelings, you make a symbolic surrender and the purging strengthens you. This point was not used as much in the Christ Family as in other cults, but I can think of a few times I saw it at work. When I was with Calvin and Jan, we had preached to a man for a few hours and he was really interested, but not ready, right then and there, to leave everything and come with us. Calvin told him he had to come now if he truly wanted to. The pressure was on him, but eventually we left without him. I thought about how long it had taken me to get into the group and how unaccepting I was of the smoking at first. If I had been this man, I would never have gotten into 'the truth;' it took me an entire winter of indoctrination. I had always felt guilty about this and therefore somewhat beneath the others and at this point I confessed my guilt feelings to Calvin and Jan. In the Christ Family, self-judgment was more widely used than public confession, but it got the same results. The more you judge yourself, the more you judge others. The more you feel purged by your judgment, the more you are able to purge others.

5. *Sacred Science:* The white robe, the self-righteousness, all-knowing attitude and the ultimate moral vision for humanity were definitely part of the Christ Family's makeup. We felt we possessed special knowledge of natural science, like the constellation that supposedly appeared when "Lightning" first hit the wind. We also believed we could achieve oneness with God if we lived the three keys of no killing, no sex and no materialism. And if oneness was possible, then man's ideas can be God. There was a strong sense of security because all questions were answered. Everything was seen in relation to the 'Family' doctrine as sacred or evil.

6. *Loading the Language:* I had lots of fun with this one, for it was widely used in the words we spoke that were exclusive to the Christ Family and we had plenty. These were thought-terminating clichés which upset normal thinking patterns. Since we feel and think in language, this was a very important tool of mind-control. Speaking a different language made us feel united and separate from the rest of the world. I could fill several pages with all of our terms, so I'll note only a few to illustrate what I mean:

- "Poison"–any food not vegetarian
- "Devil's Brew"–alcoholic drinks
- "Rotten Grain"–beer
- "Rocket Fuel"–food
- "Christian Jewelry"–handcuffs
- "Shine it on"–forget it
- "Pharisees"–preachers
- "Kick back"–be quiet, relax
- "Spaceship"–car
- "Cave or Pad"–house
- "Dusted"–died
- "Earthlings"–others, not in the Christ Family
- "Fire On"–yelling or getting yelled at
- "Blow Up"–hit someone with truth
- "Shoot Out"–debate
- "Hit the Wind"–leave
- "Rapping"–talking
- "Flip Flop"–someone who was in the robe and went back into the world
- "Open Heart Surgery"–getting to someone
- "Air Waves"–telepathic energies
- "Fried"–tired
- "Bogus"–not nice
- "Dematerialize"–leave the physical
- "Liquidation"–getting rid of new members' possessions
- "Coin"–money
- "Primo"–good
- "Yepper"–yes
- "Believe"–be and live in
- "Disease"–be dis-at-ease with God
- "Hobbit"–children
- "Communion"–eating, smoking, sharing with someone
- "Connection"–an open heart to preach to
- "Dead Man"–someone who was dead in the spirit
- "Graven Images"–drawings, photos or carvings of anything

- "Transform"–become a Christ Brother
- "Right On"–expression used to replace thank you and other words
- "Taking a Dive"–going through a hard time
- "Creature Features"–physical ills

Every cult has its own special language and words are a powerful tool for controlling people and stopping them from normal thinking.

7. *Doctrine over Person:* Cults change people to fit the mold of the prevailing doctrine. They put abstract ideas above human reality until it's more real to believe in the cult than in your own ideas. I no longer had ideas of my own; "I" no longer existed. There was little or no individuality; we were all the same; clones. The Christ Family's "truth" was all there was. This "truth" overrode myself, my children, everything.

8. *The Dispensing of Existence:* This is the final point. I believed totally that the 'Family's' doctrine was 'the truth' and merged my self with it. We believed it was the one and only way to truly live. Outsiders could be saved only if they adopted the doctrine of no killing, no sex and no materialism and repudiated the ways of the world. Everything outside the cult was false; our existence was the only reality. Ironically, though, the individual didn't exist at all.

The first thing I thought of after absorbing all of this, was Gary. "We have to rescue Gary from the clutches of this group!" I talked to Ken and pleaded with him to go and look for him; I even tried to contact Gary's mother. But, my deprogrammers were afraid that his being here would only bring me back into the cult. I also wanted them to take me to Peter's Mountain, which wasn't far at all, so that I could explain to Jake and especially Jim, but they didn't go for that, either. This frustrated me.

Although I could see the validity of the eight points described above, I still felt that the keys were a good thing. For this reason, I decided to try to approach the whole cult phenomenon with an open mind, but to hang onto the three keys with all my heart.

One morning I sat on the porch, watching the horses running free, my mind reviewing events of the past few days. Rhonda came out and sat beside me. She was one of the girls who shared the bedroom with me. Her curly, shoulder-length, black hair was pulled back on both sides by barrettes. She had big dark eyes, framed in glasses, and large, beautiful, perfectly white teeth that shone when she smiled. She had been there, sitting quietly in the shadows, through all that was going on. I had heard her speak up only a few times. There was something about us that clicked. She had a sisterly spirit. I had been aware of this feeling before, but up until now we had never been alone together.

"I sure feel for you, having to go through all of this," she said sympathetically. "I've been through it three times now. They think they can change my faith, but they can't. My parents should spend their money on something more worthwhile."

"Money?" I said. I hadn't thought about that, or realized it cost anything to be here.

"Yeah and we're talking about "big bucks," too. Ten thousand dollars or more, sometimes less, but it always costs a lot."

I was baffled. My parents paid that much money for me? They must have borrowed it, I thought. "Why does it cost so much Rhonda?" I asked.

"Well, the cost of the deprogrammers, the counselors, the security people, food for everyone, transportation for everyone, long distance phone calls, the costs of keeping the house running, the kidnapper's charges, and on, and on. There is a lot involved in running one of these places and these people are taking a big chance on getting thrown in jail, or having law suits against them. It's a risky business and every angle has to be covered," she told me.

"Why have you been here so often?" I asked her.

"Well, the first time, my group came and helped me escape. The second, I faked it and just went back when they were finished and here I am again, but it isn't doing any good. I know what I know."

I realized from this that Rhonda was here against her will and not benefiting from it much. "What are your beliefs?" I asked.

"I believe in the inner world of 'the spirit,' the sound of ethereal music, the taste of nectar. I believe in Maharaja and all he teaches us. I believe that he is the fulfillment of Christ. Jesus allowed Himself to be killed; what good did that do for the world? Maharaja is all Jesus was and more. He teaches many virtues and truths. We are vegetarian, unmaterialistic, sharing what we have. A portion of my pay check goes to him."

"You are vegetarian too?" I asked.

"Yes, but we're not quite as strict as you are. We will drink milk and we eat mainly whole grains, beans and vegetables, the macrobiotic way. I'd love to go for a walk with you, Maureen," she said.

"Right on, that would be great, it's a glorious day!" We walked onto a winding country road. I was still barefoot, finding it hard to adjust to shoes. The warm wind blew through the leaves, creating nature's own chimes. A little way down the hill we came to a spot where we could see for miles around. "God is a magnificent artist," I commented.

"He sure is," she agreed.

As we walked, we shared some of our life histories and beliefs. Parts of hers were very similar to my own, while I was in the Christ Family. She also told me some parables. They were pearls of wisdom, yet, even after my relatively brief deprogramming, I could see through her beliefs. The inconsistency and falsehood was so obvious to me. This Maharaja leader had Rhonda and all his followers working at their normal jobs while they gave him most of their money. In the meantime, he lived in several mansions across the globe with servants at his feet. Rhonda couldn't see what was wrong with that.

I could see the deception that was so tightly entwined with 'the truth' which had attracted her and kept her enslaved. In turn, she could see the deception in the Christ

Family, yet not of her own group. She was unable to let go, step back and take a look at what she was into, let alone see it from someone else's eyes. In spite of this, I liked Rhonda. She had a gentle way about her.

When we arrived at the house after our walk, our return entrance was announced with great relief. We were told not to take off again without telling someone, which made me feel like a little girl who had left her yard without permission. It was hard to be considerate of others because I was so into myself, my own conflicts and head-trips. After a minute or two, I went and sat at the kitchen table. Rhonda made some herbal tea. Cheryl and James were there too, having a snack. "So how do you feel today, Mo? Have you sorted out some of the information that we've been bombarding you with?" James asked with that chuckle of his.

"Well broth . . . um, I mean James, I can see a lot of what you are saying and I definitely see the flaws in other groups and I don't think I can go out and live 'in the wind' anymore, but I still don't see what is wrong with the three keys. I want to stick to the keys, I believe they are truth," I told him.

"It's O.K. to keep some beliefs from the cult, it had a lot of truth in it," he replied. "It had to have, or no one would have been attracted to it. It's just those subtle lies that were interwoven with that truth and the evidence that mind-control was used that make it sour. But, Maureen, you have to make sure that you want to believe in these things out of your free will, without any guilt feelings that if you don't follow the keys, then you will be condemned." James made sense, but wasn't that a fine line to walk?

"How would someone know if they were believing something out of fear, or not?" I asked.

"Well, why don't we take a good look at where you got the beliefs from? We'll go over each one of the keys and see how they were disobeyed by the very people who created them," Cheryl suggested. "Take 'no killing,' for instance. It's impossible to really live it totally. When I walk down the street even in my bare feet, how many bugs do I kill?"

"Yeah, but that's unconscious killing, Cheryl, there's a big difference," I protested.

"O.K. then, how about the fact that the Christ Family doesn't say that it's wrong to go to the hospital or use drugs if it's necessary? Those drugs have been tested on animals, first, that are kept in cages and killed in experiments. That's supporting killing. The head lice, the wool blankets . . . ," she went on.

"How about the talk around camp this spring that if Charlie died then Michael would lead the group?" James piped in. "Why would Jesus Christ die? Why was he so sick? They even got a wheel chair for him. Why would the greatest healer of all time need a wheel chair? We were told we wouldn't die, why the contradiction? We were told that disease was being 'dis-at-ease' with God, so does that mean that Charlie, who was supposedly God himself was 'dis-at-ease' with himself? No, we wouldn't even think of it, so disease was therefore defined as anything that Charlie doesn't have yet, right?" James was really fired up. I had heard that some of the sisters were worried Lightning was going to die and that if he did, Michael would take command of the Lord's Army, but at that time it caused so much confusion in my mind that I couldn't deal with it and threw it out.

"Talking about dying, what about Paul Christ?" Cheryl said.

I had heard of Francis and a sister dying, but not the story of Paul. "He was preaching near the desert camp to this 'bogus' guy named Rattle Snake," Cheryl went on. "Well, this dude didn't agree with Paul's philosophy and told him to shut up. Paul 'fired' the keys at him, just doing his job as a true Christian, right? But, Rattle Snake tied him to a fence post and whipped him to death. I think there were other brothers witnessing this, but they didn't do anything. What could they do; 'no violence,' right? Well, the older brothers justified the fact that a Christ Brother had died by saying that he wasn't a solid brother. That's ludicrous. He died for preaching 'the truth.' How much more solid can you get?" She demanded.

"How about the ridiculousness of the key 'no killing' when it comes to self-preservation?" James asked. "If someone was raping a sister, what would a brother do; just sit around and watch her get raped? Of course he would have to, because he would be bound to the key of 'no killing,' so 'no violence,' right? All these contradictions are made to keep you confused. It's absurd!" James's eyes glared.

Cheryl spoke next. "We preached 'no fear,' but they used fear itself to keep us in. If we ever took the robe off, we would live in hell, right? Then there was always the fear of the end of the world floating around the 'air waves.' As long as we were in the Christ Family it would be a breeze, but try being in the world when the end came down, it would be horrid." She stopped for a moment and then continued. "The value of human life was belittled; it was almost as if the animals were more important. We would have taken our own lives if Charlie had told us to, just like Jim Jones in Guyana.

I knew she was right. I had rehearsed this scene in my own mind. The thought of it shocked me. That's how much control I had allowed someone to have over me! This realization blew my mind. I sat there, dazed, sipping my tea.

"Let's move to the second key of 'no sex.' Cheryl's voice seemed far away as I strained to focus and listen. "We preached against lust, yet the sisters were used as tools to get things that were needed. Wasn't this working on the lust of our earthly brothers?"

"I remember a time when I was traveling with Calvin and Jan and the van broke down on the highway. Calvin told Jan and I to stand on the road and flag someone down," I said.

"There was plenty of sex going on, too. What hypocrites," James said. "Then they would justify themselves by saying they were burning off the sex vibrations in that space, or fighting off demons, or taking on the space of 'earthlings.' Garbage, they were just horny and could take advantage of their sisters because they were programmed to obey. I'm not saying that all the brothers and sisters were doing this, most of them probably weren't, but if we were all supposed to be connected to the Holy Spirit and of one mind, then that kind of stuff really wouldn't have happened. Come on, we were telling everyone we were perfect and had transcended all that stuff, then preaching 'no sex' and hopping in the sack with your sister?"

I couldn't argue with James here. This had bothered me, too.

"You see, it creates a 'catch 22' situation for the sister; you're supposed to obey your brother, yet trust your heart. It is assumed you will always be in tune, but what happens when you're not? 'Believe your brother' was just as important as the keys, it was the invisible key. So your brother tells you to go against a key and you're supposed to believe your brother because he is filled with 'the spirit' of God. Then what do you do? You feel down-right confused, but you probably will believe your brother," James said.

"There were so many contradictions, one brother saying one thing and one brother saying another. How much you believe them has to do with his rank, or how long he's been in the robe. This is a contradiction because we were told we were all equal, but we weren't all treated equal. It was all theory, not practice." Cheryl took a deep breath and then continued. "If you went up to Archangel Michael and asked him for the keys to the truck, what do you think he would do? If you told Amen it was time he trucked and that you wanted the 'Royal Coach' for awhile, what would happen? Of course, you would never dream of doing this because you were just a humble servant and all, but do you see the point I'm trying to make?"

"Yes, I do, I'm receiving a lot today," I told them.

"This kind of ties into 'no materialism,' too," James said. "Have you ever been on the 'Royal Coach?' Velvety carpeting and cushions, crystal vases, a fruit bowl full of fruit. Charlie had at least twenty robes. We never got fruit much in camp. We weren't allowed to eat when we wanted to. It had to be all of us together, when they said and we ate what they said we could eat."

"Oh yeah, that reminds me," Cheryl said giggling. "One mealtime James totally defied the 'head trips' and regulations of the space. It was the day you left camp, Maureen. On our way to the circle, a sister told us that you and Richard had 'hit the wind.' I was shocked that you left so suddenly and nervous about eating because you told me about Michael firing on all the brothers and sisters about food being just a 'prop.' I sat beside James as the bowls of pea soup were passed out and thought about how much James liked pea soup."

James bellowed out a deep laugh, anticipating Cheryl's tale. "I shared two spoons with the brother to my right, feeling the pressure to be right on," Cheryl continued. "I glanced over at James with a spoonful for him, but he didn't even notice. I couldn't believe what I saw. There was James, ravenously gulping down the soup and finishing off all the bowls that were passed around the circle and stacking them in front of him! I was so embarrassed to be his 'spiritual mate.' Yet, at the same time a part of me admired his boldness in refusing to get into the mealtime 'head trips.' My heart pounded as I watched for the reaction to his feeding frenzy.

Then Michael stood up. "Are you still hungry brother?" He asked.

"Yes!" We all laughed and Cheryl continued. "The silence was unnerving. Then Michael ordered to a brother standing by. "Bring him the pot!" Perhaps he wanted to serve James a helping of humility, but James just devoured the last tasty scrapings from the pot as everyone gazed in amazement. And can you believe that later that day, we got invited for dinner in the 'Royal Coach'?"

The things that Cheryl and James had said gave me a different perspective and I was beginning to see how closed-minded I had been. Yet still I felt that I wanted to live the keys as best I could right now. Perhaps they were the only handle I had and I felt I would be totally lost if they were taken from me. I was also helped by the fact that I had been a vegetarian before I joined the Christ Family, so I received minimal persuasion from Ken and the gang to consume flesh. Deprogrammers often try to make you break habits learned in the cult.

Each day I discovered more and more about how the brain works under mind-control, the techniques used by the cults and how we were even hypnotized. The techniques of mind-control are very similar, although each cult puts its own emphasis on them. The interesting thing, though, is that as different in dogma and beliefs as cults are, the under-current that keeps them going is the same. Here's a list of techniques:

1. Abandonment of familiar life style.
2. Severing the ties with family and friends.
3. Radical purging of personality.
4. Indoctrination with a new set of values, goals and beliefs.
5. Assumption of a totally new identity (sometimes a new name).
6. Acquisition of a new spiritual family.
7. Unquestioned submission to leaders.
8. Isolation from the outside world with its attendant evils.
9. Subversion of the will.
10. Thought reform.
11. The adoption of new social, cultural and spiritual insignia.

The Christ Family used all of them. The incredible thing for me at this time was that the Christ Family wasn't even one of the groups, or cults included in Lifton's study, yet it used these techniques like the others. The Christ Family was a pee-wee cult compared to the Hare Krishna Movement, The Children of God, The Love Family (The Church of Armageddon), The Unification Church, The Way, The Divine Light Mission (Rhonda's Group) and on, and on. The number of religious cults in North America is staggering. Then there were the scientific and political cults as well as the Manson Family, Jonestown and the cult that kidnapped Patty Hearst.

I found all this incredible. I still went through lots of what is called 'floating,' where I would think like Maureen Christ, but with the help of my friends I was able to make it through those times. It was almost like having two separate personalities. All it would take to click into floating would be a word, a smell, or some small thing that would remind me of a time in the Christ Family and I would be off and away again into those strange realms of the mind. It was like having two minds that you could switch between. This was something that occurred frequently, without warning and it would take an act of will to get my mind thinking properly again. It was as if, for a while, I had forgotten all that I had learned about cults and mind-control. My thinking mind would shut down automatically, as I had trained it to do for so long. The sensation was like having water in the gas tank of the car; my mind kept stalling.

Yet I had to know what was happening to me and why. I read many books and asked many questions. The first book I read was called "Escape," by Rachel Martin. It was an autobiography, which made it more real for me. It was simpler to read than all the technical books. Through reading her story I realized that I was just like her, a victim of the cult phenomenon. Her group, nick-named "The Garbage Eaters," wore brown robes, called each other brother and sister and took biblical names as well. The sisters were also subservient to the brothers and Rachel, like me, was coerced into believing this was 'the truth' and the only way to live.

"Not for a Million Dollars," by Una and John Cooper McManus, was another helpful book. She was in "The Children of God" and ended up suing the cult for a million dollars. Her story was also very helpful to me and I am grateful to both these women for their long hours of writing. "Youth Brainwashing and the Extremist Cults," by Ronald Enroth, was also good. Yet, I was still left with many questions. What did each group really believe in? The doctrine wasn't clear. What happened after their deprogramming? What did they think and feel before, during and afterwards?

Concentrating on the simple act of reading was incredibly difficult for me. I could clearly see just how much my mind had regressed when I started to read and re-read sentences because I wasn't able to absorb them. The technical books on brainwashing and mind-control went way over my head. I never got past the first chapter and simply could not understand what they were trying to get across. This frustrated me. I felt stupid, as if I had truly lost the thinking mind that had made me an honor roll student in high school. Cage told me that the brain is a muscle and just as I wouldn't be able to get up and walk after two years of not walking, I could not expect to regain the full capacity of my brain all at once. I had been fighting the intellect for years; shutting off that way of thinking. Many times I would find myself sitting in a room with others, an interesting conversation going on and be totally lost.

The other former-cult members at the rehab centre seemed different from me. They were happy to be out of their groups. I was told that 'snapping' is the term used to describe the sudden personality change. Your mind 'snaps back' into its former track. I wondered why I had not 'snapped.'

The others tried to persuade me to go out to movies, dancing and other activities with them, but I refused, not understanding how they could get into such worldly affairs so soon. Why was I so different?

Throughout my stay in West Virginia, there was a constant change of faces in the house. Every few days a new cult member was brought in for deprogramming.

One morning, Cheryl asked me, "Did you ever meet a sister named Theresa?"

"You mean you have a Christ Sister here?"

"Yeah, they brought her in last night and have been working on her through the night. She's just about ready to start opening her mind and listening," Cheryl told me.

"I want to see her!" I exclaimed. Then Theresa, in her white robe and cool Christ Sister moves, walked into the bedroom. For the first time, I saw the utter arrogance and false ego which we called 'Christ Ego' displayed in every pride-filled step she took. I saw myself. I had never realized how proud I had been, hiding behind the guise of humility. Ironically, instead of making me 'float' as the others feared, seeing Theresa made me look at myself and the Christ Family with new eyes. If I had thought I was being humble and instead I was portraying to the world this arrogance, then what other things had I talked myself into believing that weren't true? I didn't like what I saw. "Jesus was truly a humble man," I thought to myself. "I'd rather not know anything for sure and be humble, than think I'm right with God and be arrogant."

I also realized how the white robe set us apart from everyone else and gave us the illusion of rising above them. We preached about the 'inside,' the heart, yet in reality we judged people on the basis of appearances. If someone happened to be dressed in white on a particular day and we saw them, they would be judged as higher. I could now see how ridiculous this was. If someone gave freely to us then they were blessed, yet if someone didn't, they were cursed. How egocentrical this was. We had to kill our individual egos, only to give birth to the Christ Ego who was the king of egos. It deceived itself and others, hiding behind self-proclaimed virtues and the purity of the white robe. 'We' were the wolves in sheep's clothing! I was appalled.

Carol gave Theresa some 'funny clothes' and she took off her robe. We talked about her experiences in the cult, both positive and negative. She was another sister who had been taken advantage of sexually by a brother. Theresa and I spent a lot of time together, helping each other see a light behind all of this confusion.

As the days went by, the time for us to return to Thunder Bay drew near and the stress of the situation I would soon be facing became real. I was going to live in my parent's house and be with my children, yet not be a mother to them. I was to be their 'big sister' and to play with them, yet not have any say in their care. I was returning to Thunder Bay with the label of "child deserter." People would not understand. I had been through it and had a hard enough time understanding. I was also going to be living and dealing with people who had no idea of what I had just been through.

Then, on the other hand, I would have my friends: Don, Judy, James, Cheryl, Les, Tony and Jerry. We were all in the same boat. This would be an incredible asset to my recovery and I felt blessed for that. It was quite a miracle that we had all been rescued from mind-control and all in the same year. It's rare for people to come out of cults, let alone a whole group from the same town. This surely was the hand of God.

Had God allowed us to go through this whole thing to teach us about mind-control? It did say in the Bible that even the elect would almost be deceived. Had we gone through all this in order to be strengthened for what was in store for us? Maybe we still were among God's chosen ones?

Letting go of being a saint, a historical identity, was not an easy thing. Going from a "somebody" to a "nobody" was terrifying. When I went shopping in town, it felt strange that people weren't staring at me the way they used to. The attention was no longer there; I was no longer a mystical being.

While shopping, I also realized that I found it extremely hard to make decisions. I was used to just following and obeying. When I crossed the street I didn't even look both ways because I was still blindly following my brother. In a way, being in the Christ Family was like reverting back to childhood; just going along for the ride with your parents, not knowing where you were going; just trusting, all in your own little world. The world of fashion was so far removed from all this that I found it strange to shop. The styles had all changed. I felt as if I were in a time warp; like I was an alien.

The day finally came when Cheryl, James and I boarded the plane and said our farewells to our friends in West Virginia. These people had been good to me and I appreciated their efforts to help me see things in a different light and travel that long road to getting my reasoning mind back. As an anti-cult group named "COMA" (Council on Mind Abuse) says, "He who will not reason is a bigot, he who cannot reason is a fool and he who dares not reason is a slave."

Unlike some people who 'snap' out of cults, I crawled. In fact, I was still crawling while on the homeward-bound plane. I didn't know if my parents expected me to be totally well again, but if they did, they would soon find out that I still had a long journey ahead of me. I was like a junkie, or an alcoholic who had to be weaned from a drug. But, there was much more to it. A drug, although it affects many aspects of a person's life, does not control them completely. The victim's entire life does not have to change. It is only one part of their personality, one habit that has to be broken. A person coming out of mind-control, on the other hand, has to change and restructure their total belief system, view of life and perception of themselves.

Anxiety gnawed at me as we rode above the clouds. Would I be treated like a weirdo? What would I do with my life now? Would people understand what happened to me? I wasn't used to the stress of worrying about the future, or being understood. This was all so new to me and I knew that it wasn't going to help to worry.

When the plane landed in Thunder Bay, I was numb. Here I was on home ground, the home that I had left twice before, believing each time that I would never return. The anticipation while waiting to go through customs was almost unbearable. Just behind that steel door were my dear little ones from whom I had been separated for nearly two years. Would they even know me?

❧ CHAPTER TWENTY-FIVE ❧

I opened the heavy door, my palms sweaty and my heartbeat pulsating in my head. I watched my body walk through that door and freeze. I was crippled by emotions, caught in some sort of time warp. The children I had missed so much had grown. Sol looked at me, not a trace of recognition on his little face; he just stood there, watching the stranger. I squatted down, holding out my arms to him. He ran over to my mom, clutching her pant leg for security and burying his face in it. I watched my fear crystallize. He didn't know me!

I looked at Ariss. What a beautiful little girl. Her eyes were still shiny and blue, but her hair had darkened and straightened a bit. My, she was tall! I held out my arms to her smiling. She came to me without hesitation and threw her arms around me. "I remember you, you're my mommy Mo," she said in an angelic voice. I held her tightly and sobbed quietly, trying not to let her see me cry. I looked up at my mother and saw her crying, too. Then I stood up and embraced her. "I love you, Mom," I told her.

"I love you too, Maureen. We've been praying for you."

I went over to my dad and kissed him. "Let's go home prodigal daughter," he said with a grin.

As we walked away, I turned to Cheryl and James who were meeting Cheryl's parents: "See you guys later."

Ariss wanted to sit right next to me in the car. Sol clung to my mom. The guilt welled up in me and I felt deep regret for ever allowing them to be taken from me.

As we rode through the old familiar streets, I felt strange. Everything here remained the same, yet I had changed and been through so much. It seemed like many years since I was last here. I recalled feeling the same as when we had come home from our journey to Peru. I remembered telling my dad that I never wanted to leave town again, that I had had enough traveling. I laughed to myself.

"It's good to have you home again, Maureen," my mom told me as we walked into the house.

"It's good to be home, although it's all very strange," I answered.

"It will take some time to get into the swing of things, that's all," Dad said. "God will help us all through this."

I barely recognized my younger sister Susan. She lost weight, wore contact lenses and makeup and seemed so old.

The first person I wanted to see next was my grandmother. Dad went and picked her up. She still looked the same; elegant and beautiful, defying age. She had always been a special part of my life. I had missed her so much.

That evening I slept in the ping-pong room. This is the unfinished part of the basement where Ed and I used to play ping-pong and have parties. I thought about Ed, still living 'in the wind.' Would I ever see him again?

My old bedroom was now occupied by my mom's friend who'd had a nervous breakdown. Mom and Dad were helping her out. My mother had tried to make the ping-pong room as homey as it permitted, but I still felt cold and lonely down there. I asked if Ariss could sleep with me. Her presence gave the room and my heart a warm glow.

"Mommy Mo didn't leave you because she didn't love you, Ariss. I love you very much," I said. "I left you because I thought it was what I was supposed to do; what God wanted me to do. I missed you very much. It made me sad not to be with you," I told her.

"It made me sad, too," she replied. "But, I'm happy now cause you're home." I got so choked up looking at her innocent little face; so open, so sincere. "I'll tell you a story," she offered.

"O.K., I like stories," I answered, amused at this role reversal.

"Once upon a time," she began, "there was a mommy caterpillar and a baby caterpillar. The mommy left the baby to go and join something. The baby missed the mommy and cried every night for her. The mommy found out that it was wrong and came back. The baby hugged mommy and it was like she never left."

Wow! I was blown away at the depth of this child who wasn't quite four years old yet. She was letting me know in her own little way that she had forgiven me. I hugged her and thanked her. Here is true love, I thought; pure and simple.

"Don't cry, I'll always love you," she said.

"Oh Ariss, I love you so much. I am so sorry for what I did. You are such a big girl now," I told her.

"I prayed for you every night. I prayed that you would come home and you did. I prayed for Willy and Uncle Ed, too. They will come home, too," she said, without a doubt.

"Let's go to sleep now and I'll take you and Sol to the park tomorrow," I told her.

As her breathing changed, I looked at the sleeping child beside me and thanked God for today, for allowing me to be with my children again. I thought about Sol and prayed for our relationship, knowing that his love and acceptance would not come so easily. Thoughts swarmed through my mind all that night.

At the park, the leaves had fallen from the trees and we jumped in them and played tag. I laughed and played with the children, appreciating every moment. Later that day, Don and Judy came over. It was wonderful to see them again. I loved them both. We all had lots to tell. Both Don and Judy had been grabbed while passing through town. Don was first. He was tricked by his mother, handcuffed to his older brother Roy and dragged to a tiny trailer, then handcuffed to the trailer.

"It was intense, Mo! I was like a caged wild animal snapping angrily at everyone who got close. They tried to shock me into some kind of emotional response. They cut my hair off, took away my robe, threatened to commit me to a mental hospital, but none of those worked. I saw my family and their hired help as pawns of Satan trying to steal 'the truth' from me and I wasn't budging. I was committed to serve God no matter what." Don looked off with a distant stare. "On the sixth day, I was able to see the deprogrammer, Ed's point of view on a bible verse we had been debating for hours. It was as if a door had opened just a crack and a beam of light illuminated the fact that I had been closed to other points of views. It is a hard road to walk though, isn't it, Mo," Don sighed.

Don and I went for a walk. I still looked up to him. He was working as a deprogrammer now. He told me he felt compelled to help people out of cults. He planned to be out of town for a few months doing this. I knew I would miss him.

"I don't have all the answers anymore, Mo. It'll take a while for us to put all the pieces to the puzzle together, probably a lifetime," he told me. "But, I do know that love, true love, will see us through."

We were standing on the bridge, watching the river flow. This was symbolic to me; us standing on the bridge between two separate realities. "It feels strange to be back here. I find it so hard to relate to things," I told him.

"I know what you mean, Mo. My mom handed me my brother's baby and I was lost, I didn't know how to hold her, or talk to her. It was very uncomfortable for me," Don told me.

"Yepper, I listen to the way my mom talks to the kids, singing silly rhymes and saying weird things in a high voice. It's hard to relate to. It's like I have no humor left in me. I'm too serious and want to lighten up, but I can't let go. I can't laugh if I don't find a joke funny. I just don't fit. You know what I mean?"

Don nodded to me in agreement as he turned to the river, deep in thought. We stood there in silence for a long time.

The wind blew wildly, disarraying my hair and making the river ripple. Soon it would be trapped by a layer of ice, seemingly still on the surface, yet moving beneath. Was this what had happened to me? Were my personality, my emotions, my individuality just trapped beneath a layer of ice? Was I still here somewhere, beneath all this confusion? Cool wind stung my face. The leaves on the trees, red and gold, crackled in its force, some falling into the river, helplessly swept away by the current.

"What are your beliefs now, Don? Do you still believe in Jesus?" I asked.

"Yes, but I'm still formulating it all, sifting out the good from the bad concepts of the Christ Family. We learned a lot there and I don't want to throw it all out."

I was so relieved to hear that he felt the same way. "My greatest fear is not being right with God. How do I know that I'm doing His will, Don?" I asked.

"I don't have all the answers anymore Maureen. I really don't know much of anything, I'm just as confused as you. I think I'm starting to enjoy just being ordinary, though. There's humility in just being a common man.

"I wanted to travel with you when you came into camp, but I felt bound to Richard," I told him.

"You did? I wanted to travel with you, too," he said. "We weren't as free as we thought were we?"

"I don't know, Don. I thought I knew 'the truth' and now I don't know anything." Tears rolled down my cold cheeks.

"I know, Mo," was all Don said. We walked back to my parents' home, leaves snowing on us, sun glistening on their colors.

❄ CHAPTER TWENTY-SIX ❄

Even though I had seen the evidence of mind-control used in the Christ Family, I could not deny the truths I had learned through my experiences. What remained difficult was grasping that I might have learned those pearls of wisdom elsewhere. A secret part of me remained loyal to the Christ Family. I remained on the fringes of both lifestyles, giving way to each just enough to remain true to both.

One of the major issues bothering me was the possibility that Lightning Amen truly was Jesus Christ. I was able to see him from two points of view. I wasn't sure who he was. If he was Jesus, then I should be out there following him. But, if he wasn't, then I would be following a false Christ, and so raged the battle in my mind.

Cheryl, James, Les, Judy, Jerry and I got together often. We'd had an experience that united us through all of our differences. This invisible bond would remain forever, no matter where the future took us. One day, we found out that Tony was no longer in the Christ Family and was living in Italy. I felt compelled to write to him, to let him know about our situation.

I thought a lot about my brother Ed, Willy, Gary and Richard. I also contacted the mothers of Gary and Richard and told them all about what had happened, connecting them with the appropriate help groups. Richard's mom filled me in on a bit of what happened to Richard after I had last seen him in Florida. She said she had received a phone call from a mental health institution to say he was residing there for a while. I wondered what he had gone through; what he was still feeling. She said he was now out of there and back in the Christ Family, living 'in the wind.'

Later that year, Richard phoned me from his mom's place. It was so good to hear his voice, yet it remained a most reserved and strange conversation. He preached to me, letting me know that he knew I would undoubtedly be in the robe again. He never allowed me to explain my experience, or point of view. He was totally closed-minded. I asked Richard to come up to Thunder Bay for a visit. Of course, he replied, "If it's in the Father's will." His phone call, contrary to my parents' fears, didn't sway me towards the Christ Family; it showed me just how conditioned we all were.

I also had an opportunity to speak to Gary. He reacted the same way as Richard, preached to me and assured me I'd be back, not hearing a word I said. "You have to fully burn out on your attachment for the 'hobbits,' sister, that's the one string that's holding you in the world," he said, so knowingly. I felt frustrated because I wasn't heard, or understood.

Neither Richard, nor Gary would even allow themselves to see my point of view. It was at this point that I clearly saw how programmed and closed their minds were. I was reminded of the selfish and self-righteous know-it-all attitude I once had. I wished that both of them would pass through town so that our group of excult members could talk to them.

I also thought a lot about Willy, although I didn't feel bound to him. There was a lot of water under the bridge and I know my parents and friends saw it as a flood. No one thought we were right for each other.

In late November, Don came into town with a man named Ed who had helped deprogram him. Judy and I went with them to my dad's cottage for a couple of days. The cold north wind howled outside the cabin, the warm glow of the fire lighting up our faces.

"I still don't totally grasp it all. It's mind boggling," I said.

"What don't you understand, Maureen?" Ed asked.

"The separated realities, Ed. It seems as if it all depends what side of the fence you are on. Like when I was in the cult, I believed that Lightning was Jesus, that I was a saint, that the three keys were 'the truth.' I looked at the world and its ways and could clearly see deception. Then some people talk to me, it turns my head around and I can look at myself while I was in the Christ Family and clearly see the deception there." Ed stared into the fire. I could tell he was listening carefully. I continued. "Sometimes I wonder if I am really 'right' now. Who's to say I'm not under the mind-control of the world programming?"

"It's not an easy road to ride on," Ed told me. "But, the difference between being in a cult and being here is like night and day. Out here you have your reasoning mind, the freedom to express yourself creatively, or any way you wish. You can dye your hair purple if you want and that's your business. In a cult you don't have that freedom. You are not allowed to express your individuality; you are merely a clone, a mindless puppet, a slave." That's why I've been deprogramming all these years; to help free minds." Ed's words were one of the stepping stones to my freedom.

One cold frosty day in February, a phone call filled the household with excitement and anticipation. "Ken phoned and said they spotted Eddie," my dad told us.

"Oh, praise God!" My mother cried.

"Where is he?" I asked.

"Orlando, Florida. Let's pray he comes home soon, Maureen."

A mixture of emotions had stirred within me at the prospect of reuniting with my brother.

A few days later, we were informed that Eddie had left town before they were able to capture him. I was now able to relate to some of the anguish and pain my parents must have gone through. I missed Ed so much.

I was grateful to have such loving, accepting and giving parents. My mom, positive and pleasant to be around, gave much of herself to everyone she cared for. A bond was forming between us; we were becoming friends. I cherished this.

Dad and I talked a lot about life. This was a good learning and growing time. I discovered ways of doing things; ways of thinking I had inherited from both of them. Seeing this, I was better able to understand myself. I loved them both dearly and was sad that I had caused them so much pain.

My sister Susan was a busy lady with university courses and a part-time job. I no longer viewed her as my baby sister, but as an equal. She seemed to have her life so together, so directed and I admired this in her. She hadn't strayed off the beaten path as I had.

My relationship with the children took lots of care. Sol didn't accept me for a long time and we went through many difficult stages. I had to keep my focus on love and showing him that I wasn't a threat to him, just someone to play and have fun with.

I felt so blessed to have the opportunity to be with these little people again. I loved them so. I thought of Sister Nancy and Brother Dennis, whose child was given away to a stranger. Where was Ruben now? I thought about that other sister who roamed about the desert camp like a lost lamb, grief-stricken over the loss of her child and of Sister Martha with her baby, Robin, and all the ridicule she took for having a 'hobbit' in camp. I wondered where these people and their children were now.

During my first winter home, Bruce was found and kidnapped. Don went to British Columbia for his deprogramming and took along a tape that we had all made for him. I understand it was a tough deprogramming. Bruce came to Thunder Bay for his rehabilitation and stayed with me and my folks for a while and then with Judy and hers. He seemed to have a lot of blocks which prevented him from really understanding it all. I found it a great challenge to have him around and it actually helped me to see more clearly how wrong the group was in manipulating our minds. Shortly after this we helped out another Christ Brother, Claude, and he also took off his robe.

During that year, Don came into town now and again between deprogramming trips and we found ourselves spending time together. Coming to grips with emotions was harder for us now and the emotions we were feeling for each other went deeper than friendship. Don helped me with many struggles and battles from the cult experience.

By the end of my travels, I had really been starting to feel on top of emotion. Now feelings with which I refused to deal with, surfaced. I had to fight the Christ Family rule that first of all, it was wrong to feel and then, I was not quite sure how to handle emotions when they did come. Even opening up to someone and honestly sharing my feelings and problems was difficult to relearn. This is where Don and I became good friends. I trusted him and found it natural to be open with him.

In the beginning of May, seven months after my homecoming, I got a job at a flower shop. Working was really good for me as it made me exercise my responsible and thinking mind. I did struggle with working for man and money. Up until this point I diligently followed the three keys.

That summer, a Christ Brother came through town that I recognized. He was the same brother who had been traveling with Ed and who I meet in the winter camp. Don, James, Cheryl, Judy, Les and I successfully deprogrammed him without force, or restraint and no money was involved; the same way we helped Claude and Bruce. The power behind this peaceful method of reasoning with a cult member was the fact that all of us had been where he was. Theodore was overwhelmed by the sheer number of us who shared his experiences, yet now saw things from a different perspective. It was compelling enough to make him consider our point of view. Like a door being slightly opened in a dark room, the slightest doubts were able to fling his mind wide open. Theodore stayed in town for a few months. Sometimes he'd hang out at the flower shop and do odd jobs for my boss. Although he had a long way to go, he chose to use his thinking mind and was able to see the control the Christ Family had over him. For us, this peaceful method of rescue was a break-through because we didn't feel right traumatizing someone in the kidnapping ordeal. None of us liked it, yet it was usually 'a must' because cult members wouldn't defect of their own free will. Finding a different solution felt so good to us. There is strength in numbers, as we proved in this case and many others as well.

That summer and fall, we successfully deprogrammed five more brothers this way. All our parents helped out with a place for them to stay and food and clothing. The fact that we didn't charge money and did it out of love felt good to me. Some of these brothers didn't have parents, or parents who could begin to afford to pay the price to get their kids out of cults.

❋ CHAPTER TWENTY-SEVEN ❋

In the autumn, Don rented a basement apartment in Thunder Bay. He had spent about a year traveling and deprogramming and learning as much as possible about mind-control and religious cults. He felt he had a debt to pay because of the numerous people he had converted into the Christ Family. Every time he came to town during that year we spent as much time as possible together.

There were countless occasions when I desperately ran to the refuge of Don's arms, my mind twisted with confusion. Don had a miraculous way of making the sun shine in the middle of the night.

On one such occasion, I asked him, "What about the miracles I experienced? I can't deny them, Don, they were real! Why did they happen if it's all a lie?"

"Well, Mo, when I was in Minnesota at the rehabilitation centre, I got a chance to talk to people who had been in all different kinds of cults. Each one had his own set of miracle stories. One guy who had been in the Brother Robert's group; you know, the ones that wear the brown robes?"

"Yeah, Rachel Martin's group," I replied.

"Well, this guy told me this story . . . he had just met two brothers from that group and wanted to follow them. He was barefoot and found it hard to keep up to them. He prayed to God to let him know if it really was 'the truth' and if He really wanted him to follow these people, to show him a sign. Then he walked about twelve more steps and there beside the road were a pair of leather shoes that almost looked brand new. He tried them on and they fit perfectly. Miracle? Sign from heaven? God had answered his prayer, so he followed the brothers into coercion and mind-control. You see, Mo, to him it was a miracle. To us, leather shoes were forbidden; to him, they were a sign from heaven. Each group has its own countless miracles, Mo. We weren't unique. As far as explaining them, I don't know, but don't you think God knows our hearts? Even though we got caught up in an illusion, our hearts still wanted to serve Him, so He looked after our needs."

"Yes, Don, I can see that, but I experienced so much living 'in the wind.' I copped wonderful spaces on the 'inside.' I'm afraid of losing that special sight, afraid of being conditioned into the worldly way of seeing," I told him. "I can almost always see two points of view in any situation. If anything, I've learned that there truly is more than one way of looking at things."

"That's good though, Mo. That's called 'being aware.'"

"I know, but it also causes confusion. Didn't you doubt at times, though? Didn't you also experience confusion while in the Christ Family? You seem to remember only the good of your experience. I just can't throw the whole thing out."

Don smiled at me, his deep blue eyes sparkling. "We've got our whole lifetime, Mo," he said. "Patience girl, patience!"

That Easter, after a year and a half of being back home, Don and I watched the movie "Jesus of Nazareth" on his T.V. In the movie, the actors who played Jesus and his disciples were wearing white robes and their whole demeanor was that of a Christ Brother. The way they lived, the parables Jesus spoke, the denials of family, the way they were not accepted . . . Everything about the movie seemed to parallel the Christ Family. Don and I sat in silence watching. Once again, my mind flipped to the other side and Maureen Christ broke through the thin veil that separated her from me. Near the end of the movie, both of us were in tears.

"Don, what if Lightning really is Jesus Christ? Look! Those people of Jesus' time never recognized Him, either," I said, pointing to the T.V. "Look at them. They look exactly like Christ Brothers! The Jews probably thought He had his followers under some kind of mind control too. This movie is so close to the way we lived, so close to the 'truth' we've just turned our backs on. I don't see anyone here living anywhere close to the way Jesus wants us to. Everyone's caught up in the illusion, in working for the system, worrying about material riches . . . thinking they are in control of their lives, not God."

Don just sat there and listened to me babble on. "I can't live here anymore like this. I've been riding the fence for too long, Don. I have to 'hit the wind'!" I told him in a fit of urgency.

This time Don wasn't talking me out of it. He sat there listening to me, his eyes staring off. "You're right, Mo!" He said when he finally spoke. "Let's 'hit the wind.'"

"I wish I'd never burned my robe," I moaned.

"We'll sew new ones," he said as he went to his bedroom with a semi-crazed look on his face and grabbed the top sheet.

"I have another one in the hall closet," he yelled to me. I went to the closet and brought back the cotton sheet. My hands trembled as I unfolded it, arranging it in the familiar way for cutting. I felt rushes of energy flow through my veins; my head grew light, my heart pumped rapidly. Then, in a last effort to be heard, my 'finite mind' came to the rescue.

"What about Ariss and Sol, are you going to leave them again?" It said.

"They aren't legally mine anyway, probably never will be, they're happy," my 'Christ mind' answered.

My 'finite mind' came back for a second punch: "How about Mom, Dad, Nona and everyone? What about your job? Can you really deny everything you've learned about mind-control and cults?"

"No, I can't, I can clearly see it in other cults, but the Christ Family is different. Lightning isn't conning anyone. He truly believes he is Jesus. Look at the movie. Lightning's exactly like Jesus was two thousand years ago. It's 'the truth,' you have to follow him!"

"But, you know now that 'truth' is an individual experience, that the group 'thing' was just one experience along the road. Sure, you learned a lot in the Christ Family, but it wasn't the end of your learning. Look at all the discrepancies you saw there, the lies you were told and believed. The food stamps, the wool, the brothers screwing the sisters, the double standards!!" My 'finite mind' just wouldn't shut up this time.

Don got out the scissors and started to make a cut.

"Stop him!" My 'finite mind' screamed.

"Don, wait! I said. "We can't just forget about all the stuff we've just learned. We can't deny the control we experienced in the Christ Family and if Lightning really was Jesus, he wouldn't have to keep us under mind-control, it would be totally natural for us to follow him," I blurted out.

Don looked up at me, surprised, put the scissors down and lay down on the rug. There was an uncomfortable silence. I wondered what he was thinking, what he was going to say.

"All I want to do is God's will, Mo. We both want that," he said solemnly. "We didn't set the whole deprogramming movie up. If it's God's will, I'll 'hit the wind.' If it's 'the truth,' I'll live it, but I can't live a lie. And right now I don't know for sure if it's real, or not. Besides, what if Lightning's a false Christ? If he is, how could we follow him? But, if he isn't, how could we deny him?" He asked with anguish in his eyes.

"I didn't know that you were as confused about who he really is as me, Don. I always thought I was the fence-walker," I said.

"I've got some fears, some uncertainties, just as you have, Mo. I felt I couldn't show them to you because you are so torn and always leaning towards the Christ Family," he confessed.

"Don, did you ever think that maybe I need to be the strong one sometimes? Be real with me. Be honest," I told him.

"Well, I was tonight and look what happened!" He pointed to the white sheets, prepared for cutting. We both burst out laughing. "Whoa, talk about some major 'floating'," he added.

I threw the sheet over him playfully, then climbed on him and pulled down the sheet, revealing his handsome face. "Oh well, I really don't want to give you up anyway," I said and kissed him on the forehead. "I guess I'm attached."

"That's O.K., I am too, Maureen, I am too . . ." This whole event, a full year after our deprogramming, convinced us of the intense power of mind control.

Don got a job at the grain elevators in Thunder Bay and later that spring, he purchased a mobile home in a trailer park out in the country. I helped by putting in what I had saved in the bank, but I wasn't ready to move in with him just yet.

When the flowers started to bloom, we had an opportunity to help out another brother and sister, Ron and Maggie. They stayed with Don in the mobile for a month or two and the group of us gathered for interesting 'rap-sessions.' Cheryl, James, Judy, Les, Don and I were able to shed a little light on the way Ron and Maggie were seeing.

Countless battles of 'the spirit' and mind took place. At times, I found it frustrating because just when I thought we were making some ground their 'Christ minds' would take over and they would lose sight of it all. I saw myself in their struggles and knew what they were going through. Each time we helped a brother or sister out, I went along with them through all their struggles, feeling it all over again. Yet each time, I felt I came out with a bit more strength to believe whole-heartedly that the Christ Family was a cult; a painful admission for me. Listening to the negative aspects of the whole thing helped me gain a more balanced overview of my experiences.

In late June, my parents got a phone call from the U.S.-Canadian border patrol prison in a small town near Regina, Saskatchewan. My brother Ed was in jail there. My parents had placed Ed on a missing persons list across Canada and our local police called us. Ed was sent to Thunder Bay by plane. I nearly wore a hole in the airport floor in anticipation of his arrival. I had to be sure where I stood now if I was going to help him at all, yet I had to be cautious not to scare him away. Such a fine line and a gentle touch were needed here.

What a sight he was, walking through those doors. His white flaring robe hanging loosely on his tall form, his long brown hair bleached by the sun with highlights of auburn and gold, his beard hanging to his chest now and his sparkling hazel eyes.

"This is supposed to be a poor, lost sheep under mind control?" My 'Christ mind' tried to creep in and take a shot, but I cut it down and ignored it; the same way I used to cut down my 'finite mind.'

Ed seemed to have fewer inhibitions than I'd had in West Virginia. He smiled and wrapped his arms around my parents, sister and me and said, "Hi, good to see you all again," in a noticeable American accent. His hugging surprised me. What had changed in the group since I had left it? I wondered.

That night, Ed slept in the room beside mine. Don slept on the floor beside the door, in my room. My dad wanted him to be sort of a security man, to make sure Ed didn't take off in the middle of the night. Within a short time, Don's heavy breathing told me he was asleep, yet I lay awake, feeling my brother in the next room. Knowing that his mind was freaking out, I got up in the dark, forgot Don was beside the door and stepped on his face. He didn't even flinch, or wake. "Some security man," I thought.

Hopping over Don's body, I went to Ed's door and knocked quietly on it. I could see light filtering through the crack between it and the floor. "Come in," he said in a shaky voice.

"I couldn't sleep, you're thinking too loud and my antennae are pretty high tonight," I told him as I walked over to the bed and sat beside him. He was rolling a Bugler and kept his head down as he lit it, then looked up at me.

"Yeah, I'm pretty confused right now, sister. I can see some of the things you and Don were telling me today, but come on. All those trips and going against the keys were just other brothers' imperfections and they don't have anything to do with Lightning. Two thousand years ago, Jesus' followers didn't 'cop' the depth of wisdom He was sharing, either. Come on, Mo, don't you know in your heart that Lightning is Christ?"

"No, I don't believe he is, Ed. Would Jesus lead His people into confusion and traps of the mind? You see, Ed, in the Christ Family I was convinced that we were in 'the truth.' Yet now I can clearly see that I did not love unconditionally, the way I claimed. It was actually the opposite; extremely conditional. If you weren't in the 'Family,' or a potential convert, then you were labeled spiritually dead and in Satan's army. Our love was restricted to those who either lived the same way as we did, or believed in us. I thought that I was loving, that I was totally unselfish and had given up my life for Christ, but I was wrong. I was programmed how to love and follow the Christ Family's definition of love, not God's. I was convinced it was God's love, that it was the one and only truth, but I was gravely wrong, Ed. The Christ Family isn't the only group that claims to be 'the truth' and have all the answers; there are many of them."

Ed just looked at me, his hazel eyes filled with hurt and confusion and also a haunting emptiness, as if he were not really there. I took a puff of his Bugler and continued, "Do you believe that Jesus is compassionate, Ed?" He nodded affirmatively.

"Is it compassionate to leave a new brother with bleeding feet behind because he can't keep up? Is it compassionate for sisters to be ordered to leave their kids and then be 'fired on' for feeling bad about doing it? There was no room for feeling emotion. It was so military, cold and unloving. We truly were in an army. We were not allowed to feel or think. Our emotions and normal thinking were constantly being shut off; we were programmed to believe that our natural feelings and thoughts were tools of the devil. Through fear, our minds were being held hostage. We were told what to wear, what to eat, how to hold our bedroll and tote sack, how to go to the bathroom. Even our sexual feelings were manipulated and were to be shut off. That's control, Ed! We were not loved for who we were. We had to change every aspect of our lives and ourselves to fit the proper image. We were constantly reshaping our personalities until we were nearly devoid of them."

Ed rolled another Bugler. I wondered if anything I was saying to him was sinking in. He had been in the group almost two years longer than I had. It was all he knew at this point. I had heard of people who just could not break free from the brain-washing grip because they were in a cult for so long that their former minds and personalities were completely gone. How I felt for my brother. I knew exactly how he was feeling. His pain and confusion became mine. I felt complete empathy.

"Are you really doing what you want, Ed?" I continued. "Do you believe what's in your heart, or what someone has convinced you to believe?"

Ed just shook his head pathetically and uttered, in an almost-whisper, "I don't know!"

As the morning sun skimmed through the haze of smoke in the room, I sensed that an inner light of understanding had broken through Ed's warped vision.

After nearly a week, Ed's robe came off. Yet, like me, he too was crawling out of the relentless grip that his involvement with the Christ Family had on him. I took sometime off work to be with him. We were together night and day, breaking through the lies, one at a time.

I encouraged him to pick up his guitar again and he did find solace through playing it. It was so marvelous to watch the controlled facade of his Christ Family personality slowly leave and my brother come to life again. Right along with Ed, I journeyed. As his mind grew clearer, something inside of me that was still holding onto the possibility of the Christ Family being the real thing, let go. I experienced a new freedom of mind that I had not fully felt before.

In late July, Ed and I moved into the mobile home with Don. My parents didn't really like the idea, but agreed to let Don and I have the kids on a trial basis, so the five of us shared the mobile home. Ariss was overjoyed to move in with us. Sol wasn't. As far as he understood it, my mom was his mother, my dad his father.

This situation was hard on all of us. Sol, who was now nearly four years old, channeled his anger through various temper tantrums which all seemed to be directed at me. He seemed to hate me for taking him away from his grandparents. A new live-in relationship between a man and a woman is hard enough, but add two ex-cult members who once believed sex was a sin, plus a mixed-up brother and two young children who were also casualties of circumstance, stir, and what do you have? "You have major challenges, unnerving problems and a great opportunity to put concepts of love and patience into action," I thought.

Don and I wanted to get married, but Don was adamant about waiting until I saw Willy again and worked things out with him. He needed to know if I would feel the same way about him after meeting with Will again. Also, I had started working on a divorce, but it wouldn't become final until three years from the day Will and I separated. I knew I wanted to be with Don.

One day in early autumn, I stood in the flower shop taking thorns out of long-stemmed roses. I was alone. The store had been quite busy earlier, but now the hustle had subsided, giving me time to get some work done and to think. As I cut off the thorns of the roses, my hands were pricked and a thorn or two stuck in. This made me notice how everything was still symbolic to me as I thought about the beauty of the rose, being truth and the thorns, the pain and trials that go along with it. As I looked up towards the window at the storefront, I caught a glimpse of two white-robed people passing by. I ran to the door and out onto the street, searching for them, but they were nowhere in sight. Had it just been my imagination?

It was near closing time now. I had just served my last customer. He liked one of the fresh arrangements I had designed that day. As I cleaned up the counters, I heard the chimes above the door ring again. "Oh I don't want to wait on anyone else today," I moaned to myself. When I looked up, a hand seemed to reach in and grab hold of my heart. Standing in front of me, clothed in a white robe, was Will! A warm smile erased the initial shock on my face. "Will, it's great to see you again," I said, a bit nervous.

"My name is Zaharco now," he corrected me.

"Did you walk by here about an hour ago?" I asked, sort of ignoring the new name trip.

"Yepper, I'm here in town with Sister Catherine. My 'earth sister,' Bonnie, lives in an apartment just beside the shop here." He pointed in the direction I had seen them walking earlier. "She told me you worked here." That explained how they disappeared, I thought.

"So are you just passing through, or planning to stay a while?" I asked him.

"Come on, sister, you know the answer, it's all in the Father's will."

"Well, I was just locking up, mind if I join you over at Bonnie's?" I asked him.

"Not at all," he said.

Seeing the sister who was with him was like seeing me two, years ago. Every move she made, every gesture, every word was calculated, smooth as satin, so cool. She wasn't free to be herself; she was a clone of a Christ Sister. I could see the facade so clearly and my heart went out to her. I wanted to help her. They knew 'the truth' and were above everyone else. Their arrogance was clearly displayed in everything they said and did. Once again, God was showing me how I used to be and how opposite we truly were from what we claimed to be. Nothing I was saying to them was getting through.

That evening, Don, Ed, Will, Catherine and I spent the night at my parent's home while they were at camp with the children. Cheryl, James, Judy and Les came over and for hours we all sat in a circle in the living room, talking, debating and battling the powers of mind-control. Will wasn't budging. He wouldn't allow his mind to reason. Catherine was stubborn, too, but I could see she was hit by a few points made. Her righteous armor became riddled with bullet holes by the end of the evening.

I rested beside her that night in bedrolls on the floor. We stayed up all night talking, the battle of minds, still raging. Her questions stumped me a few times, but God seemed to give me the answers she needed to hear and I could feel I was getting through to her. It was an incredible battle just to get her open enough to listen. What a struggle this was. What powers kept her bound and so close-minded?

By the time the morning sun streamed in through the window, Catherine was ready to take a step off the carrousel and look at what she was doing. It surprised me that the first thing she wanted to do was take off her robe. This was just the first day of weeks of talking and battling with mind-control.

Catherine had been born and raised in France. She became involved with the Christ Family while traveling through the States. Although there was a bit of a language barrier, she spoke fairly good English. She spent a week or so with Judy at Don's parent's home, then the remaining weeks with us. I felt very close to her. She slept in the living room beside Ed. This was the first deprogramming that Ed had witnessed and I think it was good for him. Catherine and I became close friends and when she left for France I could see the pain in my brother's eyes. Ed and I wrote to her, keeping our friendship blooming across the miles.

Willy was harder to talk to. He knew what he knew and to him the Christ Family was 'the truth.' We tried on countless occasions to get through to him, but just as we would think we had succeeded, he would put up another barrier. He took his robe off and stayed in Thunder Bay for a while, but always held strongly to the belief that Lightning was Jesus.

❄ CHAPTER TWENTY-EIGHT ❄

Many times I would sit on a patch of moss and rock, thick forest all around me and pray. That is where I felt close to God, in the silence of nature. I took the children on many discovery walks in the woods. They loved being there, as well. Much healing took place as time wove its fabric around our lives. The guilt I had to deal with has deeply scarred me. Yet, I also realize that I, too, was a victim. I would never have left the children if I had not been under mind-control. I had to obey.

I could see at least one good thing that came out of it all, though. I felt so blessed to have the children back that I treasured the moments with them and seldom took them for granted. Ariss and I became extremely close; closer than just mother and daughter. We became the closest friends. One time in particular, I remember I was feeling very hurt about something. Ariss, who was always an extraordinarily perceptive and sensitive child, asked me what was wrong. "I just feel so sad and hurt today, Ariss," I told her. "Sometimes it's hard to be a mother. I feel like a child who needs comforting from my mother," I said, all the while wondering if I should be burdening this eight-year old with my insecurities. Her reaction told me she was more than mature enough to handle it. She was incredible. She climbed up on the kitchen chair to make herself taller than me, put her arms out to me and said, "Come here," in a soothing yet assertive voice. I went to her and wrapped my arms around her, resting my head on her shoulder. Then she stroked my hair softly as I cried like a baby in my baby's arms. "It's O.K. honey," she said, "I'm here!"

Having a group of us who were once in the Christ Family all living together in Thunder Bay was a blessing for us all. We helped each other through our struggles and felt security in knowing we were all growing in the same areas. For a long time our get-togethers usually included a sharing of road stories. I loved listening to the others' experiences and adventures. It was interesting to hear the behind-the-scenes fill in of what happened when you left the scene.

There were other Christ Brothers that we were able to influence and convince that mind-control was being used in the group. Brothers Guy, Gaeton and Randy all hung out in Thunder Bay for a while, took their robes off and started new lives.

Another Brother, James, came through town with a woman friend, Toni, who wasn't in the Christ Family. They stayed with Don and I for a week or so. Our talks were just as beneficial for Toni as for James who was walking the fence, wearing his robe half the time and taking it off the rest. Other people from other groups asked for our help. These were exciting times for all of us. We were also asked to share our experiences for different lecture classes at the local College and University. I was nervous about doing this, but felt the need to warn people. If I had been so informed, my story surely would have been different.

The year 1983 was full of change. I went through the formalities of a divorce, a marriage and an adoption. Will and my divorce was probably the most uncomplicated one the court had ever witnessed. Since we had no home, car, or possessions and the children were no longer legally ours, there was nothing to do but sign a few papers.

Don and I had a small house wedding in January of 1983. Ariss was the flower girl; Sol, the ring bearer. My brother Ed was the Best Man and Cheryl the Matron of Honor. Don and I continue to have a deep spiritual connection. Love has carried us through many challenges and I believe it always will. I truly feel blessed to be able to share my life with him.

It was weird adopting my own children. The judge was extremely judgmental of the entire situation. If my parents had not convinced him that they believed in Don and I, he would never have allowed this second adoption to take place.

Don and I also have a child now. Jesse was born November of 1984 and has been a uniting force in our family.

Will still believes Lightning Amen is Jesus. He recently spent some time living close to Amen.

Over the years, I have found my mind drifting to all the brothers and sisters still living 'in the wind.' How I still love these people and wish I could help them to at least see another point of view. Where are Richard and Gary? Will I ever get the chance to see them again?

I have learned so many lessons. Much cannot be expressed in words; they are just a part of me. One I can verbalize, though, is that over and over again, I experienced that God is. It is not because I was programmed to believe so as a child, or in the Christ Family, but because I witnessed His hand in my life, in countless confirmations of His existence.

God still remains a large part of my life. My desire to serve Him and be in His will has not diminished, though the way I perceive Him and His will has changed and will continue to do so, as I grow and learn. I can serve Him where I am in all aspects of my life.

The realization that I discovered in that cold hut in the sky village in Peru, that the kingdom of God is within, has now been expanded by the realization that the journey to finding God within our hearts is a personal journey. The lessons I learned through the journey to Peru and the Christ Family experience, will remain a part of my life forever.

God made each of us unique, as each snowflake is different and every flower scent varied. He gave us a mind to choose and to reason. He gave us a 'free will.' I think if we were supposed to all be the same, He would have created us that way.

As time goes on, I understand more and more what happened to me and why. As a young idealistic seeker of truth, I was ripe for the picking when the Christ Family shook my tree. I wanted wholeheartedly to serve God, to better the world and be a good person. Therefore, I willingly obeyed the people whom I believed could show me the way; blind to the subliminal web I was being caught in. I was one of many who got sucked up into the vacuum of a higher cause. I am one of the few who were fortunate enough to be blown out again.

As mist rises over the mountain of events that shape our lives, experiences weave in and out, some leaving patterns in the fabric of our personalities that stand out in beauty and design. But, although time keeps flowing down the river of life and fog may settle on some of the past, those intricate designs remain etched in memory, forever.

My feet have walked upon many roads and in a way the dust still remains between my toes. Truth-seeking has led me to Adventure Avenue, which gave way to Danger Road and on to Courage Highway. I've journeyed down Suffering Street which forked off to Strength Parkway. I have stumbled down Illusion Boulevard and through Dark Deception Alley. My burning feet have walked upon the Pathway of Forgiveness, around and around Compassion Crescent, to a small tunnel of light on Hope Lane and down the tiny Foot Trail of Love, the narrowest way of all.

I'm still walking . . . . I'm still praying . . . . I'm still learning . . . .

EPILOGUE

Over 27 years have past since I lived 'in the wind' as a Christ Sister and now, more than ever, I am able to understand that experience.

Although very cautious, for years I continued to seek God through books, prayer and my efforts toward perfection. How could I ever go to a church, or trust another self-appointed 'man of God' after what I had been through? I continued to try to prove myself to God through my thoughts and actions; to achieve higher levels of spiritual awareness. I tried to be a good person. I tried to follow Christ's example of love, kindness, compassion and forgiveness. Yet, there remained a haunting ache of emptiness deep within my soul. A void I was unable to fill, no matter what I did, until . . .

My eyes were opened through reading a book called "Angels on Assignment" told by Roland Buck. While reading the chapter on Yahshua's (Jesus') atonement, something profound happened at the very center of my being. It was as if a veil had been lifted and my understanding was opened. Finally, I comprehended the reason for Yahshua's death on the cross and salvation. It was as if God breathed into my being and I became alive like I'd never known before. Overflowing adoration for Him welled up inside of me and I fell to my knees 'in the spirit' and truly worshipped God.

After this, when I read and studied the Bible. His Word came alive like I was right inside those stories. Things I had read in the past, I saw and heard for the first time. I pondered all the years of striving to be good enough for God to accept me, so self-absorbed that I didn't see His hand reaching down to rescue me. I had missed the essence of the truth, that it's not about what I did for God, but rather it is about accepting what He did for me.

In the Christ Family, I worked hard at proving myself to God. I literally gave up everything to demonstrate my love and devotion to Him. Although there were pearls of wisdom and partial truths in the Christ Family doctrine, it was a counterfeit; a distraction from the simple truth and gift that Yahshua gave us. It undermined the central and essential message that Yahshua died for the sins of the world to give us eternal life. Lightning Amen is one of the false Christs the Bible warns us about. I now know that there is nothing I can do to make myself righteous, except reach out to Yahshua and accept His gift of salvation in complete and utter dependence on God.

Now my spiritual walk is dependent on a vibrant relationship with a living God; not a group, church, or set of man-made rules. This relationship is anchored through studying His word, guidance from the Holy Spirit through prayer, and fellowship with other believers. I continue to learn and grow everyday. I am so grateful for my experiences of Yahweh's (God's) guidance in my life.